SETTLER CITY LIMITS

SETTLER CITY LIMITS

INDIGENOUS RESURGENCE AND COLONIAL VIOLENCE IN THE URBAN PRAIRIE WEST

Edited by Heather Dorries, Robert Henry, David Hugill,
Tyler McCreary, and Julie Tomiak

UNIVERSITY OF MANITOBA PRESS

Settler City Limits: Indigenous Resurgence and Colonial Violence
in the Urban Prairie West
© The Authors 2019

23 22 21 20 19   1 2 3 4 5

University of Manitoba Press
Winnipeg, Manitoba, Canada
Treaty 1 Territory
uofmpress.ca

Cataloguing data available from Library and Archives Canada
ISBN 978-0-88755-843-6 (PAPER)
ISBN 978-0-88755-589-3 (PDF)
ISBN 978-0-88755-587-9 (EPUB)

Cover image by KC Adams
Cover and interior design by Jess Koroscil

Printed in Canada

The University of Manitoba Press acknowledges the financial support for
its publication program provided by the Government of Canada through
the Canada Book Fund, the Canada Council for the Arts, the Manitoba
Department of Sport, Culture, and Heritage, the Manitoba Arts Council,
and the Manitoba Book Publishing Tax Credit.

Funded by the Government of Canada | Canadä

CONTENTS

ACKNOWLEDGEMENTS

It is becoming an increasingly common practice in Canada and in other settler countries to begin public events with a territorial acknowledgement that references the original Indigenous peoples of the land. Sometimes this includes a few words of thanks for their stewardship and/or hospitality. Although these acknowledgements trace their origins to Indigenous diplomatic protocols of respect and relationship building, today this practice often seems to be treated as a minor chore, with little thought given to the importance of the acknowledgement. As editors of a book that is concerned with how relations to territory are shaped by political forces, we feel it is important to reflect upon and acknowledge the peoples, territories, and relations that have made this book possible. To acknowledge people and place requires us to locate ourselves in relation to the peoples and places we write about.

As co-editors, we came together with a shared set of questions about the ways that Indigeneity and settler colonialism are theorized—or under-theorized—in urban studies. We recognize the history of and problems with extractive work done by outsiders to the Prairies. Scholars such as Vine Deloria Jr., Linda Tuhiwai Smith, and Margaret Kovach have called upon researchers to be accountable to communities. While some of us are currently outsiders to the region, most of us have a long history on the Prairies. For some of us this relates to ancestral connections to Indigenous communities, while others descend from settlers. We all share a conviction that not only are the Prairies an important place to understand settler colonialism and Indigenous resurgence, but that this work must be done in connection with people in the region. Throughout the development of this project, we have relied upon the guidance of numerous individuals and institutions located in the region, and we are grateful for the support they have provided. Of course, the responsibility for any shortcomings in this collection belongs to the editors alone.

This project began with a workshop, held at the University of Winnipeg in the fall of 2016. This event brought contributors to this collection together with a range of activists and Indigenous community leaders to talk about the relationships between settler colonialism and urban life. Mitch Bourbonniere,

Michael Champagne, and Stan Tu'Inukuafe deepened these discussions by sharing their experiences of working with Indigenous communities in Winnipeg and Saskatoon. Erica Violet Lee generously participated in discussions about the design of the workshop, and we are indebted to her for the intellectual guidance she provided.

We are grateful to have had the support of a group of intelligent and intrepid conference assistants: Athena Bedassigae-Pheasant, Durdana Islam, Alissa Rappaport, Karine Martel, and Sarah Wood provided both organizational and intellectual support during and after the workshop. As the project progressed, a number of other individuals helped keep us on track. Jesika Allen and Elsa Hoover made maps to accompany the collection. Shaun Stevenson's editorial skills and attention to detail were instrumental in the preparation of the manuscript. Émélie Desrochers Turgeon adeptly compiled the index. Jill McConkey, Glenn Bergen, and David Larsen at the University of Manitoba Press have been skilled and patient editors and publishers.

We are thankful for the financial and logistical support for this workshop provided by the following: the Social Sciences and Humanities Research Council; Evelyn Peters, Canada Research Chair in Inner-City Issues, Community Learning, and Engagement at the University of Winnipeg; Jim Silver and the Department of Urban and Inner-City Studies at the University of Winnipeg; Bronwyn Dobchuk-Land; the Office of the Dean of the Faculty of Arts and the Office of the Vice President, Research and Innovation at Ryerson University; the Faculty of Public Affairs at Carleton University; the Faculty of Arts and Social Sciences at Carleton University; the College of Social Sciences and Public Policy at Florida State University; and the Department of Sociology at the University of Calgary.

This work began in Treaty One territory, in the territories of the Anishinaabeg, Cree, Oji-Cree, Dakota, and Dene peoples, and on the homeland of the Métis Nation. It continued as the editors returned to their residences and workplaces across the continent in Seminole territory, Treaty Seven territory in the traditional territories of the Niitsitapi, and Dish with One Spoon Territory in the territories of the Algonquin, and the homelands of the Anishinaabeg, Mississaugas, and Haudenosaunee. It concluded with an editorial retreat in Dish with One Spoon Territory. A large network of people and territories sustained us as we completed this book. We are grateful for the support we have received from many directions and hope that this work, at least in some small way, acknowledges and honours those relations.

Figure 0.1. The Prairie West. Map by Jesika Allen.

SETTLER CITY LIMITS

**JULIE TOMIAK, TYLER MCCREARY, DAVID HUGILL,
ROBERT HENRY, AND HEATHER DORRIES**

Cities are places where Indigenous peoples have continually resisted and challenged the normalizations of settler colonial violence. In 2007, members of Shoal Lake 40 First Nation, which straddles the border of Manitoba and Ontario, walked 200 kilometres to Winnipeg to protest the imposed isolation of their reserve.[1] For decades, the people of Shoal Lake 40 have been fighting for a "Freedom Road" that would connect their community to the mainland.[2] In 1916, the Greater Winnipeg Water District built an aqueduct to meet the needs of the rapidly growing city by bringing fresh water from Shoal Lake to Winnipeg. The project flooded Shoal Lake 40 and turned it into an island.[3] Today, the aqueduct meets the water needs of the city of Winnipeg, but residents of Shoal Lake 40 do not have access to clean drinking water—for years the community has relied upon bottled water transported by barge. The construction of this critical water infrastructure was not only violent in its origin; it continues to perpetuate violence on Indigenous peoples and lands far beyond the city's borders.

Politicizing this uneven linkage between city and reserve, members of Shoal Lake 40 have made their resistance a regular feature of Winnipeg political life.[4] In September 2014, Shoal Lake 40 used the launch of the Canadian Museum for Human Rights in Winnipeg to bring awareness to their experience of ongoing state violence, announcing tours of their community as a living Museum of Canadian Human Rights Violations.[5] As Roxanne Greene, a former Shoal Lake 40 councillor and one of the museum's organizers stated: "At the settlers' end of the water pipe there's economic prosperity, clean drinking water and a $350-million building that advertises 'healing' and brags about what a wonderful country Canada is. At our end of the pipe, we have 17 years of boil-water order, no job opportunities and we are forced to risk our lives for basic necessities. It's important that the world have the opportunity to see that huge Canadian contradiction."[6]

This book is about contradictions like this one. It is concerned with understanding how the original and ongoing dispossession of Indigenous peoples is both articulated and challenged through the production of urban space. It is committed, in other words, to showing how settler colonial violence is both reproduced and fiercely contested in the urban present, particularly in "settler cities" like Winnipeg.

Yet as the title of this book suggests, the term "settler city" has profound limits. To use this language is to risk reinforcing the problematic (but widespread) assumption that cities are settler spaces, both in their origin and their contemporary reality. It is also to risk reifying settler colonial entitlement to the city. Against such notions, this book highlights the fact that the sites on which North American cities sit have been parts of Indigenous life worlds for centuries, millennia, and in some cases since time immemorial. Moving beyond the limited language of settler urbanity, we highlight some of the ways that Indigenous peoples are both disrupting settler colonial city-making and producing urban space in their own right. While the concept of the settler city can draw attention to the mutual constitution of colonization, urbanization, and settler capitalism, its deployment also risks overshadowing how Indigenous peoples have actively negotiated, resisted, unsettled, and transcended the limits of settler activity. This book avoids this trap by highlighting the dynamic interplay of resurgent Indigenous world-making with the violence of urban settler colonization.

The concept of the settler city, as the example of Shoal Lake 40 illustrates, is also limited by an imaginary that sees the city as bounded by and disconnected from what (and who) is constructed as outside of it. The mythic separation of the city from its surrounds in settler colonial discourse—which imagines the city and the reserve/reservation as completely disconnected spaces—renders invisible the violence upon which settler city-building relies. Settler colonial violence entails the maintenance of a false distinction between urban and non-urban space, a distinction that in turn serves to obscure linkages between urban and non-urban space through Indigenous geographies. This book explodes that distinction, seeking instead to highlight how Indigenous resistance and resurgence rely on the assertion of Indigenous life within and beyond the urban. Indigenous people remain conspicuously absent from many North American urban genesis stories. In such accounts, the city is often presented as a settler achievement, the product of visionary arrivistes who grasped the potential of a given locale. The implication of such interpretations is that contemporary cities are exempted from the long history of settler-Indigenous spatial relations that is invariably at their root; they are discursively rendered as places that exist *outside* of the messy negotiation of colonial contestation. Insofar as settler colonial dispossession is acknowledged, it is as something that happened *back then* and *out there*. Against this view, we contend that the city is not simply an island of settler becoming but a place embedded in broader Indigenous networks and territorial relations. The city is a place where Indigenous peoples continue to make space for themselves and their relations.

Urban and reserve/reservation geographies have never existed in isolation from one another. Rather, they are relationally entwined outcomes of a particular process of geographical production grounded, fundamentally, in colonial relations. While our focus is on cities, it is evident that Indigenous strategies of resistance have relied upon connections between urban and non-urban spaces.[7] In fact, subverting the racialized division of space by, for instance, remapping urban areas as part of traditional and treaty territories is one of the most powerful ways in which Indigenous people have advanced an anti-colonial understanding of cities and the lands upon which they are built.[8]

Settler City Limits is the product of a multi-year effort to assemble a diverse range of thinkers and activists working at the intersections of Indigenous studies, settler colonial studies, urban studies, geography, and sociology. It was born of a shared a desire to contribute a regional comparative study to the growing body of work that is concerned with understanding the relationship between settler colonization and the production of urban space. The orientation of this volume is unabashedly critical in the sense that it is explicitly interested in examining radical inequities that have come to frame relationships within Prairie cities. The editors and authors of this volume come from a range of Indigenous and settler backgrounds, with a variety of kin and community connections to the Prairies, and are united by their commitment to supporting Indigenous resurgence in such spaces.

Our work starts from the premise that North American cities are contested environments. As the chapters demonstrate, Prairie cities do not exist outside of the tangled interactivity of settler colonial processes but are actively shaped by it. The contributions in this book offer evidence of the co-production of contemporary urban environments and a persistent political economy of settler colonial dispossession and exclusion. At the same time, they also show how Indigenous peoples actively refuse such impositions by asserting an urban presence, making claims that reterritorialize urban space and organizing against colonial power relations in a range of ways. To make these points is to put a new inflection on an old idea: that "the city" is not a neutral, discrete container in which things happen but an active, expanding social process entwined with both the reproduction and contestation of settler colonial relations.[9] Rather than take the city for granted, it is necessary to critically engage the relationships between settler colonialism and Indigenous resurgence in the production of urban space, and consider how settler and Indigenous practices produce different kinds of social relations. The urban environments described in the chapters that follow are understood as places that are socially and politically up for grabs, in spite of the entrenched forms of racialized inequity that continue to animate urban processes.

The historical and ongoing Indigenous occupation and transformation of the urban demonstrates the instability of settler colonial power. Settler cities are built on lands that always already belonged to Indigenous peoples. Settler colonialism reterritorializes space, constructing the grounds for the establishment of settler society.[10] However, settler attempts to effect territorial dispossession and the concomitant disavowal of Indigenous claims to space and subjectivity are necessarily incomplete. Indigenous peoples reclaim urban space through both formal political channels and informal modes of organizing urban relationships. Responding to the continual enactment and assertion of Indigenous space and subjectivity, settler colonial regimes must continually reiterate their claims to space and associated disavowal of Indigeneity. Founded on Indigenous dispossession, settler regimes continue to reproduce the colonial relation of displacement/replacement even while purporting to care for Indigenous peoples and rights. However, the Indigenous production of space is not bound to settler geographies; understanding Indigenous productions of space in the city requires attention to the ways in which cities are embedded within broader Indigenous territorialities. Thus, the major empirical, analytical, and political commitment of this collection is to frame cities as Indigenous as well as settler spaces and places. This commitment shapes how we approach the historical geographies of the regions in which cities are embedded and ongoing struggles for land, life, and self-determination. To understand how both Indigenous resurgence and settler colonial regimes shape Prairie cities, it is vital to attend to the multi-scalar, relational, and contested nature of the production of urban space.

The urban spaces considered in *Settler City Limits* are situated within a region that is often referred to as the Interior or Great Plains in the United States, and the Prairies in Canada. This region is bounded by the Boreal Forest to the north, the Red and Mississippi Rivers to the east, the Chihuahua Desert and marshy Gulf Plains to the south, and the Rocky Mountains to the west. By emphasizing the regional context, we reveal how these cities and the region in which they are located are produced through a set of multi-scalar processes, and at the same time we challenge a number of key assumptions made about cities. We wager that there is something to be gained by rejecting the methodological nationalism that has become standard in North American urban studies. Against this orthodoxy, this book is concerned with urban experiences in an admittedly porous and indistinct region that we call the Prairie West. While places like Winnipeg, Minneapolis, Saskatoon, Rapid City, Edmonton, Missoula, Regina, and Tulsa, among others, have sometimes been denigrated as "ordinary" or banal in the broader urban literature, they are also places where Indigenous marginalization has been most acute and political organizing has been most robust. As such, they present extraordinary opportunities to think critically about the normalized entanglements of coloniality, urbanity, and Indigeneity in both contemporary and historical registers.

There are a number of shared historical and contemporary elements that we feel justify the choice to consider these questions regionally. First, we want to stress that the "settling" of the North American plains was typified by extraordinary violence, on both sides of the medicine line.[11] Against exculpatory historical narratives that suggest that the Canadian variant of this invasive project was more gradualist, passive, or cooperative in character, we want to emphasize the profound brutality that has animated projects of settler accumulation and territorialization in both countries. Second, we also want to stress that while Indigenous urbanization accelerated in the period after the Second World War, it often took specific forms in the Prairie West. For example, while Indigenous urbanization in the United States tended to be typified by wide geographical dispersal—particularly through the Indian

Relocation Act of 1956, which explicitly encouraged Indigenous migration to cities that were far away from communities of origin—the process tended to be far more proximate in the region that concerns us here.[12] Cities like Minneapolis, Duluth, Rapid City, and Missoula experienced a large influx of Indigenous people in the period after 1945, but unlike the migrants who moved to official relocation centres, these tended to come from nearby reservations and communities. Roughly 60 percent of "Indian out-migrants" who left Minnesota reservations in the period between 1955 and 1960 relocated *within* the state, for example.[13] Notably, a similar phenomenon has been observed in Western Canada, where Indigenous people who relocated to urban centres have most often done so *within* the same province.[14] Importantly, then, it is critical to acknowledge that the language of "migration" is problematic. Indigenous migrants to Prairie cities often "do not arrive in cities like other migrants, national or international"; rather, they are "travelling within their traditional territories," as Evelyn Peters observes, and therefore maintain relationships to the city, reserve, and territory interchangeably.[15] Third, a regional approach offers an opportunity for refining an analysis of settler colonialism that does not lose sight of the particularity of these places. The Indigenous life of each city described in this volume is defined by its relation to both the larger territories in which it is situated, as well as to histories of mobility in this region.

INDIGENOUS RESURGENCE IN CITIES

Prairie cities have long been sites of Indigenous place-making and resistance to settler colonialism. Early research presumed an inherent opposition between Indigeneity and urbanity and focused on the problematic of how Indigenous people integrated into urban environments (or failed to do so), and particularly fixated on the construction of spaces of urban Indigenous deprivation.[16] Subsequently, researchers have demonstrated how Indigenous people have historically survived in urban environments presumed to be fundamentally non-Indigenous spaces.[17] However, as Evelyn Peters, Chris Andersen, and Nicholas Blomley have critiqued, the bifurcations of urban and rural/reserve space is fundamentally a colonial spatial imaginary imposed on prior and ongoing Indigenous spatializations.[18] Recent scholarship has sought to highlight a long history of Indigenous peoples in urban areas that both precedes colonial settlement and continues into the present.[19]

This research has emphasized how Indigenous people resist colonial spatial-izations and produce Indigenous space in and through the city.

Of course, Indigenous identities and spaces are not simply defined by settlers. In the face of colonial invasion, Indigenous peoples have maintained and continue to maintain connections to land and community within and beyond urban spaces. Prior to contact, Indigenous peoples identified with many distinct political, cultural, and linguistic national identities that continue to have meaning today. This book's contributors, both Indigenous and settler, address struggles involving Anishinaabeg, Cree, Creek, Dakota, Flathead, Lakota, and Métis peoples, among others. Within urban spaces, Indigenous identities can be complex, and researchers must approach Indigeneity as a dynamic and fluid formation that is defined by relation-ships to place and kin.[20] While settler society's capitalist orientation produces spaces of unevenness and exploitation, many Indigenous people not only resist these processes but also continue to enact alternative relations based on dignity, reciprocity, and kinship.[21]

Everyday interactions, structured by relationality and reciprocity, continue to produce distinct Indigenous forms of community and urban space. Indigenous presence is itself a manifestation of Indigenous survival, resistance, and resurgence. Gerald Vizenor describes this defiance of the logic of elimination as survivance, "an active sense of presence over absence, deracination, and oblivion." "Survivance," he writes, "is the continuance of stories, not a mere reaction . . . [s]urvivance stories are renunciations of dominance."[22] Thus, Vizenor asserts that Indigenous peoples constitute contemporary subjectivities and geographies that are in dialogue with, rather than bounded by, tradition. Many rely on complex strategies in responding to colonialism, including articulating connections between urban and terri-torial struggles, and finding ways to enact kin responsibilities within urban environments.[23] People from different Indigenous nations also form new kinds of urban connections within the city that create vibrant, diverse, and complex Indigenous communities, in which Indigenous identities and spaces are produced, reproduced, and, at times, contested.[24]

We make an analytic distinction between resurgence—movements and embodied practices focused on rebuilding nation-specific Indigenous ways of being and actualizing self-determination—and resistance—movements and embodied practices focused on addressing and fighting against settler colonial and state violence. While *resistance* tends to react to and engage the settler state, *resurgence* describes ways of being that centre on what Leanne Betasamosake Simpson refers to as the "Indigenous inside."[25] As Jeff Corntassel and Cheryl Bryce note, resurgence and decolonization include everyday practices such as reconnecting to homelands, cultural practices, and communities, which requires moving away from strategies aimed at "state affirmation and approval [and] toward a daily existence conditioned by place-based cultural practices."[26]

Activities associated with Indigenous resurgence and resistance are often organized in networks that span urban and non-urban spaces, illustrating and enacting different ways of thinking and being on Indigenous lands. While numerous scholars have theorized resurgence, the concept is best understood by looking to the work of Indigenous people in cities. Many Prairie cities are home to a remarkable concentration of Indigenous-led grassroots community organizations, including housing and food cooperatives, social service agencies, and Indigenous-focused schools.[27] As Jim Silver notes, these organizations have been built from the "ground up," in areas where de-industrialization, racism, disinvestment, and colonial practices have converged to produce concentrated racialized poverty. For example, Kinew, an Indigenous-led housing cooperative, the first Indigenous non-profit housing organization in Canada, has provided housing to low-income Indigenous people in Winnipeg for more than forty years.[28] Such organizations stand alongside vibrant cultural life and artistic production. It is important to highlight these actually existing forms of resurgence, as they complicate oversimplified narratives of Indigenous victimhood and damage, which Eve Tuck has cautioned against.[29]

The region that is the central concern of this volume is also defined by a strong history of Indigenous organizing. From the establishment of the American Indian Movement (AIM) to the Idle No More (INM) movement, to name two of the most prominent examples, the Prairie West has long been a significant centre of active Indigenous resistance.[30] Examining resistance and resurgence across this region offers an opportunity to think both regionally and relationally about the processes of dispossession, resistance, and resurgence that shape Indigenous life, and that rely on everyday practices that reaffirm connections to Indigenous territories. Organized resistance movements have been particularly effective in cities, bringing struggles against settler colonial policies of assimilation and environmental destruction into view of mainstream North America through teach-ins and round dances performed in streets, squares, and shopping malls to affirm Indigenous connections to water and land.[31]

SETTLER COLONIAL URBANISM

This collection advances a relational understanding of settler colonial urbanism, which views imperialism, colonialism, and the production of urban space as intertwined processes that are reconfigured by Indigenous resistance and resurgence. We use the concept of settler colonial urbanism to capture these connections and to assert the specificity and centrality of the production of urban space to settler colonial projects. Our aim is to contribute to conversations that are bringing the city into a critical understanding of settler colonialism.[32]

Of course, urbanization has long and substantial links to the projection of imperial violence and is linked to colonial projects on a global scale.[33] At the height of European imperialism, cities in the colonized world provided direct links to western Europe.[34] "Colonial cities" functioned "as key centers of military and administrative coordination, staging areas for incursion into continental interiors, markets and entrepots for extracted raw materials, residential collection points for missionaries, settlers and imperial agents, as well as theaters for performances of imperial strength, among other things."[35] Conversely, European urbanization accelerated through the strength of imperial accumulation. In her exploration of urban development projects in London, Perth, and Brisbane, Jane M. Jacobs shows how these lineages continue to inform urbanization in the present.[36]

In recent years, there has been an explosion of interest in understanding "settler colonialism" as a distinct form of imperial practice.[37] Theorists define settler colonial societies as sites where settlers have come to constitute a sizeable demographic majority independent of ties with any metropolitan sponsor and assert a sovereignty distinct from that of the metropolitan core. Consequently, settler colonialism makes its primary object "the land itself rather than the surplus value to be derived from mixing native labour with it."[38] (This does not mean, however, that the exploitation of Indigenous labour has not been an important aspect of racial capitalism in North America.[39]) In Patrick Wolfe's terms, settler colonial societies destroy in order to replace; thus the assailment of existing Indigenous forms of life and land use makes way for the creation of a new society on the expropriated land base.[40]

Settler colonial dispossession must disrupt Indigenous relations to the land in order to enable colonial actors to reimagine the land as a resource.[41] Resettlement enables settler communities to develop, facilitates the commodification of land, and creates extractive economies. Through fencing the fields and logging the forests, settlers materially restrict Indigenous peoples from accessing and using their territories.[42] Simultaneously, the imposition of a politico-legal order that projects settler sovereignty as absolute justifies the resettlement of the land.[43] While early relations between Indigenous peoples and colonial traders were primarily governed by a legal pluralism that acknowledged Indigenous traditions of diplomacy and relationship-building, in the nineteenth century, settler statecraft increasingly focused on perfecting territorial jurisdiction.[44] Making Indigenous peoples subject to settler regimes of sovereignty through new criminal codes as well as through legislation aiming to specifically regulate Indigenous life and destroy Indigenous political and legal autonomy, the settler state continues to homogenize the diversity of Indigenous political communities and traditions of governance under its claimed absolute authority through the Doctrine of Discovery and *terra nullius*.[45] Although the authority of settler sovereignty has always been an elaborate fiction, it has been one with powerful consequences, enduring as a structural force that limits the effective exercise of Indigenous jurisdiction over people and land.[46]

This book argues that these processes become particularly apparent in cities and that this fact makes it necessary to politicize the production of urban space. Yet while a number of theorists have made key contributions to the elaboration of a theory of settler colonization, their engagement with urban political economy remains comparatively limited. Conversely, while practitioners of urban political economy have elaborated key insights into the racialized production of urban space, their engagement with the constitutive importance of settler colonial pasts and presents has been muted at best. Although settler colonial theory has sought to think through the types of political life that projects of state formation, private property regimes, and resource extractivism enable, the discussion must be extended with regard to the complex relationships between settler colonialism and urbanization. The contributions in this volume illustrate the need to view settler colonialism through the lens of urbanization, and conversely, urbanization through the lens of settler colonialism. Settler colonial urbanism is a socio-spatial formation that is grounded in an inequitable relationship between settlers and

Indigenous peoples. It consolidates a particular system of production and social reproduction that benefits white settlers. Settler colonial urbanization is a localization of a global process that both obscures and implicates the foundational role of original and ongoing dispossession. Despite the shortcomings associated with "the city" as an analytic category, viewing settler colonialism through the lens of urbanization sharpens an understanding of how processes of dispossession, attempted assimilation, and displacement shape urban life. It also allows us to see cities as contested spaces in which the mythology of the city as a space of settler colonial progress is challenged.

Settler colonial urbanization is supported by discourses that have invariably dehumanized and framed Indigenous peoples as pre-modern/traditional, often placing them in opposition to "modern" urban spaces and development. At the same time, these narratives position dispossession and violence as part of a normal and desirable civilizing process coded as progress, which in turn legitimizes settler colonial hegemonies. Ironically, narratives of assimilation have also legitimized state efforts to relocate Indigenous people to urban centres as a "solution" to poverty and social problems in rural Indigenous communities.

In addition, technical processes of mapping and surveying and the establishment of private property regimes are integral to settler colonial urbanization.[47] They naturalize settler divisions of space and work in tandem with eliminatory and genocidal state policies that allow the city to be imagined as an assimilation machine.[48] Prairie cities are sites of specific forms of settler colonial violence and settler colonial governmentality, including displacement through gentrification and development, institutionalized physical violence and police brutality, and systemic discrimination in housing and employment.[49] With policing resembling neighbourhood occupation, community survival is criminalized while racist discourse continues to rationalize incredible rates of police violence as normal and acceptable.[50]

Settler colonialism is a necropolitical process that normalizes the destruction of Indigenous lives and peoples to the extent that genocidal policies and practices have become unremarkable.[51] From the early American Indian wars, to the Métis resistances of 1870 and 1885, to the deaths of children in Indian residential schools and child welfare systems, to the continued pattern of missing and murdered Indigenous people, there is a differential exposure of Indigenous bodies to premature death.[52] Indigenous survival is a continual reminder of the failure of a settler colonial politics of elimination and a hindrance to settler colonial fantasies of the Prairies as a vast and open space for the development of white modernity. In *Dying from Improvement*, Sherene Razack explains how settler colonialism works to validate the removal and death of Indigenous bodies. By focusing on the deaths of Indigenous men who come into contact with justice and health systems, Razack shows how their deaths, at the hands of the state, are normalized as an everyday occurrence, one that reinforces settler colonial narratives of the vanishing Indian. However, Indigenous people are not killed by the state alone. The recent killings of Indigenous youth Jason Pero, Tina Fontaine, and Jason Lafond and the acquittals of their non-Indigenous murderers, along with the high number of missing and murdered Indigenous women and girls, are striking examples of a broader normalization of Indigenous disappearance and death.[53]

Although settler colonial violence is ongoing, its modes of articulation change. While the broader literatures on colonialism have often focused on the bloodiness of dispossession as a structure built on genocide, dispossession is also effected and normalized through a more liberal politics of recognition.[54] Engaging Frantz Fanon's work on the subjective politics of colonization, Glen Coulthard has argued recognition is a form of domination "more subtle, less bloody," although no less territorially acquisitive.[55] The subjective politics of recognition rely upon a particular and limited understanding of Indigenous cultural difference while at the same time ignoring Indigenous political difference as well as colonial power relations.[56] Commenting on the growing jurisprudence on Aboriginal rights in Canada which emphasizes racial rather than political difference, Chris Andersen notes that "the justices of the Supreme Court of Canada have based the logic of their Aboriginal rights test precisely on the degree to which Aboriginal communities are able to differentiate themselves from broader Canadian norms. Yet there is little about urban Native communities that is different enough—according to judicial tests—to warrant protection by the Supreme Court of Canada."[57] Because the politics of recognition does not directly confront colonialism, it inevitably recirculates colonial forms of knowledge.[58] New forms of violence are extended as settlers demand that Indigenous peoples meet impossible standards of pre-colonial authenticity to claim rights.[59] Rather than problematizing the settler colonial city, a set of multicultural discourses and practices seeks to address the question of Indigenous inclusion within settler colonial cities. Thus, the conceptual problem is presented as the position of Indigenous people *in* settler colonial cities rather than the existence of the settler colonial city itself, normalizing settler colonial territorialized authority.[60]

Despite the centrality of settler colonial theory to our understanding of urban processes, we want to make it abundantly clear that we do not see the settler colonial framework as an adequate tool for analyzing the immense complexity of the diverse set of social realities that concern us in the following chapters. While settler colonial theory effectively highlights the violent foundations of settler society, there are very real political and analytical limitations to its framework. Alissa Macoun and Elizabeth Strakosch, for example, warn against scholarship that promotes a kind of "colonial fatalism" in which settler colonial forms of domination are presented as "highly stable" and entrenched.[61] More pointedly, the recent surge of academic energy that has been channelled into the settler colonial subfield may have the effect of undermining or silencing well-established traditions of decolonial knowledge production in the field of Indigenous studies and elsewhere.[62] Corey Snelgrove, Rita Kaur Dhamoon, and Jeff Corntassel caution that an unreflexive reliance on the core texts of the emergent settler colonial tradition may "displace, overshadow, or even mask over" existing critical work, not least "feminist and queer Indigenous work that is centred on Indigenous resurgence."[63]

Just as importantly, there is an inherent danger in theorizing settler colonial violence in a socio-political vacuum. As many have pointed out, settler colonial violence (and its resistances) appears alongside other forms of oppression and contestation.[64] The focus on the territorial dimensions of colonialism, for instance, can understate the extent to which violence against Indigenous bodies is sustained by a white supremacist heteropatriarchal social order and articulated alongside other systems of oppression.[65] Indeed, the vocabulary settler authorities draw upon to rationalize Indigenous marginalization often invokes notions of racial inferiority or unfitness. For this reason, inquiries into the violence of settler colonialism also necessitate examining other forms of violence and domination, including capitalism, white supremacy, heteropatriarchy, gender binarism, and ableism. Such investigations have the potential to create a stronger allyship with Black and other scholars of colour who have emphasized that colonial dispossession, slavery, and anti-Black racism are sustained within a logic of white supremacy.[66] Tiffany Lethabo King, theorizing the relationship between slavery and white settler colonialism, notes that they "fundamentally gave one another their structure, form, shape and even momentum."[67] We need to attend to the role of settler colonial violence in structuring multiple forms of oppression.

To reiterate, this volume addresses the relationship between settler and urban political economy by advancing four basic arguments. First, settler colonialism is operationalized at multiple scales, with the city as a central node/void; it needs to be interrogated in relation to larger-scale colonial dynamics of land and resource appropriation occurring at the level of the region and nation-state that disrupt Indigenous territorial relationships. Second, the brutality that Indigenous peoples face is long-standing and ongoing; settler colonialism endures in spite of recent legal changes that have introduced a language of reconciliation and respect for Indigenous rights, which masks foundational colonial commitments to the displacement and dispossession of Indigenous peoples and land. Third, Indigenous peoples have been and continue to be subjected to colonial violence in/through cities, in ways that are both similar to and different from the experiences of other racialized urban populations. Fourth, the colonial imagination of urban space as settler space disconnected from territorial struggles beyond the city limits is meant to obscure recognition of these dynamics.

ORGANIZATION OF THE BOOK

This volume is divided into four thematic sections. The first, titled "Life and Death," grapples with the necropolitical stakes of settler colonial urbanism but also looks beyond settler violence to draw attention to how Indigenous people have contested and countered attempts to actualize the settler fantasy of Indigenous disappearance and death. The contributors to this part not only affirm that Indigenous life in the city endures but also empirically demonstrate how diverse forms of Indigenous space-making and meaning-making continue to challenge the structural inequities that animate settler colonial politics. Heather Dorries's chapter on the now-infamous *Maclean's* article that labelled Winnipeg "Canada's most racist city" asks what it would mean to end anti-Indigenous racism in the city. Critiquing the conventional categories through which racism is rendered visible as an *Indigenous* problem in the Prairie city, Dorries argues that we must reverse this framework to truly imagine what an anti-racist city would be like. For her, problematizing settler possession and asserting Indigenous traditions provides the basis from which to foster the production and proliferation of Indigenous life. In his analysis of the "anti-Indian common sense" that normalizes Indigenous deaths in Rapid City, Nick Estes shows how urban development was and is premised on the dispossession of and disregard for Lakota lives. However, Estes's chapter also illustrates how Rapid City continues to be shaped by long-standing practices of Indigenous resistance and an anti-colonial common sense that informs ongoing struggles against racism and state violence. Meanwhile, David Hugill provides a comparative analysis of the urban politics of settler colonialism in Winnipeg and Minneapolis, highlighting linkages between the processes of territorial dispossession and housing discrimination.

The book's second part, titled "Land and Politics," offers robust evidence of the fallaciousness of analyses that represent Prairie cities as autonomously organized "settler" creations. Against such orthodoxies, this part starts from the historical fact that Indigenous peoples have long occupied and transformed urban spaces, in many cases since the very beginnings of the development of urban life in the region. Highlighting the inextricable links between urban and Indigenous life worlds, contributors to this part trouble the idea that places like Winnipeg, Edmonton, and Missoula exist *outside* of the fraught relations of settler colonial territorial politics. Julie Tomiak's chapter on the effort of Treaty One First Nations to acquire a decommissioned army base in a well-heeled Winnipeg neighbourhood demonstrates that questions of urban land in the region are anything but *settled*. By tracing the dogged efforts of settlers to disrupt Indigenous reclamations of urban space, Tomiak shows that coercion and political manipulation remain persistent features of settler efforts to retain a hegemonic grip. Nicholas Brown's chapter on the mid-century Montana Study—which he argues functioned as a regional-scale project of settler colonization—encourages us to think carefully about how particular cities are shaped by relations that extend far beyond municipal boundaries. By demonstrating how an assimilationist cultural project coordinated in the urban hub of Missoula had broad regional implications, Brown encourages us to move beyond the conventional urban/ rural binary and pay close heed to the ways in which the political life of both "city" and "countryside" are profoundly bound up with one another in the North American West. Meanwhile, Tyler McCreary's dialogue with Brenda Macdougall, Adam Gaudry, and Chris Andersen demonstrates how the distinct history of Métis peoples is irrevocably linked to the production of certain urban geographies. As they note, "settler" cities were nearly always developed in geographies that had been used or settled by Métis and other Indigenous groups before European migrants claimed to have founded them.

The third part, titled "Policing and Social Control," considers how coercive state institutions are enlisted in the project of settler colonization. Elizabeth Comack's chapter reviews the idea of "racialized policing" and situates its articulation in the city of Winnipeg. Drawing on empirical data, she argues that Winnipeg's inner city ought to be understood as a zone of "spatially concentrated racialized poverty" and makes the case that we cannot understand the conduct of police outside of that basic material context. She concludes by arguing that recent political developments (including especially the re-emergence of the Bear Clan Patrol) point to promising efforts to disrupt common-sense productions of race, space, and crime. In their chapter, Michelle Stewart and Corey La Berge examine Indigenous youth experiences within the child welfare system, and how settler colonialism has created a "rhetoric of benevolence" that continues the suffering of Indigenous youth within the Manitoba child welfare system. They focus on how the child welfare system traumatizes Indigenous children and creates a child welfare-to-prison pipeline. Meanwhile, Robert Henry's chapter mobilizes empirical data gleaned from photovoice methodologies to examine how Indigenous street gangs both challenge and reinforce the violence of settler colonization. He argues that the gangs' presence in Prairie neighbourhoods both disrupts settler hegemonies and serves as pretext for the violence of settler state institutions.

The fourth part, "Contestation, Resistance, and Solidarities," offers a thoroughgoing rejection of the idea that the city is a place of trauma and cultural loss for Indigenous peoples. Against such paternalistic analyses, contributors to this part demonstrate how Indigenous people continue to carve rich social and political space. Lindsey Claire Smith elucidates how Tulsa can be understood as an Indigenous geography rather than simply as settler space. Examining Sterlin Harjo's cinematic oeuvre, Smith considers how the meaning of places like Tulsa for Indigenous people cannot be interpreted only within the frames of the urban; rather, Indigenous Tulsa belongs to broader Creek geographies that operate across imposed settler boundaries of urban and rural. Smith's analysis not only highlights Indigenous productions of space and identity occurring in the city, but shows how they rely upon and reproduce Indigenous spatial scales of identity that stretch beyond the city. Turning to the question of solidarity, Sharmeen Khan draws on her experiences growing up in an immigrant Muslim family and uses the example of the CBC show *Little Mosque on the Prairie* to examine how narratives of multiculturalism and the figure of the "model minority" erase Indigenous presence on the Prairies. She demonstrates how historical and cultural narratives create a barrier to building solidarity between racialized immigrant and Indigenous communities and identifies pathways for creating the solidarity necessary to resist the Canadian colonial present. Finally, Zoe Todd mobilizes more-than-human kin in her narrative that refuses settler colonial understandings of Edmonton and the politics of solidarity. She shows how settler logics of dehumanization and elimination are narrated through public art, such as the sculpture of a severed red hand, and how these logics are resisted.

These chapters underline the specific urban dimensions of settler colonial violence and dispossession, while highlighting the role of cities as a locus for Indigenous resistance and reclamations of land. Together they draw attention to the ways in which both Indigenous resistance and settler colonialism shape social, political, cultural, and economic urban geographies. Moreover, contributions to this volume emphasize the need to interpret urban settler colonialism and its contestations within a broader regional context of struggles over territory. They challenge totalizing formulations of settler colonial theory, highlighting how Indigenous resistance, survivance, and resurgence operate in ways that explode the urban/rural binary. The chapters highlight the need to extend urban theory in dialogue with Indigenous ontologies and movements. In doing so, they also raise questions about the possibilities for Indigenous, anti-colonial, and decolonial urbanisms.

CONCLUSION

Returning to the place where this introduction began: the construction of Freedom Road to connect Shoal Lake 40 First Nation to the mainland began in August 2017, a century after the creation of the Winnipeg water supply cut off the community. The construction of the road is a major victory, the product of much hard work by Shoal Lake 40 community members in the face of decades of anti-Indigenous public policy. It will enable the building of water treatment facilities as well as other infrastructure that is badly needed in the community, remedying some of the enforced isolation of Shoal Lake 40. However, the colonial relation continues to be reproduced in the pipelines, fences, and other infrastructure that cut up Indigenous territories to fuel and feed cities, the regular denials of Indigenous rights to urban housing, and the normalization of Indigenous death and dispossession through institutions ranging from the media to child welfare. Yet in spite of centuries of settler colonial violence, Indigenous communities endure. We hope that this book contributes to understanding settler colonial urbanism as a contested phenomenon. Alongside the incredible violence of settler colonial urbanism, Indigenous people reappropriate urban space and reassert territorial connections, taking back the city.

NOTES

1 Kenora Online, "Shoal Lake 40."

2 Perry, *Aqueduct*.

3 Ibid.

4 CBC News, "Hundreds March in Support."

5 Levin, "A Museum about Rights."

6 Greene, quoted in Shoal Lake 40 First Nation Museum of Canadian Human Rights Violations, press release.

7 Cooke and Bélanger, "Migration Theories and First Nations Mobility," 141.

8 Simpson, "Land as Pedagogy"; Tomiak, "Unsettling Ottawa," 8.

9 See for example Lefebvre, *The Production of Space*; Edmonds, "Unpacking Settler Colonialism's Urban Strategies"; Carpio, *Indigenous Albuquerque*; Hugill, "Settler Colonial Urbanism"; Needham, *Power Lines*; Porter and Yiftachel, "Urbanizing Settler-Colonial Studies"; Toews, *Stolen City*; Tomiak, "Unsettling Ottawa"; McCreary, *Shared Histories*.

10 Tuck and Yang, "Decolonization Is Not a Metaphor"; Veracini, "Introducing Settler Colonial Studies"; Veracini, *Settler Colonialism*; Wolfe, "Settler Colonialism and the Elimination of the Native"; Wolfe, *Settler Colonialism and the Transformation of Anthropology*.

11 The medicine line is a term for the border. See for example Hogue, *Metis and the Medicine Line*; Carter, *Lost Harvests*; Hall, *American Empire*; Daschuk, *Clearing the Plains*; Waziyatawin, *What Does Justice Look Like?*; Wood, "The 'Sarcee War.'"

12 On the program's explicit efforts to disperse, see Iverson, *"We Are Still Here,"* 132.

13 Neils, *Reservation to City*, 32.

14 Clatworthy and Gunn, *Economic Circumstances of Native People in Selected Metropolitan Areas in Western Canada*; Clatworthy, *The Migration and Mobility of Canada's Aboriginal Population*.

15 Peters, *Three Myths*, 2–3.

16 Nagler, *Indians in the City*; Brody, *Indians on Skid Row*; Dosman, *Indians*; Stanbury and Siegel, *Success and Failure*; Davis, "Edging Into Mainstream"; Waddell and Watson, *The American Indian in Urban Society*.

17 Child, *Holding Our World Together*; D'Arcus, "The Urban Geography of Red Power"; Lobo, "Urban Clan Mothers"; Ramirez, *Native Hubs*.

18 Peters, "'Urban' and 'Aboriginal,'" 47; Peters and Andersen, *Indigenous in the City*; Blomley, *Unsettling the City*.

19 See for example Peters and Andersen, *Indigenous in the City*; Howard and Proulx, *Aboriginal Peoples in Canadian Cities*; Culhane, "Their Spirits Live within Us"; Peters, "Subversive Spaces"; Fixico, *The Urban Indian Experience*; LaGrand, *Indian Metropolis*; P. Deloria, *Indians in Unexpected Places*; Child, *Holding Our World Together*; Krouse and Howard, *Keeping the Campfires Going*; Lawrence, *"Real" Indians and Others*; Pitawanakwat, "Bimaadzwin Oodenaang"; Proulx, "Aboriginal Identification"; Silver, *In Their Own Voices*; Edmonds, *Urbanizing Frontiers*; Carpio, *Indigenous Albuquerque*.

20 Peters and Anderson, *Indigenous in the City*.

21 Alfred, *Wasáse*; Macdougall, *"Wahkootowin."*

22 Vizenor, "Aesthetics of Survivance," 1.

23 Baloy, "We Can't Feel our Language"; Hokowhitu, "Producing Indigeneity"; and Wilson and Peters, "You Can Make a Place for It."

24 Ramirez, *Native Hubs.*

25 Simpson, *Dancing on Our Turtle's Back*, 17.

26 Corntassel and Bryce, "Practicing Sustainable Self-Determination," 153.

27 Silver, "Complex Poverty and Home-Grown Solutions."

28 Belanger, Weasel Head, and Awosoga, "Housing and Aboriginal People in Urban Centres."

29 Tuck, "Suspending Damage."

30 See for instance Brown, *Bury My Heart at Wounded Knee*; Adams, *Prison of Grass*; Kino-nda-niimi Collective, *The Winter We Danced*; Toews, *Stolen City.*

31 McAdam, "Armed with Nothing More than a Song and a Drum"; McAdam. *Nationhood Interrupted*; Coulthard, *Red Skin, White Masks.*

32 See for example Baloy, "Spectacles and Spectres"; Edmonds, "Unpacking Settler Colonialism's Urban Strategies"; Freeman, "Toronto Has No History!"; Grandinetti, "Urban Aloha 'Aina"; Hugill, "What Is a Settler Colonial City?"; Kipfer, "Pushing the Limits of Urban Research"; Luz and Stadler, "Religious Urban Decolonization"; McClintock, "Urban Agriculture, Racial Capitalism, and Resistance in the Settler-Colonial City"; Monteith, "Markets and Monarchs"; Porter and Yiftachel, "Urbanizing Settler-Colonial Studies"; Simpson and Bagelman, "Decolonizing Urban Political Ecologies"; Tomiak, "Contesting the Settler City"; Veracini, "Suburbia, Settler Colonialism and the World Turned Inside Out."

33 King, *Urbanism, Colonialism, and the World-Economy*; Edmonds, *Urbanizing Frontiers*; Banivanua Mar and Edmonds, *Making Settler Colonial Space.*

34 Abu-Lughod, "Tale of Two Cities"; Home, *Of Planting and Planning*; Nightingale, *Segregation*; Legg, *Spaces of Colonialism*; AlSayyad, *Forms of Dominance*; King, *Colonial Urban Development*; Ross and Telkamp, *Colonial Cities*; Simon, "Third World Colonial Cities in Context."

35 Hugill, "What Is a Settler-Colonial City?," 3.

36 Jacobs, *Edge of Empire.*

37 See for example Belich, *Replenishing the Earth*; Coulthard, *Red Skin, White Masks*; Banivanua Mar and Edmonds, *Making Settler Colonial Space*; Bateman and Pilkington, *Studies in Settler Colonialism*; Elkins and Pedersen, *Settler Colonialism in the Twentieth Century*; Tomiak, "Contesting the Settler City"; Pasternak, *Grounded Authority*; Veracini, "Introducing Settler Colonial Studies"; Veracini, *Settler Colonialism*; Wolfe, "Settler Colonialism and the Elimination of the Native"; Wolfe, *Settler Colonialism and the Transformation of Anthropology.*

38 Wolfe, *Settler Colonialism and the Transformation of Anthropology*, 163.

39 See for example Lutz, *Makúk.*

40 Wolfe, *Settler Colonialism and the Transformation of Anthropology*; Wolfe, "Settler Colonialism and the Elimination of the Native."

41 Braun, "Colonial Vestiges."

42 Harris, "How Did Colonialism Dispossess?"

43 Rifkin, "Indigenizing Agamben."

44 Ford, *Settler Sovereignty*; Miller, *Compact, Contract, Covenant.*

45 Barker, *Sovereignty Matters.*

46 Pasternak, "Jurisdiction and Settler Colonialism."

47 Blomley, "Law, Property, and the Geography of Violence." See also Dorries, "Planning as Property"; Barman, "Erasing Indigenous Indigeneity in Vancouver."

48 Daschuck, *Clearing the Plains*; Dorries, "Planning as Property."

49 See for examples Broker, *Night Flying Women*; Banks and Erdoes, *Ojibwa Warrior*; Comack, *Racialized Policing*; Comack, Deane, Morrissette, and Silver, *"Indians Wear Red"*; Toews, *Stolen City;* Peters, "'I Like to Let Them Have Their Time'"; MacKinnon, "Making the Case," 277; D'Arcus, "The Urban Geography of Red Power"; Hugill, "Metropolitan Transformation and the Colonial Relation."

50 Comack, *Racialized Policing*; Perry, "Nobody Trusts Them!"; Razack, *Dying from Improvement.*

51 Morgensen, "The Biopolitics of Settler Colonialism."

52 For definitions of racism as group-differentiated exposure to premature death, see Gilmore, "Race and Globalization," 261; Morgensen, "The Biopolitics of Settler Colonialism"; Razack, "Timely Deaths."

53 See Anderson, Campbell, and Belcourt, *Keetsahnak.*

54 See for example Daschuck, *Clearing the Plains*; Taussig, *Shamanism, Colonialism, and the Wild Man*; Waziyatawin, *What Does Justice Look Like?*; Stannard, *American Holocaust*; Hinton, Woolford, and Benvenuto, *Colonial Genocide in Indigenous North America.*

55 Quoting Frantz Fanon in Coulthard, *Red Skin, White Masks*, 113.

56 Simpson, *Mohawk Interruptus*, 21.

57 Andersen, "Residual Tensions of Empire," 317–18.

58 McCreary and Milligan, "Pipelines, Permits, and Protests"; Milligan and McCreary, "Between Kitimat LNG Terminal and *Monkey Beach*"; McCreary and Milligan, "The Limits of Liberal Recognition."

59 Povinelli, *The Cunning of Recognition*; Barker, *Sovereignty Matters.*

60 As Dorries explores in this volume.

61 Macoun and Strakosch, "The Ethical Demands of Settler Colonial Theory," 435.

62 Kauanui, "A Structure, Not an Event."

63 Snelgrove, Dhamoon, and Corntassel, "Unsettling Settler Colonialism."

64 Tuck and Yang, "Decolonization Is Not a Metaphor."

65 King, "New World Grammars"; Lawrence and Dua, "Decolonizing Antiracism"; Razack, *Dying from Improvement.*

66 Harris, "Whiteness as Property"; Leroy, "Black History in Occupied Territory."

67 King, "Interview with Dr. Tiffany Lethabo King."

Part One

LIFE AND DEATH

CHAPTER ONE

"WELCOME TO WINNIPEG"

Making Settler Colonial Urban Space in "Canada's Most Racist City"

HEATHER DORRIES

In January 2015, a Canadian English-language current affairs magazine, *Maclean's*, published an article titled "Welcome to Winnipeg: Where Canada's Racism Problem Is at Its Worst."[1] The article chronicles examples of racism experienced by Indigenous people in Winnipeg, opening with the following Facebook post written by Brad Badiuk: "Oh Goddd how long are aboriginal people going to use what happened as a crutch to suck more money out of Canadians?... They have contributed NOTHING to the development of Canada. Just standing with their hand out. Get to work, tear the treaties and shut the FK up already. Why am I on the hook for their cultural support?" The post, which resulted in Badiuk being placed on paid leave from his job as a high school teacher, is used to illustrate the kind of hateful attitude endured by Indigenous people in Winnipeg on a daily basis. The article goes on to catalogue a long list of racist incidents that have taken place in Winnipeg. The *Maclean's* article prompted a flurry of responses, including a number of editorials, commentaries, and letters to the editor. Its writer, Nancy Macdonald, faced fierce criticism from those who felt her piece had unfairly characterized Winnipeg as a "racist city." Not only was the article contested in both the local and national press, it also prompted Winnipeg mayor Brian

Bowman to hold a press conference the day after the article was published in order to address the allegations of widespread racism it raised. Rather than denying the claims made by the article, the mayor acknowledged that racism is rampant in Winnipeg.

This chapter analyzes the *Maclean's* article and the responses it triggered, as represented by twenty articles from the *Winnipeg Free Press*, two articles from the *Winnipeg Sun*, and one editorial from the *Brandon Sun*. While the intent of the *Maclean's* article was to draw attention to the problem of racism in Winnipeg, in this chapter I use discourse analysis[2] to examine how the article defined racism to construct the city as settler colonial space.

Macdonald's article challenges common perceptions of Winnipeg as a friendly place populated by "smiling lefty premiers" and "pacifist Mennonite writers" and highlights the racism faced by Indigenous people, focusing on Winnipeg's North End neighbourhood. The article lists a number of social and economic problems which, according to Macdonald, shape Indigenous life in the neighbourhood, including solvent abuse, low graduation rates, high suicide rates, high hospitalization rates resulting from violence, police harassment, and funding gaps for Indigenous children in state care. The article also devotes a significant amount of space to discussing the death of Tina Fontaine, a fifteen-year-old girl from Sagkeeng First Nation who went missing and was eventually found dead in the Red River, which flows through the centre of Winnipeg. While these problems are held up as indicative of Winnipeg's racism problem, the article nevertheless paints a dark picture of the North End and its large population of Indigenous people.

Eve Tuck provides a powerful analysis of "damage-centered research,"[3] which she defines as research that focuses on hardships experienced by Indigenous communities. She observes that studies of pain and loss are often mobilized in order to make important political gains, generating damage-centred research that places hurt and loss at the forefront of analysis. Such an approach makes it difficult for communities to think of themselves as other than broken and stunts possibilities for community growth. Tuck reminds us that "without the context of racism and colonization, all we're left with is the damage, and this makes our stories vulnerable to pathologizing analyses."[4] Thus, damage-centred narratives serve to naturalize the effects of colonialism rather than effectively combating them. While Tuck's criticism is directed toward scholars of education, I propose that it explains how the *Maclean's* article discursively frames the conditions faced by Indigenous people.

In this chapter, I show how the article's use of a damage-focused approach to explain racism serves to reinforce negative perceptions of Winnipeg's North End. Moreover, I will argue that the article aids in the creation of settler colonial urban space by circulating a specific set of narratives about Indigenous people that naturalize Indigenous death and dispossession, and normalize the settler colonial logic of elimination. In particular, I will focus on the article's discussion of the murder of Tina Fontaine and argue that the discussion of her death, although intended to bring attention to the problem of racism, provides an opportunity for demonstrations of settler colonial guilt, which are then mobilized to rescue the city from the label of "most racist city." By showing how these discourses produce settler colonial space, the chapter contributes to an understanding of settler colonial urbanism as a set of discursive, material, and socio-economic practices that affirm the political and moral coherence of settler colonial society. Finally, I argue that in order to address anti-Indigenous racism, the problem of racism must be framed in a way that emphasizes the flourishing of Indigenous life rather than focusing on Indigenous death.

THEORIZING SETTLER COLONIAL SPACE

The Logic of Elimination

Settler colonialism is theoretically distinct from colonialism. While both are motivated by capital accumulation, settler colonialism is distinguished by the fact that the colonizing force does not leave but rather seeks to replace Indigenous society with settler colonial society. Thus, settler colonialism is not only motivated by the acquisition and exploitation of resources but also by the acquisition of territory for permanent settlement. Settler colonialism calculates the acquisition of territory according to a "logic of elimination,"[5] which includes the physical and murderous removal of Indigenous peoples from their territories in order to meet requirements for land. According to Patrick Wolfe, this logic of elimination is the "organizing grammar" of settler colonialism that permeates all aspects of settler society and can be read in multiple forms of physical and structural violence. The constant violence of elimination renders colonialism an enduring structure rather than a singular (past) event.[6] While this process of elimination is often marked by physical violence, settler colonialism includes more insidious forms of structural racism and violence that also serve to dispossess Indigenous peoples.[7]

Settler colonialism is enabled by an ideology of white supremacy that organizes the world into a racial hierarchy, producing a particular set of political, social, and economic conditions. Billie Allan and Janet Smylie explain that racism can take multiple forms, encompassing acts of discrimination, hostility, or antagonism toward a person based on their race.[8] However, what might begin as the subtle mistreatment of one person or group often becomes institutionalized when those in power fail to address mistreatment, or when practices in institutional contexts are premised on racist assumptions. Thus, the term systemic racism is used to describe racism that is embedded in institutions such as schools, the justice system, and the health care system. Systemic racism maintains inequalities and decreases the life chances of Indigenous peoples.[9] It is important to maintain a distinction between interpersonal and systemic racism, as locating systemic racism within social practices and government policies reveals how racist violence against Indigenous peoples is not only sanctioned by but also intentionally produced by settler colonial governance. Accordingly, geographer Ruth Wilson Gilmore defines racism as "the state-sanctioned or extra-legal production and exploitation of group-differentiated vulnerability to premature death in distinct yet densely interconnected political geographies."[10]

In Canada, settler colonialism is enacted through laws and policies that deploy racist and sexist logics in order to produce settler colonial space through the legal and physical elimination of Indigenous peoples. For example, the creation and management of a category of "status Indians" through the Indian Act serves to protect and validate non-Indigenous property ownership and occupation. For many decades, the Indian Act included a number of gendered provisions that ensured Indian status would be gradually eliminated, by stipulating that Indigenous women who married non-Indigenous men lost their Indian status.[11] Consequently, many women not only lost status through this provision but were also forced to leave their home reserves, contributing to the urban migration of Indigenous women. While years of litigation by Indigenous women has led to the removal of some of the more sexist provisions of the Indian Act, it continues to govern almost every aspect of Indigenous life. Similarly, the residential school system, which operated from the 1880s until the late 1990s, forcibly removed children from their families, resulting in the breakdown of family ties as well as kinship and governance structures.

Such policies facilitate the elimination of Indigenous peoples and the theft of Indigenous lands, thereby satisfying settler colonialism's need for territory. Racist laws and policy often operate through deeply gendered logics, making Indigenous women a target for violence. Audra Simpson has written on the significance of Indigenous women's bodies in settler colonialism and explains:

> An Indian woman's body in settler regimes such as the US, in Canada is loaded with meaning—signifying other political orders, land itself, of the dangerous possibility of reproducing Indian life and most dangerously, other political orders. *Other* life forms, other sovereignties, other forms of political will . . . Feminist scholars have argued that Native women's bodies were to the settler eye, like land, and as much in the settler mind, the Native woman is rendered "unrapeable" (or highly rapeable) because she was like land, matter to be extracted from, used, sullied, taken from, over and over again, something that is already violated and violateable in a great march to accumulate surplus, to so-called production.[12]

Thus, violence against Indigenous women is a central feature of settler colonialism. Thousands of Indigenous women in Canada have been murdered, and many more are considered missing.[13] This has prompted calls for an inquiry into the circumstances that have produced so much violence. Yet the issue of missing and murdered women did not gain much traction as a political issue until 2015, when a newly elected federal government committed to establishing a public inquiry. As Simpson explains, the reluctance to confront this problem reflects the necessary expendability of Indigenous women in the settler colonial imagination.[14]

Media Representations of Indigenous People

The media shapes public perceptions of Indigenous people in Canada,[15] while also narrating a particular national history.[16] The final report of the Truth and Reconciliation Commission of Canada (TRC) notes that "media coverage of Aboriginal issues remains problematic; social media and online commentary are often inflammatory and racist in nature."[17] Recognizing the role of the media in creating a national historical narrative, which in turn influences public opinion and policy responses, the TRC advocates for more accurate and positive media representations of Indigenous people.

Canadian media coverage of Indigenous issues typically focuses on the extreme conditions faced by Indigenous people while ignoring historical complexities that explain these circumstances. Instead, the media perpetuates "damaging stereotypes of aboriginal people and create[s] a supportive environment for state structures and practices that reproduce material and social inequality between aboriginal and non-aboriginal people."[18] At the same time, the media typically characterizes Indigenous organizing against colonial oppression in terms that position Indigenous resistance as an internal terrorist threat.[19] Consequently, problem-focused reporting makes it easier for settler colonial governments to ignore colonialism, while framing Indigenous people as a threat to dominant interests.

At the same time that the media maintains a focus on extreme conditions, other issues of critical importance to Indigenous survival are ignored entirely. For example, the news media paid scarce attention to the vast number of Indigenous women murdered and reported missing from the Downtown Eastside of Vancouver,[20] only focusing on the situation in order to sensationalize a story about a serial killer targeting street-involved women. As Jennifer England argues, the presence of Indigenous women oscillates between invisibility and "hyper-visibility" in media representations of missing women; multiple forms of state-sanctioned violence experienced by missing and murdered Indigenous women are often rendered invisible in reporting, while the deviance of their lives, bodies, and neighbourhoods is rendered hyper-visible.[21] These representations serve to naturalize Indigenous death, normalize slow police response to the murder of Indigenous women, and further underline the anomalousness of Indigenous bodies in urban space. In short, they construct the city as settler colonial space.

Indigenous peoples and cities have long been constructed as mutually exclusive,[22] with the assumption that Indigenous people in cities are merely "transient, en route to their legislated 'camp,' which is the Indian reserve."[23] The construction of Indigenous people as anomalous within the space of the city relies on the creation of clear distinctions between urban and non-urban spaces. This distinction not only allows settler colonialism to determine what kinds of spaces and categories Indigenous peoples can legitimately inhabit but also enables the designation of the city as settler colonial space, which in turn allows urban space to represent the political and moral coherence of the settler polity. The maintenance of a moral order grants settler colonialism a degree of legitimacy by allowing its inherent violence to appear as a force that restores order rather than one that destroys it.

CONSTRUCTING SETTLER COLONIAL URBAN SPACE

"Welcome to Winnipeg . . ."

The news media portrays places, events, and people, and so constructs geographic knowledge.[24] The news interprets and constructs places and contributes to the creation of a sense of place that "provides a 'grounding' for everyday life and experience."[25] Media images of places not only (re)produce local imaginaries, but also contribute to the construction of national imaginaries by creating and reflecting images of both the city and the nation.[26] The article "Welcome to Winnipeg: Where Canada's Racism Problem Is at Its Worst" constructs and mobilizes geographic knowledge about the city in order to highlight and explain the racism experienced by Indigenous people in Winnipeg.

Like many Canadian cities, Winnipeg is comprised of distinct neighbourhoods. The *Maclean's* article focuses on Winnipeg's North End neighbourhood and also introduces readers to some features of Winnipeg's geography by explaining that "Winnipeg is physically divided by CP rail yards." The article goes on to suggest that this division is not only physical but also an ethnic and moral one. Thus, Winnipeg is "deeply divided along ethnic lines" that separate the rest of the city from the "primarily Aboriginal North End." The reader learns that the North End is a neighbourhood that "looks nothing like the idyllic, tree-lined, middle-class neighbourhoods to the south." In contrast to the south side of the city, the North End is described as "the poorest and most violent neighbourhood in urban Canada," where "poor inner-city natives" experience a "shameful state of life."

The article uses statistics to describe poverty faced by residents of the North End, reporting, for instance, that "the neighbourhood is home to two of the country's three poorest postal codes," with a median household income that is "less than half of that of the wider city." However, these statistics fail to convey the socio-economic processes that have produced concentrated poverty in this neighbourhood. As in many other cities, the socio-demographic composition of Winnipeg neighbourhoods varies, reflecting socio-economic processes of uneven development. The decline of Winnipeg's inner-city neighbourhoods began in the era following the Second World War, as sweeping technological and socio-economic changes profoundly altered urban structures through suburbanization. At the same time, Indigenous settlement in Winnipeg increased during the 1960s, with many Indigenous people finding housing in inner-city neighbourhoods.[27] While the North End has always been a working-class community, decades of disinvestment in the North End mean that this neighbourhood lacks the same social and physical infrastructure that is afforded to other communities in Winnipeg.[28] Over time, increasing housing costs, low vacancy rates, and a declining supply of social housing have resulted in limited housing options for Indigenous people in Winnipeg, contributing to a concentration of poverty in the North End.[29]

The article does not shy away from painting an extreme picture of life in the North End and repeatedly describes the neighbourhood as impoverished, crime-ridden, and dangerous. In one paragraph it claims that in Winnipeg homicides are "primarily [a] North End phenomenon." In another paragraph, a fourteen-year-old informant is described as "coming off a high after huffing gas," while the physical abuse and sexual exploitation experienced by another young informant is described in tragic detail. "This is a North End childhood," the article explains.

This "North End childhood" not only describes a set of conditions faced by a few individuals; the adjectival use of "North End" suggests that these conditions characterize the entire neighbourhood. Deborah Martin argues that media representations often conflate representations of people with representation of places, with descriptions of neighbourhoods serving as proxies for descriptions of people. As crime and violence are portrayed as inherent to inner-city spaces, the people who reside in these neighbourhoods are cast in the same negative light and assumed to be degenerate merely because of their location.[30] Thus, while these descriptions of life in the North End suggest that social problems are common among residents, they also suggest that the reverse is true: the neighbourhood is a dark and dangerous place because of the people who live there. Consequently, the North End is constructed as both a deviant and Indigenous urban space, placed in contrast to predominantly white, middle-class neighbourhoods.

". . . Where Canada's Racism Problem Is at Its Worst"

As the article's title suggests, a significant portion of its content is devoted to discussing the problem of racism faced by Indigenous people in Winnipeg. While the article provides ample examples of both interpersonal and systemic racism faced by Indigenous people in Winnipeg, it makes no distinction between these experiences, nor does it explain how this racism is systematically produced. Instead, it cites opinion polling and social media analysis to show that "Winnipeg recorded the highest proportion of racist tweets" in six Canadian cities, consequently highlighting the interpersonal dimensions of racism.

As George Lipsitz notes, "By placing the emphasis on prejudice rather than on power, we lose the ability to see how race does work in our society, how it systematically skews opportunities and life changes along racial lines, and how it literally as well as figuratively 'takes place.'"[31] Thus, stories of physical and sexual violence provide a vivid backdrop for discussion of racism in Winnipeg. However, the article does little to explain possible causes of this violence and does not explore the factors that render Indigenous people vulnerable to violence. Moreover, the attempt to illuminate the problem of racism is muddied by the fact that Indigenous people perpetrated some of the violence described in the article. In the absence of a clear explanation of the causes of violence, the article merely reinforces a narrative that naturalizes the violence experienced by Indigenous people in the city and positions this violence as a product of urban life.

The article does not explore the colonial roots of state-sanctioned violence in any detail. While it makes fleeting reference to the residential school system, it does not explain how the residential school system has weakened Indigenous bodies, families, and social networks, and affected the ability of Indigenous communities to confront the unique challenges they face. Rather than situating the legacy of the residential school experience within the history of a broader project of settler colonialism, the article reinforces stereotypes as the root of Winnipeg's racism problem. Recounting the experiences of Jon C., a local musician and the child of a residential school survivors, the article explains how the after-effects of the residential school experience have contributed to the creation of negative stereotypes: "He remembers sitting through wild, all-night parties as a toddler," and concludes that "it's this sorry state of affairs that leads many in the city to look down on the Aboriginal population." Thus, these stereotypes are presented as having roots in reality, while racism is positioned as yet another problem that burdens Indigenous people in the city. The article goes on to cite examples of the kinds of harassment Indigenous people face in the city on a daily basis but does not make clear how the city is implicated in this racism, other than to show how non-Indigenous residents are occasional perpetrators of inter-personal violence.

"A body slam to the ego"
Deborah Martin notes that while the media influences common understandings of people and places, this relationship is dialogical, as media consumers often challenge news stories through letters and action, both extending and altering discourses generated by the news media.[32] This was true of the *Maclean's* article, which received significant public attention, reflected by numerous op-eds and letters to the editor in the *Winnipeg Free Press* and other Manitoba media outlets. These responses reflected and extended the ways the concept of racism was mobilized in the *Maclean's* article.

Many of these responses suggested that the *Maclean's* article had damaged the reputation of the city. These claims established the city as recipient of harm and an object of public concern. One article claimed that the city had been given a "black eye,"[33] while another argued that the city had been "publicly shamed."[34] Some were concerned about the potential economic costs of the "reputational damage" caused by the article, noting "a reputation as a racist city doesn't help anybody, whether it's local business, families or tourism."[35] By highlighting racism in Winnipeg, the article was perceived as causing damage to Winnipeg's reputation. As one article put it: "Winnipeg woke up to a body slam to the ego when *Maclean's* called it Canada's most racist city. For many it was humiliating, an epithet that's hard to swallow in a city quick to defend its virtues."[36] Some commentators sought to recover the city's reputation by calling into question the examples of racism used in the article. Rather than denying the violence and poverty highlighted by *Maclean's*, they argued that the examples cited were not, in fact, examples of racism. These responses often pointed out that the violence depicted in the article was perpetrated by Indigenous people themselves. As one editorial in the *Brandon Sun* argued: "There is more to the issue than simply blaming racism. Perhaps the attacks took place under the influence of drugs or alcohol. I hazard a guess this may turn out to be the case. If so, substance abuse is far more central to the issue than racism."[37] Such responses blamed Indigenous people for the problems identified by the article and reflect what Elizabeth Comack and Evan Bowness have called the "discourse of denial" and "discourse of responsibilization." Such discourses invoke tropes of Indian savagery and drunkenness in order to deny racism. They also suggest that experiences of racism are merely a side effect of degenerate behaviour, for which Indigenous people themselves are responsible. This discursive creation of Indigenous difference serves a unique purpose, as "it acts as a rationale on which power relations rest, justifying power imbalances and cementing the position of members of the dominant group."[38]

Not all responses denied the existence of racism. Instead, some merely challenged the suggestion that Winnipeg is more racist than other cities in Canada. One editorial questioned the extent to which racism can be measured, asking, "How does one actually quantify if Winnipeg is Canada's most racist city? Is this based on real, measurable criteria?"[39] In a similar vein, one letter to the editor conceded that racism is a problem in Winnipeg but argued, "I don't feel it is a just conclusion that we are the absolute worst."[40]

Although many responses contested the article's assertion that Winnipeg is Canada's "most racist city," the article's characterization of the North End as an exceptional and dangerous space was rarely called into question. Instead, many felt the title unfairly damaged the city as a whole. After all, according to the article, the problems described are unique to Winnipeg's North End. Thus, the defence of Winnipeg's virtue and the refutation of the epithet "most racist city" often relied on the maintenance of a set of value-laden distinctions between south and north Winnipeg, and between Indigenous and non-Indigenous life.

"It had to take my baby to die . . ."

The ways that Indigenous and non-Indigenous life are differently valued become clear when examining the article's description of the death of Tina Fontaine, which frames the discussion of the conditions confronting Indigenous people in Winnipeg.

Tina Fontaine's life is recounted in terms that mark her as transitory. The reader is told that Tina began her life in Winnipeg but moved to Powerview-Pine Falls to live with her Aunt Thelma when her father could no longer care for her. According to the article, Tina flourished in this small town, removed from both the reserve and the city. However, this all changed when Tina did not come home after a trip to the city to visit her mother. No one knows exactly what happened to Tina, but the article attempts to piece together the last weeks of her life in Winnipeg. The description of Tina's arrival and eventual disappearance traces a hazardous trajectory from a small town to the city, where her death seems inevitable given the constant danger she encountered:

strangers exploit her, the police ignore her, child welfare agents neglect her, until finally she is murdered and her body is dumped into the Red River.

In contrast to the narrative about the dangers Tina faced in the city, the grief experienced by her family is positioned within domestic space, further reinforcing the anomalousness of her body and life in urban space. The grief of Tina's Aunt Thelma is conveyed in terms that paint a picture of domesticity, from the photograph of Tina that still hangs on the wall to the description of Thelma's well-kept home. The reader is told that Thelma can't forgive herself for letting Tina go to Winnipeg and learns that since Tina's death, Thelma "has refused to leave her tidy home." She explains: "Every time I leave the house I feel like I'm having a panic attack." These details highlight the dangers represented by the city and remind the reader that within the specific context of family life and domesticity, Tina's death is a deep loss. However, the contrasts between domestic and urban spaces also reinforce the idea that Tina's multiple vulnerabilities were a product of her transitory urban life and hint at desperate reasoning: had she only stayed out of the city, she would not have been murdered.

Writing about media portrayals of women missing from Vancouver's Downtown East Side, Geraldine Pratt argues that in the context of powerful media representations, which consistently position Indigenous women's bodies as transient and deviant, Indigenous women only become grievable once they are described in terms that place them within the orbit of respectable family life and away from the space of the city.[41] While such accounts humanize murdered women, they also create a narrative that "privatizes, individualizes, and potentially depoliticizes" their experience and "establishes the family as the criterion by which their life is grievable, and it restates the missing women—not as citizens of the city—but within the private sphere of pre-political life."[42] Having established the degeneracy of Indigenous space and life in the city, the *Maclean's* article narrates Tina's life in ways that ask the reader to accept the dangers she faced as simply a consequence of her presence in the city, without questioning the ways that structural racism produces vulnerability. After all, we would expect nothing less of a "North End childhood." The narrative does not name or challenge the factors that colluded to reinforce her vulnerability and produce her death. The article pays scarce attention to the ways in which Tina was rendered vulnerable by being placed into state "care," ignoring the fact that Indigenous children placed in government "care" often face increased risks of being exposed to violence and systemic maltreatment.[43] Instead, the narrative naturalizes the exploitation she endured at the hands of strangers and normalizes the ways in which police and child welfare services neglected her life.

The *Maclean's* article serves up a number of examples of other young Indigenous women who have faced a similar fate, noting that Tina's body was in the same spot where another Indigenous woman was found murdered in 1961. The only marker of exception in Tina's story is that unlike the vast majority of Indigenous women who have been killed in Winnipeg, her death was publicly grieved. The article suggests that her death marked a "turning point" in race relations, citing public outpourings of grief and sympathy for her family as a sign of a "promise . . . of a more hopeful future for the city." The article cites a public vigil following her death—which drew a large number of non-Indigenous people and elicited public expressions of grief—as evidence that her death was a catalyst for changing attitudes within the city.

As Sherene Razack has argued, the lives of Indigenous women and girls are not valued in the colonial imagination. Instead, their disposability is continuously taken as evidence of colonial power.[44] Outside of the depoliti-cized domestic sphere, Tina's death is imbued with value insofar as it brings attention to the problem of racism. In this way, the narrative presented in the article not only positions Indigenous death as an affirmation of settler colonial urban space, it forecloses the possibility of flourishing Indigenous life in the city, as the making of settler colonial urban space is predicated on Indigenous death. The article concludes with a quote from Tina's aunt that affirms the morbid fantasy: "Tina did this. . . . It had to take my baby to die for people to realize there was a problem—and there still is."

The framing of Tina's death in this way signals the salvageability of the city and reveals a morbid settler fantasy in which the murder of an Indigenous girl is understood in ways that affirm settler sovereignty and re-makes the city as settler colonial space. The problem of racism as raised by the article casts the city as a recipient of harm and as an object to be saved. Tina's death provides an opportunity for an emotional display that saves Winnipeg from the label "most racist city." Thus, the death of this Indigenous girl serves a dual function: it removes the threat to settler sovereignty posed by Indigenous life, and it secures the moral and political integrity of the city by providing an opportunity for a performance of settler grief.

CONTEMPLATING NON-RACIST CITIES

While the *Maclean's* article was the focus of significant criticism, many—including the Mayor of Winnipeg—viewed it as a catalyst for an important public discussion about the problem of racism in Winnipeg. The ways that concepts such as "racism" and "the city" were discursively constructed in the article and in the public response it generated influenced the possibilities for redress that were discussed in the article's wake. Both the article and public response to it framed the problem of racism in ways that foreclosed a deeper discussion of how racism is related to historic and contemporary genocide in Canada. Thus, the resulting political response failed to address the ways that systematic racism renders Indigenous life vulnerable and failed to offer solutions that foreground the flourishing of Indigenous life.

On 23 January 2015, one day after the *Maclean's* article was published, Winnipeg mayor Brian Bowman convened a news conference to address the problems raised by the article. Flanked by prominent members of the Indigenous community (all male), he admitted that "ignorance, hatred, intolerance [and] racism exist everywhere." Moreover, he affirmed that "Winnipeg has a responsibility, right now, to turn this ship around and change the way we all relate—Aboriginal and non-Aboriginal Canadians alike, from coast to coast to coast." Through the mayor's suggestion that the city has the responsibility to play a leadership role in addressing racism *across* Canada, the city is positioned as both a legitimate political actor and hailed as a symbol of the settler colonial moral order. Bowman concluded his remarks by saying: "My wife is Ukrainian heritage [chokes on tears]. My family is Métis. I want my boys to be as proud of both of those family lines. And I want every young person in our community, regardless of where you come from, to be proud of Winnipeg. Be proud of who you are. I invite Winnipeggers to join us and be part of breaking down those barriers—for your kids, for my kids, and for future generations. The action has to follow the talk."[45] The cornerstone of the political response was a two-day event titled "One Winnipeg: The Mayor's National Summit on Racial Inclusion," held in the fall of 2015 at the newly completed Canadian Museum for Human Rights.[46]

The *Maclean's* article was written at a moment when the term *reconciliation* began to gain increasing political traction. The apology of Prime Minister Stephen Harper in 2008 for the residential school system, followed by public apologies in provincial legislatures, and the work of the Truth and Reconciliation Commission meant that apology and acknowledgement of

Canada's colonial past could almost be considered *de rigueur* in Canadian politics. However, political gestures such as the mayor's apology, while a positive sign, do not necessarily signal a turning point. Such admissions of bad behaviour and declarations of anti-racism can be used to signal good moral standing. As Sara Ahmed writes, through such witnessing of past injustice "shame 'makes' the nation" and "exposes the failure of the nation to live up to its ideals. But this exposure is temporary, and becomes the ground for a narrative of national recovery. By witnessing what is shameful about the past, the nation can 'live up to' the ideals that secure its identity or being in the present. In other worlds, our shame shows that we mean well. The transference of bad feeling to the subject in this admission of shame is only temporary, as the 'transference' itself becomes evidence of the restoration of an identity of which we can be proud."[47] Reflecting on damage-centred research, Eve Tuck asks: "Are the wins worth the long-term costs of thinking of ourselves as damaged?"[48] By presenting a stunning array of shocking images depicting Indigenous life in Winnipeg, the article invites readers to be spectators of Indigenous suffering. Although the article seeks to draw attention to the plight of Indigenous people by highlighting conditions of misery, the accusation that Winnipeg is the "most racist" city in Canada ultimately enables the city to perform contrition, through which it begins to recover an identity as a non-racist city. Writing in the American context, Jodi Byrd argues, "When the remediation of the colonization of American Indians is framed through discourses of racialization that can be redressed by further inclusion into the nation-state, there is a significant failure to grapple with the fact that such discourses further re-inscribe the original colonial injury."[49] Thus, the damage-focused approach fails to recognize that Indigenous life has persisted and flourished in Winnipeg in spite of settler colonial violence.

While the article describes the work of several North End community leaders, emphasizing the positive contributions they are making to their community, it does not discuss their work in terms that highlight the importance of this active resistance to colonial policies that actively produce Indigenous dispossession. Instead, these individuals are held up as shining exceptions to a dark rule, further reinforcing the negative picture of the North End projected by the article.

What if the article had focused on the vibrancy and the resilience of the Indigenous Community? Framed in this way, not only would racist violence be de-naturalized, it would invite a presentation of the multiple ways that

Indigenous people in Winnipeg are resisting colonial violence and creating vibrant communities in the face of immense challenges, and a discussion of a host of long-standing projects and new initiatives led by Indigenous people in Winnipeg.

For instance, the article might have discussed the long-standing work of Neechi Commons, a community-owned food store, catering service, and art gallery in the North End that not only provided healthy and traditional foods but also employment opportunities to both local residents and traditional food harvesters beyond the city.[50] It could have focused on a host of community organizations, such as Ka Ni Kanichhihk, Thunderbird House, or Ma Mawi Wi Chi Itata Centre, that are working to provide culturally relevant services that support the building of a vibrant Indigenous community in Winnipeg.[51] Or it might have discussed the multiple informal ways that Indigenous women and men create spaces for themselves and their communities in the face of ongoing racism.[52] It could have highlighted the work of numerous Winnipeg-based Indigenous writers, artists, and cultural institutions that actively confront settler colonialism while at the same time creating a vision for Indigenous flourishing. Such a discussion would have highlighted how Indigenous people are working to enact new forms of community, create new forms of economic organization, and invent new modes of city-building that do not rest on the oppression of Indigenous peoples. Such a framing would have shown how Indigenous people claim the city as an Indigenous space, and would have affirmed the flourishing of Indigenous urban life as a rule rather than an exception. In short, framing a discussion of racism in a way that focuses on the vibrancy of Indigenous life would set the stage for a discussion of how Indigenous people might lead processes of city-building, and affirmed the vital importance of Indigenous contributions to the making of a just and anti-racist city.

CONCLUSION: WHAT IS A NON-RACIST CITY?

As my analysis of the article "Welcome to Winnipeg" and the responses it provoked has shown, a damage-centred approach to understanding racism perversely allows Indigenous death to be understood as an antidote to the problem of racism rather than a symptom. While a discussion of racism and the living conditions of Indigenous people are ostensibly the focus of the article, its main preoccupation is not with *Indigenous* life or death but with the life and death of the city itself. In the article, as well as in the many responses it triggered, the notion of "the city" serves as a cipher for settler colonial life. In this way, the label "most racist city" is perceived as an injury to the political and moral coherence of settler colonial polity. Thus, the making of settler colonial urban space is bound up with settler colonialism's desire for life and its never-ending requirement for space, which is in turn predicated on Indigenous death.

Anti-racist and anti-colonial practice requires thinking carefully about how the problem of racism in cities is framed. Taking seriously the city as a site of anti-colonial struggle means confronting these multiple and intersecting forms of settler colonial violence. As an alternative to a politics of urban inclusion that fails to fundamentally transform the murderous logic of settler colonialism, recasting the city as an anti-racist and anti-colonial space in both discourse and policy requires understanding the city as a space where Indigenous life can flourish and subverting the logics that underlie settler colonial place making. Such a transformative project relies on multi-faceted interventions, including examining the causes of violence against Indigenous women while also foregrounding the role of women in making Indigenous space. It would highlight connections between urban and rural spaces by affirming Indigenous territorial authority, which would in turn have important implications for urban development and planning. It would highlight the intersecting logics of racism, misogyny, and capital accumulation that characterize settler colonialism. A non-racist city would not be built on human suffering. Instead, a non-racist city would ensure that the growth, governance, economy, and social life of the city did not compromise the health and survival of Indigenous women, men, and children. In short, a non-racist city would be understood as an Indigenous space, and would provide the conditions for the flourishing of Indigenous urban life.

NOTES

1   Macdonald, "Welcome to Winnipeg."

2   Tonkiss, "Analyzing Text and Speech," 367.

3   Tuck, "Suspending Damage," 409.

4   Ibid., 415.

5   Wolfe, "Settler Colonialism and the Elimination of the Native," 387.

6   Ibid., 402.

7   Veracini, *The Settler Colonial Present.*

8   Allan and Smylie, *First Peoples, Second Class Treatment.*

9   Ibid., 5.

10 Gilmore, "Race and Globalization," 261.

11 Lawrence, "Gender, Race, and the Regulation of Native Identity."

12 Simpson, "The State Is a Man."

13 Ibid.

14 Ibid.

15 Furniss, "Aboriginal Justice," 1.

16 Anderson and Robertson, *Seeing Red.*

17 Truth and Reconciliation Commission of Canada, *Honouring the Truth, Reconciling for the Future,* 196.

18 Harding, "Historical Representations of Aboriginal People," 206.

19 Adese, "Constructing the Aboriginal Terrorist," 283.

20 Hugill, *Missing Women, Missing News*; Dean, *Remembering Vancouver's Disappeared Women.*

21 England, "Disciplining Subjectivity and Space."

22 Peters, "'Urban' and 'Aboriginal.'"

23 Pratt, "Abandoned Women and the Space of the Exception," 1059.

24 Howe, "Newsworthy Spaces," 4.

25 Martin, "Constructing Place," 380.

26 Wilkes, Corrigall-Brown, and Ricard, "Nationalism and Media Coverage," 42.

27 Silver, "Segregated City."

28 Wideman and Masuda, "Intensification and Neoliberalization," 55; Hugill and Toews, "Born Again Urbanism," 69.

29 Cooper, "Housing for People, Not Markets."

30 Martin, "Constructing Place," 392.

31 Lipsitz, *How Racism Takes Place,* 41.

32 Martin, "Constructing Place," 380.

33 Paul, "Racism Is Manitoba's Shame."

34 Santin, "Summit Seen as a First Step."

35 Kirbyson, "Confronting Racism."

36 "How to Fix Canada's 'Most Racist' City."

37 Auriat, "Plight of Aboriginals."

38 Comack and Bowness, "Dealing the Race Card," 34.

39 Auriat, "Plight of Aboriginals."

40 *Winnipeg Free Press*, "Readers Divided on 'Racist City' Claim."

41 Pratt, "Abandoned Women and the Space of the Exception."

42 Ibid., 1064. See also Jiwani and Young, "Missing and Murdered Women."

43 Blackstock, "Should Governments Be Above the Law?" See also BC Representative for Children and Youth, *Too Many Victims*.

44 Razack, "Gendering Disposability."

45 *Maclean's*, Transcript: Winnipeg Mayor's Press Conference on Racism.

46 City of Winnipeg, Citizens Equality Committee, *ONE: The Mayor's National Summit*.

47 Ahmed, "Declarations of Whiteness," 23.

48 Tuck, "Suspending Damage," 415.

49 Byrd, *The Transit of Empire*, xxiii.

50 Pearce and Wuttunee, "Our Hearts on Our Street," 4.

51 See generally Cormier, "Indigenous Youth Conflict Intervention"; McKenzie and Morrissette, "Cultural Empowerment and Healing for Aboriginal Youth."

52 See for instance Silver, *Unearthing Resistance*.

CHAPTER TWO

ANTI-INDIAN COMMON SENSE

Border Town Violence and Resistance in Mni Luzahan

NICK ESTES

In 1980, when the U.S. Supreme Court verified what the Lakota people have been saying for more than a century, that the 1868 [Fort Laramie] Treaty was violated, many non-Indian people of [South Dakota] became afraid of losing their homes, businesses, and livelihoods. Are they remembering the fashion in which many of their ancestors forced the loss of the homes and livelihoods of Lakota people and think the same will happen to them, or are they afraid that the federal government will turn on them also as it has turned on Lakota people?[1]

The above epigraph is Lakota intellectual and renowned environmentalist Charmaine White Face's testimony at a U.S. Commission on Civil Rights hearing held in Rapid City, South Dakota, on 6 December 1999. The investigation brought federal, state, local, and Native leaders, community members, and law enforcement together with the intent "to conduct a public forum on Native Americans and the administration of justice in South

Figure 2.1. Map of Oceti Sakowin Treaty Territories and Reservation Boundaries

Dakota."[2] White Face succinctly explained the real problem of justice so often glossed by civil rights and law enforcement experts as "race relations" or
the ever-elusive phantom of "tribal-state relations." These so-called relations
obscure or erase the primary relationship between Native and settler: the
colonial relation. White Face suggested white settlers know, whether they
admit it or not, that their existence upon and claim to the land is premised
upon the violent forced removal, dispossession, and elimination of Indigenous peoples. Acknowledging this, however, forecloses the possibility for
anti-colonial justice by deploying the spectre of anti-white violence, a prospect White Face posed in a rhetorical question to demonstrate the double
standard of settler justice as a zero-sum game. Even in rare moments of judicial vindication, such as the landmark case *United States v. Sioux Nation* of
Indians, which found that He Sapa (the Black Hills) were in fact stolen, Native justice is made impossible.[3] This thinking keeps intact settler society by
consigning any sordid dealings, if acknowledged, to the past to make them
inconceivable, nonexistent, or a potential threat in the present.

In the months leading up to White Face's testimony, the lifeless bodies
of eight homeless men—six of whom were Lakotas—were pulled from the
city's namesake, Rapid Creek, called Mni Luzahan in Lakota. The deceased
included Benjamin Long Wolf, George Hatt, Alan Hough, Randelle Two
Crow, Loren Two Bulls, Dirk Bartling, Arthur Chamberlain, and Timothy
Bull Bear. The creek winds through the downtown area; it serves as a public
park and a municipal golf course and is also home to many poor and homeless,
who are primarily Native. Authorities ruled the deaths accidental alcohol-re-
lated drownings, in spite of Native demands to investigate them as possible
homicides. Choosing not to pursue homicide investigations, Rapid City
Police Chief Tom Hennies told the Associated Press, "There's just too many
of them to say it's coincidence. But it could be. . . . We don't know what else
to do. We've done everything we can do."[4] Everything else was shrouded in
mystery, and no other context was given as to how or why these men died.
If meaning was attributed, it was speculation and conjecture. Some on the
street blamed racist vigilantes, who often targeted Natives and the homeless
for violence and harassment. But police investigations and civil rights commission hearings remained inconclusive as to who or what was the real culprit.[5]

It was as if Rapid City, the land, and its people had no history. After all,
justice could not be served if no one or nothing were at fault. In this scenario,
the colonial project, if it is acknowledged, remains innocent and unknowable.[6]

Although we may never know what happened to these men, their deaths are full of meaning. Attributing insignificance or coincidence to homicidal tragedy is in fact, as I will show, highly significant and elicits what Raymond Williams calls "structures of feeling," the emergent or pre-emergent experiences of reality "while they are being lived" that cannot always be adequately defined and rationalized but are, instead, *felt*.[7] These feelings naturalize the colonial project by denying its existence as a kind of common sense while also attaching certain *feelings* to certain colonized bodies and subjects. These feelings are not without history and politics.

This chapter examines the historic and geopolitical contestations that produce these kinds of feelings in Rapid City, the white-dominated border town located in the heart of the moral, political, and cosmological universe of the Oceti Sakowin—He Sapa, or the Black Hills.[8] Native territorial dispossessions and violence in the founding and continued *settling* of Rapid City structure what I call "anti-Indian common sense." This idea combines Dakota scholar Elizabeth Cook-Lynn's theory of anti-Indianism and Marxist revolutionary Antonio Gramsci's theory of common sense.[9] Bridging Indigenous and Marxist traditions in this way produces more robust versions of class, class struggle, and decolonization. This includes the ways in which structural inequality, dispossession, and violence are manifest within the urban setting of border towns. Marxism and Indigenous theory are also not mutually exclusive or incompatible. Rather, they both attend to the ways in which people from different social positions, from colonizer to colonized, understand what is just and what is not, and how held-in-common senses of justice, when politically developed, can facilitate the passage from lived experiences to the formation of new political narratives and movements capable of bringing about radical social transformation.

In this chapter, I argue that Rapid City as a border town produces anti-Indian common sense. Natives are typically viewed as living in rural, isolated pockets of poverty.[10] Today, nearly four of five Natives in the United States live off-reservation, often in cities.[11] The city, which is seen as a beacon of settler progress and futurity, is commonly viewed as devoid of Indigenous presence, which is seen in contrast as the abject relic of a past and without a future.[12] Considering this majority off-reservation reality is essential to understanding how anti-Indian common sense is reproduced in border towns and how to effectively resist it.

The argument advanced in this chapter is split into four sections and a conclusion. The first section provides a brief overview of how common sense operates within settler colonialism and border towns. The rest of the chapter examines three moments in Rapid City history: militarized enclosure, urban displacement, and anti-colonial resistance. The second section shows how Rapid City emerged as a military outpost from 1876 to 1890 to fortify a supply chain for illegal mining operations in the Black Hills in violation of the 1868 Fort Laramie Treaty. The third section studies the processes of urban land dispossession in the mid-twentieth century by making clear how the destruction of Indigenous land and life secures colonial possession. The fourth section illustrates how the American Indian Movement relied on building an anti-colonial common sense through struggles against border violence. The conclusion examines present struggles against anti-Indian common sense in Rapid City and the utility of an anti-colonial common sense.

ON COMMON SENSE AND SETTLER COLONIALISM

This section develops the concept of anti-Indian common sense and locates its reproduction and utility within border town spaces. Anti-Indian common sense derives from what Cook-Lynn calls anti-Indianism and what Gramsci calls common sense. Cook-Lynn defines anti-Indianism as informing the broad array of sentiments that result in or carry out the death, elimination, and genocide of Natives through dehumanization and the disavowal of Indigenous nationhood and sovereignty. Anti-Indianism operates in a myriad of ways, such as the writing of U.S. history or literature that deliberately ignores Native existence, denigrates or insults being Native, or blames Natives for an unsatisfactory history. Cook-Lynn also develops this into a broader social theory that not only critiques the ways in which popular knowledge speaks (or does not speak) about Natives, but also understands how the enactment of law and policy targeting Natives and their lands upholds settler proprietary regimes. In the end, the state and its institutions may create laws and define parameters of normativity, but it is settler society that incubates and carries out the will of the colonial state. "All of these traits," Cook-Lynn writes, "have conspired to isolate, to expunge or expel, to menace, to defame."[13] Anti-Indianism is foundational to U.S. settler society. Even to ignore it is to participate in it.

Conceptualized this way, anti-Indianism complements Gramsci's theory of the production and utility of common sense, which at its core seeks to understand how spontaneous consent is achieved.[14] In Gramsci's *Prison Notebooks*, "common sense" in Italian (*senso commune*) does not have the same connotation in English. Whereas its English counterpart concerns pragmatism or natural intelligence, the Italian phrase conveys a generalized, class-derived world view or held-in-common beliefs. Gramsci's common sense is the "philosophy of the non-philosophers," or "the conception of the world which is uncritically absorbed by the various social and cultural environments in which the moral individuality of the average man [*sic*] is developed."[15] There is no singular common sense, but multiple, sometimes overlapping variations that develop across space and time and undergo constant transformation. Within each individual, common sense is largely inconsequential; it only takes on historic significance when operating collectively as a social force to produce consent. Particular social groups share common world views, whether they belong to an oppressed or oppressing class, making common sense into a structured system of beliefs and behaviours that governs society.

When and where a particular common sense develops is crucial. For anti-Indian common sense, the context shifts from the relations conditioned by European capitalism to those conditioned by North American settler colonialism.[16] This is an important shift, because there are fundamental differences between the type of hegemony that formed to justify class exploitation under European modes of capitalism and the type of hegemony that has formed to facilitate colonial dispossession in North America. I make three theoretical modifications to Gramsci's common sense to make it applicable in the settler colonial scenario and conclude by locating its utility in understanding how social relations in reservation border towns exemplify the dynamics of colonial dispossession more broadly. Anti-Indian common sense is also not unchallenged, but in fact arises because of mounted Native resistance and the continued assertion of a prior political, legal, and moral claim to the land, especially in border towns like Rapid City.

First, Gramsci understood bourgeois common sense as upholding the exploitation of a proletarianized labour force. Since they are essential to the capitalist system, workers must internalize (or at least consent to) the ruling class ideology to keep the system going. Colonialism, however, does not immediately mandate the consent of the colonized to keep the system operational. If consent is needed, it is imposed externally and does not always require Indigenous people to internalize it. If needed, Native consent is often achieved through coercion: forced assimilation, the withholding of rations, purposeful neglect, imprisonment, or the co-optation of leadership into state or corporate agendas. Second, although working class consent is sometimes achieved through force, it does not advance capital's interest to kill off or disappear the entire working class. In contrast, settler colonialism requires the disappearance and dispossession of Indigenous peoples, often through pure violence, to take the land. As Glen Coulthard and Patrick Wolfe argue, settler colonialism's primary acquisitive function is spatial (the theft of territory from Natives) rather than temporal (the theft of time from the labourer).[17] Lastly, anti-Indian common sense originates from the continued assertion of what Goenpul scholar Aileen Moreton-Robinson calls patriarchal white sovereignty over Native lands and lives.[18] Patriarchal white sovereignty is a form of colonial rule personified by the white male state official who administers the disciplinary and murderous apparatuses that give form to state sovereignty, most notably the police, the military, the prison, the boarding school, the Indian agency, or federal programming. Patriarchal white sovereignty is also evident in daily cultural practices that produce a settler citizenry that carries out the will of the state by policing, punishing, and sometimes killing Natives who defy imposed racial and social boundaries and colonial gender norms. As Kahnawà:ke Mohawk scholar Audra Simpson demonstrates in her aptly titled piece "The State Is a Man," Indigenous women are specifically targeted by the logic of patriarchal white sovereignty because they personify a radical counter-sovereignty, a prior political authority indelibly tied to land that fundamentally undermines the colonial project.[19]

To better understand how anti-Indian common sense operates through actual territorialization, I argue for a reframing of what we commonly conceive of as "cities," "towns," or "urban spaces" as, instead, colonial settlements—or in common vernacular, border towns. Border towns are white-dominated settlements that ring Indian reservations, where persistent patterns of anti-Indian exploitation, discrimination, violence, and criminalization define everyday life.[20] The material and ideological production of border towns directly correlates with the spatial aspects of settler colonialism. On one hand, they fortify the space between a white "civil society" and an abject "savage society." Settlers claim border towns like Rapid City as white spaces to erase and contain Indigeneity. On the other hand, Native presence in border towns gives rise to the meticulous management of space. For example, the physical frontiers between civilization and savagery are zealously enforced (through the arrangements of low-income housing, entrenched economic disparities, lack of political power, and the fabrication of a criminal "drunk Indian" that can be disciplined and sometimes murdered) by the military, the police, and citizens. For settler society, the ordering of such geographies is taken as given. It becomes naturalized with spatial thinking and is built into the physical environment: policing where Natives ought to be (or not), how they ought to behave, or in securing the myth of the disappearing Indian.

Border towns are also borders. By nature, they are unsettled frontiers defined by their own illegitimacy and contestability. Because of this, Native presence calls into question the finality of settlement. So while Native presence is heavily policed in border towns as a threat, it also represents prior claims to the land and the refusal to disappear. It is from this presence that another kind of common sense arises: an anti-colonial common sense embodied in the grounded practice of living in one's homeland or remaining in cultural or spiritual relation to it despite its continued occupation. For example, in Rapid City, the Lakotas, the original owners of the land, are a nightmarish reminder of a precarious settler belonging. In 1980, the Supreme Court confirmed this fear when it ruled that the United States had illegally taken the Black Hills and ordered a monetary settlement, to which Lakotas refused by saying resolutely, "The Black Hills are not for sale!"[21] At its core, anti-colonial common sense is the refusal to go away, to disappear, or to sell the land. It is also an affirmation of Native life and justice, an aspect I return to later in this chapter.

OFF THE RESERVATION

The history of place in the colonial context means everything. Militarization, dispossession, and enclosure to crush Native resistance were fundamental to the founding of Rapid City and continue to define the city's ongoing settling. This section explores the early history and spatial practice of anti-Indian common sense by examining the ways Rapid City emerged as a mining outpost that facilitated the taking of the Black Hills.

Rapid City was illegally founded in 1876 as the "gateway" to gold mining in the Black Hills, in explicit violation of the 1868 Fort Laramie Treaty that forbade settler intrusion. After the discovery of gold in 1874, the Black Hills required military fortification to secure the area against the intrusion of miners and settlers, to uphold the treaty boundaries. Soon federal troops, who were supposed to uphold treaty law, turned against Lakotas to protect the mass influx of miners. In its early years, Rapid City served as a base of operations for arming and deploying vigilante militias and the U.S. military to lead sorties against Native people leaving the reservation. These vigilante groups were the origins of the police force and "law and order" in the border towns in Oceti Sakowin territory, creating and enforcing the law in the absence of it. These actions were met with resistance. On 25 June 1876, in response to unabated U.S. hostility, an allied confederacy of Lakota, Cheyenne, and Arapaho annihilated five companies of the Seventh Cavalry Regiment under the command of General George Armstrong Custer, killing 268 men, including Custer, at the Battle of Greasy Grass (or the Battle of the Little Bighorn). This was an entirely defensive endeavour against continued settler incursion into the vast twenty-five million acres of treaty territory. In 1877, Congress passed the Black Hills Act, nullifying the 1868 treaty and illegally ceding the Black Hills. Although the Oceti Sakowin were never militarily defeated, settlers overran treaty lands, shrinking the land base, exterminating the buffalo, a primary food source for many Native Nations, and forcing many to seek refuge on newly created reservations.[22] "Dakota fever," the insatiable desire for cheap or free Native land, hit the early settlers from 1878 to 1887. Coming out of a five-year national economic recession, plans for a yeoman farming empire in the western half of Dakota Territory resulted in the settlement of the Black Hills and the surrounding plains of remaining Oceti Sakowin treaty territory. The population of settlers and prospectors in the area doubled in 1890, and so too did the acreage of settler land deeds.[23] What was known as the Great Dakota Boom entailed the speculative investment in railroads, mining, homesteading, and ranching operations, setting the stage for the next century of continued occupation. In 1889, South Dakota achieved statehood. The only thing standing in the way was what General Nelson Miles called the "hostile element among the Indians who want to rove at will and live as formerly in their wild state."[24]

South Dakota's "Indian Problem" has always been defined as the bodies and political sovereignties that continue to live atop desired lands and resources. To exert possession, those bodies had to be moved out of the way or eliminated altogether. To do so, the settler project has always been mobilized toward what Patrick Wolfe calls a "reproach of nomadism" that renders Native removable, killable, temporary, and defying a *settled* existence.[25] Historian Philip Hall sums up the resentment toward the Lakotas' "nomadic" proclivities: "Early developers firmly believed [that] the only way to improve economic conditions in the state was to move Indians out of the way."[26] When the "Great Sioux War" wound down, many Natives moved to reservations. Reservation life was not a choice but a means for survival—and subsequently, Natives were removed from and kept in place by border towns such as Rapid City. Businessmen and the town's newspaper, the *Rapid City Journal*, called for an escalation in arms against Natives leaving the reservations. The infamous South Dakota Home Guard, known as the Cowboy Militia, was headquartered in Rapid City and became frontier law enforcement and notorious Indian killers. In early December of 1890, the Cowboy Militia hunted down and killed seventy-five Lakotas who were on a hunting expedition.[27] Their crime? Leaving the reservation. At the apex of frontier homicide, a vengeful Seventh Cavalry, Custer's regiment, massacred about 300 Lakota men, women, and children at Wounded Knee Creek on 29 December 1890. The so-called Indian War of 1890–91 had not completely wiped out the Native population, and dissatisfied settlers further protested that Lakotas had not been adequately punished, since not an acre of land was ceded. "In frontier parlance," Hall writes, "the Indian problem had not been *settled*."[28] In this way, Natives off the reservation posed a threat to border towns like Rapid City.

"Off the reservation" is a common, seemingly innocent phrase. The *Oxford English Dictionary* defines it as an American English idiom, meaning "to deviate from what is expected or customary; to behave unexpectedly or independently."[29] The expression is also current in military and political circles, designating someone who defies limits and boundaries, who is unpredictable and therefore ungovernable. Individuals who go "off the reservation" are rogues or mavericks in military lingo—those who "cross the wire" of military bases (called reservations) or enter hostile territory without orders. Hostile territory in military jargon is also commonly called Indian Country.[30] For Native people to "go off the reservation" refers to those who historically refused reservation life or refused to respect its borders, within which Native life was contained and managed. In those days, those willfully crossing borders were renegades, outlaws, or hostiles, who were usually hunted down and summarily shot, hanged, or imprisoned. It is no coincidence this phrase arose from the parlance of nineteenth-century Indian wars, the confinement of Indigenous peoples to reservations, and the murderous consequences inflicted upon those refusing to live by imposed rules and boundaries.

"Off the reservation" is a historical question of territory and sovereignty, and most importantly, it is a political practice—a direct challenge to what produces Native life as spatially and temporally fixed and politically reprehensible. To evoke Audra Simpson, Native transgressions into the domain of what is considered "settled" territory or "settled" history calls into question the completeness, the finality, and the constant disavowal of Indigenous dispossession and elimination.[31] If territoriality is, as Wolfe reminds us, "settler colonialism's specific, irreducible element," then the erasure and elimination of Native people is not based on their race (or blood quantum, culture, civilization, religion, world view, or ethnicity), but simply to gain access to territory.[32] Once that territory is acquired—or settled—it does not become an inactive element. It requires continual *doing*—the legal, political, and ideological performance of ownership and belonging. The continued and persistent presence of Indigenous peoples atop desired or claimed land, then, presents a certain problem for that *doing*—a problem throughout history we have called the Indian Problem.

SETTLEMENT'S PRICE

Nineteenth-century frontier homicide evolved into early twentieth-century institutions of discipline, containment, and renewed rounds of dispossession. Building on previous modes of anti-Indian common sense, policing and surveilling Native bodies remained the modus operandi that furthered the dispossession of Native lands through the administration of public services in Rapid City, coinciding with the federal Indian policy of termination. This section examines how anti-Indian common sense informs the normative practice of settlement in the twentieth century.

Although expelled from their Black Hills, Lakotas returned as captives to attend boarding school at the Rapid City Indian School. On 21 June 1906 Congress granted 1,391 acres of land to the Bureau of Indian Affairs (BIA) for the construction of the Rapid City Indian School, which would annually house 250 Native students until its closing in 1934. The school was transformed into a tuberculosis sanatorium that eventually became a BIA hospital for the growing urban Native population.[33] From 1934 to 1956, more than 1,200 acres of school lands were eventually sold off or given away to the Rapid City School District, the City of Rapid City, the South Dakota National Guard (which received 673 acres for free), the U.S. Bureau of Reclamation, the U.S. Indian Arts and Crafts Board, and various Christian churches. The Indian Health Service retained forty-two acres for Sioux Sanitarium Hospital,

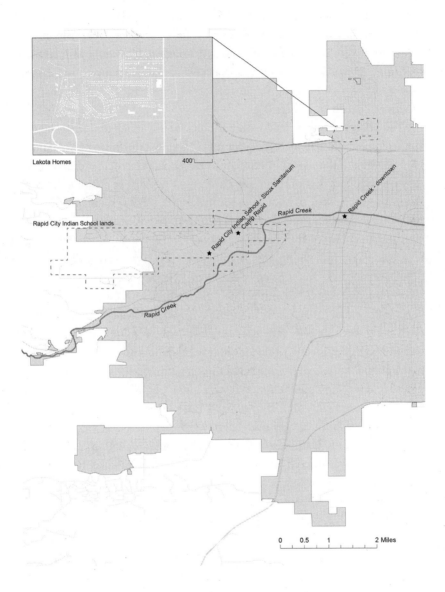

Figure 2.2. Map of Rapid City Indian School Lands and Sioux Addition Lands.

and twenty-seven acres were set aside in 1962 for the establishment of Sioux Addition, a Native housing subdivision that was located outside city limits. No Native consent was given for these land sales or the municipal assumption of jurisdiction over federal trust land.[34] Although much scholarship focuses on the usurpation of large swaths of Native land following the Great Dakota Boom and 1887 Allotment Act, little if any attention focuses on the historic practice of urban land theft.[35]

The existence of trust land within the city is an ongoing dispute alongside the counterclaim that the entire Black Hills region (including all of South Dakota west of the Missouri River) was never legally ceded and that there exists no evidence that the lands were ever purchased.[36] The creation of Sioux Addition was a result of relocating the makeshift, semi-permanent encampments of parents and relatives whose children attended the nearby Rapid City Indian School. After the school's closure, there remained federal Indian trust lands within city limits and a significant off-reservation population. The "Indian Problem" had returned in the form of "urban Indians" who left the reservation and refused to quit being Indians when they came to the city. To curb and control off-reservation migration, in 1939 South Dakota passed a series of "warning out" laws that required "transient" populations to fill out and sign "certificates of non-residence" that excluded them from poor relief, public welfare, voting, and establishing permanent residency. The legal practice of warning out stemmed from a 1662 English statute in the early American colonies, which criminalized and prevented the movements of highly mobile poor populations from one jurisdiction to another.[37]

In Rapid City, Pennington County, and South Dakota more broadly, warning out laws targeted off-reservation Natives, barring them from legally residing within certain communities or receiving basic housing, social, welfare, educational, and medical services. Ramon Roubideaux, a Rosebud Sioux attorney, described the practice at a 1962 civil rights hearing: "In Rapid City they follow that program religiously. They serve transient Indians . . . a nonresident notice. This is what they call it. In other words, by service of this notice on the individual, you prevent him [sic] from acquiring, as the statute says, a *legal settlement*."[38] Often county social service and health officials issued non-resident certificates when Natives applied for services, or they were simply denied receiving services altogether. The labelling of off-reservation Natives as "transient" did important work. It made normative the practice of settling—home ownership, citizenship, paying taxes, working, and so on—as a prerequisite for personhood versus the sensationalized and moralized lifestyle of a "nomadic" or "transient" Indian.

Two examples among many illustrate the violence of this practice and how settlement's genocidal logic structured it:

In 1956, Sarah White Bull became paraplegic after suffering a stroke while living in Rapid City. Since she had moved from the Standing Rock reservation in 1953, Pennington County denied her medical services because she was not considered a resident. She was subsequently "dumped" back at her home reservation because she was unable to work and could not afford to pay housing or medical expenses. For the medical expenses incurred, Pennington County sought liens against White Bull's allotted reservation lands. In a letter to the Indian Health Service, D.C. McCray, from the Pennington County Welfare Department, complained that because White Bull was allotted "quite a bit of land and the county can't levy against it, we feel that the county should recover to the extent of their resources on the reservation. There is no other race or color in South Dakota who are exempt from levy against their resources or property for poor relief."[39]

Chris Fire Thunder moved to Rapid City from the Pine Ridge reservation in 1951 and held a steady job. In 1960, he went to the hospital after complaining of headaches, incoordination, uncontrolled knee jerks, and unequal pupil dilation. He was denied service in Rapid City and was referred to a Pine Ridge BIA hospital, which also denied him service based on his long leave of absence from the reservation. After his condition deteriorated in January 1961, he was hospitalized in Rapid City and discharged the next morning. Following more runarounds and failure to receive proper treatment, a month later Fire Thunder was again hospitalized in Rapid City, where a neurosurgeon found a malignant tumor. He soon died, having received no treatment. Writing to the BIA area director, the Pennington County Welfare Department blamed Fire Thunder's death on the BIA, expressing dissatisfaction at the inability to place liens against federal trust lands of the surviving family to collect against medical services performed.[40]

Entire families were also denied social services, and the Pennington County Welfare Department labelled the figure of the Native mother with dependent children as "a gypsy tramp."[41] In effect, the practice of non-resident certificates and warning out laws criminalized, racialized, and hyper-sexualized Native bodies as promiscuous, transient, and in the way of the settlement. It condemned them to death precisely by implementing its own logics of settlement: to receive care, or to be cared for, Natives had to relinquish not only their lives to the state but also their property, to attain assimilation as individual proprietors through employment and private home and land ownership. (Even these aspects, however, were beyond reach.) To sum up its positions, the welfare department bluntly wrote, "If [Indians] are able bodied we have the same yardstick for them as for any nationality; namely, work or go hungry."[42]

The ableist rhetoric of a right to work simply upheld the eliminationist logic of the day encapsulated in the federal policies of termination and relocation. In 1957, termination's prophet, conservative Utah senator Arthur V. Watkins, reiterated the notion that liquidating collective Native land rights would expedite assimilation. "One facet of this over-all development," Watkins wrote in 1957, "concerns the freeing of Indians from special federal restrictions on the property and the persons of the tribes and their members."[43] He, along with other states' rights zealots such as South Dakota congressman E.Y. Berry, advocated for the programmatic liquidation of the Indian Problem, a consensus also reached by Congress. In 1953, two bills outlined this position: House Concurrent Resolution 108 declared policy to end Indian "status as wards"; and Public Law 280 granted five states immediate civil and criminal jurisdiction over tribal lands, while also allowing other states the opportunity to modify their constitutions to accommodate for the eventual assumption of state jurisdiction over Native lands. Although ostensible self-government was achieved under 1934 Indian Reorganization Act constitutions, Sicangu scholar Edward Valandra argues that termination advocated the "overthrow" of tribal governments, which also elicited a successful Oceti Sakowin resistance that defeated such an overthrow.[44]

In its arrogance, the state attempted to legislate Natives out of existence without living up to its own professed benevolence of liberal tolerance. After all, termination of land rights meant Natives would eventually integrate into dominant society—leaving the reservation to find work and housing in surrounding border towns and compelling a white-dominated state to assume the "burden" of housing, schooling, and caring for Natives as neighbours and equals. White settlers found this equally, if not more, unacceptable, thus leading to termination's failure. As cited above, Rapid City's treatment of infirmed Natives was further evidence that even if termination lived up to its name to legally *kill* the Indian, Natives nevertheless persisted, contaminated, and offended the settler body politic. Even debts to the state for medical or social welfare revealed the true intentions of Rapid City residents and the state in general: the offering of services were duplicitous attempts to acquire and liquidate tribal assets, namely land and tribal citizenship. In the eyes of settler society, Natives embodied the last remaining frontier, the last obstacle to unsettled land. Therefore, the killing of the body, whether physically or through neglect or assimilation, translated into increased access to desired lands. Assimilation, a rather soft word, should be understood as productive genocide.

The logic of termination persisted even as Indian policy shifted toward accommodation. In the 1970s, the Era of Self-Determination encouraged the devolution of federal oversight toward a tribal authority and granted more community and tribal autonomy, effectively reversing the previous policies of termination. Despite this "progressive" transition, a heightened sense of anti-colonial nationalism took shape. Rapid City became a staging ground for the Oceti Sakowin to regain stolen lands and lives in the Black Hills.

THE FLOOD

In moments of social crisis, new, counterhegemonic common senses arise, taking on a revolutionary or reactionary character. This section focuses on the 1970s as a period of crisis, its aftermath, and state and border town attempts to mediate and crush Native dissent.

The Red Power Movement arose in the 1960s in direct response to termination legislation. The American Indian Movement (AIM), formed in 1968 in response to rampant police brutality against Natives in Minnesota's Twin Cities, took on a more militant, revolutionary character. The story is well known. Historic actions from the occupation of Alcatraz in 1969, the Trail of Broken Treaties in 1972, and the famous siege at Wounded Knee in 1973 galvanized Indigenous peoples in the United States and beyond.[45] AIM is popularly viewed as a protest movement, often eliding other definitive aspects such as its border town campaigns. The era's massive Indigenous cultural and political renaissance also marked a significant shift through the creation of an anti-colonial common sense that reshaped and redefined Indigenous identity—a collective identity that took on a historic anti-colonial character. Rapid City was a key target for the mounting resentment fomenting against the established order of things that swept through the region. The struggle over the Oceti Sakowin's most prized territory, He Sapa, the Black Hills, came to a head in the 1970s. It led to violent revolt and backlash. It began with a flood.

As they had for nearly a century, most of Rapid City Natives were living in
squalor in shanty towns near Rapid Creek and downtown next to the railroad
district or in Sioux Addition, the "Indian ghetto" or "Red ghetto" outside city
limits and built upon remaining Rapid City Indian School lands.[46] On 9 June
1972, fifteen inches of torrential rain clogged the Canyon Lake dam, which
burst in the early morning hours of 10 June, sending a wall of water down
Rapid Creek. In a matter of hours, the flood rapidly swept away more than
1,300 homes, 5,000 automobiles, and 238 lives. Hardest hit were the poor,
poor Natives and poor whites who lived near the creek in mobile homes and
dilapidated structures. Although Natives made up 5 percent of Rapid City's
population, they accounted for 14 percent of those who perished in the flood
and a significant number of those displaced. The city received, in the course
of several years, $160 million for disaster relief and urban renewal programs.[47]
The relief money, however, was allocated along racial and class lines. While
all flood victims were equally entitled to relief, Mayor Don Bartlett, a liberal
Democrat, observed, "That doesn't mean that we just divvied up the money
equally all around. The Indian who lost a shack and few sticks of furniture
didn't get as much as somebody who lost a $40,000 house with 25 years
of accumulated possessions."[48] In other words, more relief was dispensed to
white, middle-class homeowners and business owners. Discrimination did not
end there. Many Natives fled to live with relatives elsewhere, including the
reservation, making them ineligible for relief. For those who stayed, temporary shelter was offered but was segregated.[49]

While white residents re-sheltered within the city, hundreds of Natives
were concentrated at "Camp Rapid" at the National Guard base, on land originally belonging to the Rapid City Indian School. The camp housed Natives
in militarized conditions that were intensely policed. What amounted to a
concentration camp merely carried out the will of the city to create a zone of
exception and exclusion. Lakota housing activist Edgar Lonehill described
conditions in the camp: "The segregating of HUD [Housing and Urban
Development] trailers, we believe, was partly done out of prejudice against
the stereotype (drunken, troublemaking) Indian. It was done, we think, so
that it would be easier for the white police and HUD to 'keep an eye on us.'
Further proof of this is offered by the fact that the Indian trailer courts are
floodlighted at night."[50]

Relief was slow, uneven, and often used to collectively punish the Native
community. Camp Rapid was supposed to be temporary. Months passed

before all the Native families were given homes, although many white families had already been rehoused. HUD homes were made available at Sioux Addition for Native families—which became the federal housing project Lakota Homes—outside city limits. Yet community harassment and policing intensified because now Natives were cordoned off into a designated neighbourhood—a permanent fix to the city's perpetual Indian Problem. It was no longer a matter of leaving the reservation but rather leaving the "Red ghetto" that made the Indian suspect.[51]

The flood accomplished what previous generations could not. It gave the city a clean slate. The built environment that kept everyone in their place was destroyed. While the city viewed it as a social equalizer that levelled not only homes but also race and class divisions, the flood instead led to a post-disaster structural racism. It removed (and killed) the undesirable, poor Natives concentrated in the city centre, literally forcing them out of town to make way for the business community's urban renewal program to rebuild the destroyed downtown area. The practice aligned with federal housing policies and community development programs targeting low-income families and disenfranchised communities. A 1974 article in HUD's serial publication *The Challenge* promoted "urban homesteading," inspired by the 1862 Homestead Act that gave rural acreage to farmers for free under the condition they migrate to it and improve it. "Just as nineteenth century homesteaders required government aid to hack out an existence as they helped to develop the West," the article reasoned, "people who are willing to undertake a difficult and rugged experience in the urban wilderness require aid designed to make the communities around them viable." In other words, urban homesteading sought to revitalize and repurpose land and housing "not worth maintaining because disease, crime, and lack of public services have made it too depressing and dangerous for anyone to live in."[52] Former slums and abandoned neighbourhoods would be made anew. It was a civilizing endeavour. Rapid City used this program to deal with its own "urban wilderness," the savage Indians who refused to go away and who brought down property values because they embodied the disease and crime of what Lonehill identified as the criminal "drunken, troublemaking Indian." Nevertheless, the city rebuilt itself and became a HUD success story. Meanwhile, Native resentment was fostered against enforced gentrification and further segregation. The fundamental challenge that the city sat atop stolen land was never addressed and was only exacerbated by the influx of federal housing programs meant to "improve" Native lives by granting community self-determination and auton-omy through federally subsidized housing.

While federal housing policies further re-entrenched Native-settler bound-aries within border towns such as Rapid City, vigilantes, police, and everyday settlers upheld the order of things to defend (often with violence) against the hyperbolic threat of Native invasion. The figure of the "drunk Indian" became a specific target. The murderous practice of "Indian busting"—the targeting of intoxicated Native men for beating, torture, and homicide—was a weekend pastime and sport for white settlers in border towns. In February 1972, four white men hunted down, beat, stripped naked, and murdered Oglala elder Raymond Yellow Thunder in the small town of Gordon, Nebraska, bordering the Pine Ridge Indian Reservation. AIM descended on Gordon demanding justice, and Yellow Thunder was immortalized in the "AIM Song" (alterna-tively known as the "Raymond Yellow Thunder Song") composed in his honour. As a result, two of the men were charged with manslaughter but given light sentences.[53] Similarly, in January 1973, after Wesley Bad Heart Bull was stabbed to death by a white man in Buffalo Gap near Custer, South Dakota, 200 AIM members descended on Custer to demand murder charges be brought against the accused. After not being allowed access to the court-house where Bad Heart Bull's murderer was being arraigned for manslaughter, a violent confrontation with police ensued. Several police cars were set ablaze. Dozens were arrested. And Rapid City became the next target for what Paul Chaat Smith and Robert Warrior call AIM's "border town campaign."[54]

The Custer fight spilled over into Rapid City's bar district, where Natives faced violent discrimination from both white patrons and the police. The figure of the "drunk Indian" is seared into the minds of the popular settler imaginary. Although being "drunk" or "Indian" or both are not definitively illegal, construct-ing Natives off the reservation as drunk is a historic political art of policing. Native presence in border towns, therefore, is always conflated with criminality and debauchery. In 1973, a white Rapid City police officer explained: "I don't think any of us go out on purpose to arrest Innuns [sic] for being drunk, but chances are an Innun's on the street by himself [sic], he'll be arrested, because chances are he's got no place to go. A drunken white man'll have a home. . . . Of course that makes our record for arresting Innuns look pretty high."[55]

To counter this, AIM called for actions in Rapid City bars and saloons—where Natives had been victimized by vigilantes and the police—to "keep the people stirred up" and to remind settlers their presence was conditional on Natives *allowing them* to be there.[56] They helped shape an anti-colonial common sense into a revolutionary consciousness to force—with violence if necessary—settlers to come to terms with their own unbelonging and conditional existence on stolen land: "You are here because we allow you to be here." Mayor Bartlett described AIM's campaign as creating "a sense of uncertainty and fear."[57] On 6 February 1973, just weeks before the armed takeover of Wounded Knee, AIM stormed a Racial Conciliation Committee hearing, a commission created partly to resolve ongoing discrimination in housing and employment that was exacerbated by the flood and more broadly to improve "race relations." About 200 Natives packed the meeting. "They weren't committed civil rights people," Bartlett described the crowd.[58] AIM leadership struck fear into the heart of the officials as they gave fiery speeches calling for revolt if their demands for equal housing, more Native police officers, and the hiring of a Native city attorney were not met. AIM leader Dennis Banks stated they were there "to declare war on every town in the Black Hills" if demands were not met. The committee agreed to host a series of meetings to discuss the demands—some demands were carried out and most were not.[59]

In response, Bartlett reminded the Native community that if they participated in "uncivil" disobedience and did not adhere to the liberal doctrine of level-headed, rational dialogue, he would respond with violence. He stated that "if [AIM] wanted Rapid City to be as famous as Selma, Alabama I could take care of that in about 15 minutes."[60] AIM did not relent. Neither did Rapid City. For several nights, AIM members took to the streets after their demand to close the bars for thirty days while they negotiated with city officials was not met. Street brawls broke out. Riot cops were deployed and hundreds were beaten, arrested, and driven out of town. Bartlett even directly participated in strong-arming AIM members from local motels and out of the downtown area.[61] White citizens were on high alert, their tenuous claims to the land made clear. To protect the sanctity of whiteness, the city offered mediation insofar as it achieved Native consent for the process. Not consenting to the process meant domination would need to be achieved through force. This demonstrated that always lurking behind consent (soft power) to "democratic" processes is violence, force, and coercion (state power) to impose it. Civil rights hearings, a hallmark of the era, attempted to mediate discontent to produce consent through civil society and settler institutions, purposely sidestepping the questions of colonialism and land. The colonial structure remained and simply entrenched itself through a consent-to-process that was not derived from Native communities but in fact, as was the case for previous policies of termination, externally imposed. In this respect, mediation reproduced the very conditions of dispossession, whether through negotiation or force.

AIM's border town campaign remained incomplete, but not over. The same month AIM took Rapid City by storm, they also occupied Wounded Knee, which further enflamed and emboldened an international anti-colonial common sense for Indigenous peoples within and beyond the United States. The outcome of Wounded Knee and the rise of AIM's internationalism through the International Indian Treaty Council, which formed in 1974, paved the way for Indigenous internationalism at the United Nations and laid the groundwork for the 2007 Declaration on the Rights of Indigenous Peoples. In 1980, AIM returned to the Black Hills and Rapid City. This time, however, Women of All Red Nations, an AIM contingent of women leadership, formed the Black Hills Alliance (BHA), a coalition of white ranchers and Native activists to halt uranium and coal mining in the Black Hills. Eleven thousand people from around the world gathered and successfully halted mining operations. After the BHA dissipated, AIM formed a short-lived encampment, named Yellow Thunder Camp (YTC) after the Raymond Yellow Thunder, on the outskirts of Rapid City. The goal was to begin to reclaim the Black Hills region under the 1868 Fort Laramie Treaty. Unlike the previous border town campaign, BHA and YTC garnered local white support under the umbrella of environmentalism and treaty rights. For example, a union of Black Hills gold miners supported both campaigns, citing the inviolability of Lakota treaty rights and a concern for corporate energy development that jeopardized "the health and welfare of working people."[62]

AIM had successfully generated anti-colonial sentiment in both Native and non-Native people, solidifying alliances with white working people and farmers who were historic enemies of Lakotas. The alliance proved vital because it demonstrated that lower-class settlers and Natives had a common struggle against corporate exploitation, and that centring Native land rights and sovereignty would protect lands both groups required for continued existence. It was the recognition that dispossession was the primary mode for exploitation in Rapid City and the Black Hills and that the liberation for both Native and settler required upholding, at bare minimum, the 1868 Fort Laramie Treaty. In this way, when poor settlers abandoned anti-Indian common sense and aligned with the interests of Natives, new anti-colonial solidarity and liberatory possibilities arose, albeit temporarily. This era of anti-colonial uprisings in Rapid City successfully evicted corporate polluters, and the dynamics of border town life for Natives improved, if even for a short while. Even one of AIM's main detractors, Mayor Bartlett, conceded "quietly behind the scenes there is an effort being made without headlines" to improve the lives of Natives in Rapid City in the wake of the uprisings.[63]

CONCLUSION

On 19 December 2014, thirty-year-old Lakota man Allen Locke, along with hundreds of Lakota people, gathered for a Native Lives Matter rally in Rapid City, South Dakota, to demand justice for rampant police violence against Natives. The next day, Rapid City police knocked at the door of an address in the low-income housing development, Lakota Homes. Police were responding to a call to remove Locke after a domestic dispute. Dispatched officer Anthony Meirose entered the residence and later, an intoxicated Locke allegedly said to him "It's a good day to die" before charging the officer with a steak knife. Meirose believed he had no other choice but to shoot Locke five times, killing him in the kitchen within earshot of his family. The South Dakota Attorney General's office ruled the shooting "justified," stressing what Locke allegedly said before Meirose killed him, implying suicide by cop. The consensus by law enforcement and the local media was that Locke was drunk and wanted to die that day.[64] There is no more stereotypical colonial encounter than one between police and the "drunk Indian." In this scenario, a violent death was expected if not inevitable.

Despite the massive gains of previous generations, anti-Indian common sense, as evident in the police killing of Locke, continues to a deadly degree in Rapid City. Locke's murder, like all police killings, was political. Lakotas in Rapid City are subject to enforced poverty, police surveillance, and mass incarceration. According to a 2013 American Community Survey, Natives in Rapid City live in poverty at rates higher than those on many reservations. More than half of the city's Natives, mostly Lakota, live below the poverty line. Most of the city's Native poor are concentrated in neighbourhoods like Lakota Homes. This rate of poverty is the highest of any urban demographic in the United States: although only 12 percent of the city's population, Natives make up half the city's jail population and more than three-fourths of its homeless.[65] Natives in Rapid City are also five times more likely to get arrested and nearly twice as likely to receive a traffic citation.[66] Locke's death simply reaffirms the pervasiveness of Rapid City's murderous anti-Indian common sense, in spite of decades of resistance.

No longer is the "drunk Indian" the only threat to the white sanctity of border town geographies. The political Indian became the uncivil, angry Indian, attracting settler ire and white backlash in the form of state violence. For example, today South Dakota's incarceration rates are among the highest in the nation. With an overall decrease in crime in the last two decades, South Dakota's imprisonment rate is ten times higher than the national average, growing over 500 percent since 1977 to 2012. Native inmates make up over 30 percent of the total population while only constituting about 9 percent of the state's population.[67] The rise of incarceration directly correlates with increased Native political militancy in the 1970s. Mass incarceration is another form of elimination—removing, imprisoning, and killing Natives—and a tool for political repression.

Simply put, Natives off the reservation represent the unfinished business of colonialism. They are the constant reminders this land is not *settled*; it is stolen. The poorest people—Natives—in the United States throw into question the entire premise of the settler project. That settler society has to invest so much material and ideological force in eliminating Native people demonstrates the weakness of its foundations and the precarity of its structure. Most of this violence does not occur on reservations, since most Natives live off-reservation. As I have shown in this chapter, it is in border towns like Rapid City where the murderous encounter between Natives, the colonial state apparatuses, and everyday settlers intensifies. Therefore, border towns are the primary engines that ideologically, materially, and spatially reproduce a state-sponsored, homicidal, anti-Indian common sense. And however perverse the murder, imprisonment, and torture of Native people may be, it is the powerful persistence of Native life—the refusal to disappear and the refusal to sell land—that continues to structure anti-colonial common sense. The resilience of an anti-colonial common sense, when studied and developed, will continue to provide the kernel of possibility for the complicated passage from the lived experience of occupation to a movement capable of bringing about decolonization. It begins in border towns like Rapid City.

NOTES

1 U.S. Commission on Civil Rights, *Native Americans and the Administration of Justice*, 86–87.

2 Ibid., 1.

3 For the Black Hills case, see Gonzalez and Cook-Lynn, *The Politics of Hallowed Ground*, 41–46; Lazarus, *Black Hills/White Justice*, 403–28; Ostler, *The Lakotas and the Black Hills*, 139–66.

4 Quote from Brokaw, "Officials Look for Answers in Rapid Creek Mystery Deaths."

5 Brokaw, "Multiple Drownings." For a parallel case study on the "mysterious" premature deaths of Indigenous men and the failure of settler law enforcement in the Canadian context, see Razack, *Dying from Improvement*.

6 Tuck and Yang call this "settler moves to innocence," which "are those strategies or positionings that attempt to relieve the settler of feelings of guilt or responsibility without giving up land or power or privilege, without having to change much at all." In "Decolonization Is Not a Metaphor," 10.

7 Williams, *Marxism and Literature*, 131–32.

8 For Oceti Sakowin historical, cultural, political, and spiritual understandings of the importance of He Sapa, see Howe, Whirlwind, and Lee, *He Sapa Woihanble*.

9 See Cook-Lynn, *Anti-Indianism in Modern America*; Gramsci, *Selections from the Prison Notebooks*.

10 For reservation-specific histories, see Biolsi, *Deadliest Enemies*; Biolsi, *Organizing the Lakota*; Clow, *The Sioux in South Dakota History*; Fixico, *Termination and Relocation*; Gonzalez and Cook-Lynn, *The Politics of Hallowed Ground*; Iverson, *The Plains Indians*; Ostler, *The Lakotas and the Black Hills* and *The Plains Sioux and US Colonialism*; Valandra, *Not Without Our Consent*; Wilkinson, *Blood Struggle*.

11 Statistics for off-reservation population are from U.S. Census Bureau, *The American Indian*, 12. For contemporary Native life in Rapid City, see Estes, "Off the Reservation" and "Racist City, SD."

12 For studies on contemporary Native urban experiences, see Andersen, "Urban Landscapes of North America," 139–70; Blomley, *Unsettling the City*, 105–38; Denetdale, "No Explanation, No Resolution, and No Answers"; Fixico, *The Urban Indian Experience*; Ramirez, *Native Hubs*; Razack, "Gendered Racial Violence and Spatialized Justice"; Thrush, *Native Seattle*, 3–16; Yazzie, "Brutal Violence in Border Towns."

13 Cook-Lynn, *Anti-Indianism in Modern America*, x.

14 My interpretation of Gramsci's common sense builds in part on Crehan's work. In *Gramsci's Common Sense*, 4.

15 Gramsci, *Selections from the Prison Notebooks*, 419.

16 I build on Glen Coulthard's reframing of Marx's primitive accumulation. To make Marxism applicable to North American settler colonialism, Coulthard argues for "shifting the contextual analysis" from the capital relation to the colonial relation. In *Red Skin, White Masks*, 10.

17 Ibid; Wolfe, "Settler Colonialism and the Elimination of the Native."

18 Moreton-Robinson, *The White Possessive*, 34–35.

19 Simpson, "The State Is a Man."

20 See Estes, "Off the Reservation."

21 Ostler, *The Lakotas and the Black Hills*, 188.

22 Korsgaard, *A History of Rapid City*, 522–24; Ostler, *The Plains Sioux and US Colonialism*; Ostler, *The Lakotas and the Black Hills*.

23 Schell, *History of South Dakota*, 158–59.

24 Miles, quoted in Hall, *To Have This Land*, 136.

25 Wolfe, "Settler Colonialism and the Elimination of the Native," 396.

26 Hall, *To Have This Land*, 2.

27 Gonzalez and Cook-Lynn, *Hallowed Ground*, 177.

28 Emphasis added; Hall, *To Have This Land*, 128.

29 *OED Online*, "reservation, n."

30 See LaDuke and Cruz, *The Militarization of Indian Country*; Dunbar-Ortiz, *An Indigenous Peoples' History*, 133–61.

31 See Simpson, "Settlement's Secret."

32 Wolfe, "Settler Colonialism and the Elimination of the Native," 388.

33 See Riney, *The Rapid City Indian School*.

34 U.S. Department of Interior, *Sioux Sanatorium Lands*.

35 For example, see Gonzalez and Cook-Lynn, *Hallowed Ground*; Lazarus, *Black Hills/White Justice*; Ostler, *The Plains Sioux and US Colonialism*; Ostler, *The Lakotas and the Black Hills*.

36 Eagle, "A Ripe Rank Case."

37 At the time, only Iowa and South Dakota had warning out laws. See Mandelker, "Removal and Exclusion Legislation."

38 Emphasis added. Quote from U.S. Congress, *Constitutional Rights of the American Indian*, 603.

39 Ibid., 668.

40 Ibid., 670–72.

41 Ibid., 675.

42 Ibid., 671.

43 Watkins, "Termination of Federal Supervision," 47.

44 Valandra, *Not Without Our Consent*, 10.

45 Smith and Warrior, *Like a Hurricane*.

46 Smith and Warrior, *Like a Hurricane*, 179; Emery, Interview by Ward, 11.

47 U.S. Congress, *Federal Disaster Relief Legislation*, 291, 297.

48 Quoted in Kentfield, "A Letter from Rapid City."

49 U.S. Congress, *To Investigate the Adequacy and Effectiveness of Federal Disaster Relief Legislation*, 452.

50 Ibid.

51 Ibid., 455.

52 Berry, "Homesteading," 2.

53 See Magnuson, *The Death of Raymond Yellow Thunder*.

54 Smith and Warrior, *Like a Hurricane*, 171–93.

55 Kentfield, "A Letter from Rapid City."

56 Ibid.

57 Bartlett, Interview by Hausle, 11.

58 Ibid., 13.

59 Ibid., 14.

60 Ibid., 11.

61 Ibid., 16–19.

62 See Black Hills Alliance, *The Keystone to Survival*; Miners for Safety, Yellow Thunder Camp Press Release.

63 Bartlett, Interview by Hausle, 20.

64 Lakota People's Law Project, *Native Lives Matter*, 2–3.

65 U.S. Census Bureau, *Poverty Rates*, 10; Pennington County Sheriff's Office, *Annual Report 2013*, 23; Estes, "Racist City."

66 Estes, "Off the Reservation."

67 South Dakota Criminal Justice Initiative, *Final Report November 2012.*

CHAPTER THREE

COMPARATIVE SETTLER COLONIAL URBANISMS

Racism and the Making of Inner-City Winnipeg and Minneapolis, 1940-1975

DAVID HUGILL

For most Indigenous people, it was hard to find an apartment in Minneapolis, Minnesota in the decades that followed the Second World War. Municipal civil rights complaint records confirm this explicitly, detailing the varied forms of racism that prospective tenants encountered. In rare instances, landlords were honest about their racialized preferences. But in most cases they were shrewd enough to disguise them as confusion or misunderstanding. Indigenous applicants routinely booked appointments to view apartments, only to be told that they were filled once the landlord had had a chance to get a look at the prospective renters.[1] Vacancies, it seems, were disappearing in the time between a phone call and a visit.

Roughly 700 kilometres north—in the city of Winnipeg, Manitoba—a nearly identical pattern was unfolding. Research conducted by the Manitoba Indian Brotherhood (MIB) in the late 1960s and early '70s reveals that Indigenous renters had long been facing the same hurdles as their contemporaries in Minnesota's Twin Cities. In words that could easily have been written about Minneapolis, one MIB report described a typical situation encountered by would-be renters.

> When a prospective Indian tenant inquires by telephone, the landlord, ostensibly unaware of his caller's ancestry, confirms the vacancy indeed exists. When, however, the would-be tenant subsequently calls in person, the landlord, upon perceiving that his prospective tenant is of [I]ndian descent, quickly reverses himself and declares that he was previously in error and that the vacancy has already been filled. This series of events has been repeated with such frequency that it is something of a bitter joke with a large segment of the Indian community. They know if they were again to contact such landlords by telephone (and many have) they would be told that a vacancy still existed.[2]

Yet what might have appeared to be a "bitter joke to some and an isolated occurrence to others," the authors continue, was far more significant when it was placed in its proper context. Above all else, they observed, racist contempt remained the animating principle of a society bent on "placing and keeping the Indian in substandard ghetto housing."[3]

What is the significance of these coterminous patterns of discrimination? Is it merely a coincidence that Indigenous renters were encountering such similar forms of exclusion in Winnipeg and Minneapolis? Or is there something more significant that unites the postwar urban histories of these two places? Is there something broader about the history of the region encompassing both of these urban areas that can be gleaned from looking at them in a comparative context?

Conventional scholarly wisdom suggests not. In their frequently cited *The Myth of the North American City*, for example, Michael Goldberg and John Mercer argue that urban dynamics in Canada and the United States defy easy comparison.[4] Like many others, they insist that key differences in history, demographics, political organization, and economic structure, as well as less tangible attributes such as national "character" and "values," make Canada-U.S. comparisons a foolhardy enterprise.[5]

While such approaches can promote a laudable degree of investigatory caution, they also often enforce a dangerous insularity. By privileging elements (either real or imagined) that distinguish national cultures from one another as ontologically distinct entities, such approaches encourage audiences to train their analytic energies on questions that emerge from *within* national containers while stifling comparative conversations. Research grounded in methodological nationalism diminishes the possibility of encountering something different by venturing outside of conventionally proscribed boundaries.

In this chapter, I draw on empirical data from Winnipeg and Minneapolis to trouble the insularity of methodological nationalism and bring a transnational experience of postwar urban racism into sharper relief.[6] I ask what can be learned by shifting focus away from single-city studies and toward a comparative approach that seeks to understand the colonial relation as an enduring and formative aspect of urban life in North American Prairie cities. The analysis that follows is concerned with understanding the sustained potency of practices and mentalities that privilege the social forms, economic interests, territorial ambitions, and interpretive frames of colonial settlers and their descendants over and above those of the continent's original inhabitants and their descendants. Of course, it is important to point out that my objective here is not to conflate distinct urban experiences or suggest that colonization is a unitary process that takes the same form in different environments. (I emphatically agree with Wolfe's insistence that all racialization be contextualized in its historical and geographical specificity.)[7] Rather, the objective is to think carefully about whether or not there is something to be gained by breaking out of the national containers that generally frame discussions of urbanization and colonialism.

In this spirit, the chapter engages evidence from the postwar urban histories of both cities to show how comparable forms of spatially concentrated racialized exclusion emerged on both sides of the Canada-U.S. border. Specifically, I trace how a politics of structural and cultural anti-Indigenous racism contributed to the remaking of both Winnipeg and Minneapolis in the period between 1940 and 1975. To do so, I begin by demonstrating how and why inner-city districts in both communities emerged as sites of acute group-differentiated inequity *and* sites of impressive anti-racist mobilization and community building. With this established, I turn to a discussion of how the knowledge produced by mainstream commentators—including journalists, urban bureaucrats, and representatives of social service agencies—obscured the centrality of the colonial relation in interpretations of the situation. Here, I argue that such "authorized knowers"—who were almost always non-Indigenous—operated to depoliticize and naturalize inner-city Indigenous marginality by promoting explanations that identified particular forms of Indigenous *deficiency* as its primary cause while disavowing broader patterns of colonial inequity in their explanations. Writing against such disavowals, I close the chapter by reiterating the analytical importance of re-centring the colonial relation in considerations of these cities.

Yet the analysis that follows is intended to do more than identify similarities in the postwar histories of two urban sites. My broader aim here is to demonstrate that the racialized inequities that animated postwar development in both Winnipeg and Minneapolis were also reflections of a more generalized pattern of injustice. While both were (and are) sites of extreme anti-Indigenous racism, as well as sites of potent challenge to it, they also were (and are) socio-spatial reflections of a politics of a racialized inequity that extends far beyond the life of any one city, region, or nation-state. Indeed, the extraordinary violence shouldered and challenged by Indigenous people in both cities cannot be adequately explained through an analysis of the particularities of local racisms. What have sometimes appeared to be discrete events take on a new urgency and broader importance when they are reassessed as part of a pattern of colonial injustice. Accordingly, this chapter starts from the premise that to understand the meaning of anti-Indigenous urban racisms in Winnipeg and Minneapolis, it is helpful to contextualize both cities in a broader discussion about the persistence of the colonial relation in settler societies in general. Against those who argue that group-differentiated outcomes are reducible to a set of aberrational place-specific problems (a local housing shortage, a few bad landlords, the actions of individual racists, for example), my aim in bringing these cities into a trans-border comparative conversation is to demonstrate that both Minneapolis and Winnipeg are animated by inequities that are intrinsic to all settler colonial societies.

In spite of the manifold differences that exist between and within national contexts, settler colonial societies like Canada and the United States remain indelibly marked by the persistence of a politics that systematically advantages colonial settlers and their descendants. To stress this point of unity across settler states is to undermine the potency of national narratives that disavow the enduring persistence of colonial inequity by emphasizing the uniqueness of their own developmental trajectories. As Gabriel Piterberg points out, the comparability of settler colonialism's various national cases is a reminder that settler colonization itself is a "global process" and not a "haphazard array of discrete phenomena."[8] His point is not to deny historical specificity or national particularity but to contribute to the political work of undermining nationalist "claim[s] to uniqueness" (be they appeals to the good intentions of settlers or any number of contextual justifications) that operate to obscure the core inequities that undergird *all* setter colonial societies.

URBAN CONTEXTS

The geographies on which Winnipeg and Minneapolis now sit have been Indigenous places of gathering, commerce, habitation, and exchange for thousands of years. Importantly, too, those patterns of inhabitation remained significant as both cities began to be transformed into regionally formidable "frontier" hubs in the nineteenth century. While this basic fact is well known, it is important to reiterate it here because the presence of Indigenous people in both cities is too often interpreted as something that *began* in the decades after the Second World War. Indeed, while "settler cities" have often been reimagined as the creations of rugged European arrivistes who erected great towns in an unforgiving wilderness, the reality is different. Because the land upon which settler outposts were constructed was used and inhabited by Indigenous people, settler forms of urbanism are explicitly rooted in dispossession.[9] In spite of this history, however, Indigenous people remain vitally linked to urban geographies. As Nicholas Blomley points out, dispossession may be complete but displacement is not. "Physically, symbolically, and politically, the city is often still a native place," he writes.[10] Settler seizures of land, in other words, have never erased Indigenous claims and contributions to urban space. Thus while it is true that many Indigenous people moved to Winnipeg and Minneapolis in the period after 1945, it doesn't make sense to describe this development as a "migration" in the conventional sense. In relocating to the city, Indigenous people were responding to conditions of colonial deprivation and reoccupying lands within their traditional territories.

With that said, the number of Indigenous people living in both cities did grow very considerably in the period between 1940 and 1975. In Minneapolis, Indigenous residents numbered only a few hundred at the start of the Second World War, but that figure would grow to roughly 6,000 by the formal end of hostilities.[11] This trend continued in the years that followed, and by the late 1960s conservative counts suggested that the Indigenous community now numbered more than 10,000.[12] In Winnipeg, the pre-war Indigenous community was also rather small. That began to change rapidly around the mid-century mark, however, and by the late 1950s, approximately 5,000 Indigenous people were thought to have migrated to the city over the course of the preceding decade and a half.[13] In the 1960s, the number of self-identified Indigenous persons living in Winnipeg is estimated to have grown by roughly 400 people per year. In the 1970s, that figure tripled.[14] Today, Winnipeg is home to roughly 100,000 Indigenous residents, the highest number in any Canadian census metropolitan area.

Those who moved to Winnipeg and Minneapolis from the mid 1940s on arrived in cities that were being rapidly and substantially transformed. In the immediate aftermath of the Second World War, North American public policy actors embarked on a range of ambitious urban projects aimed at "modernizing" infrastructures, housing growing populations, and sustaining high levels of accumulation in a time of peace. Little had been invested in urban development during the war, and cities everywhere were grappling with serious challenges. Addressing these issues was front of mind as state planners promoted the dramatic physical expansion of North American cities and underwrote the production of an increasingly suburban consumer society. In this context, the private development industry boomed as it leveraged public spending and subsidy to pursue suburban projects with an unprecedented zeal. These efforts had a dramatic effect. From Montreal to Modesto, urban regions were radically remade as governments across the continent built sprawling automobile-based transportation networks, facilitated unprecedented levels of suburban decampment, and razed large sections of historic downtowns through comprehensive programs of "urban renewal."[15] The cumulative result of these strategies was a dramatic decentralization of urban systems and a mass exodus from urban centres. In many cities, core neighbourhoods were sapped of their commercial and reputational vitality.

These transformations had potent effects in Winnipeg and Minneapolis. Both cities were relatively compact places when combatants began arriving home in late 1945. But over the course of the years that followed they sprawled to immense proportions. By the end of the 1950s, suburban areas in Minnesota's Twin Cities region were growing more than five times faster than their central city counterparts, and the urban region as a whole began to rank among the country's least dense metropolitan regions.[16] Collectively, Minneapolis and St. Paul hemorrhaged more than 400,000 residents in the generation that followed 1945.[17] Winnipeg was also dramatically decentralized and suburbanized in that period, though the political and cultural context differed considerably north of the border. While the city's urban footprint covered roughly 150 square kilometres in 1961, it would more than double in size over the course of the next thirty years.[18] These changes entailed a significant exodus from core residential districts and a considerable fragmentation of the urban population (which has grown only at a modest pace since the mid-century mark).[19] In both cities, the urban core came to be associated with economic and infrastructural decline, substandard dwellings, disinvestment, and the racialized communities that had largely been excluded from the spoils of postwar prosperity.

Indigenous people were dramatically affected by this process of uneven urban development and, for the most part, the publicly subsidized benefits of suburban life were not made accessible to them. Many (though by no means all) of those who relocated to Winnipeg and Minneapolis ended up securing housing in the inner-city neighbourhoods that had been abandoned by participants in the great march to the suburban fringe. In Minneapolis, for example, the Southside Phillips neighbourhood emerged as the cultural, residential, and political centre of Indigenous life in the city, often described as a de facto "urban reservation." By 1970, nearly two-thirds of the Twin Cities' Indigenous population had taken up residence in Phillips, many in the immediate environs around East Franklin Avenue.[20] The demographic picture in Winnipeg is slightly murkier, but the evidence suggests a comparable degree of Indigenous concentration in core districts, particularly in the neighbourhoods north and west of the central business district. The findings of an urban housing survey conducted by the MIB in the late 1960s and early '70s (published in 1971) suggest that more than 60 percent of Indigenous households were located in the city's twelve core-area census tracts.[21] In 1975, meanwhile, a report prepared by an urban consultancy found that nearly half of the city's Indigenous residents were living in the city's inner-city residential districts.[22]

It is critical to point out that Indigenous residential congregation in both cities was the product of numerous dynamics. Certainly, the shared desire to build community in a context of considerable adversity is one of them. Importantly, though, the historical evidence suggests that pernicious forms of racialized exclusion and discrimination played the decisive role.

Indigenous people who took up residence in the abundant subpar rental units that dominated the inner city of Minneapolis in the postwar decades often did so because they had limited options in a hostile housing market.[23]

In 1969, a municipal official summarized the situation bluntly: "There is a higher concentration area [of Indigenous people] in the south . . . [because] that is the only place they are allowed to move to."[24] Legally speaking, of course, Indigenous people were *allowed* to move anywhere they liked. The municipal official's point, however, was that any such legal right was impeded by the persistence of a complex set of interlocking obstacles, including housing market discrimination, slum landlordism, circumscribed economic opportunities, and, in many cases, grinding poverty. For this reason, Indigenous urbanites were often only able to secure shelter in dilapidated inner-city dwellings, units that another municipal official described as "barely liveable."[25]

The evidence from Winnipeg suggests a similar set of circumstances. By the early 1960s, inner-city "hollowing" had begun to couple with a high rate of Indigenous in-migration to yield a particular form of "spatially concentrated, racialized poverty" in the residential districts north and west of the central business district.[26] The MIB's 1971 urban housing survey offers visceral evidence of the perniciousness of this patterned inequity. It found, for example, that Indigenous urbanites were occupying the "most squalid" residences in the entire metropolitan area and documented landlord neglect through a series of jarring photographs.[27] Indeed, the survey's authors argued that Indigenous people so frequently found themselves in the "lowest level of housing in the city" that it had become possible to "consider such accommodation the *private preserve of the native populace*."[28] Importantly, too, they insisted that such conditions were merely one of a broad series of burdens shouldered by Indigenous people that had recently migrated to Winnipeg. "We contend that the chain of circumstance by which the newly-arrived Indian is confronted often irrevocably shackles him to an existence of hopelessness and degradation," they wrote. "We further contend that the first link in this blighted chain of events is forged by the type of accommodation into which he is thrust."[29]

In Winnipeg and Minneapolis, then, the evidence is clear that Indigenous tenants had to contend with a hostile housing market. In the inner cores of both cities, dilapidation remained widespread as absentee landlords continued to collect rent without investing in serious upkeep. This was not merely a matter of interpersonal disrespect. As urban geographers have long observed, property owners sometimes have an "inherently 'rational' reason" for putting off upgrades and repairs in areas where the housing market is in decline, particularly in cases where "undermaintenance" will yield surpluses that can be invested elsewhere.[30] Such strategies were certainly employed in the inner-city contexts considered here, as opportunistic landlords traded on lax code enforcement to turn a healthy profit.

Yet landlord predation was not merely a question of cold economic rationality. The evidence suggests that attitudinal racism against Indigenous people was so widespread that even finding accommodation in "slum" housing could be a considerable challenge. The historical record from both cities demonstrates that landlords frequently denied tenancy on the basis of Indigenous identity, either directly or by more surreptitious means.[31]

And yet, the hostile housing market that Indigenous urbanites encountered in both cities is only one way to look at what is in effect a broad pattern of enduring inequity. In nearly every domain of urban life, Indigenous residents in both cities were structurally disadvantaged. They were dramatically more policed than their counterparts in other parts of the city.[32] They had far fewer opportunities than others to make a living in post-industrial urban labour markets.[33] And they had to shoulder the deleterious effects of a diverse range of interpersonal racisms, operating in a range of registers, to name only a few examples.[34]

Of course, Indigenous urbanites have not been passive recipients of such oppression. In the inner-city neighbourhoods of both cities, marginalization has been challenged by some of the most impressive traditions of urban anti-racist organizing in the continent. In Minneapolis, for example, the shared experience of sustained exposure to the challenges of poverty, slum housing, police violence, and widespread discrimination created a "shared sense of embattlement" that hastened the emergence of an "activist community" and led to the establishment of a very serious set of urban social movements.[35] Indigenous organizations had existed in the Twin Cities before the Second World War, but it was not until the community became geographically concentrated in Phillips and other inner-city districts that groups began to organize explicitly around contesting patterns of inequity.

The vast majority of the literature on this coordinated fightback is concerned with the work of the American Indian Movement (AIM), which was formed in Minneapolis in the summer of 1968.[36] But the historical evidence reminds us that organizational challenges to Indigenous marginalization had begun in earnest by the mid-1960s.[37] Importantly, then, AIM did not emerge in a political vacuum and its varied successes are in many ways indebted to a culture of contestation that began well before the organization came on the scene. Nor are its most celebrated actions and personalities necessarily the most consequential expressions of the local culture of Indigenous resistance. Brenda Child argues, for example, that an outside focus on the mediagenic and charismatic male protest leadership that emerged in the 1960s has sometimes overshadowed the critical role that Indigenous women, in particular, have played in building and sustaining a broad range of organizations (including the AIM itself) and institutions that have been critical to Indigenous survival in the urban region.[38] These include, for example, the establishment of one of the first urban Indian Health Boards, the establishment of a range of community schools, including two AIM survival schools, and key activism against police brutality, inadequate housing provision, slum landlordism, child apprehension by state adoption authorities, racist textbooks and school curricula, among other things.

In Winnipeg, meanwhile, there has been a comparably impressive tradition of Indigenous resistance. From the 1960s on, a shifting matrix of organizations sought to render visible and contest a range of grievances, just as they did in Minneapolis. In the inner-city North End, in particular, there has been a long tradition of community-based organizations that have "emerged from the ground up" to pursue anti-racist projects, including local development efforts aimed at healing and empowering those who have been adversely effected by the inequities of colonization and poverty.[39] The impressive demonstrations that took place in Winnipeg as part of the Idle No More mobilizations are a testament to the enduring strength of Indigenous organizing in the city.[40]

Perhaps most significantly, the two traditions of urban Indigenous political organizing have done the important work of clarifying what lies at the root of the varied oppressions that Indigenous people have encountered in both cities. Indeed, political challenges to housing discrimination, police brutality, and various forms of insecurity in both Minneapolis and Winnipeg have often gone beyond the immediacy of a given grievance to point to what Glen Coulthard calls the "deep seated structural features" at the core of the colonial relation. In so doing, such challenges have done the important work of providing an analytical and evidentiary counterweight to the often contextually vapid interpretations that have been routinely offered by institutionally affiliated commentators. Unfortunately, however, the latter have played a decisive role in defining how the lives of Indigenous people in Winnipeg and Minneapolis have been understood by the broader population.

OBSCURING THE COLONIAL RELATION

As we have seen, then, many of the Indigenous people who moved to Winnipeg and Minneapolis after 1940 had to contend with a complex range of quotidian privations. Simply put, they encountered what Jim Silver has called a "wall of racism" as they sought to build lives in the city.[41] And while a range of Indigenous organizations and activists sought to communicate the brutality of this experience, their voices were only rarely taken seriously in local policy conversations. Far more influential were the host of bureaucrats, social service agency researchers, reporters, and "authorized knowers" who were charged by their employers with interpreting the emergence of economically distressed inner-city "Indian neighbourhoods" for a range of audiences.

In the context of rapid change that defined postwar Winnipeg and Minneapolis, a diverse range of institutional, governmental, and journalistic attention was heaped upon inner-city "decline" and the Indigenous people so often associated with it. The accounts that emerged from this surge of interest took a range of forms. Some were nakedly castigatory, openly declaring Indigenous people to be the authors of their own misfortune. Others were more sympathetic, stressing that the "plight" of Indigenous urbanites was rooted in the fundamental difficulty of integrating into the purportedly "alien" world of the city. What nearly all explanations had in common, however, was that they mobilized theories of Indigenous deficiency as definitive and identified Indigenous "integration" into the urban "mainstream" as the most desirable form of remediation. In doing so, they operated to *depoliticize* and *naturalize* the racialized production of marginality, while obscuring what Sarah Schulman calls its "machinery of enforcement."[42] Because these accounts were widely influential, it is worth considering some of the recurring themes that emerge from the explanations they provided.

In the first place, mainstream explanations of spatially concentrated Indigenous marginality often cited the trauma of adjusting to a new environment as a decisive cause. Indeed, non-Indigenous commentators in both cities, speaking from a range of institutional positions, often lamented that Indigenous urbanites were "failing" in the city because they were either ill equipped to adjust to the norms of the "dominant" society or unwilling to accept the presumed impossibility of sustaining "traditional" lifestyles in the face of the juggernaut of urban modernity. The broad prevalence of this attitude has been observed by analysts in a range of contexts, but examples from Winnipeg and Minneapolis offer particularly striking evidence of its potency.[43] In 1968, for example, a *Minneapolis Star* report summarized the situation in that city starkly: "The American Indian living in Minneapolis is beset by problems inherent in his move from the reservation," it observed. "He is faced with adjustment in a competitive, urban society which is alien to his culture." [44] North of the border, non-Indigenous commentators were making nearly identical assessments. In 1972, the City of Winnipeg's Director of Planning published a report that defined "cultural disorientation" as a definitive cause of the "suffering" of Indigenous people. Once established in the city, the report observed, Indigenous people can find "no basis for self-identity and no basis for social and economic motivation." [45] In fact, it was precisely this "cultural disorientation" that was "the hard core of the urban Indian and Métis dilemma, and no solution is possible until the native people themselves perceive the nature of the problem and are prepared to seek the means to resolve it," the report concluded. These quotations illustrate the potency of the idea that the "problems" shouldered by Indigenous urbanites were "inherent" to the trauma of migration. This idea was so widely circulated in the postwar period that it came to function as the central element of the mainstream explanatory framework.

Indeed, among non-Indigenous interpreters in both cities, the sources of Indigenous marginalization were identified as originating within the purportedly *damaged* psychologies of Indigenous individuals themselves; they were interpreted as side effects of a clash between "traditional" and "modern" cultures.[46] In 1958, for example, officials with the Welfare Council of Greater Winnipeg cited the possession of "cultural traits which strongly contrast with ours" as a definitive explanation for Indigenous impoverishment.[47] In the council's view, these "traits" were functioning as obstacles preventing full Indigenous inclusion. They were the primary reason that Indigenous people frequently had trouble "securing and holding a job," finding a place to live, and engaging in "social participation on par with other residents of the city." Meanwhile, in Minneapolis, some officials mobilized the "trauma" of migration as an explanation for the disproportionate entanglement of Indigenous people in the criminal justice system. The Community Welfare Council of Hennepin County's Indian Committee, a group established in the 1950s to respond to the rapid growth of the Minneapolis Indigenous community, surmised that the large number of Indigenous urbanites that had begun to appear in Hennepin County courts, generally arraigned on minor charges, was a result of the migrants' unfamiliarity

with city life and a series of connected difficulties, including the various discour-
agements of joblessness, the strain of substandard living conditions, and, most
condescendingly, an "improper use of leisure time."[48] Less than a decade later,
in 1965, the (Minnesota) Governor's Human Rights Commission reiterated
this sentiment, noting that while some Indigenous migrants had "succeeded" by
finding work, shelter, and "identify[ing] themselves with their new community," others had found "nothing but trouble in the city."[49]

Mainstream commentators also often interpreted urban spaces that came
to be associated with Indigenous people—such as the Phillips district in south
Minneapolis and Winnipeg's inner-city North End—as *chaotic* and *disorganized* zones. Perhaps not surprisingly, Indigenous people themselves were
routinely identified as the active producers of blight in such narrations. This
line of interpretation was articulated at a number of scales. For example,
commentators often interpreted Indigenous marginality as the product of
a culture of *chaotic* living and pointed to the "inherent" *disorganization* of
urban Indigenous family units and the community as its key source. One
report prepared by the Minneapolis League of Women Voters explained that
"a *disorganization* of family life brought on by poverty and heightened by
the need to balance new ways with old in a complex, urban society" was
at the very centre of the "disproportionately large" percentage of the local
Indigenous community that found themselves "in trouble with the law."[50]
Meanwhile, the Welfare Council's Indian Committee lamented that "slum"
housing was part of a "total environment" that represented "a serious hazard
to Indian children and young people, morally, physically, and in relation to
their educational opportunities," whether "Indian families realize it or not."[51]
The broader community could not afford to "let such conditions persist," the
committee contended, because "they breed delinquency and backwardness."
In both cities, non-Indigenous observers often presumed that Indigenous
children lacked adequate supervision or guidance, that Indigenous women
lacked skills in household management, and that Indigenous men had little
sense of how to spend their time responsibly, among other things. Taken
together, these depictions consolidated a common-sense impression of urban
communities that were fundamentally at odds with an abstract standard of
mainstream urban propriety, though the latter was rarely defined.

Non-Indigenous commentators often associated the structural dilapidation of the inner city with the presence of Indigenous people.[52] Journalists
and bureaucrats routinely insisted on an organic link between Indigenous

tenancy and the structural deterioration of rental units, often by deploying a perverse urban arithmetic that ignored the profitable political economy of slum landlordism. In both cities, the presence of Indigenous people in "barely liveable" housing was generally interpreted as an effect of the moral and proprietary failing of the tenants themselves. The MIB was clearly so accustomed to contending with this view that they felt the need to explicitly call it out in their 1971 housing survey report.

> It is apparent that the white community—leaders as well as average citizens—is sadly lacking in knowledge of the situation of the urban Indian. Members of the white community point their fingers at Indian-occupied slums and trot out the age-old stereotype of the Indian as one who feels at home in filth and disrepair. If such individuals could remove the blindfold which prejudice and ignorance have placed over their perceptual faculties, they would realize that these residences were in a decayed state prior to any Indian family assuming tenancy and that Indian people are occupying them through necessity rather than choice.[53]

Meanwhile, the evidence from Minneapolis demonstrates the prevalence of similar associations in the mainstream discourse about the Phillips neighbourhood.[54] Indeed, there is perhaps no more striking example of the way that this interpretive line seeped into the broader culture than a series of letters responding to a *Minneapolis Tribune* report by Gerald Vizenor about the deplorable housing conditions that Indigenous Southsiders encountered in 1969.[55] While his dispatch from the inner city was a rare attempt to identify pernicious public policies and profiteering slumlords as *culpable* for these inadequacies, readers chose to read their own interpretive biases into his piece. Despite the clear evidence of criminal landlord neglect and racialized structural disadvantage that Vizenor marshalled, one of his readers saw only the "filth and garbage all over the place" on the part of "Indians" living in the Southside's unclean dwellings.[56]

What all of these explanatory strategies have in common is that they identify the activities and behaviours of Indigenous people themselves as the definitive cause of concentrated racialized poverty. By mobilizing such culturalist explanations these strategies operate to absolve non-Indigenous people of the burden of pursuing a more rigorous examination of the sources of group-differentiated marginality. In this way, they both depoliticize and individualize racialized exclusion by encouraging the curious to interpret Indigenous marginality in terms of Indigenous deficiency rather than racialized structures of inequity. Even more critically, such strategies have the effect of bracketing off considerations of colonization as a system of social relations that continues. Insofar as mainstream interpretations like the ones cited above mention the effects of colonization at all, they tend to do so by treating it as a regrettable series of historical events. Colonial violence, in such interpretations, is never treated as a persistent set of structural arrangements that continues to facilitate the consolidation of advantages by settler colonists and their descendants, often at the expense of Indigenous people. The colonial relation, in other words, is fundamentally disavowed.

CENTRING THE COLONIAL RELATION

How would engaging the colonial relation challenge and transform the facile interpretations of mainstream commentators? In the first place, doing so would provide a means to grasp the interpretive bankruptcy of explanations that stress cultural alienation and the trauma of migration as the *definitive* cause of Indigenous marginality in the postwar city. There are many problems with this line of thinking, of course, but I want to isolate and dwell on the idea of the city as a place that is "alien" to Indigenous people. While it is certainly true that many of the Indigenous people who migrated to cities in the postwar city faced considerable challenges, descriptions of these challenges that define the city as a "foreign" universe betray a host of prejudicial misinterpretations.

Specifically, these descriptions promote a spatio-historical imaginary that obscures the ways in which contemporary urban environments such as Minneapolis and Winnipeg are actively shaped by settler colonial processes. In this view, colonization is interpreted as something that belongs to a time and place that is separate from the life of the city; it is a series of events that happened *out there* and *back then*.[57] Indeed, the contemporary city in such presentations is generally imagined as a neutral time-space, a geography of the present in which diverse peoples come together and negotiate their lives on more or less even terms. In this thinking, the problem of Indigenous marginality is not the product of urban relations so much as a *cultural* problem that is imported from elsewhere. In this thinking, the contemporary city is exempted from the long history of settler colonial spatial negotiation and rendered an exceptional place, cut off from the exigencies of colonization and bounded by a kind of postcolonial *cordon sanitaire.*

Critically, though, urban and Indigenous geographies did not (and do not) exist in absolute isolation from one another. Rather, they are relationally entwined spatial products of a unitary process of territorialization that is grounded in the inequity of the colonial relation. As William Cronon has shown, we cannot tell the story of North American urbanization in a vacuum; the lives of cities have always hinged on a broader series of connections that link them explicitly to a range of non-urban geographies.[58] Moreover, as Nicholas Brown reminds us in Chapter 5 of this volume, drawing on the work of Andrew Needham, it is not enough to simply expose the connections between "city and countryside." It is also necessary to pay close heed to the ways that these connections are fundamentally unequal, differential, and predatory. In the context that concerns us here, this means, in part, thinking carefully about how the production of settler prosperity and advantage in the city is intractably linked to processes of dispossession and the production of Indigenous privation. To make this point is to counter the idea that the city is a neutral time-space in which the privations of Indigenous people can be explained as an effect of the trauma of migration. It is to insist that the city be understood as a spatial reflection of the colonial relation, a site where the social, political, and distributional inequity of colonization continues to be reproduced.

By analytically centring the colonial relation, it becomes possible to think critically about the pervasive idea that "integration" into the urban mainstream is the most desirable solution to Indigenous marginalization. The non-Indigenous commentators cited above routinely argued that the "solution" to Indigenous urban privation was to broker points of entry into that mainstream; in doing so, they betrayed their conviction in the essential desirability of dominant forms of social organization. By assuming that all individuals in a society share a common foundation that transcends "particular historical, social, and cultural differences," they minimized the degree to which North American life was and is organized around an economy of power relations that has been consistently hostile to the needs, aspirations, and desires of Indigenous people.[59] By setting the horizon of their ambition as the inclusion of Indigenous people into the ranks of the comfortable, relatively prosperous, and wage-earning dominant society, they failed to engage with more comprehensive demands for a rethinking of the colonial order of things. As such, they failed to grapple with the degree to which the colonial relation functioned as a "structural" dimension of contemporary life. Accordingly, the "problem" they sought to address was one of individual trauma or interpersonal prejudice. To engage with the constitutive importance of the colonial relation, however, is to take a step back from the individualizing obfuscations of this thinking. It is to question the very desirability of a "mainstream" animated by the entrenched inequity of settler colonial politics.

Additionally, centring the colonial relation offers a means of articulating the contemporaneity of settler colonial inequity. Doing so is a critical task because commentators like the ones cited above have so often endorsed a temporal politics that operates to confine colonial violence to a historically concluded past. In so doing, they have tended to relegate the transgression of colonization to a distant horizon. The violence of settler colonization is thereby compartmentalized as a series of past events, while contemporary manifestations of that violence, insofar as they are acknowledged, are categorized as residual symptoms of that "past" treatment. If colonial violence is understood to continue, it is presumed to do so only as an echo of the original sin of historical colonization. The idea that contemporary settler prosperity was won at the cost of an earlier period of violence implies a debt, but denies the persistence of an economy of privilege and disadvantage that functions as a constitutive dimension of contemporary life. Accordingly, the moral imperative for those who seek to overcome this original violence is understood as one of settling accounts. But debts, like apologies, create a sense of "pastness" in which the transgression for which the debt is owed is no longer present.[60] Decolonization, in this limited view, is understood as a matter of acknowledging historical wrongs rather than a process of actively dismantling colonial structures in the politics of the present. As we have already seen, the solution to urban marginality is understood as one of bringing Indigenous people into that standard of living rather than challenging its basic foundations. It is worth noting that while Indigenous activists have often made similar demands— insisting that Indigenous people be adequately housed, be able to access state benefits, not have to fear police violence, for example—they have often done so in ways that insisted on the ongoing nature of colonial violence.

Furthermore, centring the colonial relation reveals the profound absurdity of analyses that characterize inner-city Indigenous communities as "disorganized." Indeed, the evidence from Minneapolis and Winnipeg suggests that the opposite is true. But despite this robust history of organized contestation, non-Indigenous observers have frequently interpreted inner-city Indigenous neighbourhoods as chaotic and disorganized, as the evidence cited above attests. Why? The answer to this question is complex, but surely part of the answer is that in settler colonial societies like Canada and the United States, colonial inequities are both legitimated and rendered opaque through prevalent *ways of seeing* that obscure the functioning of a discrete "machinery of enforcement."[61] Such exculpatory thinking operates to absolve the beneficiaries of colonial power relations from the burden of examining the politics that undergird settler privilege. What George Lipsitz calls the "white spatial imaginary" is instructive here. In his terms, it is precisely this way of seeing that allows "whites" to see themselves as "individuals whose wealth grew out of their personal and individual success in acquiring property on the 'free market'" rather than as a disproportionately privileged tranche of the larger population that includes many who benefited from their capacity to access racialized financial advantages.[62] This same "spatial imaginary" has allowed "whites" to view racialized people living in the inner city not as "fellow citizens" who are denied certain advantages but as "people whose alleged failure to save, invest, and take care of their homes forced the government to intervene on their behalf."[63] Thinking about the ways in which "Indigenous neighbourhoods" in Winnipeg and Minneapolis have been interpreted in this way reminds us that they are inseparable from the processes through which settler colonists and their descendants have consolidated material advantages for themselves. "White supremacy does not exist or persist because whites foolishly fear people with a different skin color," Lipsitz observes. "It survives and thrives because whiteness delivers unfair gains and unjust enrichments to people who participate in and profit from the existence of a racial cartel that skews opportunities and life chances for their own benefit."[64] Settler colonization establishes a spatial and political order in which "unfair gains and unjust enrichments" are funnelled to settler constituencies, above all others. This process does not simply end at the conclusion of a founding moment of colonizing violence but continues through "structured advantages" that persist in contemporary life in a diverse range of forms.

CONCLUSION

What is to be gained by putting Winnipeg and Minneapolis in conversation with one another? What can we learn about the politics of the colonial relation by engaging in comparative urban analysis? Importantly, these questions have been made all the more urgent by current trends in the two main disciplinary literatures that animate my thinking in this chapter. In the first place, the idea that we ought to be far more cautious about putting discrete urban environments in comparative conversation with one another has been a recurring theme in recent debates in critical urban studies. As Jamie Peck critically summarizes, a spate of recent contributions to the field have made the case for the "provincialization of urban theory; for the recognition of divergent circumstances, localized complexity and unpatterned diversity; for explanatory circumspection and humility; and, in some cases, for a retreat from generalized urban theories themselves," among other things.[65] "Uniqueness and particularity are back (again) and finding exceptions to—as well as taking exception to—general urban-theoretical rules have become significant currents in the literature," he writes. In the second place, however, the emergent subfield of settler colonial studies has moved in almost exactly the opposite direction, embracing theoretical abstraction as a means of linking struggles and patterns of inequity at almost planetary scale.[66] As analysts working in this tradition have sought to contribute to the development of a thoroughly multi-sited and multi-national concept of settler colonization, they have often downplayed the importance of localized particularity in the service of building a more generalizable conceptual apparatus. And while this approach risks conflating heterogeneous phenomena into an overly coherent frame, it also offers opportunities to challenge the naturalization of settler hegemonies by revealing their proximity to other historical formations.

In this chapter, I have adopted a comparative framework in the interest of accomplishing such a denaturalization. My objective is to demonstrate both that Winnipeg and Minneapolis were and are shaped by the persistence of the colonial relation *and* that they are not unique in doing so. While there manifestly are key differences in the ways Canadian and American cities have developed, there is also something appealingly political about emphasizing their similarity. Indeed, to demonstrate that cities on both sides of the Canada-U.S. border have been shaped by comparable forms of racialized inequity is to contribute to the refutation of core features of hegemonic settler narratives of self-legitimation, including the presumption of national uniqueness and the view that the dispossession of Indigenous inhabitants is aberrational rather than "an intrinsic part of what settler nations are."[67] This work is important because it is precisely on grounds of national uniqueness and exception that settler colonial myths of self-legitimation are constructed in both countries.

NOTES

1   Hugill, "Metropolitan Transformation and the Colonial Relation."

2   Manitoba Indian Brotherhood, *Urban Housing Survey*, 22.

3   Ibid., 22.

4   Goldberg and Mercer, *The Myth of the North American City*.

5   See for example Filion, "Concepts of the Inner-City and Recent Trends in Canada"; Lipset, *Continental Divide*; Adams, *Fire and Ice*.

6   Of course, the "nations" at play here are not merely Canada and the United States but also the Dakota, Lakota, Cree, Anishinaabe, Métis, and other Indigenous nations that are also key players in this story.

7   Wolfe, *Traces of History*, 10–18.

8   Piterberg, *The Returns of Zionism*, 55.

9   Blomley, *Unsettling the City*, 109.

10 Ibid., 109.

11 Shoemaker, "Urban Indians and Ethnic Choices."

12 *Minneapolis Tribune*, "The Plight of the Urban Indian."

13 Hall, "The Early History of the Winnipeg Indian and Métis Friendship Centre," 224.

14 Silver, *In Their Own Voices*, 13.

15 Jackson, *Crabgrass Frontier*; Harris, *Creeping Conformity*.

16 Saunders, "Surburbia Booms as 'Blue Collar' Workers Arrive"; Adams and Van Drasek, *Minneapolis-St. Paul*, 90.

17 Martin and Goddard, *Past Choices/Present Landscapes*, 5.

18 Milgrom, "Slow Growth versus the Sprawl Machine."

19 Leo and Anderson, "Being Realistic about Urban Growth."

20 Davis, *Survival Schools*, 26.

21 Manitoba Indian Brotherhood, *Urban Housing Survey*, 9.

22 Damas and Smith Ltd., *Neeginan*, 1.

23 See Hugill, "Metropolitan Transformation and the Colonial Relation."

24 Committee on Urban Indians, *Public Forum before the Committee on Urban Indians in Minneapolis-St. Paul*, 68.

25 Statement of Dennis Wynne, Minneapolis Housing and Redevelopment Authority, in ibid., 146.

26 Comack, Deane, Morrissette, and Silver, "*Indians Wear Red*," 7, 49–51.

27 Manitoba Indian Brotherhood, *Urban Housing Survey*, 7.

28 Ibid., 7; emphasis added.

29 Ibid., 7.

30 Ibid., 544; Smith and LeFaivre, "Class Analysis of Gentrification," 49.

31 Hugill, "Metropolitan Transformation and the Colonial Relation," 176–80; Manitoba Indian Brotherhood, *Urban Housing Survey*, 22.

32   Minnesota Human Rights Commission, *Police Brutality*; Banks and Erdoes, *Ojibwa Warrior*; Birong, "The Influence of Police Brutality on the American Indian Movement's Establishment in Minneapolis"; D'Arcus, "The Urban Geography of Red Power"; Comack, *Racialized Policing*.

33   Silver, "Segregated City: A Century of Poverty in Winnipeg"; Comack, Deane, Morrissette, and Silver, *"Indians Wear Red"*; Silver, "Winnipeg's North End."

34   Comack, Deane, Morrissette, and Silver, *"Indians Wear Red"*; Hugill and Toews, "Born Again Urbanism"; Vizenor, *Crossbloods*; Broker, *Night Flying Woman*; Smith and Warrior, *Like a Hurricane*.

35   Davis, *Survival Schools*, 30.

36   For a relatively thorough consideration of Indigenous organizing in the years before 1965, see Child, *Holding Our World Together*; and Shoemaker, "Urban Indians and Ethnic Choices."

37   See accounts in Vizenor, *Interior Landscapes*; Child, *Holding Our World Together*; and Brunette, "The Minneapolis Urban Indian Community."

38   See Child, *Holding Our World Together*, 139–60.

39   Silver, "Winnipeg's North End."

40   Kino-nda-niimi Collective, *The Winter We Danced*.

41   Silver, "Winnipeg's North End."

42   Schulman, *The Gentrification of the Mind*, 27.

43   On this point and the enduring tendency of analysts to interpret Indigeneity and urban life as radically incommensurable, see Peters, "'Urban' and 'Aboriginal.'"

44   Hovik, "Urban Indians Must Conquer Problems of 'Alien' Culture."

45   Levin, *A Proposal for the Urban Indians and Métis*.

46   Hall, "The Early History of the Winnipeg Indian and Métis Friendship Centre," 224.

47   Ibid., 224–25, quoting Welfare Council of Greater Winnipeg, "Indian and Métis 4th Annual Conference Proceedings."

48   CWC Indian Committee, *The Minnesota Indian in Minneapolis*, quoted in League of Women Voters of Minneapolis, *Indians in Minneapolis*, 55.

49   Governor's Human Rights Commission, *Minnesota's Indian Citizens*, 42–43.

50   League of Women Voters of Minneapolis, *Indians in Minneapolis*, 49, emphasis added.

51   CWC Indian Committee, *The Minnesota Indian in Minneapolis*, 4.

52   See Dorries, this volume.

53   Manitoba Indian Brotherhood, *Urban Housing Survey*, 8.

54   Hugill, "Metropolitan Transformation and the Colonial Relation."

55   Vizenor, "Indian's Lot: Rent, Ruins and Roaches."

56   Johnson, Untitled letter to Gerald Vizenor. For a full discussion of Vizenor's piece and the response to it, see Hugill, "Metropolitan Transformation and the Colonial Relation."

57   Hugill, "Settler Colonial Urbanism," 267.

58   Cronon, *Nature's Metropolis*.

59   Goldberg, *Racist Culture*, 5.

60   Mackey, "The Apologizer's Apology."

61   Schulman, *The Gentrification of the Mind*, 27.

62 Lipsitz, *How Racism Takes Place*, 27.

63 Ibid., 27.

64 Ibid., 36.

65 Peck, "Cities beyond Compare?," 161.

66 See for example Banivanua Mar and Edmonds, *Making Settler Colonial Space*; Bateman and Pilkington, *Studies in Settler Colonialism*; Elkins and Pedersen, *Settler Colonialism in the Twentieth Century*; Piterberg, *The Returns of Zionism*; Piterberg, "Settlers and Their States"; Stasiulis and Yuval-Davis, *Unsettling Settler Societies*; Veracini, "Introducing Settler Colonial Studies"; Veracini, *Settler Colonialism*; Wolfe, "Settler Colonialism and the Elimination of the Native"; Wolfe, *Settler Colonialism and the Transformation of Anthropology*.

67 Piterberg, *The Returns of Zionism*, 55–56.

Part Two

LAND AND POLITICS

CHAPTER FOUR

CONTESTED ENTITLEMENT

*The Kapyong Barracks, Treaty Rights,
and Settler Colonialism in Winnipeg*

JULIE TOMIAK

*All Canadian cities are on Indigenous lands. Indigenous presence
is attacked in all geographies. In reality, the majority of Indigenous
peoples move regularly through reserves, cities, towns and rural
areas. We have found ways to connect to the land and our stories
and to live our intelligences no matter how urban or how destroyed
our homelands have become. While it is critical that we grow
and nurture a generation of people that can think within the
land and have tremendous knowledge and connection to aki,
this doesn't have to take away from the contributions of urban
Indigenous communities to our collective resurgence. Cities have
become sites of tremendous activism and resistance, and artistic,
cultural and linguistic revival and regeneration, and this too comes
from the land.*[1]

Leanne Betasamosake Simpson and other scholars and activists have drawn
attention to the significance of cities for Indigenous peoples as well as to the
importance of refusing settler colonial conceptualizations of space that com-
partmentalize the urban as the exclusive entitlement of settlers.[2] Against this

settler common sense,[3] a group of Indigenous people set up camp outside the fenced-off Kapyong Barracks in May 2016 and eventually gained access to the former armed forces base "to bring ceremonies to the people," as Kylo Prince, one of the organizers, explained.[4] The abandoned military base in Winnipeg provided an opportunity to engage in ceremonies and to affirm connections to the land in the city. (Re)connecting to the land is foundational to anti-colonial resistance and Indigenous resurgence at and across all scales.[5] However, the spiritual, physical, emotional, and intellectual aspects of relationships with and responsibilities to the land have been most aggressively targeted and policed in cities.

The project to disconnect and disappear Indigenous peoples, rights, and title from urban space has been integral to the history of settler colonialism in what is now known as North America and continues to motivate state violence today, involving a wide range of actors, policies, legislation, institutions, discourses, and everyday practices.[6] Indigenous peoples have resisted both original and ongoing dispossession in/from/through the city based on Indigenous histories and geographies that fundamentally contest the settler city. Most importantly, Indigenous people who live in cities, often in their homelands and/or treaty territories, continue to assert a presence and collective visibility as Indigenous people. Urban Indigenous place-making includes reclaiming space for ceremonies, as well as creating service infrastructures and community spaces that nurture connections to culture, language, and both local and translocal communities.[7] The specific form of urban Indigenous place-making this chapter examines is the struggle of Treaty One First Nations to acquire the Kapyong Barracks and turn the 160-acre site into an urban reserve.

More specifically, I present a case study of settler attempts to prevent a collective Treaty One First Nations presence and Indigenous place-making in one of the wealthiest areas of Winnipeg.[8] My analysis draws primarily on documents obtained through access to information requests from Aboriginal Affairs and Northern Development,[9] the Department of National Defence, and Justice Canada, as well as four court rulings to highlight the framings that have informed discourses on the contested Kapyong Barracks.[10] In conjunction with an examination of policy, this chapter makes visible how the state has perpetuated the ongoing dispossession and displacement of Treaty One First Nations. Among the questions of interest in my analysis are: How have settler state agents attempted to insulate urban space from Indigenous and treaty rights? What ideas about the city are enacted in these discourses and practices? And how should we understand the role of urban reserves beyond the entrepreneurial script of neoliberalized settler colonialism?

Organized into four sections, this chapter begins with a brief review of the literature on settler colonialism and the city. I then situate the Kapyong Barracks case. In particular, I draw attention to reclamations of urban space through the treaty land entitlement process and the opportunities for and regulation of First Nations place-making through urban reserves. This is the backdrop for understanding the ongoing struggle to create a common Treaty One reserve in Winnipeg. This is followed by a discussion of the legal battle that involved Federal Court rulings in 2009 and 2011 and decisions by the Federal Court of Appeal in 2012 and 2015. In the last section, I contextualize the creation of a new policy category in 2001 for the "strategic" disposal of federal surplus properties. I read it as a direct reaction to the prospect of First Nations ownership of valuable land and control, however limited, over the production of urban space and thus part of a larger strategic effort, over a period of seventeen years, to prevent the sale of Kapyong Barracks to Treaty One First Nations.

CITY-MAKING ON INDIGENOUS LANDS

The discursive framings of the Kapyong Barracks case are consistent with dominant legal and public discourses in Canada. They reflect the core logics of settler colonialism—the dispossession and elimination of Indigenous peoples—and are constitutive of the settler city as a material and ideological terrain. Territoriality, as "settler colonialism's specific, irreducible element,"[11] and the production of space are the medium and stake in settler colonial regimes that seek to emplace settlers as the legitimate owners of the land. This emplacement is incompatible with the existence of Indigenous nations and the historical geography of Turtle Island. In this sense, it is useful to think about settler colonialism as a set of processes and assemblages of institutions, policies, discourses, knowledges, and everyday practices that cohere around its core objectives of displacing and erasing Indigenous peoples.[12] As theorists of settler colonialism like Glen Coulthard,[13] Joyce Green,[14] and Leanne Simpson[15] remind us, this is an ongoing project, yet one that has not remained static. Different strategies and technologies of power have been employed at different times. What has remained relatively stable, however,

is the narrative validating the fantasy of the settler city—that cities are new
and modern and, by virtue of this logic, cannot be Indigenous places. This
version of *terra nullius* is at the core of settler colonial urbanism and, by extension, the process of (re)producing a settler nation "that has and continues
to constitute itself as a white possession."[16]

Despite the historical geographies and contemporary realities of cities
as Indigenous places,[17] where a large and growing number of First Nations,
Métis, and Inuit people live,[18] the displacement of Indigeneity through the law
and public policy has remained persistent in the Canadian context. Dominant
narratives essentialize Indigenous peoples as incompatible with modernity, in
the way of progress and antithetical to city life.[19] Given that the view of the
urban as settler space is so entrenched as the contemporary settler colonial
common sense, it is important to place cities at the core of settler colonialism
and as spaces that continue to benefit from settler capitalism and Indigenous
dispossession elsewhere and everywhere.

This chapter analyzes the normalization of urban settler colonialism by
examining the dispossession of Indigenous peoples not only as a constitutive historical moment but also as a foundational dynamic of contemporary
cities across Turtle Island. Settler colonial state power and its specific regimes
of producing urban space have been normalized to the extent of becoming
invisible.[20] This has also entailed actively disappearing Indigenous bodies,
especially Indigenous women. Writing about resistance to this erasure in the
context of the 14 February day of remembering and honouring murdered and
missing Indigenous women in Vancouver, Dana Culhane notes that "visibility and recognition are inseparable from the goals of material survival."[21]

Against such dispossession and erasure, Indigenous peoples have resisted
and subverted the settler common sense and state power, with cities as
important places of and nodes in multi-scalar networks of resurgence.[22]
Contestations and reclamations of land in particular make the profoundly
unsettled nature of urban space visible. While a focus on the production
of space often tends to disembody the specific processes of urbanization as
colonization (and colonization as urbanization), it is important to keep in
mind that these violences are experienced at the scales of the body, family,
and community. For many Indigenous people—many living in their homelands—the violence perpetrated by police and the child welfare system is
compounded by the violence of poverty and lack of access to adequate, safe
housing, services, and employment. Indigenous city-making has focused on

(re)creating safe spaces and community infrastructures.[23] For First Nations in the Prairie provinces, urban reserve creation is an additional avenue to greater control over traditional territory, economic self-sufficiency, and improved services and programming.[24]

SITUATING THE KAPYONG BARRACKS CASE

First Nations efforts to use and acquire the Kapyong Barracks site are not new but have been ongoing since 2001. Treaty One First Nations have been asserting their right to buy the 160-acre operational section of the former base since 2001, when it was announced (and when Treaty One First Nations learned through the media) that the military base would be decommissioned.[25] The former base has sat idle since the Second Battalion Princess Patricia's Canadian Light Infantry vacated it in 2004. Based on the provisions of treaty land entitlement (TLE) agreements with Long Plain First Nation, Swan Lake First Nation, Roseau River Anishinabe First Nation, Peguis First Nation, and Brokenhead Ojibway Nation, First Nations' interests in what the federal government declared surplus land should have been prioritized as a right of first refusal, or should at least have resulted in meaningful consultation prior to the decision to sell the land. Instead, the federal government decided to ignore the rights of Treaty One First Nations and invented a category of exception that would exempt the sale of the Kapyong Barracks from the government's legal obligations under TLE agreements. In November 2007, Treasury Board approved the sale of the site to the Canada Lands Company (CLC), a for-profit Crown agency tasked with redeveloping former government properties.[26] This initiated a set of legal challenges, the only available recourse, resulting in the courts siding with Treaty One First Nations, as will be discussed in more detail below.

The Kapyong Barracks is located between two affluent neighbourhoods, Tuxedo and River Heights, in the southwest of Winnipeg. The land is invariably described as "the most valuable piece of underdeveloped real estate in the province"[27] and "a developer's dream."[28] Together with the property values in the surrounding area, the market value of the site plays an important role in explaining settler resistance to a collective property-owning First Nations presence, especially if this presence could be residential in nature.[29] The site also provides a rare opportunity for Indigenous city-making on a relatively large scale. I argue that the long-standing refusal to deal with the treaty right

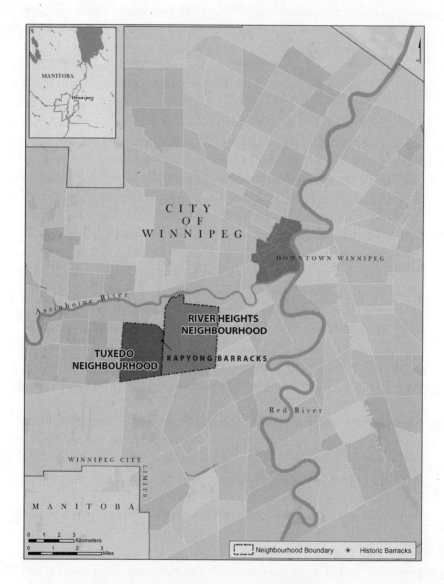

Figure 4.1. Map of Kapyong Barracks, Tuxedo, and southwest Winnipeg. Map by Jesika Allen.

to land is linked to an entrenched sense of settler entitlement to the production of urban space and to a discursive and non-discursive state investment in Winnipeg as white settler space—an investment in a racist/settler city.

Now called Winnipeg, the area around the confluence of the Assiniboine and Red Rivers has been an important meeting and trading place for Anishinaabeg, Cree, Oji-Cree, Dakota, and Dene peoples for thousands of years. More recently, it became part of the territory covered by Treaty One, signed in 1871, and is also the homeland of the Métis Nation. According to the 2011 National Household Survey, 72,335 Indigenous people reside in Winnipeg, the largest number of Indigenous residents of any city in Canada. Representing about 11 percent of the city's population, Métis make up 57 percent and First Nations 41 percent of Indigenous people living in Winnipeg.[30] As an instrument of settler state sovereignty, the census represents distinct political, ideological, and methodological strategies to subvert Indigenous nationhood by categorizing and racializing Indigenous people as Canadian subjects.[31] The census is also problematic in its chronic undercounting of urban Indigenous people. The available data therefore provide a conservative estimate of the actual number of Indigenous people who live in Winnipeg.

The legal dispute about the Kapyong Barracks dates back to 1871, when Treaty One was signed on 3 August. Treaty One is part of the so-called numbered Treaties (One to Eleven) covering much of the Canadian Prairies and entered into in the context of a rapidly expanding and consolidating settler colonial regime between 1871 and 1921.[32] It is clear that throughout Treaty One negotiations at Lower Fort Garry (or Stone Fort), different concepts of land, tenure, law, and jurisdiction were at play. Settler understandings of land transfer remain incompatible with Anishinaabe law and principles of ongoing relationships and responsibilities to and continued use of the land "for their traditional activities of hunting, trapping, fishing and harvesting, with shared use by the settlers for agricultural purposes, and with a promise to have selected lands set aside for their farms, should they choose to engage in agriculture."[33] As Aimée Craft explains, while different understandings of the spirit and intent of treaties existed at the time of the signing of Treaty One, in order to appreciate the ongoing significance of this arrangement to "share the land in a spirit of peace and coexistence" Indigenous perspectives and legal orders need to be considered.[34] This, however, has not

Figure 4.2. Map of Treaty One. Map by Jesika Allen.

happened, and settler law has reinforced self-serving interpretations of treaties, "often limiting the treaty rights in space and in time."[35]

The written text of Treaty One provides that "one hundred and sixty acres for each family of five, or in that proportion for larger or smaller families" be set aside for the exclusive use of First Nations.[36] The land promised in the per capita provision was not set aside for the First Nations signatories.[37] The Manitoba TLE framework agreement and TLE agreements with First Nations are mechanisms that are supposed to remedy this ongoing breach of Treaty One.

Although the Kapyong Barracks site accounts for only a small portion of the land debt owed to Treaty One First Nations, seven First Nations have been involved in efforts to acquire it and turn it into an urban reserve. In contrast to existing reserves, new urban reserves are created through the federal additions-to-reserve (ATR) process at the request of First Nations who have acquired land. The creation of urban reserves has geographically expanded but not fundamentally challenged the Indian Act regime of colonial governance. Rather than being a mechanism to reverse dispossession, urban reserve creation is implicated in perpetuating a framework that erases Indigenous sovereignty and relationships to the land. Made possible through TLE and specific claims settlements, new urban reserves are the direct outcome of the retroactive pseudo-legalization of dispossession and extinguishment of rights elsewhere. Most common in Saskatchewan and Manitoba,[38] these satellite land holdings of First Nations communities located outside of the city tend to primarily serve economic development and, to a lesser extent, service provision or community-building goals.[39] The ATR policy forces First Nations, through development corporations, to buy their own land and restricts First Nations to roles as entrepreneurs and investors, not as sovereign rights- and title-holders.[40] The fact that proposals for new urban reserves have tended to face significant barriers, delays, and settler opposition supports the view that they are contradictory spaces that do not fit neatly into the socio-spatial order of the settler colonial city.[41]

In relation to the Kapyong Barracks, the settler state reflex to reproduce settler colonial logics of dispossession and displacement through policy directives and mundane bureaucratic practices appears particularly strong in the context of a proposed urban reserve that might involve residential in addition to commercial uses. In this sense, settler resistance to First Nations' place-making in the city must be read as directly linked to the foundational tenets of settler colonialism, racism, and property in Treaty One territory. Property is one mode in which settler colonialism normalizes and invisibilizes its violence. The conceptualization of space as fee simple title—as if Indigenous title and treaties did not exist—has material consequences in the continuation of the de- and reterritorialization of Indigenous lands.[42] Much of this work is performed by private property and the primacy of settler notions of what it means to relate to lands and waters. Blomley points out that "the establishment of a Western liberal property regime was both the point of these violences and the means by which violent forms of regulation were enacted and reproduced."[43] This violent transformation of Indigenous land into settler property continues to be pursued aggressively in relation to urban space. The creation of new urban reserves, however, illustrates that binaries—essentializing Indigenous/land and settler/capitalism as opposites—are not useful in an analysis of urban Indigenous resistance. As I discuss in more detail elsewhere,[44] property can also serve as a "ground for resistance."[45] First Nations as collective property owners in the city, especially as title holders based on Indigenous and treaty rights, destabilize the settler entitlement to the production of urban space—and thereby expose the fantasy of the settler city itself.

JUDICIAL REVIEW, 2008–2015

Indigenous peoples have resisted dispossession and displacement through a number of strategies, including through settler law. Using settler law to fight colonialism comes with its own set of contradictions and challenges.[46] Treaty One First Nations were left with no other option but to file for judicial review—that is, to have the Federal Court review the legality of the sale to the Canada Lands Company—if they wanted to retain the option to acquire the Kapyong Barracks site. In April 2001, a number of Treaty One First Nations immediately expressed their interest in acquiring the site, as per TLE agreements that provide for what essentially amounts to a right of first refusal in cases of the sale of so-called surplus federal lands. For years the federal government was uncooperative and unresponsive to requests by First Nations to gain more information about the site and to negotiate the terms of transfer as part of a TLE selection. Long Plain First Nation, for example, received no response to their 2001 correspondence or to 2002 and 2003 follow-ups expressing interest in the site.[47] After the Treasury Board's decision to sell to the Canada Lands Company, as part of a process that would most likely put the land out of reach for First Nations, Treaty One First Nations filed for judicial review in early 2008 to stop the sale.[48]

The judicial review was to determine whether the federal government had fulfilled its duty to consult Treaty One First Nations. Articulated in the *Haida*, *Taku*, and *Mikisew* cases,[49] Maria Morellato asserts that the duty to consult and accommodate can serve as an important legal instrument to dismantle colonial practices, noting that "if government actions infringe potential or existing Aboriginal rights [. . .] a subsequent court challenge could very well render a Crown decision, license or permit unconstitutional and invalid."[50] At a minimum, the duty to consult should ensure that the federal government cannot simply ignore the rights and interests of First Nations, here in relation to TLE, but must make a meaningful effort to consult and accommodate before any third parties, which cannot be held legally responsible in the same way, become involved. Governments must engage directly with First Nations to provide detailed information on projects and address First Nations' concerns and adverse impacts. The intertwined principles of the honour of the Crown and its duty to consult are to ensure First Nations participation in decision making and prevent Crown unilateralism.[51]

More broadly, this was a legal challenge to hold Canada accountable to its obligation to implement Treaty One and settle the land debt owed to First Nations. The case was also centrally about disrupting state narratives that have spatially confined Indigenous and treaty rights as relevant only in relation to land outside of the city and/or deemed not valuable.[52] The fear of an urban reserve, particularly in conjunction with the adjacent section of the decommissioned military base, the married quarters with 356 homes, figures prominently in state and media discourses on the Kapyong Barracks case.[53]

In addition to remaining inactive when First Nations requested information and meetings, the federal government was quick to respond to First Nations' expressions of interest by creating a new category of disposal in the summer of 2001. The *Treasury Board Policy on the Disposal of Surplus Real Property* introduced a new "strategic" disposal category that effectively put designated properties out of reach of First Nations, as exceptions to the TLE agreements and legal framework that would apply in "routine" sales of federal surplus lands.[54] The directive gave the federal government the power to unilaterally designate properties of very high market value and/or of any sensitive nature as exceptions to lawful obligations. The "strategic" disposal process legitimized the practices of officials with the Departments of Defence, Indian

Affairs, and Justice to ignore Indigenous and treaty rights and to dismiss Treaty One First Nations as potential buyers of the Kapyong Barracks.

The legal challenge resulted in Federal Court decisions in 2009 and 2012, which were appealed, and decisions made by the Federal Court of Appeal in 2011 and 2015, respectively. In the 2009 Federal Court ruling, Justice Campbell stated that the First Nations who launched the case successfully established that "a Treaty right to land currently exists; the right is currently in the process of being implemented; and there are legal expectations upon Canada with respect to the conduct of the implementation which have not been met."[55] The 2009 Federal Court decision starts with recounting the importance of Treaty One, according to Justice Campbell, "still very much in the implementation stage."[56] Land rights are here framed in relation to this agreement with Canada and the per capita land promise rather than as also fundamentally based on the recognition of inherent rights and underlying title to the land. Canada argued that entering into TLE agreements extinguished treaty rights. But Justice Campbell found that Canada has to consult with Brokenhead and Peguis First Nations, as per the provisions of their specific TLE agreements.[57] Brokenhead First Nation's TLE agreement stipulates that notice of surplus federal land must be provided, along with an estimate of the fair market value.[58] Indigenous and Northern Affairs Canada did not provide any information that would have made it possible for First Nations to enter into negotiations. Instead, and underscoring the willful disregard for the TLE process, the federal government decided in November 2001 to carry out a strategic property disposal through the Canada Lands Company.

The court found that Canada failed to live up to its legal obligation.[59] The ruling further notes that "the Kapyong Barracks is prime land for commercial development. Canada's decision making with respect to the disposition of the land is specifically for this purpose. The Applicant First Nations' interest in the land is for the same purpose, but under their control, including a long standing interest is the creation of an urban reserve."[60] The decision declared the transfer of the Barracks to the Canada Lands Company invalid until meaningful consultation takes place.[61]

The federal government appealed this decision, and in 2011 the Federal Court of Appeal decided that "the right to acquire land on a priority basis essentially amounts to a right of first refusal. . . . The priority does not, however, give any of the respondents an entitlement to acquire the land because all of the agreements specify that land will be transferred only on a willing buyer/willing seller basis."[62] The insistence on "willingness" is problematic, because it frames a legal right, in this case a treaty right to land, as a voluntary market transaction. Making Indigenous rights a matter of settler willingness (and, one might assume, the right price) further illustrates how Canadian law upholds a regime of dispossession. Even if one accepts that First Nations have to buy their own land in order to have their title recognized under Canadian law, a serious commitment to remedying the breach of Treaty One would entail ensuring that First Nations can acquire the amount of land to which they are legally entitled. Finding procedural problems with the previous ruling, Justice Nadon sent the case back to Federal Court for re-trial with a different judge.[63]

In the 2012 decision of the re-trial, Justice Hughes reiterated that "the decision to sell the property will be set aside and any further decision to sell is enjoined until after Canada has fulfilled its duty to consult in a meaningful way."[64] What emerges clearly from the documents entered as evidence is that there was a pattern of reticence and unresponsiveness when it came to communication among federal departments and, more importantly, between Canada and Treaty One First Nations.[65] Letters with requests for meetings to the Minister of Indian Affairs, Attorney General of Canada, and Treasury Board were left unanswered.[66] As stated in the decision, "The Applicants were simply ignored. After the fact, the Applicants were told to take their concerns to Canada Land Company. I find the treatment of the concerns raised by the Applicants and other aboriginal bands to be far short of the scope of even the minimum duty to consult."[67] Canada appealed the ruling in January 2013.

On 14 August 2015, the Federal Court of Appeal released its decision, allowing the appeal in relation to remedy. Justice Stratas clarified that "Canada was well aware that the four respondents might have an interest in the Barracks property,"[68] but failed to inform Treaty One First Nations of the 2001 decision. Furthermore, the decision confirmed that Canada failed to contact First Nations and failed to provide any information about the site and its estimated value.[69] The decision goes on to state that "to the extent that each of the First Nations' treaty land entitlement agreement applies to the Barracks property, Canada is no ordinary vendor. Canada's exercise of discretion concerning how to go about the sale of the Barracks property must be guided by the treaty land entitlement agreements it has signed, its commitment to the purpose of those agreements, and the concepts of honour, reconciliation and fair dealing. In this case, honour, reconciliation and fair dealing—often expressed as the obligation to avoid sharp dealing—are particularly important because of Canada's broken promise in Treaty No. 1."[70] All four rulings are consistent in their finding of Canada's breach of its own laws and due process.

While Justice Stratas saw "no particular *animus* on the part of Canada"[71] and voided the restraining and supervision orders preventing the sale, the decision asserts that "Canada must act like the willing seller contemplated in the treaty land entitlement agreements."[72] The judge also pointed out that there is nothing preventing Canada from reclassifying the property as a "routine" disposal to ensure that Treaty One First Nations are considered as buyers on a priority basis.[73] Then prime minister Stephen Harper surprised many by announcing in September 2015, in the midst of a federal election campaign, that the federal government would not appeal this decision and "is consulting with First Nations."[74] Under the Trudeau government, an agreement-in-principle was signed with the seven Treaty One First Nations in April 2018. However, the details of the current agreement and what the final agreement will look like remain unclear. In the meantime, the Department of National Defence has begun a two-year demolition project, destroying the remaining buildings, including housing, on the former army base.[75]

STRATEGIC RESISTANCE TO AN URBAN RESERVE

The 2015 decision points to what is at stake, the value of the site and the unique opportunities it presents for redevelopment, as well as the significance for Treaty One First Nations to reclaim and reconnect to their lands. As Justice Stratas notes, "from the perspective of the four respondents, the Barracks property is unique and important. It is a large parcel of land in an urban area that is available for sale and could be redeveloped by the respondents. Some of the traditional lands formerly inhabited by some of the four respondents now constitute the City of Winnipeg. These days, large pieces of available land in an urban area are not commonplace."[76] The evidence suggests that the size and location of the site in an affluent area of the city and its high market value intensified settler resistance to the reclamation of the Kapyong Barracks, based on the deeply entrenched sense of entitlement to the production of urban space.

Between 2001 and 2018, there has been a persistent effort on the part of several federal departments to prevent the sale of the former military base to Treaty One First Nations. At times, this strategic orientation was expressed through public servants refusing to engage and remaining unresponsive when First Nations requested information and meetings to advance their vision of an urban reserve. This is not simply a matter of ignoring First Nations requests for information and meetings. For instance, Indigenous and Northern Affairs advised the Department of National Defence in June 2004 that "Long Plain and Brokenhead had expressed an interest."[77] Neither federal department pursued this further. The strategic nature of this bureaucratic inertia was documented in the 2012 Federal Court decision. A 10 July 2004 article in the *Winnipeg Free Press* reported that Long Plain First Nation was abandoning its plan to buy the military base. "The newspaper clipping obtained from the Canadian government files bears the handwritten note 'Peter – Well done – Fraser.'"[78] Long Plain First Nation's giving up its bid in the face of the government's refusal of due process was evidently considered a success. This mindset is further documented in reports that federal official signalled willingness to negotiate with First Nations "as long as the bands promised not to turn Kapyong into an urban reserve."[79]

Treasury Board's creation of a category of exception for the sale of former federal lands takes properties off the table for TLE land selection, based on the assessment of state agents of which parcels of land are too valuable for First Nations and/or too sensitive.[80] Here, "too sensitive" can be assumed to mean that federal bureaucrats anticipate that it would require more effort to manage the racist backlash of residents mobilizing against a collective Indigenous presence in "their" neighbourhood. A settler category such as "surplus federal land" already performs crucial work in insulating land-as-property from First Nations title and interests in the land. But creating a "strategic" disposal process that simply bypasses the federal government's legal obligations based upon unilateral criteria illustrates a concerted effort to shut out First Nations' rights, title, and jurisdiction (even a delegated form of jurisdiction under the Indian Act and one subject to de facto municipal veto).[81]

It appears that, at least for the period between 2001 and 2018, there has been a strong investment of the settler state to keep an urban reserve out of Tuxedo.[82] By transferring the Kapyong Barracks to the Canada Lands Company, the federal government could count on First Nations having a much smaller chance, if any, of acquiring the site, since it would be sold on the open market. While it is difficult to quantify this investment, the *Winnipeg Free Press* reported that since 2005 at least $14.7 million had been spent on the empty barracks (this includes the married quarters, not just the operational section) for operations and maintenance, taxes, security, and so on, with another "several hundred thousand dollars on legal fees" spent fighting First Nations in court.[83] Incurring these costs to fight the inclusion of the Kapyong Barracks as TLE lands is particularly revealing in light of the fact that the property was initially appraised at $8.6 million.[84]

This investment in preventing a common Treaty One reserve in Tuxedo is also ideological, and shared by settlers in Winnipeg. Discourses on the Kapyong Barracks are pervaded by themes of Treaty One First Nations standing in the way of progress and creating a burden of insecurity and anxiety for non-Indigenous residents. Racist fears have been mobilized by speculation that impacts of reserve creation would be overwhelmingly negative, including ghettoization, crime, and dropping property values. Another persistent theme in settler discourses, ironically, is the alleged lack of local control and consultation.[85] Rallying around the undemocratic nature of urban planning is a deliberate strategy to discredit and regulate a potential First Nations development project, especially since Treaty One First Nations are on the record as consistently stating that they plan to consult with Tuxedo residents. In the media, Treaty One First Nations have been very careful to stress that they "want to build a neighbourhood that blends seamlessly with River Heights and Tuxedo—a mix of houses, condos, apartments, parks, shops big and small, maybe a training facility or offices. They want this to be a high-quality, progressive development. It won't include a casino."[86] In attempts to pre-empt local settler resistance, Treaty One First Nations have tended to emphasize how the urban reserve would "blend seamlessly" and be unrecognizable as such, or, more accurately, unrecognizable as a space imagined by settlers as an urban reserve and therefore incongruous with city life and middle-class respectability. First Nations' assurances of normalcy are in direct response to often and openly expressed concerns about "lifestyles" and "housing values," code for the racist perceptions of what an Indigenous urban presence represents in the minds of the settler majority.[87]

In relation to the alleged democratic deficit identified with respect to treaty rights and the prospect of First Nations' production of space, it is instructive to consider a similar conflict in the city of Winnipeg in 2010, only in this case the controversial development went ahead without any consultation and against strong local opposition. David Hugill and Owen Toews describe how the Christian organization Youth for Christ was able to bring on board all levels of government to establish a strong presence in a part of the city with a significant number and density of Indigenous institutions and residents. In fact, local Indigenous organizations were also interested in the same parcel of land across from Thunderbird House and the Aboriginal Centre of Winnipeg, but it was Youth for Christ, an organization targeting "at-risk youth," that was able to leverage support, including financial support, to build a flagship service agency, the Centre for Youth Excellence, within two years of introducing the proposal. Vocal and organized Indigenous opposition to the project was simply ignored.[88] This is a marked contrast to the situation in Tuxedo. The different levels of support illustrate the workings of racial capitalism that make it im/possible for the settler state to ignore the needs and sensibilities of settler and Indigenous residents in different parts of the cities.

This enduring sense of settler entitlement to the city is linked to and has maintained the socio-spatial discipline of urban settler colonialism— with Treaty One First Nations to this day fighting for their right to the city. Lefebvre conceptualized the right to the city in relation to the appropriation of existing and future cities.[89] I use the concept here to more broadly mean the right to the production of space, in a more expansive sense of what is considered urban, and who and where.[90] In this sense, the concept refers not only to a right to live in the city but to the collective right to produce urban space, including the larger political economic relations in which cities are embedded and which they shape. In a settler colonial context like Canada, this entails addressing the foundational and ongoing role of Indigenous dispossession in the production of urban space.

CONCLUSION

In a letter to Treaty One First Nations dated 3 December 2007, then minister of Indigenous and Northern Affairs Chuck Strahl stated that "it is the position of Canada that the Treaty One First Nations have no Aboriginal title in, or claim under treaty to, any lands in the City of Winnipeg."[91] This position has been reflected in policy, as well as procedural and popular resistance to First Nations' right to land in the city. Officials actively worked against TLE claims and urban reserve creation—which, as the Kapyong Barracks case illustrates, included willful inactivity. The prospect of an urban reserve, especially one that could perhaps in part be residential in nature, demonstrated the state's long-standing investment in city-making that excludes First Nations. This resonates with the popular settler imagination of the implementation of treaty rights and a collective First Nations presence as detrimental to city life. Settler resistance to Indigenous reclamation of urban space, especially when it involves the active production of space, remains a persistent feature of the colonial present.

Treaty One First Nations have resisted dispossession, and the struggle to reclaim the Kapyong Barracks site is ongoing. The struggle has contributed to politicizing Winnipeg as Treaty One territory. It is also part of a larger trend of First Nations leaders stressing the importance of urban reserve creation.[92] Regardless of the problems with the process under the Indian Act and ATR policy, the prospect of a property-owning and city-making presence of First Nations appears to be unsettling to settler sensibilities in Winnipeg. Restitution of land is a foundational aspect of decolonization,[93] and it needs to include the affirmation of land rights and Indigenous place-making in cities. First Nations residents have continued to affirm connections to the land in Winnipeg, including by reclaiming the Kapyong Barracks for and through ceremony.[94] In addition to the importance of visibility and reterritorialization, a common Treaty One reserve could provide significant material benefits, including collective opportunities for economic self-sufficiency and access to affordable homes for Treaty One First Nations people in their homelands.

Despite a strong demographic presence in the city, First Nations people have faced settler resistance to place-making and self-determination in Winnipeg. Settler politicians and pundits regularly posit migration to cities as a solution to the systematic underfunding of First Nations communities,[95] as part of an effort to dispossess and remove Indigenous peoples who are seen as in the way of development, that is, extractive industries. Framing cities as a solution to Canada's settler colonial problem in this way implies an understanding of the urban as a site and process of erasure. Within this necropolitical logic of the settler city, urban spaces are projected to automatically disappear Indigeneity through assimilation or by spatially containing and policing urban Indigenous communities. Accordingly, settler publics and state agents have demonstrated strong resistance to Indigenous rights and collective visibility—as nations and communities—in the city. To make this settler fantasy true, Indigenous people are instead dehumanized, expelled, and controlled;[96] collective Indigenous rights, title, and agency are dismissed or tightly regulated to ensure that the production of urban space occurs strictly on settler terms.[97] However, resistance to erasure through Indigenous place-making, such as the project of creating an urban reserve at the Kapyong Barracks site, demonstrates that urban settler colonialism is always incomplete and, ultimately, unable to actualize its objectives.[98]

NOTES

1   Simpson, "Land as Pedagogy," 23; Aki means land in Anishinaabemowin.

2   Simpson, "Land as Pedagogy"; Simpson, *As We Have Always Done*; Goeman, *Mark My Words*; Coulthard, *Red Skin, White Masks*. See Flowers, "Refusal to Forgive" for discussion on settler as a political identity.

3   Rifkin, "Settler Common Sense;" Estes, this volume.

4   CBC News, "First Nations Group Granted Access."

5   Simpson, "Land as Pedagogy," 23.

6   Blomley, *Unsettling the City*; Mays, "Pontiac's Ghost in the Motor City."

7   Krouse and Howard, *Keeping the Campfires Going*; Silver, *In Their Own Voices*.

8   This chapter was originally submitted in December 2016, focusing primarily on the time period between 2001 and 2015. Canada and Treaty One First Nations entered into an agreement-in-principle about the transfer of the Kapyong Barracks site in April 2018, but it remains unclear if a final agreement and/or an urban reserve will result from this.

9   This was the name of the department at the time of the ATI (access to information) request. It was subsequently changed to Indigenous and Northern Affairs Canada and, in its latest iteration, separated into Crown-Indigenous Relations and Northern Affairs Canada and Indigenous Services Canada.

10 I am a researcher of mixed Anishinaabe (Algonquin) and European descent and want to acknowledge my positionality as an outsider to the struggles around urban reserve creation in Treaty One territory.

11 Wolfe, "Settler Colonialism and the Elimination of the Native," 388.

12 Coulthard, *Red Skin, White Masks*; Wolfe, "Settler Colonialism and the Elimination of the Native;" Simpson, *Mohawk Interruptus*; Simpson, "The State Is a Man."

13 Coulthard, *Red Skin, White Masks*.

14 Green, "Decolonization and Recolonization in Canada."

15 Simpson, *As We Have Always Done*; Simpson, *Dancing on Our Turtle's Back*; Simpson, "Land as Pedagogy."

16 Moreton-Robinson, *The White Possessive*, 52.

17 Blomley, *Unsettling the City*; Peters and Andersen, *Indigenous in the City*; Howard and Proulx, *Aboriginal Peoples in Canadian Cities*; Krouse and Howard, *Keeping the Campfires Going*; Newhouse and Peters, *Not Strangers in These Parts*; Barman, "Erasing Indigenous Indigeneity in Vancouver"; Mawani, "Genealogies of the Land."

18 Statistics Canada, *Winnipeg: 2011 National Household Survey*; Statistics Canada, *Aboriginal Peoples in Canada in 2006*.

19 Lawrence, *"Real" Indians and Others*; Razack, *Race, Space, and the Law*; Razack, "Memorializing Colonial Power."

20 Blomley, *Unsettling the City*; King, *Urbanism, Colonialism, and the World-Economy*; Jacobs, *Edge of Empire*.

21 Culhane, "Their Spirits Live within Us," 595.

22 Kino-nda-niimi Collective, *The Winter We Danced*; Dhillon, *Prairie Rising*.

23 Krouse and Howard, *Keeping the Campfires Going*; Silver, *In Their Own Voices*; Peters and Andersen, *Indigenous in the City;* Howard and Proulx, *Aboriginal Peoples in Canadian Cities*.

24 Barron and Garcea, *Urban Indian Reserves*; Peters, *Urban Reserves*; Tomiak, "Contesting the Settler City."

25 See also Tait, "Kapyong and Treaty One First Nations" for an overview and discussion of Crown obligations in relation to treaty rights.

26 Aboriginal Affairs and Northern Development Canada, *Fact Sheet*; Aboriginal Affairs and Northern Development Canada, documents obtained through ATI request, A201301457; Department of National Defence, documents obtained through ATI request, A-2010-01212; Department of National Defence, documents obtained through ATI request, A-2010-01225.

27 Welch, "Kapyong Is a Symbol of Sabotage."

28 *Winnipeg Free Press,* "No Need to Appeal Kapyong."

29 Paul, "Residents Voice Concerns over Urban Reserve."

30 Statistics Canada, *Winnipeg: 2011 National Household Survey.*

31 See Andersen, "From Nation to Population," for discussion on the role of the census in racializing the Metis.

32 Miller, *Compact, Contract, Covenant.*

33 Craft, *Breathing Life into the Stone Fort Treaty*, 64.

34 Ibid., 12.

35 Ibid., 14.

36 Treaty One, cited in Craft, *Breathing Life into the Stone Fort Treaty*, 117.

37 *Canada v. Brokenhead First Nation.*

38 According to a 2014 departmental document, sixty-five urban reserves were created since 1981; Aboriginal Affairs and Northern Development Canada, documents obtained through ATI request, A201301457, 19.

39 Barron and Garcea, "The Genesis of Urban Reserves and the Role of Governmental Self-Interest"; Gertler, "Indian Urban Reserves and Community Development"; Makela, "Legal and Jurisdictional Issues of Urban Reserves"; Peters, *Urban Reserves*; Tomiak, "Contesting the Settler City."

40 Tomiak, "Contesting the Settler City."

41 Ibid.

42 Harris, "How Did Colonialism Dispossess?"

43 Blomley, "Law, Property, and the Geography of Violence," 129.

44 Tomiak, "Contesting the Settler City."

45 Blomley, "Making Space for Property," 1303.

46 Monture-Angus, *Journeying Forward*, 52; Coulthard, *Red Skin, White Masks*; Coulthard, "Subjects of Empire"; Blomley, "Mobility, Empowerment and the Rights Revolution."

47 *Long Plain First Nation v. Canada*, 29.

48 *Canada v. Brokenhead First Nation.*

49 *Haida Nation v. British Columbia; Taku River Tlingit First Nation v. British Columbia; Mikisew Cree First Nation v. Canada Minister of Canadian Heritage.*

50 Morellato, *The Crown's Constitutional Duty to Consult and Accommodate Aboriginal and Treaty Rights*, 8.

51 Ibid., 25–26.

52   The first urban reserve in Winnipeg was created by Long Plain First Nation in an industrial area on the outskirts of the city; Paul, "City's First Urban Reserve Born."

53   Paul, "Residents Voice Concerns over Urban Reserve"; Welch, "Kapyong Is a Symbol of Sabotage"; Kusch and Rabson, "First Nations 1, Ottawa 0."

54   Treasury Board of Canada, *Treasury Board Policy on the Disposal of Surplus Real Property.*

55   *Brokenhead First Nation v. Canada,* 1–2.

56   Ibid., FC, 6.

57   Ibid., FC, 3.

58   Ibid., FC, 11.

59   Ibid., FC, 16.

60   Ibid., FC, 17.

61   Ibid., FC, 20.

62   *Canada v. Brokenhead First Nation,* 3.

63   Ibid.

64   *Long Plain First Nation v. Canada,* FC, 2. The application was originally filed by seven applicants: Brokenhead First Nation, Long Plain First Nation, Peguis First Nation, Roseau River Anishinabe First Nation, Sagkeeng First Nation, Sandy Bay Ojibway First Nation, and Swan Lake First Nation.

65   Ibid., FC, 30.

66   Ibid., FC, 31.

67   Ibid., FC, 43.

68   *Canada v. Long Plain First Nation,* 13.

69   Ibid., FCA, 10.

70   Ibid., FCA, 33.

71   Ibid.n, FCA, 46.

72   Ibid., FCA, 35.

73   Ibid., FCA, 17–18.

74   Latt, "Desperate Times Call for Desperate Measures."

75   CBC News, "Few Details in Kapyong Deal between Federal Government, Treaty 1 First Nations."

76   *Canada v. Long Plain First Nation,* FCA, 9–10.

77   *Long Plain First Nation v. Canada,* FC, 30.

78   Ibid., FC, 30.

79   Welch, "Kapyong Is a Symbol of Sabotage"; Kusch and Rabson, "First Nations 1, Ottawa 0."

80   In 2006, Treasury Board amended the policy to include consideration of possible impacts on any relevant Aboriginal rights or claims.

81   As noted in the 2015 Federal Court of Appeal decision, the designation as a strategic disposal had "a significant practical effect: the Barracks property would be transferred from an entity subject to duties to consult with Aboriginal peoples (Canada) to a private entity free from any such duties (Canada Lands Company). On this view of things, the Canada Lands Company could then transfer the Barracks property to any third party free from any need to consult with Aboriginal peoples." *Canada v. Long Plain First Nation,* FCA, 12.

82   The federal government was considering a plan to ship all or some of the 356 houses to First
     Nations in the Interlake Tribal Council region. In addition to the prohibitive cost of moving them,
     these homes also "likely contain asbestos-tainted flooring and drywall, lead paint, mercury, arsenic
     and other toxins, says a government report." Rabson, "Land Claim Prevents Transfer of Homes."

83   Rabson, "Tories Appeal Kapyong Ruling a Second Time."

84   Department of National Defence, documents obtained through ATI request, A-2010-01212, 33.

85   Tomiak, "'Too Valuable for Indians.'"

86   Welch, "Breaking Down the Kapyong Saga."

87   Paul, "Residents Voice Concerns over Urban Reserve."

88   Hugill and Toews, "Born Again Urbanism."

89   Lefebvre, *Writings on Cities*; Marcuse, "Whose Right(s) to What City?," 35.

90   Brenner, *Implosions/Explosions*.

91   Department of National Defence, documents obtained through ATI request, A-2010-01225.

92   Paul, "Grand Plan for Prosperity."

93   Corntassel, "Re-Envisioning Resurgence"; Tuck and Yang, "Decolonization Is not a Metaphor."

94   CBC News, "First Nations Group Granted Access."

95   See Gilmore, "The Hard Truth about Remote Communities."

96   Culhane, "Their Spirits Live within Us;" Green, "From Stonechild to Social Cohesion"; Razack,
     "Memorializing Colonial Power."

97   Razack, "Memorializing Colonial Power"; Razack, *Race, Space, and the Law*; Sandercock,
     "Commentary"; Shaw, *Cities of Whiteness*; Walker, Jojola, and Natcher, *Reclaiming Indigenous Planning*.

98   Simpson, "Mohawk Interruptus;" Pitawanakwat, "Bimaadzwin Oodenaang"; Silver, *In Their Own
     Voices*; Tomiak, "Unsettling Ottawa."

CHAPTER FIVE

EXPERIMENTS IN REGIONAL SETTLER COLONIZATION

Pursuing Justice and Producing Scale through the Montana Study

NICHOLAS BROWN

Speaking at the thirty-first annual convention of the Montana District of Kiwanis International on 14 August 1951, Bert Hansen offered reassurance about the congeniality of social relations in western Montana. "The Indian, like his white neighbor," Hansen asserted, "is fundamentally a simple, sincere, democratic individual who can be completely relied upon, even after years of abuse by the white man, if he feels the cards are fairly dealt, not stacked against him."[1] A professor of speech and drama at Montana State University, Hansen was reflecting on the Montana Study and the efficacy of "sociodrama" as a form of "interracial therapy." An ambitious and multi-faceted project funded primarily by the Rockefeller Foundation, the study sought to empower rural communities throughout western Montana over a three-year period ending in July 1947. In his speech, Hansen acknowledged the therapeutic limitations of sociodrama, a type of historical pageantry that had become synonymous with the Montana Study. "It would be altogether wrong," he stated, "to assert or to assume that these dramas will in themselves solve the interracial antipathies and misunderstandings between Indians and whites of western America grounded as they are in one hundred years of distrust in the motives of each other." Emphasizing the importance of intercultural understanding, albeit unidirectional, Hansen continued, "The initiative must rest with the white man. He alone has the power, the drive and the will to do something about it. But in using this he must learn to know and to respect the Indian."[2] Here, Hansen sought to convince the presumably all-white audience of its common bond with the Indian as fellow "democratic individuals," and to include the Indian in a broader vision of liberal humanism.

Hansen's comments expose the settler colonial ideology at the core of the Montana Study, but they reveal little about *how* the project actually worked (i.e., how it operationalized this ideology). Often described as an experimental program in adult education and community outreach, the Montana Study was also an experiment in regional settler colonization, with Missoula as its urban hub. It produced space—settler colonial *and* racialized space—and it also produced *scale*. The Montana Study, which linked small towns, universities, philanthropic organizations, and government agencies in an effort to modernize the rural West, in part by furthering the project of Indigenous assimilation, is an important case study in both regional settler colonization and settler colonial urbanism. It demonstrates not only that questions about scale are crucial for apprehending what Cole Harris calls the "principal momentum" of settler colonialism, but also that a regional field of analysis is essential if we aspire to construct a *relational* theory of settler colonial urbanism.[3] The case of the Montana Study demonstrates that the regional is not simply a convenient framing device but the precise scale at which certain settler colonial structures coalesce, and also a scale produced in part through settler colonization. The Montana Study also reveals how the oppositional politics of scale can function in colonial contexts to reproduce settler colonial power, and thus how settler colonial (oppositional) politics of scale differ from anti-colonial (oppositional) politics of scale.[4]

The title of Hansen's speech, "Move Over, Pardner, Let's Talk," captures the folksy spirit of the Montana Study while also hinting at the liberal character of its settler colonial ideology.[5] The presence of different, often antagonistic, and sometimes contradictory, regimes of settler colonialism—which still share elimination as the end goal—is enabled partly through the production of scale. In other words, scale amplifies what Jodi Byrd terms "colonial cacophony."[6] A theory of regional settler colonization will help us parse "settler common sense" and identify the layers—or scales, as the case may be—that give the structure its strength and resilience.[7] In the case of Missoula, it helps explain how the Montana Study, by cultivating a liberal settler imaginary, refashioned the city as a progressive non-Native space and a "settler city" with circumscribed relationality.[8]

This chapter consists of three parts. The first part revisits the Montana Study as a case study in regional settler colonization and settler colonial urbanism, paying close attention to overlooked aspects of the project that dealt with Indigenous-settler relations, and also political opposition to the project. Building on recent theoretical work on regional formation in urban history and regional racial formation in critical ethnic studies, the second part applies a "critical scalar lens" to the Montana Study in order to "denaturalize the [simultaneous] settler colonial production of urban [and rural] space," thereby decentring Missoula within the region.[9] The third and final part considers how the Flathead Nation, particularly the Séliš-Ql̓ispé Culture Committee, is decolonizing regionalism—producing new scales, partly through historical pageantry and place-based commemoration, that align with ancient and evolving bio-cultural landscapes rather than the geopolitical coordinates of the settler state.

THE MONTANA STUDY

On 4–5 July 1947, more than 8,000 people gathered near Fort Connah to witness an outdoor pageant, "A Tale of the Shining Mountains (Skol-loomts Ska-kel Whoo-zo-zoot)," that marked the 100th anniversary of the fort's establishment at Post Creek.[10] Relating the "true story of a hundred years of white and Indian relations" in northwestern Montana, the pageant-drama was the culmination of months of intensive dialogue and rehearsals by residents from the small reservation towns of Arlee and Dixon.[11] The *St. Ignatius Post* reported that the spectators "were conscious of the fact that they were seeing something out of the ordinary."[12]

"A Tale of the Shining Mountains" was one of a handful of historical pageants that were produced as part of the Montana Study. As the study's most visible outcome, the pageants reflected the belief that learning is a lifelong

Figure 5.1. "A Tale of the Shining Mountains" pageant, Post Creek, Montana, 4–5 July 1947. Archives and Special Collections, Mansfield Library, University of Montana.

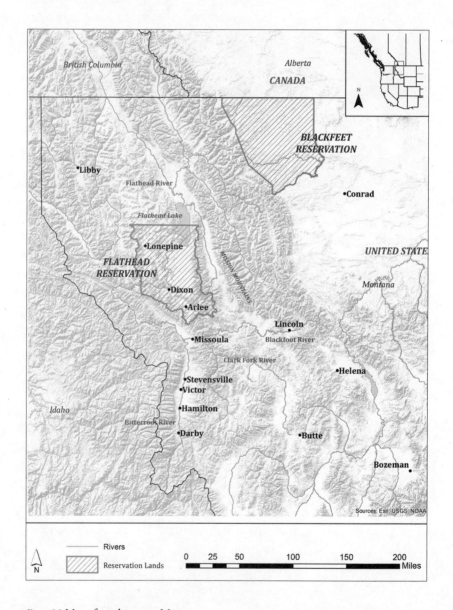

Figure 5.2. Map of northwestern Montana.

endeavour; the pageants also embodied the study's goals of "getting the university off the campus" and "making the humanities more relevant to everyday life."[13] What made the Montana Study "something out of the ordinary" was partly its commitment to using commemoration as a tool to address questions about justice and reconciliation in the present. And what made this particular pageant extraordinary was the fact that it incorporated both Indigenous and settler perspectives in an attempt to answer these questions. However, despite its good intentions, the Montana Study remained fully ensconced within a settler imaginary, imbued from the start with "colonial good intentions."[14]

In other respects, the Montana Study was just ordinary, and this too makes it a useful case study. The project existed somewhere between "capital's interest in uncluttered access to land and settlers' interest in land as livelihood," and yet it contributed substantively, I argue, to the principal momentum of settler colonialism—not on its own so much as in combination with other "minor" interests.[15] This cumulative effect is similar to the jurisdictional "micropowers" mapped by Shiri Pasternak, which in their singularity mask "the total effect of accretion and layering of authority that governs the land."[16] Part of what makes the Montana Study so intriguing is the fact that it was an *event*—a relatively obscure, even quotidian one—that clearly ended.[17] Yet its interaction with other minor and place-specific interests and events, especially antagonistic ones, produced lasting effects, enabling, almost like an adhesive, settler colonial structures to coalesce and endure.

Study Groups and Sociodramas: Experiments in Regional Settler Colonization

Directed by Baker Brownell, a philosophy professor on leave from Northwestern University, the Montana Study was at once pragmatic and utopian. The short-term objective was to make the state's small towns economically viable and culturally appealing—to facilitate a rural revitalization in order to stem the tide of migration to urban areas. The long-term goal, however, was more far-reaching. According to historian Carla Homstad, the project aimed to strengthen "American democracy by bolstering its mainstay, the American small town."[18] Brownell was assisted by Bert Hansen, David Stevens, director of the Rockefeller Foundation Humanities Division; Arthur E. Morgan, former director of the Tennessee Valley Authority; Paul Meadows, Northwestern University sociologist; and Ernest O. Melby, chancellor of the University of Montana system, all of whom agreed that the arts and humanities had an important role to play in improving community life in rural Montana.

Yet the study was more than just an effort to bring the humanities to the people. It aspired to "use the humanities for the promotion of democratic ideals on a worldwide basis."[19] The decline of family farms in the postwar years and the migration of rural residents to cities resulted, by Melby's estimation, in a "lack of independence in political and social thought." The erosion of self-reliance, exemplified by these demographic trends, made it easier for people to be "herded politically."[20] To counteract these trends, the Montana Study featured a study group process that was designed to promote self-reflection and community empowerment.[21] Joseph Kinsey Howard, a muckraking journalist hired by Brownell to be part of the Montana Study's field staff, felt the project could serve as a bulwark against the state's colonial economy and empower its (settler) citizens to protect themselves against further exploitation by outside corporate interests.[22]

With the help of professional facilitators, residents from participating towns were encouraged to collectively research community histories and to analyze local economic and social problems. The process was predicated on a belief that small-town neighbourliness, particularly face-to-face interaction, was necessary to produce a vital sense of belonging and civic responsibility.[23] Over the course of three years, from September 1944 through July 1947, fifteen rural communities, located mostly in western Montana, participated in the Montana Study. *Life in Montana*, a study guide developed by Brownell, Howard, and Meadows, was used to lead participants through a series of ten topics over a ten-week period.[24]

The study group process constituted the first phase of the Montana Study. The second phase, undertaken by seven of the fifteen study groups, focused on the "artistic and appreciative aspects of life in Montana, including the graphic arts, literature, music, and folk interests in general."[25] Elaborate historical pageants, such as "A Tale of the Shining Mountains," were the signature outcome of this "more action-oriented" second phase.[26] Working in collaboration with study group participants, Hansen, who believed strongly in the possibility of "community unification through dramaturgy," played a key role in developing these pageants or "rehearsed sociodramas." "An annual historical pageant in which a community looked at its past in a genuinely analytical and critical way over a number of years could do much to integrate community life," Hansen argued.[27] The professor eschewed "colorful spectacle" and un-reflexive glorification of the past in which "truth is sacrificed for effect, realism for sentimentality, simplicity for tomfoolery, and trained judgment for enthusiasm."[28]

On 18 August 1946, a crowd of 2,500 people—more than three times the town's population—gathered at the rodeo grounds in Stevensville to witness "A Tale of the Bitter Root." The oldest settler community in western Montana was regarded as the "chief center of experimental field work" by organizers of the Montana Study, due in part to its "living and proud record of social disintegration."[29] Given the prominence of Stevensville in the region's settler colonization, it is not surprising that this pageant was the first to deal explicitly with the contentious history of Indigenous-settler relations.[30] Researched and written entirely by a committee of Stevensville residents, including "a Harvard graduate, a day laborer, a college student, and the wife of a cattle ranch foreman," the pageant, Hansen insisted, "dealt realistically, truthfully, and without elaborate overtones, with what had happened to the native Indians of the Bitter Root Valley between the years 1841 and 1891 as the result of the white man's invasion of their lands."[31]

One of the major characters in the pageant was Peter Ronan, who had served as Indian Agent on the Jocko (Flathead) Reservation from 1877 to 1893. During the performance, Ronan articulated an outlook toward Indians that was emblematic of the Montana Study in general. "The chief difficulty all along has been that the government and most of the people, including the bulk of settlers in this valley, have never understood the Indian; never seen him as a human being with emotions of love of home, of love of justice and fair play."[32] The pageant sought to humanize Indians and promote mutual understanding and respect, but its benevolence was conditioned by the logic of elimination. In other words, Indians were humanized so that they might be more efficiently assimilated into a liberal democracy.

Like "A Tale of the Bitter Root," the 1947 Post Creek pageant, which Hansen described as "objectively critical," also highlighted Indigenous-settler relations.[33] "A Tale of the Shining Mountains" was unique among the Montana Study pageants, however, because it was a collaborative production between two separate study groups, the Dixon Agency Study Group and the Full Blood Flathead Indian Study Group. As the names suggest, the former group was comprised of white settlers from Dixon, whereas the latter group was comprised of full-blood Indians from Arlee. Although the two worked independently through the study group process, the subsequent pageant was

Figure 5.3. "A Tale of the Shining Mountains" pageant, Post Creek, Montana, 4–5 July 1947.
Archives and Special Collections, Mansfield Library, University of Montana.

"the result of many conferences between Indians and whites." According to historian Maurice Lokensgard, the pageant "dealt with fundamental differences in the Indian and white approaches to problems involving communal justice."[34] "A Tale of the Shining Mountains" established an important precedent by framing practices of commemoration in terms of justice, even if the purview of the concept was *a priori* limited. Like Hansen, who described the pageants as cathartic, Richard Poston—professor of community development at Southern Illinois University and author of *Small Town Renaissance: A Story of the Montana Study*—characterized them as a form of "spiritual therapy" for the Indians' "drooping morale."[35] In this sense, justice simply entailed rationalizing dispossession; treating the symptoms rather than root causes of injustice. In his account of the Montana Study, which often reads like a hagiography of Hansen, Poston goes so far as to suggest that the Full Blood Flathead Indian Study Group offered "a new start" for the Indians and marked an important step in restoring their faith in the white man.[36] "When the Indian and the white man, with his inventions, his educational resources, and his wealth that has been gained from Indian lands, are ready to begin together where the Indian Study Group left off," Poston wrote, "a richer and fuller life will be created for both races. And it will not be a one-way proposition—for neither race will find the other lacking in culture or intelligence."[37] Comments like these underscore the extent to which the Montana Study can and must be understood partly as an experiment in regional settler colonization.

While Indigenous-settler relations were not the primary focus of the Montana Study, they were a common feature in the historical pageants and a subject of particular interest to Hansen, who believed it necessary "to face squarely the problem of interracial adjustment."[38] Hansen therefore conceived of the study group process as a form of "interracial therapy" and insisted that "to understand is to tolerate."[39] Elsewhere, he stated, "The playing together of white men, who now prosper in the fertile Valley, and the Indians, whose ancestors once roamed that land at will and in freedom, is in itself an example of the tolerance a common effort can create."[40] Despite his relatively progressive objectives, Hansen's personal views about Indians were shaped by numerous stereotypes, including expectations about cultural authenticity and investments in blood purity. He claimed, for example, "Group discussion is a natural medium of expression with the Indian. Even today the Indian mind is at its best when working, not alone, but with his group—a fact constantly demonstrated in our discussion sessions."[41] Hansen also contributed to the production of white innocence.[42] "The early settler wasn't characterized by, or in any way educated to, a humanistic approach to the Indian 'savage' he was replacing in the wilderness," Hansen claimed. "He wanted land, a farm, and he knew nothing of the 'force and fraud' methods being employed to make this land available and safe for him."[43] Hansen's statement reveals how white innocence contributes to the "principal momentum" of settler colonialism.[44] If "the momentum to dispossess derived primarily from the interest of capital in profit and of settlers in getting somewhat ahead in the world," as Cole Harris suggests, white innocence cleaves these two interests and exonerates individual settlers who benefit materially from structures of settler colonialism. Put differently, it launders profits derived through processes of settler accumulation.[45]

PRODUCING SETTLER SCALE AND RECONFIGURING THE URBAN

As an experiment in regional settler colonization, how exactly did the Montana Study produce scale? Like regional racial formation, which Wendy Cheng defines as "place-specific processes of racial formation," the Montana Study can be understood simply as a place-specific process of settler colonization.[46] Cheng's call for "a regional field of analysis," which, she argues, "allows a fine-grained analysis of the production of both hegemonic ideologies and counterhegemonic ways of thinking in everyday landscapes and institutions of civil society," is deeply relevant not just to questions about the scales of racial formation, but also to the scales of settler colonialism, including the oppositional politics of scale.[47] In the case of the Montana Study, Cheng's intervention reminds us that the project, which sought to racialize what was in fact political difference and used blood purity as a marker of authenticity, was also an experiment in regional racial formation, and that regional racial formation and regional settler colonization often go hand in hand, with apparent contradictions only adding to the colonial cacophony.[48] Recognizing this example of "colonial racism" troubles "theorizations of settler colonialism as a stand-alone analytic."[49]

The regional scale produced by the Montana Study can in turn be understood simply as the area defined by the fifteen rural communities that participated in it, with Missoula functioning as the urban and institutional hub.[50] But the regional scale is more than just an area. It is also a means of "organizing space politically," as the urban historian Andrew Needham argues in his book *Power Lines*, which explores intimate linkages between Phoenix and the Navajo Reservation as manifest in regional energy infrastructure.[51] The Montana Study, an outgrowth of the broader regionalist reform movement, self-consciously cultivated a regional identity. Joseph Howard articulated a definition of regionalism—contra provincialism—that would guide the study during its short life: "Regionalism . . . means fullest recognition and utilization of the resources of one's area and their integration into the national and world scene; and of course it welcomes new brains and new blood for the regional effort. Provincialism means sitting around on one's fat rump and yelping that everything is rosy as it is and we mustn't be disturbed and asked to think. Montana isn't regional enough and it's too damned provincial and always has been."[52] In a letter to Howard, study director Baker Brownell reaffirmed his commitment to Howard's brand of regionalism. "Whether or not we in the United States can move toward the kind of regionalism which you support seems to me the most critical question that this country now faces," Brownell wrote.[53]

The Humanities Division of the Rockefeller Foundation, fiscal sponsor of the Montana Study, was also deeply invested in regionalism, and thus can be considered another agent in the production of scale. Between 1933 and 1947, the Humanities Division spent over $3 million on regional studies. The area studies program, launched in 1933, initially funded research in four broad geographical areas, including North America, where it focused on four specific regions.[54] Historian Philip Nelson contextualizes the Rockefeller Foundation's investment in area studies, particularly the bolstering of regional identity in the domestic sphere, in relation to the imperatives of the Second World War: "This effort at identification of unity within diversity; the bridging of gaps between occupations, classes, and civil boundaries; and the encouragement of a grass-roots, participatory movement, rather than the often inflexible, traditional, and sometimes esoteric ruminations and procedures of time-bound institutions, not surprisingly coincided with the all-out effort required of Americans by the reality of total war."[55] By the late 1940s, with war in the rear-view mirror, regionalism as "an intellectual organizing principle," exemplified by the Humanities Division, was on the decline.[56] Although the scale produced by the Montana Study was fleeting, its ideological effects were more persistent.

As a case study in settler colonial urbanism, what exactly does the Montana Study reveal about the urban? Howard's idea of regionalism, which resonates with William Cronon's account of the inextricable bonds between country and city in his book *Nature's Metropolis: Chicago and the Great West*, offers clues about how the study functioned as an urban, or *urbanizing* project.[57] "Regionalism . . . means fullest recognition and utilization of the resources of one's area," Howard wrote, "*and* their integration into the national and world scene." By linking or integrating small towns, universities, philanthropic organizations, and government agencies, the Montana Study exerted a strong centripetal force, acting as "social infrastructure."[58] Although it was designed to offset the pressures of urbanization and to counter the "growing cultural hegemony of urban over rural areas, as well as regional dominance of East over West," the study actually functioned as an instrument of regional consolidation and repossession, cultivating new relationships and inter-scalar configurations in the process.[59]

By telling the "city-country story as a unified narrative," Cronon follows in the footsteps of Raymond Williams; however, he explicitly frames his story of Chicago in terms of the *geography* of capital and the "landscape of obscured connections" that capitalism produces.[60] Indeed, while Cronon calls attention to both "capitalist expansion and colonization," the former is clearly the primary driver of the region's physical transformation. In the book's opening chapter, Cronon evokes the land's deeper history and he also acknowledges prior inhabitants, including the Potawatomi, who knew the area as "Chigagou" or "the wild-garlic place." Despite these prefatory remarks, Cronon's telling of Chicago's metropolitan story begins in 1833 at the conclusion of the Black Hawk War.[61] Cronon thus engages mostly with second-order colonization, which mirrors in some ways his focus on "second nature."[62] This emphasis on second-order colonization—a form of exploitation, often based on class and regional hierarchies, that *follows, effaces, and naturalizes replacement*—resonates with the Montana Study, which was founded partly on the belief that the project could serve as a bulwark against the state's "colonial economy" and protect its own citizens from exploitation by outside corporations. This belief is ironic, of course, since it disavows a much broader colonial economy predicated on Indigenous dispossession. Howard failed to recognize ongoing processes of settler accumulation and to differentiate these from other modes of extraction. Put differently, by focusing only on second-order colonization, the Montana Study promoted municipal and regional self-determination at the expense of tribal self-determination.

This apparent contradiction actually makes sense within the context of settler colonial urbanism. If settler colonialism produces a "landscape of obscured connections," settler colonial urbanism produces disconnected cities, or cities with circumscribed relationality, which are akin to Julie Tomiak's "settler city" and Zoe Todd's "city-as-terminus."[63] Tomiak insists that de-essentializing the city—or "fundamentally re-thinking how the city is conceptualized and by whom"—requires attention to "the connections to relations outside of the city."[64] The Montana Study also suggests spatial equivalents to Elizabeth Povinelli's concept of the "autological subject" and "genealogical society," which are associated with "discourses of individual freedom and social constraint," respectively.[65] Arguably, settler colonial urbanism produces autological cities and genealogical reservations.

Needham's account of linkages between Phoenix and the Navajo Reservation is a case in point. If Cronon focuses more on capitalism than settler colonialism in describing processes of regional formation, Needham shifts the emphasis from the capital relation to the colonial relation. Echoing Cronon, Needham advocates "remapping metropolitan history at the regional level."[66] In so doing, he demonstrates how "metropolitan development and Indian underdevelopment went hand in hand in postwar America," describing the Colorado Plateau, dominated by the Navajo Reservation and its vast coal fields, as Phoenix's "plundered province."[67] Like Neil Smith, Needham cautions against taking the "region for granted conceptually."[68] The modern Southwest, for Needham, is not simply a regional description but "a form of organizing space politically, a means towards claiming resources and contesting their proper distribution."[69] His book, therefore, is an argument for "an understanding of regional formation produced both in the material ties that connected spaces and in the shared understandings of space that those connections abetted."[70] With power lines—both literal and figurative—in mind, Needham describes the Navajo Reservation as "a vital part of urban space," effectively collapsing the distinction between city and country.[71] What sheds the most critical light on the *differential* production of geographical scale—and what Needham, in particular, excels at—is exposing not just connections between city and country but "unequal connections" between the two.[72]

If settler colonial urbanism describes a set of relations or processes, it involved ideological diffusion rather than material concentration in the case of the Montana Study. In other words, the study disseminated—albeit unevenly—settler colonial ideology throughout a region rather than extracting and importing material resources from a hinterland, which is the inverse of the scenario in Chicago described by Cronon. This diffusion is embodied by the Montana Study's stated desire to "get the university off the campus."[73] The study pursued its goal of offsetting the pressures of urbanization by integrating small towns with cities in Montana and other eastern states. Even though it was ostensibly about rural development, the Montana Study ultimately consolidated or urbanized a liberal settler imaginary. In this sense it is also an example of "rural urbanism," which Laura Barraclough defines as "the production of rural landscapes by the urban state, capital, and other urban interests."[74] It is partly the Montana Study's anti-urbanism that makes it such an intriguing case study in settler colonial urbanism—one that resonates with Ruth Wilson Gilmore's theory of the "anti-state state" and Jodi Byrd's theory of cacophony.[75]

These examples, all of which blur the boundaries between city and country, demonstrate the value of a regional field of analysis in constructing a relational theory of settler colonial urbanism.[76] Increased geographical specificity, including more nuanced understandings of the differential production of space and scale, helps explain what Scott Lauria Morgenson describes as settler colonialism's "inherent relationality."[77] A critical scalar lens, in particular, reveals that settler colonialism is inherently obfuscatory, producing, like capitalism, its own "landscape of obscured connections." If settler colonialism preserves "the narrative estrangement of urban and Indigenous histories," which Coll Thrush defines as "the deeply held notion that urban and Indigenous histories, like urban places and Indigenous peoples, have little to do with each other except as mutually exclusive opposites," a counterhegemonic and relational theory of settler colonial urbanism must necessarily refuse this false division.[78]

The Smear of Socialism, Colonial Cacophony, and False (Settler) Antagonism

Despite limited successes, the Montana Study moved against the political current for most of its short life, encountering resistance of one sort or another at almost every turn. This political context is important because it reveals how the production of scale amplifies "colonial cacophony." The Rockefeller Foundation ended its financial support of the study after the initial three-year grant, and the Montana legislature declined to make any further appropriations. A growing rivalry within the state's university system, combined with the departure of key organizers, also hastened the project's demise. In addition, the study's reputation suffered when other organizers, particularly Joseph Howard and Paul Meadows, were painted with the "smear of socialism." "Critics went so far as to label the Study a 'communist front'—an incendiary charge in the postwar era," Carla Homstad writes.[79] It was not just the study's goal of collective self-analysis and mutual aid that aroused suspicion. Even the concept of "sociodrama" was linked—rather crudely—to socialism.[80] Bert Hansen characterized opposition to the Montana Study as "surprisingly bitter, considering the mild nature of the program." "This opposition came from what might roughly be called the conservative-minded citizens," he wrote in an evaluation of the project two years after its conclusion.[81] "The program of the study was definitely concerned with the rights of human beings as such, and placed emphasis on decision by groups arrived at through group discussion. To some, this philosophy seemed both radical and dangerous."[82]

In addition to opposition from settlers who viewed it as a radical left-wing project, the study also encountered resistance from the opposite end of the spectrum. Undertaken during an era when termination dominated federal Indian policy, the Montana Study was greeted with scepticism on the Flathead Reservation, where many assumed it was a harbinger of termination. Participants in the Full Blood Study Group, for example, frequently sought reassurance from Hansen that the study was not simply a means of "turning the Indians loose."[83] Although tribal concerns about the study group process were unfounded in a policy sense—Hansen spoke openly against termination, performing his (colonial) good intentions—the Montana Study clearly advanced the project of assimilation, thus contributing to termination in a social sense. Participants' "fear of social and political death" therefore was not unwarranted.[84] But their concerns were overshadowed by the clamour on the right. Indigenous critique of the Montana Study was erased in real time, much as it has been overlooked in historical assessments of the project. Importantly, this discord on the right was productive, in the sense that it calcified what Manu Vimalassery, Juliana Hu Pegues, and Alyosha Goldstein refer to as "structuring events."[85] We might further unpack the productivity of clamour by accepting Jodi Byrd's invitation to understand colonialism "as a cacophony of contradictorily hegemonic and horizontal struggles."[86]

The Montana Study disseminated progressive or "liberal colonialism," which emphasizes inclusion, tolerance, and respect.[87] In short, it was based on principles of recognition.[88] This contrasts with conservative regimes of settler colonialism that can be characterized by more willful ignorance and/ or outright hostility toward Native peoples. Framing these seemingly antagonistic modes of settler colonialism in the context of Bert Hansen's speech to the Kiwanis International, one could argue that the progressive settler colonist believes he must know and respect the Indian in order to eliminate him, whereas the conservative settler colonist does not.[89] This distinction revolves around what Vimalassery, Hu Pegues, and Goldstein describe as "colonial knowing" and "colonial unknowing," with the Montana Study exemplifying a "more inclusive regime of colonial knowing."[90] This distinction also pivots around the question of white innocence, which is coveted by the liberal settler and rejected by the conservative one. Recall Hansen's comment about the ignorance of settlers concerning the "force and fraud" methods of dispossession. "Had [the settler] known," Hansen would go on to say, "he would in all probability have approved for, in his willful ignorance, the Indian was a useless and distasteful weed which had to be controlled and, if necessary, eradicated."[91]

The production of geographical scale also creates cacophony by allowing these antagonistic and contradictory regimes of settler colonialism to reverberate, thereby reinforcing the overarching logic of elimination. Cacophony resonates with Pasternak's notion of "interlegality" or the "interlegal space of settler colonialism," which is produced when "legal orders meet across epistemological difference and overlap on the ground."[92] Importantly, this space is characterized not by a "unified logic" but rather the "*tangle* of authorities that creates the overlays of Indigenous and settler claims to territorial jurisdiction."[93] The cacophony and interlegality amplified through the production of scale is one way that settler colonialism is "relationally constituted to other modes of imperialism, racial capitalism, and historical formations of social difference."[94] And it suggests that scale is an integral part of the "ongoing construction of settler geographies," and, following Tomiak, "a useful tool for thinking about how the settler city is constituted and normalized."[95]

In contrast, Pasternak invites us to think *beyond* scale to better grasp the production of space under settler colonialism. Focused on the Algonquins of Barriere Lake, her book *Grounded Authority* is "an argument to foreground jurisdiction as an approach to understanding how authority is established, exercised, and contested in settler colonies."[96] "Jurisdiction exceeds scale," Pasternak suggests, characterizing the latter as "an aspirational order of settler jurisdiction" that "implies a functioning chain of command."[97] As such, scale fails to explain what is often a dysfunctional chain of command, including "imperfect geographies," "the tangle of authorities," and "patterns of partial and uneven state sovereignty."[98] If jurisdiction reveals these "details of interlegality," the case of the Montana Study shows that scale remains a powerful analytic for understanding "social infrastructure" and the *cultural* production of settler colonial space.[99] In addition, scale remains useful for deciphering how settler common sense is "renewed and recreated in ordinary phenomena by nonnative, nonstate actors."[100]

As a spatial analytic—a corollary to Byrd's temporal analytic of cacophony—scale enables us to "imagine cacophonously" and to understand that the *geographical* processes, in addition to "the historical processes that have created our contemporary moment have affected everyone at various points along their transits with and against empire."[101] Scale also helps us to see the *structuring* of settler colonialism. To see, in other words, discordant settler affects consolidate into a singular common sense, and thereby to "dissolve the implied divide between structure and event."[102]

The cacophony or dialectic between liberal and conservative colonialism is significant because it creates a false antagonism that centres and further entrenches the settler imaginary by deflecting attention from foundational tensions between Indigenous peoples and settlers. It shifts the focus from the Indigenous-settler relation to the settler-settler relation; or, following Chadwick Allen, from struggles between "native indigeneity" and "settler indigeneity" to struggles exclusively over the latter.[103] The production of scale calls forth a "cacophony of competing struggles for hegemony," in Byrd's words, and enables it "to misdirect and cloud attention from the underlying structures of settler colonialism."[104] In terms of the oppositional politics of scale, this false antagonism enables a settler usurpation of oppositionality, such that oppositionality itself becomes a mechanism for settler indigenization.

Scale matters, Neil Smith argues, precisely because it "is as much the project of opposition as it is the project of capital."[105] Emphasizing the oppositional politics of scale—or the role of social struggle in the production of scale, which includes "the power to determine the scale of the struggle"— Smith argues that "the oppressive and emancipatory possibilities of space, its deadness but also its life," are all distilled in scale.[106] The oppositional politics of scale are integral to settler colonial urbanism, contributing to the production of landscapes of obscured connections. The Montana Study is a valuable case study of settler colonial urbanism because it highlights the oppositional politics of scale, including internal tensions, and also reveals how these oppositional politics shift within settler colonial contexts, producing false antagonisms that contribute to the structural resilience of settler colonialism. The study nuances oppositionality, calling attention to a subtle but important distinction between settler colonial (oppositional) politics of scale and anti-colonial (oppositional) politics of scale.[107] By revealing how what we might call a "cacophonous politics of scale" functions, the Montana Study suggests that the emancipatory possibilities of space are *different* in relation to the project of settler colonialism than to the project of capital. The study therefore helps us construct, more deliberately, an anti-colonial oppositional politics of scale, cultivate "an unsettling relational politics of entanglement and possibility," and unlock the emancipatory possibilities of space.[108]

De/Centring Missoula

The false antagonism also shifts the terrain of struggle in a more geographical sense. In the case of the Montana Study, specifically its urban hub, the false antagonism evacuated Indigeneity from the city—pushing it to the margins of the new regional formation—and rendered Missoula a non-Indigenous space. In this sense it materialized what Coll Thrush describes as "the narrative estrangement of urban and Indigenous histories" and re-articulated Missoula as the mutually exclusive opposite of the Flathead Reservation. "Cities have been central to this [estrangement]," Thrush argues, "both as primary technologies of the colonial dispossession of Indigenous lands—there is no better way to expropriate territory than to build a city—and as spaces imagined as free of Indigenous bodies, minds, and histories."[109] The urban/rural dichotomy thus emerges as another false antagonism as our focus shifts from the Indigenous-settler relation to the settler-settler relation. The dichotomy was often expressed in subtle ways that reinforced "autological and genealogical imaginaries" and denied the inextricable link between Missoula and the Flathead Reservation.[110] For example, Hansen separated Missoula from "Indian Country" in a comment about the Montana Study's commitment to inclusion. The project of "bringing the Indians and whites together in a common enterprise" was "something"—a notable achievement—only in "Indian Country." In separating city from (Indian) country, Hansen also framed the settler city as always already progressive.[111]

Since Missoula functioned as the urban hub for a liberal regime of regional settler colonization, the city was not entirely unwelcoming to Indigenous people. Rather, it sought to manage the terms of engagement in ways that gave spatial form to white innocence while also fostering assimilation. By way of contrast, if we turn our attention from the Montana Study to Fort Missoula—a permanent military post established in 1877 by the United States Army to protect settlers from Native Americans—we can appreciate how Missoula served as the urban hub for an earlier, more conservative regime of regional settler colonization.[112]

Reflecting the principles of inclusion, tolerance, and respect, the Montana Study cultivated a liberal settler imaginary that welcomed Indians to the city, just as it welcomed them to the study group table. But inclusion was on settler terms, and in this case, it came with the caveat that Indigenous people were but a temporary presence, always only passing through. Evidence of this attitude can be found in the numerous pageants and festivals that were staged in Missoula during and after the Montana Study's three-year run. On 12 and 13 August 1955, for example, "Your Land Forever"—a historical pageant-drama commemorating the Lewis and Clark sesquicentennial, the Council Grove Treaty centennial, and the U.S. Forest Service's golden anniversary—was performed at Dornblaser Field in Missoula. Throughout the weekend, visitors were encouraged to tour the "Indian Encampment" at Island Park, under the Higgins Avenue Bridge. "These original Americans (about 100) will be encamped on the Island for four days and have invited the public to visit their temporary homes during this stay for a nominal admission fee. Indians will be in native historical garb during their stay in Missoula and will be living in tepees and lodges which are duplicates of those used by their ancestors."[113] In addition to listing the times for "Indian Ceremonial Dances" and Sunday Mass at the island encampment, the souvenir program contained an implicit message: these "original Americans" are not from here and will not stay here. These festivals functioned as "structuring events," or, in the words of Mark Rifkin, "performative regularities of settler colonialism."[114] And they were essential for maintaining the city's status as a progressive non-Native space.[115] In this way, Missoula became peripheral to its own settler colonial history.

Stepping back, we can appreciate how liberal colonialism on the ground is mirrored by a liberal form of "methodological settler colonialism" that can critically engage second-order colonization while overlooking first-order or settler colonization, even though the latter remains "an ongoing structure of dispossession."[116] The false antagonism that shifts the focus from the Indigenous-settler relation to the settler-settler relation also facilitates the shift away from the colonial relation to the capital relation in liberal accounts. Once again, settler colonial urbanism helps us resolve, analytically, this apparent contradiction and, in this instance, make sense of Howard's conceptualization of the Montana Study as a bulwark against the state's "colonial economy."

Revisiting the Montana Study as a case study in regional settler colonization and settler colonial urbanism challenges liberal methodological settler colonialism and contests interpretations of "the urban region as a strictly settler creation."[117] It also denaturalizes Missoula by decentring it and repositioning it spatially, temporally, and discursively within a much larger Indigenous territory—weaving it, in the words of Zoe Todd, "into a much broader constellation of stories, histories, legal frameworks, and movement." This contributes to work, well underway, by the Flathead Nation, especially the Séliš-Qlispé Culture Committee.

DECOLONIZING REGIONALISM

On 4–7 September 2002, exactly fifty-five years after the Post Creek pageant, a large crowd gathered at the Arlee Powwow Grounds to watch a new pageant, "Salish and Pend d'Oreille People Meet the Lewis and Clark Expedition."[118] Directed by Johnny Arlee, a Salish author and spiritual leader who founded the Flathead Culture Committee in 1974, the pageant told the story of "how Indian people experienced the expedition and how later generations of Native Americans [came] to interpret the meaning of the expedition."[119] Over its four-day run, more than 4,000 people witnessed the pageant.

Staged just prior to the start of the Lewis and Clark Bicentennial, the pageant contested the expedition's status as the preeminent marker of the beginning of history in Montana.[120] According to Arlee, the pageant "respectfully presented our people as an organized culture in 1805—one with rules, teachings, and languages of our own."[121] In addition, he argued, "The Lewis and Clark Expedition entered an ancient tribal world, and the expedition cannot be fully understood unless we understand this world that preceded them."[122] In short, the pageant situated the 200-year-old expedition in the fold of the tribe's 10,000-year history in Montana and within its vast Aboriginal territory.[123] Tellingly, Arlee had been exposed to the Montana Study as a child. He noted that his interest in "the pageant as an art form stemmed from the 1950s when he participated with his great grandfather in pageants organized by Montana State University."[124] Arlee's personal connection to the Montana Study is significant, in part because it reveals an intergenerational or slow aspect of the oppositional politics of scale.

Augmenting the pageant, the Séliš-Q̓lispé Culture Committee—directed by Tony Incashola since 1995—published a book, *The Salish People and the Lewis and Clark Expedition*, on the occasion of the bicentennial.[125] Like the pageant, its purpose was to provide tribal perspectives on the encounter and also to reframe the expedition in the context of the much longer trajectory of tribal history and geography.[126] The Culture Committee also sought to pre-empt the "celebratory din" of the bicentennial, asserting that "the expedition was less an innocent 'Corps of Discovery' than a reconnaissance for invasion."[127] Acknowledging that this message may be "difficult" for those more invested in the romantic story of Lewis and Clark, the book's authors also contend that "many people are interested in a more realistic assessment of American history, even if it is a less comfortable assessment."[128] The book reflects briefly on Arlee's pageant, arguing that it offers something other than "blind celebration:" "The pageant performers, like the authors of this book, were motivated by a simple idea: that an unflinching reconsideration of that first encounter, and of the past two centuries, is essential if we are to reach for a different relationship—if the next 200 years are to be seen by our descendants as an era of greater respect, and of deeper understanding."[129] If the Montana Study used historical pageantry in part as an attempt to assimilate the Indians, Johnny Arlee and the Séliš-Q̓lispé Culture Committee have turned the tables and are now using it to "assimilate the newcomers."[130] By grafting settler history onto the "main trunk" of native history, Arlee invites us to "reassess [our] place within an Indigenous nation."[131] Unlike Hansen's sociodramas, these new projects emerge from the "third space of sovereignty," which Kevin Bruyneel describes as "a space of sovereignty and/or citizenship that is inassimilable to the modern liberal democratic settler-state and nation."[132] Importantly, this space is forged through struggle "against and across the boundaries of colonial rule," which is to say the third space of sovereignty is created partly through resistance to the scales of settler colonialism and partly through the (re)articulation of scales of Indigeneity. The work of the Culture Committee is also an example of "the stretching of anti-colonial resistance across and against settler colonial boundaries and scales," which Tomiak argues "is crucial in the re-politicization of the urban."[133] Additionally, it is an "exercise of jurisdiction," which, following Pasternak, can be understood as an "ontology of care."[134]

For Zoe Todd, bodies of water, especially those interfacing cities, are useful for tracing connections between city and country and understanding Indigenous-settler relations. "The river-city edge is a site that weaves the city-as-terminus into a much broader constellation of stories, histories, legal frameworks, and movement," she writes. "Whereas cities guard their boundaries quite jealously with ring-roads and ordinances, rivers permeate and implode these boundaries, necessarily drawing city-dwellers into broader awareness of, and responsibilities to, the watersheds with which they are enmeshed."[135] Todd's "river-city edge" disrupts "methodological settler colonialism," which Tomiak defines as "the assumptions, values, principles and ways of knowing through which settler cities have become known and normalized."[136] It is also a powerful tool for understanding efforts by the Séliš-Qlispé Culture Committee to decolonize regionalism and decentre Missoula, which sits at the confluence of Rattlesnake Creek and the Clark Fork River, and is known to the Salish and Pend d'Oreille people as Nł̓ay or "Place of the Small Bull Trout," one of many place names within their traditional territories that refer to bull trout or other fish.[137]

The Confederated Salish and Kootenai Tribes of the Flathead Nation are working methodically to revitalize relationships with the land and water both on the present-day reservation and within the traditional territories of the Salish, Pend d'Oreille, and Kootenai peoples, territories that together comprise a vast region extending outward from Missoula in the four directions. In so doing the tribes are redefining and decolonizing regionalism—producing new scales that align with ancient and evolving bio-cultural landscapes rather than the geopolitical coordinates of the settler state. The work reflects, in Pasternak's words, "the vitality of Indigenous territorial jurisdiction" and also "represents the reclamation of Indigenous space [and scale]," which Clint Carroll describes as "a sovereign act of reterritorialization in a settler colonial context."[138] The tribes are constructing a truly oppositional politics of scale. By shifting the focus from the settler-settler relation back to the Indigenous-settler relation and by carving out space for the Indigenous-Indigenous relation, the false antagonism gives way to one that is full of decolonial possibility. The emancipatory possibilities of space that are distilled in scale are therefore no longer fully eclipsed by the oppressive ones. In short, the Confederated Salish and Kootenai Tribes are producing scale in ways that enable us, if we listen carefully, to discern a distinctly decolonial cacophony. In the process they are slowly reclaiming Missoula as a Native place at the centre of a much larger Native region.

On 29 April 2017, Missoula County and the City of Missoula celebrated the grand opening of Fort Missoula Regional Park. The culmination of a twenty-year process, the new park features an interpretive trail that includes a sign designed by the Culture Committee. "Homeland of Séliš & Qlispé People," it states matter-of-factly. Accompanied by a few photographs and a map with selected place names, the sign articulates a dynamic relationship with the land and water.

> For millennia, the Missoula Valley has been a place of great importance to our people . . . This is a vital part of our aboriginal territories, a landscape filled with cultural meaning . . . The west side of the valley, including the prairies around Fort Missoula, was the greatest bitterroot digging ground in all of our vast aboriginal territories . . . In 1855, just a few miles west of this sign, our tribal nations met with U.S. officials to negotiate the Hellgate Treaty. The treaty established the sovereign Flathead Nation, and guaranteed our continued use of tribal homelands for traditional purposes . . . Today, Séliš and Qlispé people maintain a vital connection to the Missoula area. We are active members of the community, engaging in this transformed world even as we maintain and revitalize our connection to the ancestors.[139]

NOTES

1   Lokensgard, "Bert Hansen's Use of the Historical Pageant," 158.

2   Ibid.

3   Harris, "How Did Colonialism Dispossess?," 179.

4   Mitchell, "Neil Smith, 1954–2012," 219.

5   Bruyneel, "The American Liberal Colonial Tradition."

6   Byrd, *The Transit of Empire*, 84.

7   Rifkin, *Settler Common Sense*, 10.

8   Julie Tomiak uses the term "settler city" to "denote specific, yet unstable and varied, socio-spatial formations that are at once the products and vehicles of settler colonialism and its logic of displacing Indigenous bodies, peoples, ontologies, and rights." More generally, she denaturalizes the settler colonial production of urban space in Canada by critically engaging the politics of scale from anti-colonial and feminist perspectives. Focusing on Ottawa, or "the *city-region* that has come to be known as Ottawa," Tomiak illustrates "the efficacy and diversity of anti-colonial scale politics" through a series of case studies, including the Algonquin land claim process and Chief Theresa Spence's hunger strike on Victoria Island. Scale politics, for Tomiak, refers to both settler colonial and anti-colonial spatial politics, thus capturing strategies used by the settler state to normalize "specific ways of knowing and governing," and also to Indigenous resistance to settler state power and the articulation of other socio-spatial imaginaries and "inter-scalar configurations." Tomiak, "Unsettling Ottawa," 9, 10, 11, 12.

9   Ibid., 9.

10 Established in 1846, Fort Connah was part of the Hudson's Bay Company's vast network of trading posts. It was also the last post the company built within the boundaries of the United States. Believed to be the oldest standing building in Montana, the fort is now listed on the National Register of Historic Places. Lokensgard, "Bert Hansen's Use of the Historical Pageant," 48.

11 Poston, *Small Town Renaissance*, 182.

12 "8000 People See Thrilling Centennial Pageant-Drama."

13 Nelson, "Community Dreaming in the Rural Northwest"; Nelson, "Regionalism and the Humanities Division of the Rockefeller Foundation," 14, 12.

14 Contesting "structural good intentions" in post-secondary institutions, Sarah de Leeuw, Margo Greenwood, and Nicole Lindsay argue that "good intentions present a set of deep colonizing (unintended) consequences that obscure ongoing relations of inequity and conquest." de Leeuw, Greenwood, and Lindsay, "Troubling Good Intentions."

15 Scale is implicit in Cole Harris's oft-quoted analysis of colonial power: "Combine capital's interest in uncluttered access to land and settlers' interest in land as livelihood," he argues, "and the principal momentum of settler colonialism comes into focus." Harris, "How Did Colonialism Dispossess?," 179.

16 Pasternak, *Grounded Authority*, 21.

17 Despite its relevance to contemporary debates about the so-called crisis in the humanities and the attendant public, spatial, and digital turn of the humanities, surprisingly little has been written about the Montana Study. Like Richard Waverly Poston's definitive assessment, *Small Town Renaissance: A Story of the Montana Study* (published in 1950, three years after the study concluded), most accounts are celebratory, even nostalgic, and do not engage aspects of the project that deal with Indigenous-settler relations. Instead they emphasize the project's civic virtues. Homstad, "Two Roads Diverged"; Lewis, *In the Footsteps of Lewis and Clark*; Nelson, "Community Dreaming in the Rural Northwest"; Poston, *Small Town Renaissance*.

18 Homstad, "Two Roads Diverged," 18.

19 Nelson, "Regionalism and the Humanities Division of the Rockefeller Foundation," 12.

20 Homstad, "Two Roads Diverged," 20–21.

21 The Montana Study's pedagogical approach grew out of an earlier project, Northern Plains Studies, which was also sponsored by the Rockefeller Foundation. This project's shortcomings, chronicled in *The Northern Plains in a World of Change*, inspired the humanistic approach that characterized the Montana Study. Homstad, "Two Roads Diverged," 18–20.

22 Howard, *Montana*. Echoing Howard, Philip Nelson writes, "Observing that the West might free itself from its traditional 'colonial' status only to lose its way in the developing national society, a handful of small community reformers challenged the direction of mass culture by tapping into the neo-Jeffersonian, decentralist, adversarial tradition. From this intellectual base, they posed an alternative vision of modernity based on the idea of the progressive small community, which in the West found its most noteworthy expression in the Montana Study. In essence these reformers tried to do for the small town and rural West something akin to what the war was doing for urban areas, while rejecting the technocratic, urbanized, centralized nature of modern society." Nelson, "Community Dreaming in the Rural Northwest," 258. See also Lehman, "Wrong Side Up," 220–21.

23 Brownell, Howard, and Meadows, *Life in Montana*, 3.

24 The tiny town of Lonepine launched the first study group in January 1945. At the first weekly meeting participants were asked to reflect on why they lived in Lonepine and whether it was by choice. By the fifth week, they were pondering the meanings of modernism as manifest in their community. Poston, *Small Town Renaissance*, 195–96.

25 Brownell, Howard, and Meadows, *Life in Montana*, 3.

26 Homstad, "Two Roads Diverged," 23. Six sociodramas were produced during the final two years of the Montana Study. The first one, "Darby Looks at Itself," was performed in the town of Darby on 7 December 1945.

27 Hansen, "A Tale of the Bitter Root," 162.

28 Ibid.

29 "All the evils of the decaying small community life have settled upon Stevensville," Hansen observed. "It is a town in which either you belong or you do not." According to Hansen, "Those who do are conservative, complacent, and quite satisfied to let well enough alone. They dislike anything that stirs their imagination or that requires energy." Hansen was not surprised, therefore, that "there was some 'name-calling,' based on an idea that any discussion group concerned with human welfare was radical." Precisely because of this resistance, Hansen believed Stevensville was an ideal host and a "real test" for the Montana Study. Hansen, "An Evaluation of the Montana Study," 22.

30 Historian Stephenie Tubbs writes, "Stevensville residents had never, publicly, acknowledged, together with the Native people, the intricacies of their forefathers' relations. This time the injustice of the Salish people's story of forced removal from the homeland came to life." Tubbs, "Bert Hansen," 186.

31 Hansen continued, "It was a drama of willful aggression, the tragedy of a minority people first frustrated, then demoralized in order that the aggressor might take over their lands. This was the pageant the Stevensville people had the courage to conceive, to write, to produce, to see, and to let others see. They were fully aware, of course, that it was not without a contemporary parallel." Hansen, "A Tale of the Bitter Root," 162, 163, 166.

32 Ronan continued, "To the white man the Indian is a savage, a beast lower than his own domestic animals. This attitude has made a frustrated being out of the Indian and has demoralized him." Lokensgard, "Bert Hansen's Use of the Historical Pageant," 74.

33 Hansen, "An Evaluation of the Montana Study," 26.

34   Lokensgard added, "Actually the several cases of misdemeanor dramatized seemed to suggest that the old-time Indian method of solution by community opinion after the case had been tried before all members of the tribe was more democratic and many times more humane than similar cases tried before a court of law and settled by a judge or by a selected group of jurors." Lokensgard, "Bert Hansen's Use of the Historical Pageant," 155. During the performance, one of the characters, Father Hoecken, stated, "Times have taught us that justice for the Indian has little meaning in the minds of the white settlers when they are on the trail of a good piece of land. But we must be patient, trust God, and hope for the best." Ibid., 174.

35   Poston, *Small Town Renaissance*, 180.

36   Ibid., 183. Prefacing these comments, Poston observed, "There was a time not so long ago when the Flathead Indians had faith in the white man. They welcomed him to their native land, fed him when he was hungry, clothed him when he was cold, and defended him against hostile tribes. In that day the Indians were supreme and the newcomers were a minority. Then this state of affairs was reversed and the white man became dominant. He called the Indian a savage and destroyed his faith. What happened in the process is history. But through the Full Blood Indian Montana Study Group a new start was made toward the restoration of that faith."

37   Ibid.

38   Hansen, "An Evaluation of the Montana Study," 23.

39   Lokensgard, "Bert Hansen's Use of the Historical Pageant," 153, 155.

40   Ibid., 166. For an incisive critique of tolerance as a form of governmentality, see Brown, *Regulating Aversion*.

41   Hansen, "An Evaluation of the Montana Study," 26.

42   For more on the production of white innocence, see Cothran, *Remembering the Modoc War*; Biolsi, *Deadliest Enemies*.

43   Lokensgard, "Bert Hansen's Use of the Historical Pageant," 154.

44   Harris, "How Did Colonialism Dispossess?," 179.

45   Brown, "The Logic of Settler Accumulation."

46   Questions about scale are foregrounded in Wendy Cheng's book, *The Changs Next Door to the Díazes: Remapping Race in Suburban California*, which focuses on "everyday landscapes" of Los Angeles's West San Gabriel Valley, described by Cheng as "crucial terrains through which racial hierarchies are learned, instantiated, and transformed." Building on Michael Omi and Howard Winant's influential theory of racial formation, Cheng articulates a theory of *regional racial formation* that emphasizes the relational, spatial, *and* scaled character of racial formation, particularly its geographical specificity. She defines regional racial formation as "place-specific processes of racial formation, in which locally accepted racial orders and hierarchies complicate and sometimes challenge hegemonic ideologies and facile notions of race." In contrast to Omi and Winant, who theorize racial formation at the scale of the nation—albeit without talking explicitly *about* scale or space—Cheng asserts that "regional racial formation is concerned instead with the ways in which [social processes and movements] are situated in smaller-scale contexts (neighborhoods, localities, regions), important to the production of these scales themselves and intertwined with complex geographies of race." Cheng, *The Changs Next Door to the Díazes*, 3, 10, 211.

47   Cheng, *The Changs Next Door to the Díazes*, 211. Echoing Cheng, Cole Harris makes a similar case for greater geographical specificity in analyses of settler colonialism. "Assumptions about the location of civilization and savagery were widespread, and assimilation was a common goal," Harris writes, "but geographical, historical, and institutional contexts were very different, even in adjacent places, and broadly similar ideas and policies worked themselves out differently in different contexts." See Harris, *Making Native Space*, xxv.

48 TallBear, *Native American DNA*; TallBear, "DNA, Blood, and Racializing the Tribe."

49 Bruyneel, "Race, Colonialism, and the Politics of Indian Sports Names and Mascots," 3; Vimalassery, Hu Pegues, and Goldstein, "Introduction."

50 Communities included Lonepine, Dixon, Arlee, Libby, Darby, Hamilton, Stevensville, Woodman, Victor, Conrad, and Lewiston.

51 Needham, *Power Lines*, 15.

52 Lehman, "Wrong Side Up," 209.

53 Ibid., 220.

54 The Humanities Division funded research in the Far East, Latin America, the Slavic countries of Europe and Asia, and North America, primarily the United States. Nelson notes, "By 1943, the Humanities Division had authorized studies of four regions in North America: French Canada, the Eastern Maritime area, the Connecticut Valley, and the Northern Plains," which included the Montana Study. Nelson, "Regionalism and the Humanities Division of the Rockefeller Foundation," 13.

55 Ibid., 13.

56 Ibid., 14.

57 In 1991, William Cronon published *Nature's Metropolis: Chicago and the Great West*, an innovative history of Chicago's explosive growth in the nineteenth century. Focusing on the material resources and technological innovations that fuelled metropolitan growth, Cronon recounts the "twin birth of city and hinterland," arguing that "neither was possible without the other." That his story is as much about the Great West as it is about Chicago reinforces his central point that country and city are inextricably linked. "One cannot understand the environmental or economic history of the Great West," Cronon argues, "without exploring Chicago's nineteenth-century hinterland and the urban-rural relationships that defined it." Cronon, *Nature's Metropolis*, 264, 265.

58 Cowen, "Infrastructures of Empire and Resistance."

59 Nelson, "Community Dreaming in the Rural Northwest," 258.

60 Cronon, *Nature's Metropolis*, xiv, 340.

61 Cronon writes, "If, then, we take 1833 as the beginning of Chicago's metropolitan story, the Indians' and boosters' different notions of land and empire marked a great cultural divide on human maps of the Great West in the 1830s." With great self-awareness about the implications of his story's timeline, Cronon continues, "The Potawatomis finally sold their lands to the United States and moved west to prepare for their next encounter with American land hunger. The removal of these 'dusky nuisances' fulfilled an imperial ideology that viewed the 'idle and dissolute Indians' as 'the first obstacle to the growth of Chicago.' Henceforth the Potawatomis played only the most marginal roles in the marketplace they had once dominated. The proof of their tragedy is that the history of Chicago can be written from 1833 forward as if they had never lived there." Cronon, *Nature's Metropolis*, 53, 54.

62 Ibid., xvii.

63 Tomiak, "Unsettling Ottawa," 10; Todd, "From Classroom to River's Edge," 91.

64 Tomiak, "Unsettling Ottawa," 10, 16.

65 Framed as examples of liberal sociality, Povinelli explains, "By the *autological subject*, I am referring to discourses, practices, and fantasies about self-making, self-sovereignty, and the value of individual freedom associated with the Enlightenment project of contractual constitutional democracy and capitalism. By *genealogical society*, I am referring to discourses, practices, and fantasies about social constraints placed on the autological subject by various kinds of inheritances." Povinelli, *The Empire of Love*, 3–4.

66 Needham, *Power Lines*, 9.

67   Ibid., 8, 154.

68   Ibid., 16.

69   Ibid., 15.

70   Ibid., 16.

71   Ibid., 156. This strategy of blurring boundaries is also used by historian Coll Thrush in *Native Seattle*, when he incorporates "the lived experiences of Native people in the city and its hinterland" and grounds the city "within particular Native places ranging from a fishing camp buried beneath fill in the heart of the city to a British Columbia village linked to Seattle by trade and migration." Thrush, *Native Seattle*, 13.

72   Needham, *Power Lines*, 251.

73   Nelson, "Regionalism and the Humanities Division of the Rockefeller Foundation," 14. Lehman writes, "Advocating a blend of adult education and public humanities, [Howard] urged the entire state 'to become one vast university in which all of you are teachers or research students.'" Lehman, "Wrong Side Up," 221.

74   Using California's San Fernando Valley as a case study, Laura Barraclough highlights the process of "rural urbanism," which occurs through "the dialectics of myth making about rural land and western heritage and the formulation of urban policy." Barraclough notes, "The concept [of rural urbanism] builds on Raymond Williams's and William Cronon's insights . . . that the development of city and countryside go hand in hand, both in terms of their material, physical development and their cultural and symbolic meanings." An example of "relational racialization," rural urbanism is also key, Barraclough argues, to understanding the relationships between imperialism, racial formation (especially whiteness), and urban geographies. Barraclough, *Making the San Fernando Valley*, 2.

75   Gilmore, "What Is to Be Done?," 252; Byrd, *The Transit of Empire*, 53.

76   Other scholars such as Ruth Wilson Gilmore, Renya Ramirez, and Laura Barraclough have pursued similar lines of inquiry, deepening our understanding of the city-country nexus and the differential production of geographical space and scale. See Gilmore, *Golden Gulag*, 17; Ramirez, *Native Hubs*, 1; Barraclough, *Making the San Fernando Valley*, 2.

77   Morgensen argues that settler colonialism, by definition, is "*a relationship* between something that may attempt totalization and all that it attempts (forever incompletely) to suppress. Indeed, settler colonialism's inherent relationality continually invokes interdependence, *not* independence—whether that to which it relates seems present or absent, in the imagination or in interactions with those who survive attempted erasure." Morgensen, *Spaces between Us*, 51.

78   "At its core," Thrush writes, "the narrative estrangement of the urban from the Indigenous has reflected a broader perceived estrangement of Indigenous peoples from modernity, framed in binaries such as civilized versus savage, rational versus irrational, or historical versus timeless." Thrush, *Indigenous London*, 13. See also O'Brien, *Firsting and Lasting*.

79   Homstad, "Two Roads Diverged," 27.

80   Lokensgard, for example, notes, "A suspicious visitor at a study group meeting in Stevensville, in 1946, heard little more than Bert's mention of the word when he jumped to his feet, raised his arm, pointed his finger at Bert, and angrily exclaimed: 'I knew it! I knew it all the time! Socialism! That's what you're promoting! And the very word, sociodrama, proves it!' With no further words the man stomped from the meeting." Lokensgard, "Bert Hansen's Use of the Historical Pageant," 46–47.

81   Hansen observed that Montanans were generally "uninterested" in "town meeting democracy," and considered the study to be an "impotent" program. Hansen, "An Evaluation of the Montana Study," 20.

82   Ibid. Echoing this sentiment, literary critic Leslie Fiedler published a provocative essay, "Montana; or The End of Jean-Jacques Rousseau," in the *Partisan Review* in 1949. Distilling attitudes common

among the state's citizenry into a single image, which he condescendingly referred to as the "Montana face," Fiedler asserted that it was "a face developed not for sociability or feeling, but for facing into the weather." Evoking Hansen's "conservative-minded citizen," the "Montana face" emerged, according to Fiedler, only after Montana became "psychologically possible." To make his point, Fiedler referred to the Montana Study. "Under the compulsion to examine his past (and there have been recently several investigations, culminating in the Rockefeller Foundation-sponsored Montana Study), the contemporary Montanan, pledged to history though nostalgic for myth, becomes willy-nilly an iconoclast." Fiedler, "Montana."

83 Poston, *Small Town Renaissance*, 172–73.

84 Simpson, *Mohawk Interruptus*, 43.

85 "It may be useful to dissolve the implied divide between structure and event," argue Vimalassery, Hu Pegues, and Goldstein. "How would our critical perspective open up if we began to understand (settler) colonialism as a structuring event, an ongoing elaboration of a structure, a suspension of time, tense, and timeliness? In order to interrogate settler colonialism as a unique structuring event or events in a structure of power, close attention to process and relationship, to structures of power as they transform in specific places and times, seems to be a useful approach for clarifying the stakes of decolonial possibility." Vimalassery, Hu Pegues, and Goldstein, "Introduction."

86 Byrd writes, "In geographical localities of the Americas, where histories of settlers and arrivants map themselves into and on top of indigenous peoples, understanding colonialism as a cacophony of contradictorily hegemonic and horizontal struggles offers an alternative way of formulating and addressing the dynamics that continue to affect peoples as they move and are made to move within empire." Byrd, *The Transit of Empire*, 53.

87 Simpson, "Whither settler colonialism?," 441.

88 For more on the politics of recognition, see Coulthard, *Red Skin, White Masks*; Simpson, *Mohawk Interruptus*; Povinelli, *The Cunning of Recognition*.

89 Parallels can also be drawn to Martin Luther King's distinction between the "white moderate" and the "Ku Klux Klanner" in his famous 1963 "Letter from Birmingham City Jail." "I have almost reached the regrettable conclusion," wrote King, "that the Negro's great stumbling block in the stride toward freedom is not the White citizens' 'Councilor' or the Ku Klux Klanner, but the white moderate who is more devoted to 'order' than to justice; who prefers a negative peace which is the absence of tension to a positive peace which is the presence of justice." In conclusion, he stated, "Shallow understanding from people of good will is more frustrating than absolute misunderstanding from people of ill will. Lukewarm acceptance is much more bewildering than outright rejection." King Jr., "Letter from Birmingham City Jail."

90 Vimalassery, Hu Pegues, and Goldstein, "Introduction."

91 Lokensgard, "Bert Hansen's Use of the Historical Pageant," 154.

92 Pasternak, *Grounded Authority*, 7.

93 Ibid., 8.

94 Vimalassery, Hu Pegues, and Goldstein, "Introduction."

95 Rifkin, *Settler Common Sense*, 193; Tomiak, "Unsettling Ottawa," 11.

96 Pasternak carefully disentangles jurisdiction from sovereignty, arguing that "the *legitimacy* and *legality* of sovereignty can be called into question in the register of jurisdiction." Conflict over jurisdiction, she observes, is conflict over "the authority to have authority," or "the inauguration of law." Pasternak, *Grounded Authority*, 2, 3, 15.

97 Ibid., 16–18.

98 Ibid., 7–8.

99 Cowen, "Infrastructures of Empire and Resistance."

100 Rifkin, *Settler Common Sense*, 10.

101 Byrd, *The Transit of Empire*, xxxix.

102 Vimalassery, Hu Pegues, and Goldstein, "Introduction."

103 According to Chadwick Allen, "The Fourth World condition is marked by a perennial struggle between 'native' indigeneity and 'settler' or 'New World' indigeneity. Stated briefly, aboriginal inhabitants of what are now First World nations have been forced to compete for indigenous status with European settlers and their descendants eager to construct new identities that separate them from European antecedents." Allen, *Blood Narrative*, 9. Jean O'Brien identifies a similar tension, arguing that "non-Indians stake a claim to being native" through the processes of firsting and lasting. O'Brien, *Firsting and Lasting*, xv.

104 Byrd, *The Transit of Empire*, xvii. "As liberal multicultural settler colonialism attempts to flex the exceptions and exclusions that first constituted the United States to now provisionally include those people othered and abjected from the nation-state's origins, it instead creates a cacophony of moral claims that help to deflect progressive and transformative activism from dismantling the ongoing conditions of colonialism that continue to make the United States a desired state formation within which to be included. That cacophony of competing struggles for hegemony within and outside institutions of power, no matter how those struggles might challenge the state through loci of race, class, gender, and sexuality, serves to misdirect and cloud attention from the underlying structures of settler colonialism that made the United States possible as oppressor in the first place."

105 Smith, *Uneven Development*, 229.

106 Smith explains, "Geographical scale is political precisely because it is the technology according to which events and people are, quite literally, 'contained in space.' Alternatively, scale demarcates the space or spaces people 'take up' or make for themselves." He adds, "A spatial politics not only puts into practice the metaphor that events 'take place,' but that the true contest concerns the locus of the power to determine the scale of the struggle: who defines the place to be taken . . . and its boundaries." Smith, *Uneven Development*, 230, 232.

107 Following Tomiak, the Montana Study illustrates "the efficacy and diversity of anti-colonial scale politics." Tomiak, "Unsettling Ottawa," 9.

108 Vimalassery, Hu Pegues, and Goldstein, "Introduction."

109 Thrush, *Indigenous London*, 14.

110 Povinelli, *The Empire of Love*, 3.

111 Hansen argued, "The project is bringing about better relations and better understandings. They are bringing the Indians and whites together in a common enterprise in which they share and share alike in all its aspects. And in Indian country, that's something." Lokensgard, "Bert Hansen's Use of the Historical Pageant," 158.

112 Koelle, "Pedaling on the Periphery."

113 "Lewis and Clark Sesquicentennial."

114 Rifkin, *Settler Common Sense*, 193.

115 On 16 and 17 August 1957, another pageant-drama, "Move Over, Indian" was presented at the Field House in Missoula as the highlight of the inaugural Western Montana Indian Festival. As the title suggests, "Move Over, Indian," was partly *about* dispossession—specifically, it was about the 1891 removal of the Salish from the Bitterroot Valley just south of Missoula—but the pageant-drama was equally about *dispossessing*, which is to say that it had a lot more to do with the present than the past.

116 Audra Simpson defines settler colonialism as "an ongoing structure of dispossession that targets Indigenous peoples for elimination." Simpson, *Mohawk Interruptus*, 74.

117 Hugill, "Settler Colonial Urbanism."

118 Arlee, "Salish and Pend d'Oreille People Meet the Lewis and Clark Expedition." See also Greene, "Pageant to Provide Education"; Greene, "Johnny Arlee, Cultural Leader, Has Walked Many Roads"; Stromnes, "Salish Showcase"; Robbins, "Setting the Record Straight."

119 Arlee, "Salish and Pend d'Oreille People Meet the Lewis and Clark Expedition," 2. The Séliš Qlispé Selis Qlispe Culture Committee (originally called the Salish-Pend d'Oreille Culture Committee/ Flathead Culture Committee) and Kootenai Culture Committee were established in 1974–75 for the purpose of preserving and revitalizing the traditional cultures and languages. Today, the committees play an important role in tribal governance. "The culture committees have also served to reintegrate traditional culture into the decision-making structure of tribal government, from which it was formally excluded in 1935 after the reconstitution of the tribes under the terms of the Indian Reorganization Act, which phased out the traditional chiefs." Salish-Pend d'Oreille Culture Committee, *The Salish People and the Lewis and Clark Expedition*, 120. See also Séliš Qlispé Culture Committee, accessed August 1, 2018, http://www.csktribes.org/history-and-culture/salish-culture-committee; Kootenai Culture Committee, accessed August 1, 2018, http://www.csktribes.org/history-and-culture/ kootenai-culture-committee.

120 For more on the Lewis and Clark Bicentennial (2003–2006), see Howe and TallBear, *This Stretch of the River*; Hoxie and Nelson, *Lewis and Clark and the Indian Country*; Fresonke and Spence, *Lewis and Clark*.

121 Robbins, "Setting the Record Straight."

122 Arlee, "Salish and Pend d'Oreille People Meet the Lewis and Clark Expedition," 2.

123 Salish-Pend d'Oreille Culture Committee, *The Salish People and the Lewis and Clark Expedition*, 109.

124 Robbins, "Setting the Record Straight."

125 Fehrs, "The Good Life of Tony Incashola."

126 The arrival of non-Indians is thus depicted as "another chapter" in this long history, not the beginning of history. "Lewis and Clark were much less discoverers than visitors, venturing into the territory of a sovereign native nation—a tribal world that was older, richer, and more complex than the expedition members could have possibly imagined. Rather than examining the role of native people within the history of the expedition, we are examining the role of the expedition within the history of our tribe—within the history of one tribe's struggle for cultural and political survival over the past several centuries." To emphasize this point, the book includes a timeline stretching back 15,000 years to the draining of Glacial Lake Missoula and the warming of the region after the last Ice Age. A caption states, "If we were to compress the last 9,000 years of this timeline into a single 24-hour day, Lewis & Clark would arrive at 11:28pm—about a half an hour before midnight." Salish-Pend d'Oreille Culture Committee, xi–xii, 8–9.

127 "The historical meaning of Lewis and Clark must be understood within the broader context of the sudden, and relatively recent, non-Indian invasion of native North America." Salish-Pend d'Oreille Culture Committee, *The Salish People and the Lewis and Clark Expedition*, xii, 9.

128 Ibid., xii.

129 Ibid.,122. Prefacing this comment, the authors write, "And so, despite the misunderstanding, the injustice, the loss and tragedy reflected in these pages, there is also hope to be taken from this history. That hope depends on our continuing to work together to create a deeper understanding of our history. In 2002, the tribe was given a much louder voice when former culture committee director Johnny Arlee presented a theatrical pageant on the Salish and Pend d'Oreille encounter with the Lewis and Clark expedition. In several days of performances at the Arlee Celebration Grounds on the Flathead

Reservation, some fifty tribal members gave audiences totaling more than four-thousand people a sense of the tribal cultural world that the expedition was entering in 1805, and the historical meaning of the encounter itself."

130 Muecke, *Ancient and Modern*, 6.

131 Advocating for Native literary nationalism, Craig Womack writes, "Tribal literatures are not some branch waiting to be grafted onto the main trunk. Tribal literatures are the *tree*, the oldest literatures in the Americas, the most American of American literatures. We *are* the canon. [...] Without Native American literature, *there is no American canon.* . . . Let Americanists struggle for their place in the canon." Womack, *Red on Red*, 6–7; Birch, "'The Invisible Fire,'" 114–15.

132 Bruyneel, *The Third Space of Sovereignty*, 217.

133 Tomiak, "Unsettling Ottawa," 16.

134 Pasternak, *Grounded Authority*, 6.

135 Todd, "From Classroom to River's Edge," 91.

136 Tomiak, "Unsettling Ottawa," 9–10.

137 Salish-Pend d'Oreille Culture Committee, *The Salish People and the Lewis and Clark Expedition*, 46–47.

138 Pasternak writes, "The ongoing exercise of Indigenous jurisdiction over land, resources, and bodies on their homelands today reveals the continuity of this suspended space between settler assertions of sovereignty and the vitality of Indigenous territorial jurisdiction." Pasternak, *Grounded Authority*, 4; Carroll, "Native Enclosures," 33.

139 Azure, "Small Signs Carry Big Messages."

CHAPTER SIX

URBAN MÉTIS COMMUNITIES

The Politics of Recognition, Reflexivity, and Relationality

**TYLER MCCREARY
IN DIALOGUE WITH CHRIS ANDERSEN,
ADAM GAUDRY, AND BRENDA MACDOUGALL**

Métis relationships to urbanization need to be understood against the backdrop of the distinct history of Métis communities and their encounters with colonialism. Networks of kinship relationships and a shared history of political struggle have enabled Métis communities to recognize themselves as a distinct people; however, Canadian government discourse and practice have racialized Métis communities as defined by their "mixed blood" and legislatively differentiated them from Indigenous communities racialized as "Indian" in Canada.[1] While research on "Indian" urban life has been expanding, the distinct Métis urban experience remains relatively understudied, particularly in relation to the ways in which Métis families maintain relations and produce Métis spaces in the city.

The prevalent approach to urban Métis has been through an analysis of colonial racial formations. As Evelyn Peters et al. argue, the legal construction of a racial boundary between the categories of Métis and Indian placed

Métis people in a different relationship to the federal government, the provincial government, and the city.[2] While historically Indian life was regulated by the Indian Act, Métis people were positioned in a liminal space as non-white and non-Indian. The government did not recognize Métis possession of Indigenous land rights; instead, Métis title claims were recognized on an individual basis that created distinct processes of dispossession. Relatedly, federal reserves were not established for Métis communities, and Métis access to Indian reserves was controlled. From the perspective of the state, Métis constituted a position of racial liminality—too white to claim Indigeneity and too Indigenous to claim whiteness.[3] Doubly excluded, Métis *qua* mixed race communities were relegated to an urban fringe. Interrogating these historic exclusions, Jaimy Miller and Bonita Lawrence have positioned the construction of categories of Métisness as a means to deny certain groups of Indigenous people access to Indian status.[4] However, focusing on the category of Métisness as a mechanism to exclude people from Indian status fails to recognize that the Métis constitute a distinct political community.

The association of Métisness and mixed race within settler colonial discourse has obscured the nationhood of Métis people. Chris Andersen and Adam Gaudry argue that the techniques the Canadian state has used to render Métisness legible—specifically, conceptualizing the Métis as a mixed race community in court cases on Métis rights and obscuring the distinction between Métis citizenship and mixed race heritage on the census—have obscured the history of the Métis as a distinct political community.[5] Rather than approaching Métisness through mixed race definitions, Andersen argues, it should be understood as a particular form of nationhood linked to the political histories of the Red River region (a portion of which would later become the city of Winnipeg). Building on the conceptualization of Métis nationhood, Ron Laliberte argues that urban Métis identities on the Prairies draw together identities based on notions of Métis nationhood and racial hybridity.[6] While Laliberte finds people self-identify in Saskatoon as Métis based on mixed race ancestry as well as ancestral connections to historic Métis communities, he argues that the history and culture of the Métis nation provide the foundation for the emergence of a "pan-Métis" community in the city.

Recent research on Métis identities has suggested that Métis identities can be better understood through Indigenous concepts than via Western political theory. Brenda Macdougall particularly argues for a focus on the importance of Métis relations of kinship.[7] She uses the concept of *wahkootowin* to emphasize the importance of family connections to the historic emergence of a self-defined Métis community. In contrast to political histories of Métis nationhood that centre on struggles against the Hudson's Bay Company and Canadian state around the Red River, Macdougall highlights the emergence of distinct Métis communities in northwest Saskatchewan based on the way in which community was self-defined and actively built through relations of kinship and networks of mutual responsibility.

To examine how the politics of recognition, reflexivity, and relationality shape urban Métis experience, I asked Chris Andersen, Adam Gaudry, and Brenda Macdougall to join me in conversation. Through what follows, they examine how Métis identities and geographies are expressed within and beyond the city. The conversation highlights the importance of critiquing the politics of state recognition, exercising reflexivity to situate Métis urban experience within the history of Métis struggles with settler colonialism, and remembering and continually renewing relations of kinship with the broader Métis community.

FOUNDATIONS OF MÉTIS URBAN EXPERIENCE

In this interview, I want to discuss relations between Métis and settler colonial urbanism on the Prairies. To begin, I think it's necessary to provide some historic context. Who are the Prairie Métis people, and how do they emerge as a distinct Indigenous people?

CHRIS: Well, I think it's safe to say that there is a great deal of complexity, even within the Métis academic communities. Even among those of us who respect each other's work but come from different disciplinary backgrounds. From my perspective, I see Métis as being rooted in and around Red River and see that as being the heart of it, but it's certainly not just in that area.[8] I think about Métis in terms of nationhood, in terms of peoplehood, and in terms of their connections to other Indigenous peoples and their connection to the territories that they lived upon, as opposed to thinking about Métis in the way that most Canadians are used to thinking about it, which is in terms of mixed Aboriginal and non-Aboriginal ancestry.

BRENDA: I would agree with Chris in that last part absolutely. We can't talk about this in a mixed race capacity. It's not about being mixed blood, about being a loose collection of individuals. While I would agree with peoplehood and nationalism, my sense is that it is much more expansive and probably rooted in very specific historical circumstances that exist outside of the core of the Red River Settlement in particular time periods. I think the people of Red River come from the Prairies and that this is a place that is fuelled by a bunch of different trajectories that create a particular kind of space by the end of the nineteenth century.

ADAM: My interest in this history is in the political institutions that the Métis have created, so I see Métis as a political community as well. One that's self-conscious and has common political institutions, all of which play a role in constituting a Métis people, a Métis nation. A lot of that, as both Brenda and Chris have already noted, is connected to two places, the Red River Settlement and the broader Prairie society, which allow Métis to move between many of those places with relative ease. So I think that Métis are fundamentally a political unit and that political unit is constituted based on the buffalo hunting practices of Métis largely in the nineteenth-century Prairies.

Conventionally, people imagine Indigenous spaces as rural and Indigenous people only coming to the cities in recent years. However, Indigenous urbanization often preceded the establishment of white settler towns. Indigenous peoples across North America lived in urban communities long before white people came. Would you similarly argue that the story of urban Métis people should begin prior to white settlement? How should we understand the beginning of Métis urbanization?

BRENDA: If you look at Prairie cities, they all exist where Métis communities existed, whether they were fur posts or encampments. That includes Regina, Winnipeg, Saskatoon, Edmonton, all of the cities that we see as major centres. Those are all historical fur trading locations. Of course, First Nations people were there. That should be a given. But people who lived in and around and populated those posts are our people. Cities were built around us. Absolutely. Winnipeg is obviously the best example, but Edmonton is a stellar example as well.

ADAM: Both those places had communities of Métis for generations, and we can probably call them urban for lack of better terminology. In some instances, these communities were "urban" for over a century and a half. And so there are a lot of families that haven't left their traditional territory but are now urban without ever having moved. Those communities were also supplemented by Métis from more rural areas when they were pushed out of their own communities by various social and political forces. So I think a lot of this is a swelling of Métis communities that were Métis communities at their origins.

BRENDA: Absolutely, by the end of the nineteenth century, Métis people are on the move. Their homeland is being consistently reduced, their opportunities are reduced as the cities become a place where they head. You know, the road allowances are burned out and people go to the cities.[9] Some of them go further into the bush but a lot of people end up in urban spaces.

CHRIS: Just to add to what both of you are saying—it is very important to think of urban spaces as hubs rather than locales. People are both on the move into and out of these spaces. I always recall that line of Malcom X's where he talks about how Black people didn't land on Plymouth Rock, Plymouth Rock landed on them.[10] This is a similar kind of situation—we have a concentration of Métis people living in a particular area, and as urbanity expands opportunities get reduced and in some cases change. This has an enormous impact on people's ability to stay or move. Of course, people do stay and move, and when they come back, they return to places they knew, even if those places have been transformed, or they move back to where they know they still have family. Thinking of urban spaces in terms of hubs, you start to see where and why movements happen.

BRENDA: Also, as opportunities in rural and remote regions became constricted, very specific kinds of places developed on the edges of Prairie cities—the shanty towns or road allowances, places like Fox Farm in Prince Albert, or Round Prairie just outside of Saskatoon, or Rooster Town in the City of Winnipeg. There are very clear regional associations within those urban spaces, at least historically up until the last decade or two.

Before we get too far in talking about the relationship to settler space, I think
it would be worth talking about the larger sense of Métis territoriality and
the way that Métis produced urban spaces in relation to broader political
relationships, but also family relationships. I would be interested in how you
understand a Métis production of space in terms of its political qualities and
kinship obligations. What are the structures that regulate the relationships
Métis people maintained to one another and to particular places?

ADAM: There is a memoir by Louis Goulet.[11] When he's young, his family
travels between Red River and Fort Edmonton almost on an annual basis.
Basically for them, Red River was always referred to as home. And in that
era, a lot of Métis from Red River go to the Prairie and come home. That's
kind of the language used. Even though they're spending more time on the
Prairie, home for them is still connected to Red River. I think that's true
in places like Lac St. Anne, Fort Edmonton, and Île-à-la-Crosse— there
was this sense of home, but also this constant movement to and from other
places. A lot of it is economic: to hunt buffalo, to trade, to freight goods for
companies and governments, or to get buffalo robes and then sell them in
St. Paul, Minnesota. The Métis covered a lot of space, which was all shared
territory, of course. But I still think that certain centres, at least until 1870,
were very much hubs, like Chris said, to which Métis constantly returned
and conceptualized as their home.

BRENDA: While I don't think Red River is the centre for all those
people, I agree with Adam that there are hubs where people end up. I'll
use another example from Cheryl Troupe's research on Métis people in
Saskatoon,[12] and this is also borne out in the work that Evelyn Peters has
done on Rooster Town in Winnipeg.[13] When people came to the city,
they very much congregated in spaces where they recognized people.
Certainly, whole communities shifted into the city and settled in specific
neighbourhoods. They took over streets, and while their children might
have moved out of that neighbourhood, there is still a definable space based
on kinship relations within urban centres. And those kinship relationships
I think were borne out in political governing structures. So the ways that
the locals tried to organize in urban spaces were initially built on kinship

relationships. They worked to put in place things that other people would be able to use when they came into the city, that they would be able to connect to. And so I think there is definite kinship within urban settings.

CHRIS: This is not in disagreement with anything that's been said, but when we think of urban spaces specifically, urban spaces become these incubators of Indigenous culture, if you will, that don't fit the hard-and-fast delineations that we often take for granted around First Nations and Métis. We get these spaces that are distinctively Indigenous, for sure, but they're tied together politically and socially to the place that they're in. Rob Innes, who is a professor at the University of Saskatchewan who grew up in Winnipeg, talks about how everyone was Indian and you didn't think or talk about the term Métis.[14] Which is not to say that there wasn't anyone who was Métis. It's just that people thought about themselves as being specifically Indigenous to that particular space. So when we talk about Métis in a particular area, for sure there's chain migration, there are people moving to where they have family and extended family, but think about the community that gets created there—it ends up being a community that transverses these legal constitutional definitions.

BRENDA: And I think that's a reality because that's the way people live outside of the city. It's not a big deal to live among your First Nations relatives even if they're not your biological relatives—they're now your urban-dwelling relatives. There's this sense that we're all in this space together, absolutely; it's an unconscious acceptance of anybody who needs to be there.

THE PLACE OF URBAN MÉTIS WITHIN SETTLER COLONIAL GOVERNANCE

What is settler colonialism and how does it transform Métis geographies, and particularly, Métis urban geographies?

ADAM: For me, settler colonialism was primarily a way of moving settlers onto Indigenous lands. As the power of the state expanded, it was more difficult for Indigenous peoples to move across those lands. It was a closing up of Indigenous lands and a limiting of the ability of Indigenous peoples to move across their territory, to practise their laws and assert authority over those territories. Their authority was increasingly replaced with Canadian laws. Canada sought a very different future for Métis than Métis sought for themselves.

CHRIS: I agree. I see settler colonialism as being a particular way of talking about the capitalist projects that end up being imposed on these particular territories. You get a number of different projects that impose particular social, cultural, political schemes onto areas that already have forms of political, social, and cultural agency, and when this occurs you get the attempted erasure of these pre-existing formations and you get these arrogant impositions of new schemes and projects.

BRENDA: The reality of colonialism or settler colonialism is that it starts as an intellectual process. You have to start delineating the "us" from "them." And Métis sat for a period of time in an awkward space of are they "us" or are they "them"? And what are the conditions under which they are "us"—colonialist, settlers—and what are the conditions under which they are "them"—Native? And eventually, Canada and the United States both decide it's a "them." Unless you meet certain kinds of standards of behaviour, you must automatically be a "them," and the "them" then gets erased from the intellectual memory of that space. So you can walk through a city completely invisible no matter what your colour is, because you're not legitimately there, because you don't exist in a civilized space, you exist in an outside space, and eventually we can forget that you're even in that outside space. It's about erasure. These complex categories that get developed are all about that constriction, constriction of space, constriction of identity, constriction of opportunity to be Indigenous.

ADAM: The idea that Métis are urban is, especially in policy terms, a rather recent phenomenon. I think early settler colonialism envisioned Métis to be farmers, that was the civilizational goal. The highest achievement of "Indigenous-people-turned-civilized" was to be able to farm productively. As a sort of best-case scenario, it was envisioned that most Indigenous people would move away from these centres, take up reserves, and turn them into farms. I think a lot of Métis in Red River, during the settler colonial moment just preceding the Red River Resistance, when Canada arrives to claim ownership over their territory, are really trying to set themselves up to be at the centre of the province.[15] I think that means that Red River Métis really set themselves up to consolidate their lands there. Not quite urban, because much of it is river lots, but still quite densely populated. They were looking to hold onto that land but also have a land reserve elsewhere. I think Métis saw things very differently, in those days, than the settler colonial project. It took quite a while to recognize that Indigenous people did live in cities. And that kind of project, from a policy standpoint, I think, arrives fifty, sixty years later.

BRENDA: But you still hear this mythology of the city that Native people didn't arrive until the 1960s. Maybe the 1970s. It doesn't matter if we're talking about Winnipeg or Saskatoon. It's this constant reproduction of a mythology that puts us outside of it. And therefore we're not really entitled to the space.

CHRIS: And I think part of the problem, or the conditions under which that mythology takes hold or is able to maintain itself, is that the state hasn't done a good job of actually measuring urban Indigeneity. When we look at an urban context, we say, "Well, this is when Aboriginal people started coming to the city—from the late 1960s and early '70s onward." And while it's partly true that, for various reasons, after 1951 with the "double mother clause" and changes to the Indian Act, more people were pushed off reserves, the other thing going on is that the state was getting better at measuring populations at that time.[16] So, it's not just this unvarnished truth that more Indigenous people were moving [to the city], it's that the Canadian state starts seeing that as a policy imperative worthy of building measures for, and they start creating statistical formats for actually measuring this stuff. And just because we start measuring something doesn't mean that it wasn't there before; that's not the case. Most people treat statistics as the self-evident truth of things encountered on the ground, but we lose that previous context of things because we don't have a way of intelligibly translating it into the language of policy, which almost always tends to include statistical measurements.

Pulling at this a little more explicitly, what does this kind of statistical proliferation and imagination of three categories of Aboriginal people and the mobilization of populations of Métis, First Nations, and Inuit mean for the ways that we understand these political communities and their experiences, the ways in which urban services are delivered, the ways in which communities mobilize themselves?

ADAM: Obviously, there's a lot of complexity there. Regarding First Nations, Métis, and Inuit, the terminology is interesting given that Métis and Inuit are pre-existing peoples that pre-exist those categories. The state adopted those categories to name people that already existed. First Nations, of course, is a construct that encompasses many, many nations. Whereas Métis and Inuit are much more specific terminology. And so I think that those constructs, in the way that Chris already mentioned, differentiate how the state conceives of those peoples and our organizations, and up until recently there has been some jurisdictional confusion over where Métis fit in all of this. I guess all nations face the same sort of jurisdictional confusion off-reserve and there's been buck-passing by the federal and provincial governments for all kinds of urban services, but Métis in particular, in the contemporary era up until the *Daniels* decision, were considered to be under provincial jurisdiction.[17] Which meant we had different funding pathways and service organizations. Métis essentially lobby a different set of governments than First Nations and Inuit do for their service provision. So I think this has created a distinction between these groups in terms of policy and in terms of service provisions in a way that pulls apart the complex relationships that Brenda mentioned earlier. Belonging in these communities is connected more by kinship and a common approach to living rather than by jurisdictional and funding boundaries, which are in a lot of ways more arbitrary than these older connections.

CHRIS: I would say that statistics become important because they are the lenses through which states look at what is otherwise a fairly undifferentiated mass of humanity, right? It's the way in which it picks certain elements of populations that are deemed important for policy purposes. States take data out of local context, bring official statistics together in an essentialized format, rescale them, reorder, rejig them, and send them back into these disparate geographical and cultural contexts— as Bruce Curtis argues in his classic text *The Politics of Population*.[18] So if you understand statistics as the lens through which the state looks at humanity then you start to see, if you think about the complexity of our communities—and this particularly comes out of work that Brenda has done, both in her book and in her work with Nicole St-Onge around mobility—you start to see the ways that states have no interest and no ability in understanding that complexity.[19] You get these three lenses for looking at this complexity, and that's problematic enough in and of itself, but the other issue is that in many cases, the people who are Inuit, First Nation, and Métis start to become invested in these tripartite divisions as well. Because there are policy and financial implications for becoming invested in them. So they see large parts of themselves in the way in which those divisions get created. None of these census categories would work if at least some part of us didn't recognize ourselves in the context of those categories.

In an urban context, people will say this becomes less important because very often urban service delivery tends to be status blind. And that's true for a very large part, but the other thing it means is that it tends to be needs based rather than rights based. And when things are needs based, it means that whoever has the money can withhold it whenever they want, because they view it as charity. It's seen as a gift rather than something that's owed, in terms of building a moral relationship between peoples that were there before and newcomers. And so the big thing that this racialization does is that it moves the argument from a rights-based argument to a needs-based argument. I think rights-based arguments are still deeply racialized as well, but the way in which this plays out in an urban context is that you start to see a needs-based ethos or ethic. And the reason that becomes important is that if things are needs based, the funding tends to be year to year and precarious rather than something that's stable and long term, based on rights, based on the idea that different people involved are equal partners in terms of figuring out how to solve these policy issues.

BRENDA: I agree with everything that Chris and Adam just said. But this is the ultimate colonial distraction. Right? We spend all of our time worrying about these things instead of who and what we actually are and this rights-based agenda: the inherent rights that we possess as Indigenous people. We start to talk even less about that as we deal with certain service delivery. Service delivery is the deepest colonial distraction that we have, because we have very real needs. People need education, people need health, people need glasses, people need the kinds of services that they're fighting for. But even Indigenous leadership doesn't see these necessarily within an Indigenous rights complex. And so they squabble. We all squabble. Nobody wants to talk about that, but let's be clear, we argue about this constantly. Because what [the federal Department of] Indigenous Affairs tells us is that there is a finite block of money and the more people that want it, the more finite it's going to be as it's systematically cut up and distributed. Even though they created the colonial structure, they say: "You guys just sort it out among yourselves. And if you can't stop fighting, what are we going to do about it?" So it's a constant distraction.

One of the major forms of resistance for Indigenous peoples in Canada has been through the courts. This has secured significant victories for Indigenous peoples, including the Métis; however, the courts have produced or reproduced problematic constructions of authentic Indigenous culture as rural and land based. What do these legal strategies and forms of legal recognition mean for

Métis people, and particularly urban Métis people, and what are their short-comings as a strategy to achieve justice?

BRENDA: While I would agree that there have probably been some interesting gains, nothing radical has happened through the courts. Every court decision reifies the distinctions, boundaries, and categories, and there's nothing radical about it. It's not a recollection of anything Indigenous, it's a complete reproduction of settler colonial categories of them and of us. And we shouldn't be too excited about any of it.

CHRIS: I would largely say that I agree with Brenda—the big thing that court cases have done over the past thirty or thirty-five years is that they have reproduced the idea that they're necessary as a way of resolving the difficulties and injustices we're experiencing. They have also deeply reproduced racialized understandings of mainstream Métis, First Nations, and Inuit. I agree that the big radical impact of these court cases has been that as an Indigenous people, the Métis people in particular have started to somehow think that our authenticity as Métis people is something that the courts (a) have the right to pronounce on; and (b) when they do pronounce on it, we have to listen to them. I'm the wrong person to talk to about the great victories that these court cases have produced. *Powley* was supposed to be a sea change in how Métis relate to the Canadian state.[20] It could have been a worse decision, for sure, but it could have been a far more dignified decision than it was. And when I see people invest deeply in these court-based definitions, it makes me sad because it means we're not looking to our families or our communities to have the kinds of complex discussions that we need to have about these things. Instead, we're expecting the courts to do this work for us, and of course the courts are as deeply mired in colonialism as any of the other institutions that Canada holds dear. So I don't see any great gains in the courts, and I think that given the cultural power of Canadian law in particular, there have been a number of enormous impacts on our ability to conceive of ourselves as Métis and the ways in which we conceive of ourselves as Métis.

BRENDA: The minute you ask the Canadian courts to legitimize you, you've already lost the fight.

CHRIS: And I do want to be clear, though—I don't mean this as a
simplistic critique of the fact that the Métis are going to court over the past
thirty or thirty-five years. There's a great story that the late Cree leader
Harold Cardinal used to tell: if you're outside and it's minus 40, you need
a jacket, and people say, "Well, I'm not going to give you a jacket, but I'll
give you a sweater." What do you do—do you take the sweater or do you
wait to see whether a jacket comes along? I think in many cases, our going
to the courts was the equivalent of our taking a sweater because that was
what was offered to us. Having said that, I get into arguments with my
jurisprudential friends a lot where they say, "Well, what else is there?" You
feel like saying, "Well, what the fuck else have we tried?" Like when's the
last time you've seen Métis marching in the streets or all the different kinds
of political agonism that constituted a very diverse form of politics in the
1960s and '70s? We don't do that anymore. We put all our eggs into this
juridical basket. And whenever the courts get it right, it's a big victory for
Canada; when the courts get it wrong, we whine about the fact that the
courts get it wrong. Courts by definition don't get things wrong, at least
not the Supreme Court.

BRENDA: It's the same distraction as service delivery, right? So, service
delivery is the sweater and courts are the sweater, to continue with your
analogy borrowed from Harold Cardinal.

ADAM: I was just thinking back to the 1970s, when there was this very
big debate among Métis leaders over whether or not to take government
funding. Many Métis leaders in the 1970s were against taking government
funding, as there had been an established concern for decades that
funding would co-opt Métis organizations and make them extensions of
federal or provincial policy, and we'd lose our autonomy.[21] But there was
a recognition, I think, in the '70s around that debate, of what will we pay
for taking this funding? For giving up this control? And it seems when
the decision was made to actually take the money, there was more of a
discussion about it. I think today we take for granted that the courts are
there and that they are an avenue to pursue; that there's funding there.
We don't often have those sorts of deep conversations about the costs of
doing these things.

THE PRODUCTION OF MÉTIS URBAN SPACE IN THE PAST, PRESENT, AND FUTURE

So how could Métis traditions provide a way—an alternative to state frames that create land-based rights outside of the city—to fulfill urban needs inside the city? We've identified both of those legal and service frameworks as maintaining the colonial structure. What would be an alternative way of conceptualizing Métis relationships, particularly a Métis urbanism that can start to break through that mould?

BRENDA: We're good at critiquing, we're less good at knowing the answers. [Laughter]. I think that people need to re-engage with their relationships with each other. We need to stop putting each other down in order to actually build something. I don't know how to do that, it's not easy. People are invested, as Chris has said, in the production of these categories, and it's so hard to think of yourself outside of that world.

CHRIS: I'm pretty cynical because we Métis make up about 2 percent of the population, probably in reality a lot less than that, depending on how you measure Métis identity. I don't think having a discussion about how Métis sociality can exist completely outside colonialism gets us very far in terms of a concrete strategy. I just don't know what that would look like. You have people like Christi Belcourt, who moved back to the land and is doing all of these really amazing things.[22] But not everybody is in a position in their lives to do that, and not everybody wants to do that, and yes, it's incredibly difficult. I agree with Brenda that in many cases we're much better at critiquing than we are at proposing alternatives. I think partly that's because it's incredibly difficult to propose alternatives, given the elemental power of states to produce a sense of normalcy and what's possible in any given context. I went for a vacation a couple of years ago with my wife to Rarotonga, the Cook Islands, and they have no internet really, and I—honest to god—thought I was going to die from not having the internet. It's incredibly difficult to get outside of the gravitational pull of states. It just is. Even if we think we're turning away from states, it's not that easy.

ADAM: One of the conversations Chris and I had this morning, actually, was around how few rural Métis communities that were thriving in the 1960s and '70s continue to thrive. And there's been urban migration from a lot of small Métis communities to the point where Métis don't necessarily have those communities anymore. So I think much of the ability to move back and forth between these spaces, the kind of fluidity that was once very normal, is increasingly restrained for a lot of the reasons Chris stated, and for economic reasons too. We're being forced to choose urban or rural, and increasingly it's urban for economic reasons. Métis aren't the only rapidly urbanizing culture. Pretty much every single culture that has accepted modernity as the norm, or has been forced to accept modernity as the norm, is urbanizing on a rapid scale and facing massive social upheavals because of it. And I think these questions are difficult because many Métis young people who grew up in the city have little access to land outside of it.

CHRIS: Even access to family, for that matter, or extended family.

BRENDA: That's what I'm saying about family inside of urban spaces— I grew up with no family other than my immediate family in an urban space, but it didn't make me disconnected. You have to connect in a different way, and that's partly what those organizations and neighbourhood structures created. There is a gravitational pull toward one another.

So, despite the devastation and violence that settler colonialism has occasioned, Indigenous people continue to survive, contest colonial structures, and produce their own space in the city. In your writing, you have all argued that research-ers need to go beyond an analysis of colonialism to recognize the histories of Indigenous struggle. Why is it important to analytically centre a history of Métis resistance and resurgence?

CHRIS: From my perspective I would say that the reason it becomes so important to centre Métis is because it's a way of getting outside of the purity/racialization discourses through which most people think about Indigeneity in Canada. When you begin with the perception that Métis are equally Indigenous to all other Indigenous people, it radically changes the lens through which you can understand what Indigeneity is, because it's always relational. So if you're thinking about Métisness differently, if you're getting outside of that Métis-as-mixed palindrome, then it means you're doing the same for First Nations, or should be doing the same for First Nations and Inuit as well. And once that happens you get these radically reconfigured notions of sociality, and that's where we get into the stuff around peoplehood and nationhood. Regardless of arguments we might have about the limits and boundaries of those kinds of things, it's really important to move away from the racialization element because if we don't, then the Canadian state has all the categories we need to make sense of ourselves, and we've dealt with them for almost 150 years. No, 150 years exactly!

[Laughter]

BRENDA: What's really interesting about being a scholar of things Métis is that when I write about Métis people, I'm asked to explain that language, replay that moment of ethnogenesis so the reader knows who these people are. Nobody's asked to explain that about Cree or Dene or the word First Nations. And so I won't do it. Right? Like no, it's not up to me to tell you, I'm telling you already who they are by the very content of this article. You figure it out. It's not my job to continuously describe ethnogenesis.

ADAM: And to speak specifically to the stories of resistance, I taught an intro class this year and I was amazed at how initially confused students were when we talked about Indigenous power. We talked about when Indigenous people were dominant political forces, when Métis were wealthy, powerful, and sought-after allies. I think a lot of students, particularly non-Indigenous students, are very comfortable with the idea of Indigenous people as weak. I think that that has been normalized in the colonial context in which we're living. I think that telling stories about power, resistance, and strength challenge that narrative in fundamental ways. People still struggle with the idea of Indigenous power; of powerful Indigenous people who are grounded, smart, articulate; and of the tactical nations that sought to benefit from the arrival of Canada into their territory and manage that process in a way that benefited them. These stories are really tough to tell, and I think that Métis history is largely a history of resistance. Sometimes it's physical, but almost always intellectual and political. Métis are constantly resisting, constantly attempting to structure a narrative which pushes back against colonial forces. Métis have been prolific history writers, because it's central to who we are. And so these stories of resistance are very much about reaffirming with one another who we are. And that's why they are so important. That's why they feature so prominently, not only in intellectual or scholarly works but in the everyday discussions about who we are. The history, regardless of whether we're looking at urban or rural, is in many ways a unifying factor. It's something that we share. It's something that has had a nationalist outlook. It's something that can bring us together across geography and across the urban-rural divide. And Métis are a diasporic people, right? I grew up well outside of the Métis homeland. I spent time on Vancouver Island where there's a fairly large urban Métis community, and these sorts of things are a way to bridge people back to the Métis homeland.

Urban Métis are continuing to make space for themselves in the city. How does the creation of Métis urban space contribute to the maintenance of Métis identities grounded in Métis relationships of kinship and responsibility?

CHRIS: It really differs from city to city, right? One of the things that we know about Indigeneity in general is that it's quite powerfully shaped by the genealogical context of the cities that it exists in. However, the kinds of racialization that we've been talking about up to now circulate in cities as much as or more so than they do anywhere else. One of impacts that has had is a lot of people self-identifying as Métis who aren't Métis— people who are of mixed Aboriginal and non-Aboriginal ancestry but for any number of different reasons decide to self-identify as Métis. That sometimes makes it difficult to get into any of the complexity of the urban Métis sociality that is tied into a particular history and a particular sense of kinship relationships.

Personally, most of the time that I interact with other Métis people is in seeing certain family who used to crash with us (before we got a small apartment) when they came into the city. My experience is that I don't see much in the way of Métis communities outside of a family context. I see nodes of Métis coming together in particular times. But I never grew up in the urban Métis community, outside of the family and extended family that I existed in. The formative context in which I knew Métis community was always through family and extended family, and then from there outwards.

BRENDA: I don't come from a large family and I'm not in a province where there is family. So, I get involved with Métis community stuff as much as possible in the places that I live, because it's important to me. Because I can't fall back on that family relationship in an urban setting. Those kinds of community events are critical for people not just to come together and socialize, but because social events are the things that allow you to move away from that constant political discourse—of work for service delivery organizations, political organizations, provincial governments—into a different kind of affirmation.

ADAM: I moved around after I left home to go to university, usually living in smaller centres. I was surprised that so many places outside of the Métis homeland, like Victoria and Vancouver, have a self-aware and self-sufficient Métis community. I think there was a feeling that if we don't get together, you know, this will be lost. On the Prairies it's just there, present in a way that it may not be outside of the homeland. I think that studies of Métis diaspora are going to be important, because a lot of Métis families are living in some sort of diaspora. A lot of the communities that existed twenty-five to fifty years ago either don't exist today or exist today on a much smaller scale than they once did. And many of those communities are actually formed from an older diaspora, right? Métis being pushed out of someplace else. What does that mean for us culturally? What does that mean in the urban context? And what kind of common histories are there? I think these are important questions.

Finally, I would like to turn from the past to the future. I'd like to ask what a decolonized city might look like. What should we be fighting for?

ADAM: It's just interesting because we don't often think about decolonization and the city. I think in a lot of Indigenous discourse, decolonization means leaving the city for the bush, at least metaphorically. That's the assumption behind it.

CHRIS: To me, a decolonized city is a city that sees Métis people in particular, but Indigenous people more generally, as partners to be engaged with rather than problems to be solved.

BRENDA: I like that. Nice summation.

CHRIS: To understand and work through those power differentials and to see us agentic partners with alternative visions that just because they're alternative doesn't mean they're worse. To be willing to engage with us in that complexity and just see us as partners rather than problems.

NOTES

1   Andersen, "From Nation to Population."

2   Peters, Stock, and Werner, *Rooster Town.*

3   Mawani, *Colonial Proximities.*

4   Lawrence, *"Real" Indians and Others*; Miller, "The Papaschase Band."

5   Andersen, *"Métis"*; Gaudry and Andersen, "Daniels v. Canada."

6   Laliberte, "Being Métis."

7   Macdougall, *One of the Family.*

8   Drawing on Nicholas Vrooman's research, Chris Andersen has argued elsewhere that Métisness histor-
     ically emerged around what he termed the Red River Settlement Zone (RRSZ). This historic core
     Métis region, as defined by Vrooman, had "a circumference that runs counter-clockwise from the east,
     at the Lake of the Woods, Minnesota, northwest to the mouth of the Red River at Lake Winnipeg, in
     Manitoba, farther west to the confluence of the Souris with the Assiniboine River at today's Brandon,
     Manitoba, south through the Turtle Mountains on the North Dakota/Manitoba border, southeast
     to the source of the Red River at Lake Traverse (where Minnesota, North Dakota, and South Dakota
     meet), then northeast, back to the Lake of the Woods." See Vrooman, *"The Whole Country was . . .
     'One Robe,'"* 19, and Andersen, *"Métis,"* 110–111.

9   As settlement pushed Métis people off their traditional lands and land speculators defrauded Métis
     families of the government-issued scrip recognizing their title, Métis communities re-formed on road
     allowances. When the Canadian Prairies were surveyed, public land was designated around each
     township to allow for road construction. This became a space that dispossessed Métis appropriated
     for their own use.

10   Malcolm X, "It Shall Be the Ballot or the Bullet."

11   Louis Goulet, as told in Charette, *Vanishing Spaces.*

12   Troupe, "Métis Women."

13   Peters, Stock, and Werner, *Rooster Town.*

14   Innes, *Elder Brother and the Law of the People.*

15   In the Red River Resistance, the Métis led a political movement that declared a provisional govern-
     ment in order to negotiate the terms of their confederation into Canada. The Resistance followed
     the Canadian Dominion's purchase of the Northwest Territories from the Hudson's Bay Company.
     This transaction occurred without the consent of the Métis people.

16   Amendments to the Indian Act in 1951 codified sexually discriminatory provisions regarding Indian
     status. Any Indian woman who married a man without Indian status (regardless of his ancestry) would
     lose status. Conversely, a non-Indian woman who married a man with Indian status would gain that
     status. However, the "double mother" clause would remove status from Indian children at age twen-
     ty-one if their mother and grandmother had both acquired Indian status through marriage.

17   The *Daniels v. Canada* decision found that the federal government has jurisdictional responsibility
     for Métis and non-status Indians, and cannot simply presume that services for these communities are
     the responsibility of the provincial governments.

18   Curtis, *The Politics of Population.*

19   Macdougall, *One of the Family*; St-Onge, Podruchny, and Macdougall, *Contours of a People.*

20   Centring on whether Métis people had protected hunting rights under s. 35 of Canada's 1982
     Constitution Act, *R. v. Powley* was the first major Métis rights case to reach the Supreme Court of

Canada. The decision established criteria to define a legitimate Métis right and offered a definition of the meaning of community from which those rights flow.

21   As noted by Brenda Macdougall in review, this critique emerged at least as far back as the organizing of the 1930s and '40s. Malcolm Norris stressed this in the 1960s, and it framed the work of organizers such as Rose Richardson from Green Lake and Maria Campbell (who would later discuss the issue in *Halfbreed*). Howard Adams also later wrote about the need to refuse government money in *Prison of Grass*.

22   Christi Belcourt is a Métis visual artist and author; see christibelcourt.com/.

Part Three

POLICING AND SOCIAL CONTROL

CHAPTER SEVEN

POLICING RACIALIZED SPACES

ELIZABETH COMACK

Canada is a settler colonial society. Historically, the appropriation of Indigenous territory and resources and the political and legal subordination of Indigenous peoples were key elements in establishing the imperial rule of the European settlers.[1] But settler colonialism is not simply a historical artifact that has no bearing on contemporary events. As Haudenosaunee scholar Patricia Monture pointed out, colonialism "is a living phenomenon.... The past impacts on the present, and today's Aboriginal peoples in Canadian society cannot be understood without a well-developed historical understanding of colonialism and the present trajectories of those old relationships."[2] One of those trajectories is the role of police in the reproduction of a settler colonial order in Canada. Historically, the North-West Mounted Police (NWMP) played a key part in creating a white settler society. In contemporary times, this role is nowhere more evident than in the policing of the racialized spaces of inner-city communities on the Canadian Prairies. Similar to the role played by the NWMP, contemporary police forces in Canadian society have been tasked with the management and containment of Indigenous people. This is especially the case in the urban centres of the Prairie provinces. From the more obvious practices—such as "red zoning" and "starlight tours"—to the seemingly mundane operation of searching for the "usual suspects" who "fit the description," urban police forces engage in racialized policing.

In this chapter I attend to the relevance of the interconnected issues of race, space, and crime for understanding the role of the police in the reproduction of an urban settler colonial order. To do so, I focus on the Prairie city of Winnipeg, Manitoba, which is located on Treaty One territory, the traditional lands of the Anishinaabeg, and the homeland of the Métis people. Drawing on interviews conducted with Indigenous people in Winnipeg, my purpose is to elaborate on what this racialized policing involves. I conclude the discussion by entertaining the prospects for realizing a decolonized future—one that does not involve racialized policing.

RACE, SPACE, CRIME, AND THE REPRODUCTION OF ORDER

Scholars have emphasized that both "race" and "space" are abidingly social constructs. As Robert Miles tells us, race is "an idea created by human beings in certain historical and material conditions and is used to represent the world in certain ways."[3] To differentiate between people on the basis of race is to engage in a process of racialization: "the process through which groups come to be designated as different and on that basis subjected to differential and unequal treatment."[4] Racialization, therefore, involves the production of difference; it is the process of constructing racial categories, identities, and meanings. While engaging in racialization—recognizing difference between people—does not in and of itself constitute a problem, it is the attachment of negative meanings to this difference that is problematic. In these terms, the idea of race becomes ideologically problematic when it is used as a rationalization for the dominance of one racial group over another;[5] in other words, when it is used to promote racism.

Racism can be defined as "ideas that delineate group boundaries by reference to race or to real or alleged biological characteristics, and which attribute groups so racialized with other negatively evaluated characteristics."[6] But more than this, racism is a social practice connected to power; it is the use of racial categories to define an Other. The idea of race, in this sense, is an effect of power. Racism organizes, preserves, and perpetuates the power structures of a society;[7] it rationalizes, legitimizes, and sustains patterns of inequality.[8]

Racism is not only systemic—embedded in institutional and social practices—it also occurs at the level of everyday experience. Philomena Essed defines "everyday racism" as a complex of practices (both cognitive and behavioural) that integrate racism—and its underlying power relations—on a daily basis.[9] These daily situations become part of the expected, the unquestionable. They are what the dominant group in society sees as "normal." To this extent, everyday racism becomes part of common sense; "a way of comprehending, explaining, and acting in the world."[10] Racist beliefs and actions that infiltrate everyday life thereby become part of a wider system that reproduces racism and racial inequality.

Similar to race, space "plays an active role in the construction and organization of social life";[11] it is "constituted through social relations and material social practices."[12] Spaces not only have a materiality in that they connect to social relations that produce and use them but also have a symbolic meaning attached to them. Spaces can variously come to represent places of home, work, or leisure, sites of comfort and the familiar, or places of danger and disorder. Together, the material and the symbolic work through each other to constitute a space.

These racializing and spatializing processes are "co-constitutive and dialectical in nature" in that "racial interactions and processes (e.g. identities, inequalities, conflicts, and so on) are also about how we collectively make and remake, over time and through ongoing contestation, the spaces we inhabit. In turn, the making and remaking of space is also about the making and remaking of race."[13] From this standpoint, racialization processes can be directly experienced as spatial: "When police drop Aboriginal people outside the city limits leaving them to freeze to death, or stop young Black men on the streets or in malls, when the eyes of shop clerks follow bodies of colour, presuming them to be illicit, when workplaces remain relentlessly white in better paid jobs and fully 'coloured' at the lower levels, when affluent areas of the city are all white and poorer areas are mostly of colour, we experience the spatiality of the racial order in which we live."[14] It is in this sense that particular spaces become *racialized* spaces; "racial difference is also spatial difference."[15]

In the same manner that "race" and "space" are social constructs, so too is "crime." While popular and legal discourses construct "crime" as a straightforward matter, attributed to the actions of "criminals" and "offenders," crime is actually a social construction that varies over time and place. As Stuart Hall and his colleagues note, crime is not a "given, self-evident, ahistorical, and unproblematic category."[16] Crime cannot be separated from the social context in which it occurs; it is "differently *defined* (in both official and lay ideologies) at different periods; and this reflects not only changing attitudes amongst different sectors of the populations to crime, as well as real historical changes in the social organization of criminal activity, but also the shifting *application* of the category itself."[17]

Acknowledging that crime is a social construct directs our attention to the process of criminalization. Like the process of racialization, the process of criminalization involves the exercise of a particular form of power: the "power to criminalize" or "to turn a person into a criminal."[18] In the same way that racialization involves a "representational process of defining an Other,"[19] criminalization involves establishing a binary between "the criminal" and "the law-abiding." This dualism reinforces the view that those who are deemed to be criminal are not like "the rest of us"—not only in terms of what they have done but also who they are and the social spaces in which they move. The net result is that the criminal justice system reproduces a very particular kind of order, one in which gender, race, and class inequalities figure prominently.[20]

At its core, the goal of criminalization is "to target those activities of groups that authorities deem it necessary to control, thus making the process inherently political."[21] Criminologists have long noted that the criminal justice system devotes far more resources to the policing of the poor in society than it does to controlling the harmful activities of the wealthy.[22] And there is a spatiality to this process. Crimes that are promulgated "in the suites" of large corporations (tax evasion, environmental pollution, and workplace health and safety) have been documented as producing great harm in lives lost and financial costs incurred. Yet these actions receive far less attention in the criminal justice system than those that occur "in the streets" (assaults, robbery, and theft). One result of this focus of criminal justice intervention is that measures taken to control and contain the threat posed by crime have resulted in the construction of particular groups as troublesome "problem populations"[23] and particular spaces—such as inner-city neighbourhoods in the Canadian Prairies—as dangerous and disorderly.

This understanding of race, space, and crime as social constructs holds implications for how we approach the role of the police, especially in relation to the policing of Indigenous people. In his now-classic study, Richard Ericson developed the argument that contemporary police forces "are essentially a vehicle for the reproduction of order." Their mandate is "to transform troublesome, fragile situations back into a normal or efficient state whereby the ranks of society are preserved." But as Ericson clarified, "it is not the mandate of police to produce a 'new' order." Rather, "their sense of order and the order they seek to reproduce are that of the status quo." As well, Ericson specified, "the term 'reproduction' implies that order is not simply transmitted in an unproblematic manner but is worked at through processes of conflict, negotiation, and subjection.[24]

Ericson's formulation has relevance for situating policing within the context of race and racialization, that is, as racialized policing. While the order that police are assigned to reproduce will differ in certain historical periods and between societies, it will nonetheless be an order of a particular kind. In other words, the very order that police are consigned to reproduce can be a racialized one. Drawing on Michael Omi and Howard Winant's notion of racial formation,[25] with its focus on how racial projects work to produce race at the level of cultural representation (that is, as a descriptor of groups or individual identity, social issues, and experience) and on how particular institutional arrangements are organized along racial lines, racialized policing can be said to constitute one of the colonial projects through which race is interpreted and given meaning and the means by which the settler colonial order of a society is reproduced.

Moreover, in reproducing order, police work involves not just the policing of individuals but the policing of spaces. Over time, certain spaces come to be identified as places in which crime and violence are most likely to occur. For instance, inner-city communities populated by impoverished Indigenous people come to be seen as "disordered" and "dangerous" places, whereas suburban white middle-class neighbourhoods—with their tree-lined streets, manicured lawns, and spacious homes—become spaces of "civility" and "respectability." In carrying out their task as reproducers of order, then, police concentrate their attention and activity on the former and not on the latter racialized spaces. In the process, they help to constitute and normalize particular spaces—and the Indigenous people found within them—as "disorderly" and "dangerous." Such is the case with Winnipeg.

SPATIALLY CONCENTRATED, RACIALIZED POVERTY IN WINNIPEG

Much like other Prairie cities in Canada, Winnipeg is home to a large number of Indigenous people. In 2011 about one-third of all Indigenous persons in Manitoba lived in Winnipeg. Of major cities in Canada that year, Winnipeg had the highest density of Indigenous people (72,335), representing 11 percent of the total Winnipeg Census Metropolitan Area population.[26] Many Indigenous people have taken up residence in Winnipeg's inner-city neighbourhoods, making up some 21 percent of the population of those communities;[27] in some inner-city neighbourhoods the Indigenous population is 50 percent or more.[28] Jim Silver observes that "the spatial distribution of Aboriginal people in cities . . . parallels their spatial distribution outside urban centres." That is, just as they have historically been confined to rural reserves, now in cities Indigenous people are being set apart from mainstream Canadian life. Their "move to the city is too often a move from one marginalized community to another."[29]

Like other inner-city communities across North America, Winnipeg's inner city has undergone drastic changes with the advent of capitalist globalization—the integration of national economies into a global network—and the accompanying shift from industrial to "non-standard" and service-sector jobs.[30] Many industrial jobs that were unionized, paid a living wage, and offered reasonable benefits have relocated to other, lower-wage jurisdictions or, in some cases, have dramatically reduced wages in the face of external competitive pressures. At the same time, the process of suburbanization that began in the post–Second World War era has seen large numbers of people who can afford to do so moving away from inner-city locations to the suburbs. Many businesses followed suit. The result has been a hollowing out of many inner cities, Winnipeg's included. Those left behind in inner-city communities have been, for the most part, those least financially able to move.

The abandonment of Winnipeg's inner city by the more financially well-off placed downward pressure on housing prices in an area where housing was already the oldest and in need of repair.[31] Ten percent of Winnipeg dwellings are in need of major repair, which significantly exceeds the national average of 7 percent and is the highest percentage among Canada's twenty-five metropolitan areas.[32] In many cases cheap inner-city housing was acquired by absentee landlords who used it as a "cash cow" while allowing it to further deteriorate. Close to two-thirds of Winnipeg's inner-city residents rent their living accommodation and are therefore reliant on landlords to ensure that buildings are properly maintained.[33] Cheaper housing attracts people with the lowest incomes, not surprisingly, thus concentrating poverty in large numbers in the inner-city neighbourhoods.

While over half of the Indigenous population of Canada now live in urban centres,[34] few Indigenous people were living in urban centres such as Winnipeg up to the 1950s.[35] When Indigenous people began arriving in Winnipeg in the 1960s, many came unprepared for urban industrial life, in large part because the residential school system had left them without adequate formal educational qualifications.[36] They became concentrated in Winnipeg's inner city, at first because housing there was least expensive, and in subsequent decades because that is where other Indigenous people already lived, among other factors. But they were moving to neighbourhoods in which jobs—and particularly the kinds of industrial jobs that had historically been available to those with limited formal educational qualifications—had disappeared. With few well-paid jobs available, and facing a wall of systemic racism and discrimination because they were "different," many Indigenous people became effectively locked out of the formal labour market.[37]

In more recent years, growing numbers of immigrants and refugees arrived in Winnipeg, many with low levels of formal education as a result of poverty and war. Most of them located in the inner city, and for the same reasons that low-income people had for decades located there.[38]

The result of these various processes—globalization, suburbanization, internal migration, and immigration—has been the spatial concentration of racialized poverty in Winnipeg's inner city. While inner-city residents take pride in their community and see its many strengths and benefits,[39] the neighbourhoods are characterized by extreme poverty, inadequate housing, high unemployment, and limited recreational and other resources.[40] The rate of poverty in the inner city is almost twice as high (39.6 percent) as it is for the rest of Winnipeg (20 percent).[41] As Silver notes, "the median household income in the inner city is just under two-thirds—about 64 percent—that of Winnipeg as a whole."[42] While Indigenous people make up some 21 percent of the population of Winnipeg's inner-city communities, 65 percent of Indigenous households in those inner-city communities were living in poverty in 2006.[43]

It is not surprising that crime and violence flourish in this context of spatially concentrated, racialized poverty. This is particularly so when street drugs are readily available as a means of escape and can be bought and sold at prices and in volumes sufficient for the upper-level traffickers to earn a living well beyond what they could earn from menial service-sector "McJobs."[44] A self-reinforcing dynamic is set in motion. Many inner-city people reject such jobs on the grounds that the wages are insufficient to support themselves and their families and to create an economically secure future. Instead, some turn to the hidden economy—especially the drug and sex trades—to make a living. The illegal trade in drugs has become more and more insidious in Winnipeg over the last two decades, with drugs such as crack cocaine and crystal methamphetamine being distributed on the street and via "crack houses" in inner-city neighbourhoods. For young—and disproportionately Indigenous—women, working in the street sex trade is often their only recourse for getting by, which puts them at risk of violence and leads to drugging and drinking as a means of coping with the work.[45]

The drug trade constitutes a major source of income and activity for street gangs. In the mid-1990s Winnipeg gained the reputation as the "gang capital of Canada," and the names of Indigenous street gangs became part of the public discourse. As I have argued elsewhere along with my colleagues Lawrence Deane, Larry Morrissette, and Jim Silver, this emergence of Indigenous street gangs in Winnipeg is a "natural outgrowth" of the impoverished conditions, social exclusion, and experiences of racism encountered by inner-city youth—and a form of resistance (albeit a damaging one) to colonialism: "Creating or joining street gangs offered young Aboriginal men a means of exerting power, of resisting their impoverishment. . . . Moreover, given the colonized space that the North End [one of Winnipeg's inner-city communities] had become, it is no accident that Aboriginal street gangs in Winnipeg adopted names such as Indian Posse, Manitoba Warriors, and Native Syndicate; their self-identity as 'gangsters' is a racialized feature stemming from a recognition (however underdeveloped) of their colonial condition and their resistance to that condition."[46] While only some people may choose this pathway, all those who reside in the inner-city communities where the gangs operate are tasked with negotiating the violence that pervades their social spaces.

Increasingly, therefore, in Winnipeg, concerns about the prevalence of crime and violence in inner-city communities have figured prominently. By and large these concerns are a product of broader processes tied to global economic restructuring and the neoliberal response of the state to the deepening inequality between rich and poor that these economic changes have produced.[47] In this regard, Winnipeg is not alone in experiencing the effects of globalization, suburbanization, internal migration, and the concomitant intensification of spatially concentrated and racialized poverty. As Loïc Wacquant documents, the widening gap between rich and poor has created a class of "urban outcasts" in Western cities worldwide, leading to aliena-tion and disaffection and spawning heightened anxiety over crime, violence, and disorder.[48]

The key state institution assigned the job of responding to these concerns is the criminal justice system. At its front lines, the police are relegated to managing the fallout created by these broader processes.

RACIALIZED POLICING

At its core, settler colonialism has been about physical space: the appro-priation of Indigenous lands. As Brooke Neely and Michelle Samura note, "racialized bodies and groups have always been linked to the theft of land and the control of space."[49] Historically, the NWMP occupied a prominent place in the settling of the Canadian West. Like other frontier police forces, the primary role of the NWMP was "to ensure the submission of Indigenous peoples to colonial rule."[50] The spatiality of this colonial process was evident not only in the seizure of Indigenous lands but also in the containment of First Nations peoples onto reserves. The NWMP were tasked with enforcing the laws and policies of the colonial state, including ensuring that Indige-nous people stayed on the reserves.[51] In more contemporary times, urban police forces in the Canadian Prairies have been tasked with the job of repro-ducing order in inner-city spaces.

One event that has come to symbolize the colonial relationship between the police and Indigenous people in contemporary times is the shooting death of Indigenous leader John Joseph (J.J.) Harper by a Winnipeg police officer. Early on the morning of 9 March 1988, Harper was walking home along an inner-city street when he was approached by a police officer. The police had been looking for a suspect in a car theft. Despite the fact that the suspect was reported to already be in police custody, and that Harper was much older and of a stockier build than the young man police were looking for, the officer made the decision to stop Harper anyway. A struggle ensued and Harper was shot with the officer's revolver. Harper's tragic death became one of two incidents—the other being the murder of Helen Betty Osborne by four white men in The Pas, Manitoba, in 1971—that led to the establishment of the Aboriginal Justice Inquiry of Manitoba in April 1989. In their report, commissioners Alvin Hamilton and Murray Sinclair attributed Harper's death to the racism that existed in the Winnipeg police department.[52]

More recently, the freezing deaths of three Indigenous men—Neil Stonechild, Rodney Naistus, and Lawrence Wegner—and the experience of Darrel Night in Saskatoon set off a tidal wave of controversy revolving around the issue of "starlight tours"—a seemingly benign term that refers to the police practice of detaining people, driving them to another location, and leaving them there to find their own way home.[53] Stonechild's body was discovered on the outskirts of Saskatoon in November 1990. Some ten years later, in January 2000, the bodies of Naistus and Wegner were found within five days of each other. The day after Wegner's body was found, Darrel Night told a police officer that he had escaped a similar experience. Night said that he had been taken out of town by two Saskatoon police officers and dropped off not far from where the bodies of Nastius and Wegner were discovered. Despite being dressed in only a jean jacket and summer shoes, Night managed to survive the bitterly cold weather by attracting the attention of a worker at a nearby power plant. The worker let him into the building to warm up and phone for a taxi. A commission to investigate the death of Neil Stonechild deemed the police investigation into his death to be "insufficient and totally inadequate."[54] The two officers who had Stonechild in their custody that night were subsequently dismissed from the Saskatoon Police Service. While no one was ever held to account for the deaths of Naistus and Wegner, the two officers who had Night in their custody were found guilty of unlawful confinement, sentenced to eight months' imprisonment, and dismissed from the Saskatoon Police Service. Indigenous activists and organizations, meanwhile, declared the practice of "starlight tours" to be evidence of the racism that was rampant on the Saskatoon police force.

Saskatoon is not the only Prairie city in Canada where troubling relations between Indigenous people and the police prevail. In 2008 and 2009 I had the opportunity to interview seventy-eight Indigenous people residing in Winnipeg's inner city about their encounters with police.[55]

THE "USUAL SUSPECTS"

When interviewed, Indigenous men report being regularly stopped by the police and asked to account for themselves. When the men ask "What did I do wrong?," the typical response is "You fit the description" because the police are looking for an Indigenous man as a suspect in a crime. In other words, the men are stopped precisely because they are Indigenous. For many

Indigenous men living in Winnipeg's inner city, this experience has become an all-too-normal occurrence.

One twenty-year-old man, for instance, reported that he was accustomed to being stopped by police "once a week, guaranteed. I can't even, like, count the number of times where I've been stopped just for walking down the street wearing, like, all black or something." When asked what the police say when they stop him, he replied, "Nothing. Just, like, put some cuffs on me and say, 'Oh, we have a guy fitting your description. He's breaking into garages or throwing stuff at houses.' It makes me mad. But, like, there's nothing you can do." A twenty-four-year-old man had similarly frustrating experiences with police. Since the age of sixteen he had been stopped "at least twice a month" by police because he apparently fit the description of someone police were looking for. Another man in his early forties also said that he attracted the attention of the police because he "fit the description." He recalled one incident:

> One day, this was last summer [at about two in the afternoon], there was a cop car parked behind Mac's on Selkirk and Arlington, and they came across the back lane really fast. A cop got out and grabbed me without asking me, like, without even telling me what the hell is going on. Like, I asked him, "What's going on?" He says, "Quiet. You fit the description of somebody we're looking for." "Well, what's the description?" "White T-shirt, blue jeans, long hair, ponytail." I says, "Don't forget where you are, man. You're in the North End. How many Native people in the North End have long hair and a ponytail and are wearing a white T-shirt? Come on now, use your fucking head." Cop grabs me, throws me against the car, puts me in the car, doesn't, I'm not under arrest or anything but he's throwing me in the car and they want to take me for a ride. So they take me for a ride. And they're trying to get me, like, do I know this, do I know that. Like, I don't know anything.

One of the challenges confronting Winnipeg police officers in their endeavour to reproduce order is quelling the illegal trade in drugs that goes on in the inner city. Several men talked about how the police just assume they are involved in the drug trade. One thirty-year-old man, for instance, told of an incident when he had been standing in front of his house, "and my friend, my neighbour, he was giving me ten dollars so I can go get some beer for him. 'Cause I had a bike so I was going to the beer store for him." The police happened by and saw the exchange. "They grabbed me, searched me and everything, thinking I got drugs or something. I didn't have nothing." A nineteen-year-old man told of being pulled over by police "countless times." The police, assuming he was dealing drugs for a street gang, would ask him: "Who are you selling for?" "Who are you banging for?" "Where's the shit?" A man in his thirties said that police would assume he was gang-involved when he wore a white track suit (associated with the Deuce gang) or a red one (Indian Posse). "They would beat you up and they would try to make you rat out where drug houses are and that. It was scary, scary growing up being Native in this neighbourhood."

While Indigenous men are assumed by police to be involved in the drug trade and/or affiliated with a street gang, Indigenous women encounter a different kind of stereotyping. Given the concerns with the street sex trade that operates in Winnipeg's inner-city neighbourhoods, police often assume that Indigenous women found in those spaces are sex workers. One thirty-three-year-old woman told of being stopped by police on her way to the corner store. The police assumed she was a sex trade worker: "I live in an area where there is prostitution happening there and, like, sometimes I go to the store and, like, right away they're driving by and then they slow down. Like, 'I'm going to the store,' and, like, 'Oh, you're lying.' Like what—a woman can't even walk the street today? Every woman that walks the street today is what, supposed to be a hooker?" Simply, then, because of their location in the racialized space of the inner city, Indigenous people are subject to the racialized and gendered stereotypes associated with the "usual suspects." Racialized policing, however, runs deeper than the use of stereotypes; it is also implicated in the particular cultural frames of reference that officers adopt in the course of their work.

RACIALIZED FRAMES

Winnipeg police officers are tasked with the difficult job of responding to situations when—as Egon Bittner describes it—"someone-had-better-do-something-now!"[56] These situations include break-ins, assaults, robberies, and other forms of crime. In the course of fulfilling that role, and particularly in their encounters with Indigenous people, the police see matters through racialized frames. As officers go about their daily work, these frames inform what Clifford Shearing and Richard Ericson refer to as the "storybook" or particular way of seeing that develops over time.[57]

One young man had been at a birthday party for a friend who had just turned eighteen. It was a hot summer's night and they were sitting in the backyard of a North End house. Earlier that evening, the young man and his friends had heard a house alarm going off, but thought little of it. He explained what happened next:

> After a while a cop came, just one cop in a car, like, not two of them, just one guy. And he came out and he approached us. We were sitting in the backyard. And he said, "Where's your guys' IDs?" And he pointed at me and my girlfriend . . . and he only wanted our IDs, like, he didn't care for anyone else's around, like my friend or his sister. So I gave him my ID and I told him my name or whatever and he wrote it down in his little log book. And my girlfriend told him her name too, but she didn't have her ID on her, so he started giving her attitude. Like, he said, "How am I supposed to believe you if you don't have ID on you?" And he came onto our property there, you know, and giving her heck for not having ID when she's on private property anyway. So she gets pretty steamed and she walks inside. And he continues talking to me, "Where have you guys been all morning?" and "Where are you guys going?" or whatever. And I said, "We've been here the whole time, like, I slept here last night. I've been here since yesterday." Then my friend's sister was outside, like, they were kind of standing around and she starts going inside, and he goes, "Hey," and he goes, "Where did that other girl go?" And he was talking about my girlfriend. And she's like, "I don't know." And then she walked inside and he said, "Jesus, how come I can never get a straight answer from you people?"
>
> So then my friend walks inside and I'm starting to walk inside too at that point, 'cause I'm just kind of, like, it feels like it's just a waste of all of our time, right. Like, we didn't do anything. There was no reason for him to come onto the property. So I was about to walk inside and then he starts stepping into the door. And then I stood in the doorway and I said, "You have no warrants. You can't come in here." And then he goes, he steps back and he goes, "What. You want to fuckin' fight me?" And I'm like, "No." And he's like, "Well"—and then he leans in the doorway 'cause he sees my friend's sister, the one that had gone in

earlier and he says, "Where's that girl? Go get that girl and bring her out here." And then, so then my girlfriend comes back outside and we're both standing there and he goes, "So this is your real name?" And she's like, "Yeah." And he's like, "Well, if I look up both your names in my computer right now, you guys aren't going to have any warrants?" And we both said, "No." I said, "Why would we have warrants?" And he said, "'Cause most of you people do." And I said, "What's that supposed to mean?" And he said, "Figure it out." . . . He sat around in his car there and probably ran the names through first and then he took off.

Comments such as "Jesus, how come I can't get a straight answer from you people?" and "'Cause most of you people do" signal the racialized frame that the police officer adopted in carrying out a routine investigation. One has to wonder if the response would have been the same if the citizens the officer encountered resided in a wealthier neighbourhood instead of being Indigenous residents of Winnipeg's North End.

THE USE OF RACIST AND SEXIST LANGUAGE

For many Indigenous people living in Winnipeg's inner-city communities, how the police chose to interact with them is a matter of importance. In particular, many people spoke of the way police officers put them down. As one woman queried, "Why do they have to treat us with such disrespect?" More often than not, this attitude shows up in the language they use.

According to many of the people interviewed, police officers regularly use words like "squaw," "dirty Indian," or "fuckin' Indian" in their encounters with Indigenous people. As one woman said, "I've heard it so many times from their mouths I just don't say anything anymore." The use of racist and sexist language by police obviously runs counter to the professional image of the police officer and the Winnipeg Police Service's mission to perform its duties with "compassion, integrity and respect."[58] While the use of such language may emanate from the effort to reproduce order, at its core it constitutes a power move that has the effect of silencing and marginalizing Indigenous people. When such language is heard "so many times from their mouths" it becomes a routine part of the everyday life—and experiences of everyday racism—of Indigenous people living in Winnipeg's inner city, thereby contributing to the perpetuation of a colonial order.

TROUBLESOME POLICE PRACTICES

Even more concerning are the troublesome police practices reported by Indigenous people. While the use of force by police officers is officially sanctioned, the conditions under which officers use force and whether the amount of force used is reasonable under the circumstances are contentious issues.[59] One of the ironies to emerge from the interviews with Indigenous people in Winnipeg is that police are tasked with the job of responding to the violence that occurs in the inner city, but in the process, violence appears to have become one of the strategies that police themselves use in the reproduction of order.

People who are involved with street gangs appear to be especially prone to encountering violence from the police. One twenty-eight-year-old man, for instance, reported that he was part of a street gang when he was a teenager, and that brought him into conflict with the law. He acknowledged that his crimes were "pretty violent." So too was the response of the police. He told of one night when he was arrested and taken to the police station with two of his friends: "They put us each in a cell and they confined us to three cells, side by side. And they started doing interviews? And the interviews, they were not interviews, there were five guys walking, five un-uniformed officers walking into the cell and beating the living daylights out of you to try to make you confess for what you did. And so I listened to the guy in the next cell. And he was just screaming and hollering. And then my turn came around and then I just gave up." The young man said that he told the police "everything because I couldn't stand the assaults. I couldn't take it. So I just, whatever they said, I just agreed, and that was it."

Participants also spoke of other troublesome police practices, including getting "red zoned," or banned from certain areas of the city, and being taken on "starlight tours." While inner-city communities are cast as spaces of disorder and danger, other spaces are cast as respectable, as spaces of civility. In reproducing order, police officers maintain this divide by cleansing certain spaces and containing "disorderly" people in other spaces. Being found "out of place," therefore, prompts police attention and action. One twenty-seven-year old man told of being stopped by police when he was visiting a cousin in Tuxedo, which, as the name suggests, is one of the wealthiest neighbourhoods in Winnipeg:

And they asked—I was coming back down where the number 18 bus stops, and I was walking through Tuxedo—and they were, "Oh, what are you doing out here?" I was like, "I'm visiting a cousin." "You don't have a cousin out here." I was like, "Why can't I have cousins out here?" "Oh, because you're a dirty bum, blah, blah, blah. We see you in the Village all the time." I was like, "Whatever. You don't know nothing." And then they were, "Okay, we're going to write you up for jay walking. We just saw you jay walk." I was like, "I didn't jay walk. I used the crosswalk thing." Then they told me to sit on a bus bench, and I sat down. And they said, "If you move, we're going to pepper spray you." And I was like, "Whatever." I didn't say anything. I just sat there. And I told them, "I'm going to sneeze." He's like, "You move, we're going to pepper spray you." And I said, "I'm gonna sneeze." And then I sneezed. Just—sprayed me down. And then they left. So I was just sitting at the bus stop, rubbing my eyes.

Another young man said that he had been "banned more than once in Winnipeg." On one occasion he was living in the Elmwood area and got picked up there by police. "They said I lived in the North End. They said, 'Get back on Mountain [Avenue].' I said, 'My address is down the street.' [They] said, 'We're banning you from Elmwood.'" The young man ended up moving to one of the city's suburbs to avoid being stopped and harassed by police all the time.

Similar to the events in Saskatoon, the matter of "starlight tours" emerged in thirteen of the seventy-eight interviews. While some of these "tours" had occurred several years previously, others were much more recent. One woman in her thirties told of an experience that happened to her just a few months before our meeting. It was a minus-40-degree-Celsius evening when the police came along and "grabbed" her. They drove her to the outskirts of the city, where they took her shoes and jacket and then abandoned her there to find her own way back, telling her, "Well, it gives you time to think." As she remarked, "I was thinking about freezing and all that." The woman managed to make it back to an inner-city homeless shelter, but did not want to tell the staff about her experience "because I was scared they were going to call the cops and I'd get more harassed again. So I just left it at that and I didn't want to tell nothing to nobody."

Another woman told of an experience that had happened two years prior to our meeting. She was coming home from a social event on a winter evening when she was picked up by two male police officers outside of the Northern Hotel on Main Street. The police had another woman in the back of the car. At first the woman thought they were both being taken to the district police station. Instead, "they dropped off that other woman first" and then dropped her off "way on the outskirts of the city." She recalled that the police officers "took my jacket. But I kept my shirt, like, my arms in my shirt like that tucked in, and I was freezing." When asked what the police officers said when they dropped her off she replied, "They just called me a 'stupid Indian.' 'You guys won't be missed,' that's what he said. And I said, 'What about my jacket?' and then he threw my, just tossed my jacket in the trunk. And they just drove off and just left me there. And I started crying 'cause I was cold." Luckily, a car drove by. The woman said she "was screaming and that car stopped and pulled over and gave me a ride back to the city and dropped me off at home. And I just took a hot bath and I just cried to myself."

WHAT IS TO BE DONE?

The experiences of Indigenous people with the policing of Winnipeg's inner-city communities suggest that racialization is ingrained in the routine practices of police officers. In reproducing order, police concentrate their attention and activity on the racialized space of the inner city. Not only is that space constituted as disorderly and dangerous, so too are the people who inhabit it. But the issue is more complicated than simply racial profiling or the stereotyping of Indigenous people. Having defined Indigenous people as troublesome, the police respond with troublesome practices of their own.

So what is to be done? How a problem is framed will govern the particular ways of responding to it. For instance, the current trend is to frame the problems confronting inner-city communities in criminal justice terms, as located in the prevalence of crime and violence in these communities. With this framing, "law and order" strategies such as heightened police surveillance make sense. If, however, the problem is reframed as being rooted in the impoverished social and economic conditions in these communities, then crime and violence become symptoms of a deeper problem that requires solutions beyond "fighting crime" to ameliorate it.

Inner-city communities where Indigenous people are found in large proportions are the site of a growing number of community-based organizations and initiatives. Their mandate is to attend to the complex material, cultural, and emotional needs of the residents.[60] By and large these organizations—many of which are Indigenous driven—adopt a community development approach that involves strategies by which people participate directly or through organizations that they control in bottom-up planning and community action.[61] Community development, in other words, is geared toward enabling communities to overcome poverty and social exclusion in ways of their choosing.

More specifically, Indigenous community development is aimed at decolonization, or the process of undoing settler colonialism by attending to the devastating effects that it has wreaked on Indigenous people, in terms of not only their material circumstances but also their identity. In contrast to criminal justice strategies that focus on punishment, discipline, and control, Indigenous community development focuses on healing, wellness, and capacity building. Honouring Indigenous traditions and cultures becomes an important part of that healing process. So too does reclaiming a sense of self-worth and pride that has systematically been stripped from Indigenous people by colonial strategies manifested in the residential schools, the reserve system, and the Indian Act, and dominant discourses that other them as "welfare recipients" and "criminals." By adopting a holistic approach that focuses on strengthening the individual, the family, and the community, Indigenous community-based organizations and initiatives aim to move Indigenous people out of and beyond colonialism's straightjacket.[62]

In that regard, one promising development in Winnipeg's inner-city communities is the work of the Bear Clan Patrol. Based on the teachings of the Bear Clan, the patrol was a prominent feature in Winnipeg's North End in the 1990s. Modelled after the Peace Makers Patrol based in Minneapolis, the patrol "came about as a result of the ongoing need to assume our traditional responsibility to provide security to our Aboriginal community." The rationale of the patrol "is community people working with the community to provide personal security in the inner city in a non-threatening, non-violent and supportive way."[63] The patrol has been recently reactivated. Volunteer members patrol inner-city communities in cars and on foot to ensure the safety and security of the residents. The patrol has also been active in conducting searches for missing individuals. In this respect, the patrol is disrupting the ways in which the production of race, space, and crime has played out in Winnipeg's inner-city communities. By reinvigorating the traditional justice system of peacekeepers and peacemakers that the Bear Clan historically performed in the clan structure of Indigenous communities, the patrol restores to the local community "the responsibility and the capacity to protect the unprotected members of our society"—especially children, youth, women, and elders.[64] Through their everyday social relations and material practices, therefore, Indigenous people are (re)claiming urban spaces as their own. In the process, the racialized space of Winnipeg's inner city is being transformed. In a sense, that space is still racialized, but to very different effect. It becomes a space where Indigenous people feel they belong, where they are protected and safe.

Such community development initiatives open up possibilities for the role of the police in this project of decolonization, albeit a very different role than has traditionally been assigned to them. Rather than an outside force brought in to contain and control the "usual suspects," the police could play a part in community mobilization, walking the beat and getting to know people in the community, using conflict-resolution and problem-solving skills, earning the trust of the people they are mandated to serve and protect; in short, working *with* the community to collectively build safer and healthier neighbourhoods. In this way, the role of police as "reproducers of order" would be transformed. Rather than reproducing the status quo of the settler colonial order, police could participate in fashioning a new form of social order—one not founded on racialized policing.

NOTES

1   Green, "Honoured in Their Absence," 2.

2   Monture, "Racing and Erasing," 207.

3   Miles, "Apropos the Idea of 'Race,'" 137.

4   Block and Galabuzi, *Canada's Colour Coded Labour Market*, 19.

5   Miles, "Apropos the Idea of 'Race,'" 137.

6   Miles, *Racism*, 75.

7   Henry, Tator, Mattis, and Rees, "The Ideology of Racism."

8   Barrett, *Is God a Racist?*, 17.

9   Essed, "Everyday Racism," 188.

10 Omi and Winant, *Racial Formation in the United States*, 60.

11 Neely and Samura, "Social Geographies of Race," 1936.

12 Massey, *Space, Place, and Gender*, 70.

13 Neely and Samura, "Social Geographies of Race," 1934.

14 Razack, "When Place Becomes Race," 75–76.

15 Ibid., 80.

16 Hall et al., *Policing the Crisis*, 188.

17 Ibid., 189.

18 Comack and Balfour, *The Power to Criminalize*, 9.

19 Miles, *Racism*, 75.

20 Comack and Balfour, *The Power to Criminalize*, 9–10.

21 Chan and Mirchandani, "From Race and Crime to Racialization and Criminalization," 15.

22 Snider, "Making Corporate Crime Disappear"; Reiman and Leighton, *The Rich Get Richer and the Poor Get Prison*.

23 Spitzer, "Toward a Marxian Theory of Deviance."

24 Ericson, *Reproducing Order*, 7.

25 Omi and Winant, *Racial Formation in the United States*, 55–56.

26 City of Winnipeg, *Aboriginal Persons Highlights*.

27 MacKinnon, "Tracking Poverty in Winnipeg's Inner City," 32.

28 Silver, "Spatially Concentrated, Racialized Poverty as a Social Determinant of Health," 228.

29 Silver, *In Their Own Voices*, 17.

30 Broad, *Capitalism Rebooted?*; Broad, Cruikshank, and Mulvale, "Where's the Work?"

31 Deane, *Under One Roof*; Silver, *North End Winnipeg's Lord Selkirk Park Housing Development*.

32 Skelton, Selig, and Deane, "CED and Social Housing Initiatives," 55.

33 Cooper, "Housing for People, Not Markets," 22.

34 Statistics Canada, *Aboriginal Peoples in Canada in 2006*.

35 Loxley, *Aboriginal, Northern, and Community Economic Development*, 151.

36 Truth and Reconciliation Commission of Canada, *Honouring the Truth, Reconciling for the Future*; Milloy, *A National Crime*.

37 Cheung, *Racial Status and Employment Outcomes*; Silver, *North End Winnipeg's Lord Selkirk Park Housing Development*.

38 Silver, "Segregated City"; Kazemipur and Halli, *The New Poverty in Canada*.

39 CCPA–MB, *Step by Step*; Comack and Silver, *Safety and Security in Winnipeg's Inner-City Communities*; Silver, *In Their Own Voices*.

40 MacKinnon, "Tracking Poverty in Winnipeg's Inner City"; Deane, *Under One Roof*; Lezubski, Silver, and Black, "High and Rising."

41 MacKinnon, "Tracking Poverty in Winnipeg's Inner City," 30.

42 Silver, "Spatially Concentrated, Racialized Poverty as a Social Determinant of Health," 228.

43 MacKinnon, "Tracking Poverty in Winnipeg's Inner City," 32, 30.

44 Ritzer, *The McDonaldization of Society*.

45 Brown et al., "Challenges Faced by Women Working in the Inner City Sex Trade"; Seshia, *The Unheard Speak Out*.

46 Comack, Deane, Morrissette, and Silver, *"Indians Wear Red,"* 62.

47 Bourgois, *In Search of Respect*; Hagedorn, *A World of Gangs*; Rios, *Punished*.

48 Wacquant, *Urban Outcasts*.

49 Neely and Samura, "Social Geographies of Race," 1934.

50 Nettelbeck and Smandych, "Policing Indigenous Peoples on Two Colonial Frontiers," 357.

51 Brown and Brown, *An Unauthorized History of the RCMP*.

52 Hamilton and Sinclair, *Report of the Aboriginal Justice Inquiry of Manitoba*, 2:93; see also Sinclair, *Cowboys and Indians*; Comack, *Racialized Policing*.

53 Reber and Renaud, *Starlight Tour*; Comack, *Racialized Policing*.

54 Wright, *Report of the Commission of Inquiry into Matters Relating to the Death of Neil Stonechild*, 212.

55 See Comack, *Racialized Policing*, appendix.

56 Bittner, "Florence Nightingale in Pursuit of Willie Sutton."

57 Shearing and Ericson, "Culture as Figurative Action."

58 Winnipeg Police Service, *Annual Statistical Report*.

59 Hoffman, "Canada's National Use-of-Force Framework for Police Officers"; Iacobucci, *Police Encounters with People in Crisis*.

60 Silver, *In Their Own Voices*; CCPA–MB, *Step by Step*.

61 Wharf and Clague, *Community Organizing*.

62 See Silver, Ghorayshi, Hay, and Klyne, "Sharing, Community and Decolonization."

63 Morrissette and Blacksmith, "Winnipeg's Bear Clan Patrol."

64 Ibid.

CHAPTER EIGHT

CARE-TO-PRISON PIPELINE

Indigenous Children in Twenty-First-Century Settler Colonial Economies

MICHELLE STEWART AND COREY LA BERGE

This chapter interrogates a contemporary settler colonial project that mobilizes the rhetoric of benevolence in conjunction with racialized care and policing practices to generate economies predicated on the ongoing suffering of Indigenous children (and families). Focused on the role of the "child welfare" system and the insidious relationship it has to expanding settler colonial projects in Canada, this chapter will draw together critical Marxist theory and critical perspectives on the school-to-prison pipeline. In so doing, we will consider the various actors that contribute to this project that includes work performed by lawyers, judges, social workers, correctional staff, probation officers, foster parents, child-serving agencies, youth and group home workers, psychologists, psychiatrists, nurses, and researchers. And while some of this work is critically informed and holds central an analysis of racialized oppression, the overwhelming majority of this work on *behalf* of Indigenous children fails to address the social injustice(s) taking place in this settler state. The opportunity cost of all of this benevolence—and the potential impact of redistribution of these resources to better meet the material needs and circumstances of Indigenous families and communities—needs to be addressed. If we are serious about the work of reconciliation, there must necessarily be a reckoning in these colonial economies that evolve around the ongoing displacement of Indigenous children. This chapter argues that the ongoing expansion of settler colonialism is clearly articulated through child welfare practices that fuel a "care-to-prison" pipeline for Indigenous youth in the Canadian Prairies—a pipeline that generates surplus value through a complex contradiction that at once commodifies Indigenous children while concurrently devaluing Indigenous lives.

This chapter will focus on four central examples—one child and three youths, who in their short lives offer emblematic examples of processes of displacement that enact and re-enact the violence of settler colonialism. These four stories are the central anchor from which we will unpack how such experiences, while tragic and horrifying, are not unique. The four stories from a Prairie city a tell a familiar tale: of a benevolent state that "steps" into the lives of Indigenous families, takes children out of the home in the name of child welfare, and in so doing extends the ideologies that drove settlement and residential schools. These are practices that first and foremost will not empower Indigenous parents to be active agents in the lives of their children. These are practices carved and polished from ideologies that date back to the Doctrine of Discovery and *terra nullius*, colonial fantasies of expansion and displacement that play out through daily and routinized practices of racialized child welfare. While the chapter tells four stories from Winnipeg, the photos deliver a concurrent story about displacement in another Prairie city, Regina. Taken together, these stories and photos demonstrate how the Plains are still being cleared, one child at a time. Using a settler colonial framework, this chapter shows how such ongoing displacements are fuelling pipeline economies—care-to-prison pipelines.

PIPELINES, CHILDREN, AND ECONOMIES OF SCALE

The literature on the school-to-prison pipeline argues that there are tangible links between how youth are treated (in relation to punishment regimes) and justice encounters in adulthood. This has included school disciplinary practices that mirror or hail the justice system[1] with direct links to the rise of so-called zero tolerance practices.[2] These disciplinary practices aggressively displace students from the classroom. Within the school-to-prison literature attention is paid to the role of systemic oppression, inequality, race, and class.[3] Researchers point out the link between privilege and positive outcomes in educational settings[4] and the need for further understanding of the internal variables that can contribute to poor educational outcomes,[5] the need for educational reform,[6] and for legislative changes.[7] The practices of expulsion and suspension are expanding at alarming rates such that upwards of 30 percent of African American youth are on suspension in some states[8]—the largely U.S.-based literature focuses on the disproportionate impact on Latinx and Black American youth.[9] These disciplinary actions in schools are then mirrored as youth emerge into adulthood and face disproportionate surveillance and sanction, leading Smith to note the "blurred pedagogical distinctions" between the justice and educational systems such that they actually have a "symbiotic relationship" in many respects.[10] This symbiotic relationship and configuration of oppression will be central to our argument about the care-to-prison pipeline.

While there is some research in the area of the "foster-to-prison" pipeline, it is largely based in the United States and is focused primarily on causal arguments,[11] the role of risk,[12] as well as on program and policy developments to address youth to adult challenges.[13] However, in drawing on these clusters of literature from the United States, our aim is to look at the role of capitalism at the centre of these phenomena. Indeed, in the United States the pipelines all lead to neoliberal forms of incarceration in which adult jails are increasingly privatized, leading some to suspect that there is an early economic investment in pushing youth into this pipeline that profits from incarceration over education[14] through the "soft coercive migration of youth of color."[15] In this way, some states easily spend more on prisons than on education,[16] predicated on a pipeline that is understood to have a "predictable and steady flow."[17] While the literature on school-to-prison pipeline is dominated largely by U.S. research, Raible and Irizarry note that similar phenomena can be extrapolated in places like Canada, where Indigenous peoples make up less than 4 percent of the overall population but are overrepresented in the justice system.[18] Unapologetic about the displacement of children to state care systems and concurrently cognizant of the disproportionate representation of Indigenous people in the justice system, the Canadian state generates economic activity off the bodies of Indigenous children *and* adults through practices of valuation and devaluation as it grows economies through nuanced articulations of extraction and occupation.

In her book on the deaths of Indigenous people (at the hands of the state), Sherene Razack argues that Indigenous bodies are framed as "remnants" in

Figure 8.1. Aerial shot of the Regina Indian Industrial School, Saskatchewan, that operated from the late nineteenth to early twentieth century. Provincial Archives of Saskatchewan, R-A21262.

Figure 8.2. The unmarked graveyard of the Regina Indian Industrial School stands in the distance from the old footprint of the school. The only marked graves belonged to the priest and his family. The location has been surveyed and it is believed that dozens of young children are laid to rest here, likely stacked one atop the other, having died and never been returned to their families and homes. Photo by Michelle Stewart.

Canada and therefore treated as always withering, unfit, and always broken in the settler state, which justifies acts of violence as part of ongoing dispossession.[19] The Canadian Plains were aggressively cleared first through tactics of starvation and disease,[20] then by broader policies of state violence directed at family disruption through the forced removal of children in residential schools that sought to "kill the Indian in the child." Such policies inflicted wide-scale abuses, contributing to the intergenerational trauma many families endure today.[21] And while residential schools began to close in the 1950s and '60s, with the last school closing in 1996, the removal of Indigenous children from their families has increased. The Assembly of First Nations notes there are more children in state care today than at the height of the residential schools[22]—"by a factor of three."[23] Some have called this the Millennium Scoop— an extension of the ideologies that facilitated the residential schools and the Sixties Scoop.[24] Concurrent with the operation of the residential schools, the Sixties Scoop was an intervention that ran from 1960 to the 1980s in which the state actively intervened to remove Indigenous children from their biological homes and then place them with primarily white, middle-class families. Patrick Johnston coined the term in part because adoption workers would describe "scooping" children away from their families[25]—often without the family's knowledge of where the child was placed. Both generational scoops (Sixties and Millennium) have mobilized the same ideologies and state violence(s) as the residential school did in ripping children out of their family homes,[26] and we are currently witnessing the full maturation of this process as whole budget lines are created to "accommodate" ongoing influxes of Indigenous children, youth, and adults into pipelines that flow from child welfare to adult corrections. We align our analysis with those who consider colonialism to be a "living phenomenon" by looking to specific stories from one Prairie city to demonstrate economies that are predicated on the ongoing displacement and marginalization of Indigenous people.[27] The intergenerational trauma and displacement resulting from the residential schools and Sixties Scoop that is now being extended and mirrored by the so-called Millennium Scoop leaves one asking if these are best described as distinct eras or if they are just reconfigurations of a constant: settler colonialism.

While colonialism and colonial expansion were predicated on lucrative plans of extraction, from first contact and the subsequent seizing of lands to contemporary practices of mining and damming,[28] settler colonialism reconfigures the encounter such that the "invasion is a structure not an event,"[29] in

Figure 8.3. The Paul Dojack Youth Correctional Facility. This facility now sits on the former footprint of the Regina Indian Industrial School. Photo by Michelle Stewart.

which the encounter is meant to be sustained—and it does so through practices that are intended to permeate and displace. Or as Woroniak and Camfield argue, "unlike the kind of colonialism experienced in places such as India, the main goal of settler colonialism was not to take advantage of the labour of Indigenous peoples. Instead, it was to displace Indigenous peoples from their lands, break and bury the cultures that grew out of relationships with those lands, and, ultimately, eliminate Indigenous societies so that settlers could establish themselves."[30] As it relates to this chapter, settler colonialism is an ongoing occupation that predicates economic expansion on structural inequalities as naturalized through biopower, governmentality, and ideologies of white supremacy.[31] Seen this way, settler colonialism works to produce particular subject formations. As Audra Simpson points out, subject formation goes hand in hand with historic formation.[32] Historic and contemporary manifestations of settler colonialism must therefore interrogate the specific structures that Patrick Wolfe draws our attention to alongside the particular mechanisms that facilitate ongoing expansion, including but not limited to popular media and public policy.[33] This chapter focuses on the care-to-prison pipeline to demonstrate the overall need to interrogate settler colonialism. Settler colonialism serves to naturalize structural racism, making a tangible impact on the health of individuals and families,[34] both within and between generations. At the centre of settler colonialism are the material practices that actively traumatize and displace. We offer this chapter as settlers who are actively seeking to interrogate but also dismantle these programs and practices that are predatory, violent, and colonial—and formulated exclusively to exploit the bodies and lives of children.

PLACING THE STORIES

Winnipeg is a city with approximately 700,000 people. The city is home to half of Manitoba's total population, making it the largest city and primary urban hub in the province. As with many cities across Canada, the influx of Indigenous people into urban centres has been a steady phenomenon for the past few decades, with many Indigenous people framed within research and demographic analyses as "social misfits" or "lacking social adjustment" to urban living.[35] While Alan Anderson characterizes this as a challenge that must be faced, Sherene Razack, as well as Elizabeth Comack, Lawrence Dean, Larry Morrissette, and Jim Silver draw explicit attention to the ways in which settler colonialism perpetuates particular forms of displacement as part of ongoing colonial activity.[36] In the case of Winnipeg, it has long been a "segregated city," dating back to the turn of the twentieth century when the railway cut the city in half and migrants were among the earliest people to live in the North End—an area where it was hard to plant and grow food, and where developers built quick and shoddy housing.[37]

In the years following the Second World War, the North End of Winnipeg experienced considerable suburban out-migration and concurrently an influx of Indigenous people who were leaving the reserves because of poor conditions. Poor conditions on reserves that have contributed and still contribute to urban migration include lack of employment opportunity, lack of appropriate housing, resource depletion, lack of access to services, and poverty.[38] Urban migration is also a gendered experience, reflected in the feminization of poverty experienced in larger urban centres in Canada.[39]

Today, the North End confronts a range of challenges including housing, employment, crime, and the realities of a food desert—"this is what colonialism looks like today."[40] As de-industrialization occurred within urban centres, many manufacturing jobs that supported neighbourhoods such as the North End were removed for cheaper labour overseas. In response to calls for a return to a "real" economy, Neferti Tadiar calls into question the binary of material and immaterial labour as it relates to ideas and ideals of industrialization. She writes that "what makes financial processes of value extraction symmetrical to these new processes of value production is precisely the extension of such processes beyond factory production and into the sphere of circulation and reproduction, i.e., in the sphere of bios, of life."[41] In this way, the economy continues to expand and grow as new ways of extracting surplus value are identified. Tadiar, drawing on Marx, is exploring conceptual frameworks around how "value extraction" is realized. Thinking about Marx's concept of surplus value, we understand surplus value as the "value" that is *produced* after the costs of labour (and raw materials) are accounted for, specifically, increase in the value of capital. Surplus value is what is left after "necessary labour" is accounted for, and necessary labour consists of all of the elements required to reproduce the worker (this could be anything from food and shelter to emotional support or affective labour). Surplus value is the excess—what is often described as "profit" but is in actuality better described as the remainder of that labour *and life*. Going back to Tadiar, this excess is the result of specific forms of exploitation—exploitations—that have long permeated the factory floor and entered into the circulation of everyday life, where different bodies have different value.

In the following section we turn to four stories about young Indigenous children and youth who are taken into state "care." Individuals who are taken into care in Manitoba are part of a half-billion-dollar industry designed to "protect" children and act as a "caring and responsible parent."[42] This industry of care is also an industry in which 88 percent of children and youth are Indigenous, and the majority of the workers are non-Indigenous.[43] In the four stories, we find two deaths and one vicious assault. The last case features a person who moves from care to prison, transitioning from being the subject of institutionalized state violence to being the perpetrator of violence. This configuration of the care-to-prison pipeline, we argue, has a particular relationship to settler colonialism. We analyze these four stories to examine how the pipeline—an entire industry—forms around young bodies. We do so to highlight the ways in which twenty-first-century economies are continuing to identify new ways to extract surplus within a settler state context.[44] Glen Coulthard argues that the Canadian state was never invested in developing colonial economies through the exploitation of cheap labour, but rather predicated its expansion on displacement: the settler economy needed land and the way for that to happen was to clear Indigenous bodies from the land.[45] We put Coulthard in conversation with the works of Tadiar and Melissa Wright[46] and their conceptual frameworks to understand how particular bodies are constructed as disposable or waste.[47] We do so to illustrate that one way the settler colonial economy continues to generate surplus is through the ongoing clearing of the land, which includes the ongoing "scoops" of young Indigenous children under the auspices of care who are then later transformed into prisoners. In this way we are blending post-colonial, post-Fordist Marxian theorists to argue that the extraction of surplus value in the Canadian settler state has a particular articulation. It is an articulation predicated on the displacement of Indigenous children through a care-to-prison pipeline that has the net effect of ongoing and long-term displacement of marginalized and excluded individuals; individuals who enter the pipeline configured as waste in the making and whose true value lies in the ongoing management potential that is predicated on their ongoing displacement.

The populations that are excluded and marginalized become manageable/managed objects for state institutions like social services, child welfare, and the justice system, as well as for a multitude of private contracted companies.

Tadiar places these managed bodies as the flip side of the "mercantilization of life" that produces "immeasurable surplus of the 'living labor' of life subsumed within capital."[48] She argues there is an absolute commodification of life that is produced by managing excluded and dispossessed populations in industries of security and protection. Here the capitalist subsumption of life is more than mere consumption where life is spent, but a production of *life as waste*, as Tadiar writes, "disposable material whose management has become an entire 'province of accumulation,' spawning proliferating industries of militarization, security, policing, and control."[49] We will return through the text to Tadiar's economic analysis of expansion and waste; it will be coupled with Razack's concept of remnants and the disposability of Indigenous bodies to explore this twenty-first-century settler colonial economy. Social technologies such as race, gender, nationality, and sexuality become central for biopolitical interventions over what lives are worth—which lives yield value as living labour and which lives yield more value as a "disposable existence." We start with the story of young Phoenix Sinclair, whose death fuelled economic activity in the name of care—Phoenix would drive industry through her very disposability.

PHOENIX SINCLAIR

In June 2005, five-year-old Phoenix Sinclair died as a result of homicide. She lived in Manitoba. She was Indigenous. Her death went undiscovered for months. News of the horrific circumstances of her death (her mother and her mother's boyfriend were ultimately held criminally responsible for torturing and killing her before disposing of her body in a nearby garbage dump) triggered a firestorm in the media. Media noted that concerns about Phoenix had previously been reported to child and family services, putting Manitoba's Department of Child and Family Services and the government ultimately responsible for the department's administration under the spotlight. By way of response, the government of the day called a public inquiry, and commissioned the Honourable Ted Hughes, a retired judge, to inquire into the circumstances of Phoenix's death. The inquiry concluded with a report, released some eight-and-a-half years after Phoenix died.

According to government media releases and other news reports, the inquiry into Phoenix's death cost $14 million.[50] Seven lawyers were among the commission staff. Twenty-five more lawyers went on record on behalf of seventeen parties and intervenors. Nineteen lawyers appeared on behalf of thirty-six witnesses. The inquiry heard from 126 witnesses over ninety-one days, many of them professionals who provided evidence by way of having direct knowledge relevant to the inquiry, or by offering "expert opinion" evidence used to assist the commissioner.

The final report made sixty-two recommendations, with poverty cited as the most significant factor for the protection of Manitoba's (Indigenous) children.[51] Subsequently, the government commissioned a further report to inquire into "options for action" for implementing thirty-one of the sixty-two recommendations. This second "implementation report" was reported to have cost a further $350,000. Since the time of Phoenix's death, child-in-care totals in Manitoba have increased from approximately 6,629 children in care to 10,501.[52] A full 88 percent of these children are reported to be Indigenous.[53] The Department of Child and Family Services' annual budget for "child protection" has increased from $155 million to $495 million.[54]

The final report of the inquiry, submitted to government in December 2013, included an examination of the overrepresentation of Indigenous children and families within Manitoba's child and family services system. Commissioner Hughes stated that "research shows that Aboriginal children are taken from their homes in disproportionate numbers, not because they are Aboriginal but because they are living in far worse circumstances than other children. . . . When Aboriginal families are compared with other families in the same circumstances, there is no significant difference in rates of apprehension."[55] However, the commissioner also wrote that "many of the reasons why Aboriginal children and families are more vulnerable and more likely to come into contact with the child welfare system, according to several witnesses, have to do with the legacy of colonization and residential schools."[56] Given that experiences of colonization and residential schools in Canada have been specific to Indigenous peoples, it could be argued that it is precisely because they are Indigenous that these children are taken from their homes in disproportionate numbers.

Had Phoenix been identified as "a child in need of protection" and apprehended from her mother and brought into care, her life might have been spared. However, while there is a presumption that the state provides an appropriate level of care for children who are "Crown wards," the evidence suggests that the outcomes for these (Indigenous) children are not positive. Evidence put to the inquiry from Manitoba's Centre for Health Policy cited poor outcomes for children in care, including outcomes related to education, health, and reliance upon social assistance as young adults. And while Manitoba was found to have some of the highest rates of children in care in the world, it was noted that "thousands of Manitoba children are being placed into care each year, with little evidence that this intervention is effective and will result in the best possible outcomes for the children."[57] Which of course begs the response, framed as a rhetorical question: Is the system ultimately invested in the "best possible outcome for the children"?

The issue of how the Canadian state is investing in children, particularly First Nations children[58] who are vulnerable to jurisdictional disputes respecting funding, as between federal and provincial governments, was addressed by the inquiry. While there was no finding that funding directly contributed to Phoenix's death, the commissioner posed the question of whether investment is better made in protection or prevention, before citing testimony from Cindy Blackstock of the First Nations Caring Society: "We know from good research that for every dollar you invest in a child you save six to seven down the line, as a government. . . . And the reason for that is that you maximize the opportunities of raising a generation of children who not only are proud of their traditions and their peoples, but are also best prepared to be able to implement the career of their dreams and take full advantage of the opportunities that are presented to them."[59] On 26 January 2016, after almost nine years of litigation, the Canadian Human Rights Tribunal issued a landmark decision, finding that the federal government had been discriminating against First Nations–status children by way of failing to fund child welfare services to First Nations children at a level equitable to that provided to other children by provincial jurisdictions.

Subsequently, the Human Rights Tribunal has issued two orders of non-compliance relating to the federal government's failure to end discrimination as ordered by the tribunal, and litigation is ongoing. In March 2017, the federal government filed a respondent's factum with the tribunal, arguing that the tribunal lacks statutory authority to enforce its own orders and that "they should generally operate under a presumption that their rulings will be executed with reasonable diligence and good faith."[60]

Citing the devastating impacts of the mass apprehension of Indigenous children in their critique of child welfare systems in Saskatchewan and elsewhere in Canada, Caroline Tait, Robert Henry, and Rachel Loewen Walker highlight a false presumption regarding state care: "A 'benevolent culture of care,' or what is commonly referred to as 'acting in the best interests of the child' [within provincial child welfare legislation] assumes that the State takes children into foster care and places them in nurturing, stable, and supportive foster home environments where they are able to thrive as children. However, existing C W S [child welfare services] environments in Saskatchewan (and in other areas of Canada) continually fail to accomplish this goal."[61] Such assertions can lead one to ask if there is another goal?

While it is horrible to analyze Phoenix's story on economic terms, it is necessary because it is a story about how surplus value was extracted from this young child—in life and death. Indigenous bodies—children and adults—hold a particular type of value and have a particular relationship to the colonial state. In a settler state where state care is arguably a misnomer, Phoenix was the forgotten child. There was no child welfare that attended to young Phoenix; the warnings and calls for assistance and intervention went unattended. Rather than rely on notions of a caring and benevolent state, there is a need to recall that Phoenix is an Indigenous child and one who is easily forgotten by the "care making" industry because, as Razack points out, Indigenous bodies are the remnants[62]—the remainders that have not yet been settled. Building on Razack and Tadiar, we argue that no one took action to intervene and help save Phoenix's life because no one cared about yet another Indigenous child who was experiencing neglect. Phoenix becomes Razack's remnant: a remainder of a citizen-subject who is understood to always be in a state of decay because of being out of place in a contemporary settler state. We offer this story as a stark reminder that children are lost in this machinery—Manitoba boasts some of the highest rates of children in state care. Again, 88 percent of those children are Indigenous, and we can see with Phoenix's case and many others that these children are often forgotten or rendered invisible once they are in state care. Phoenix received more care and attention in death than in life—and economic activity was mobilized around her. Economic activity and surplus value were extracted through the management regimes previously discussed.

In death, Phoenix is transformed into an economic object that has potential value—something to be acted upon. Phoenix as a subject of public inquiry mobilizes a wide range of state actors. Suddenly there is concern and care; concern and care that is then transformed into recommendations; recommendations that are then transformed into increased budget lines for social services. Millions of dollars are spent investigating Phoenix's death and millions more are "invested" in the apprehensions of thousands more

Indigenous children identified as being "at risk" and "in need of protection" from their families. Phoenix's life is valorized in death by the expansion of the child welfare industry.

Within these industries, race, religion, nationality, gender, and sexuality operate as social "technologies of biopolitical decisions over life worth, critical markers for distinctions not only between rates of remunerable life (high value vs. low value, skilled vs. unskilled labor) but also between life worth living, that is, life with the capacity to yield value as living labour, and life worth expending, that is, life with the capacity to yield value as disposable existence."[63] Tadiar draws out what the violence of twenty-first-century capitalism looks like. We have violence that surrounds both material and immaterial forms of labour, but here her analysis helps to highlight that we also have lives that have value through their disposability. Like the detainee Tadiar analyzes, Indigenous lives are "simply a unit of measure of capitalist temporality, a form of currency of trade (with the state as market), a means for carrying out processes of value extraction that do not issue from the labor of those lives."[64] This economy is founded on the "forced expenditures" of "at-risk" populations, lives increasing wealth. Seen this way, the twenty-first-century settler colonial economy in Canada expands through narratives of welfare and care—where there is neither welfare nor care in these cases, but rather the extraction of surplus value found in disposable lives that render value through their management.

RIVERS AND HOTELS

On 17 August 2014, the body of fifteen-year-old Tina Fontaine was found wrapped in plastic in the Red River, a few hundred metres downstream from the Canadian Museum for Human Rights. She had been reportedly living in the care of a child and family services agency and was "placed" in a downtown hotel.

Many Indigenous children in state care in Manitoba have found themselves living in downtown hotels in the care of low-paid and unskilled contract staff from private companies. That is, until two tragedies resulting in extensive media coverage and public outcry ultimately led the Minister of Child and Family Services to issue a directive to end the practice. As early as 2001, the Office of the Children's Advocate publicly reported that they had received a complaint about the use of hotels in 1999.[65] In particular, the complaint had been in regard to the number of children being placed in hotels and the quality of care being provided. Upon review of one agency, the Children's Advocate found that over 2,500 children had been placed in hotels between 1995 and 2000, for a total of more than 60,000 days. The average cost was determined to have been $305 per day, while offering little in the way of resources for treatment or care. At the time of Tina's death in 2014, provincially mandated child and family services agencies were allotted budgets of $1,300 per year for purposes of "family enhancement"—funding for agencies to support (Indigenous) families so as to prevent them from having their children apprehended. Prior to and at the time of Tina's death, it was still well-known that large numbers of children in care were living in downtown hotels, without adequate care and supervision.[66]

In December 2015, fifty-three-year-old Raymond Cormier was charged with Tina's murder. Media reports suggested that she had been experiencing sexual exploitation while living in the downtown Winnipeg hotel—an experience that was reported to be common to many children who were housed in the hotel.[67]

While Tina's murder caused a great deal of public outcry and advanced calls for a national investigation into missing and murdered Indigenous women and girls, it was not until the 2015 assault upon another fifteen-year-old Indigenous girl in the care of child and family services, placed in the same downtown Winnipeg hotel, that the minister responsible for the administration of child and family services directed staff to put an end to the practice.

A fifteen-year-old Indigenous boy, also in care and placed in the same hotel, was charged with aggravated sexual assault and aggravated assault against the girl. It was reported that the boy and the girl had been drinking and attempted to return to their hotel "placement," but had been refused entry. The two children left and the girl was subsequently seriously assaulted by the boy, resulting in her being admitted to hospital, placed on life-support, and sustaining life-long injuries that included permanent brain damage.

The boy was described as having come from a First Nations community north of Winnipeg prior to his apprehension at birth, whereupon he had been placed in a foster home in the city. Media further reported that the boy was described as having been diagnosed with Fetal Alcohol Spectrum Disorder (FASD), "intellectual disabilities," and "attachment disorder," and that "doctors . . . [had] assessed the teen as being 'very early in his emotional and social development.'"[68] It was further reported that he had been struggling after being removed from his foster care home and placed at the hotel, where he had little in the way of support. The boy was reported to have no criminal record. The Crown, though, which had been responsible for the boy's care as he was a "ward" of the state, asked the court to sentence him as an adult—a sentence reported to carry a maximum penalty of seven years and normally reserved for extraordinary cases where the presumption of a young person's "diminished moral blameworthiness" or "culpability" is rebutted.

While the boy was held to account for his behaviour within the context of Manitoba's youth criminal justice system, the media did not report upon any accountability for the state or the Crown in discharging its duty of care to the boy and the girl. The media also did not report on whether the care provided to a fifteen-year-old struggling with a constellation of diagnoses and unique care needs by placing him in a downtown hotel without adequate supports and turning him back out onto the street while intoxicated was "prudent" or appropriately "mitigated the risk of foreseeable harm," as required under Canada's common law. It was the boy who was told by the sentencing judge that "there was no one who egged you on or encouraged you or anyone that provoked you to commit this offence. You committed it in a rage against your own circumstances."[69]

The boy received a three-year sentence, described as "allow[ing] the teen to receive individualized rehabilitation including treatment from a psychologist, an occupational therapist who can teach him life skills and an individual tutor, along with one-on-one monitoring while in custody."[70] Media headlines described this (benevolent?) response by the state as "intensive help for teen who brutally assaulted friend in parkade."[71]

While Manitoba has experienced an increase of (Indigenous) children living in the care of the state, so has the province experienced an increase in (Indigenous) children becoming involved in the criminal legal system. In a notice to the profession issued in December 2013, Legal Aid Manitoba reported "growth in all areas of legal aid with respect to legal matters issued, [with] the most significant growth . . . in the area of administration of justice offences, and in particular breach of probation charges . . . Youth breaches increased by 961 legal matters (200.6%) between fiscal years 2008/09 and 2012/13."[72] Economies are expanding through the trafficking of Indigenous children between various state systems—from care to incarceration.

This idea of Indigenous children making significant contributions to Manitoba's Prairie settler economy is not new and has been articulated by many within Manitoba's Indigenous communities, including the Assembly of Manitoba Chiefs' Grand Chief Derek Nepinak: "The child welfare industry in Manitoba puts about 500 million dollars in play, each year. . . . That half billion dollars is a very very significant contributor to Manitoba's economy, so what we've done is we've turned our children into money. We've turned children into a commodity. . . . [I]t's speculated on the tragedy of our families and it's a very good business. . . . [W]e cannot commodify our children, we cannot turn them into money . . . the commodification of them is contributing to the tragedies that we're seeing every day."[73] The "problems" of "youth crime" and "child protection" have been addressed in a variety of institutional responses. These responses have not tended to address the "far worse circumstances" that too many Indigenous children, families, and communities find themselves living in, as described in the findings of the Phoenix Sinclair Inquiry. Rather, institutional responses have largely focused upon identifying "children at risk"—effectively constructing individual children as constituting the problem that requires intervention. This perspective, rather than understanding children, their families, and communities as experiencing "social suffering" resulting "from what political, economic, and institutional power does to people," particularly as it relates to the colonization of Canadian Prairie Indigenous peoples, frames children as a specific locus of risk requiring the (benevolent) care or intervention of settler professionals and institutions who rely upon ever-increasing amounts of state funding for the purposes of their work.

Swadener and Lubeck have argued that "the generalized use of the 'at risk' label is highly problematic and implicitly racist, classist, sexist, and ableist, a 1990s version of the cultural deficit model which locates problems or 'pathologies' in individuals, families and communities rather than in institutional structures that create and maintain inequality."[74] Indeed, a great deal of attention was given to actuarial-based assessment tools within the context of the Phoenix Sinclair Inquiry. Testimony was heard that Manitoba child and family service authorities, upon advice from professional experts, had made the decision "to adopt a set of actuarial tools known as the Structured Decision Making tools (SDM), which was developed by the Children's Research Center[75] in the United States."[76] Components of the SDM tools include a "safety assessment" used "to make an immediate determination as to whether a child needs to be apprehended," a "probability of future harm (risk assessment)" "which will guide a worker in determining the likelihood of children being harmed in the future if services are not provided," as well as a "family strengths and needs assessment." It was noted that "[a]doption of the SDM tools required a license from the Children's Research Center," which monitors the use of their system and provides "training and works with users to adapt its tools to local circumstances."[77]

While the SDM tools can be used to assess whether or not to apprehend a child, its ability to determine the "probability of future harm" is limited: "it doesn't accurately predict which families will re-harm their kids; it only provides a classification of families that are more likely to harm their kids."[78] Testimony at the Phoenix Sinclair Inquiry suggested that "the decision to keep a case open, and the intensity of services to be provided, will be informed by this tool." However, further testimony also revealed that family enhancement funding, used to pay for these services for families whose children have not been apprehended, was capped at a mean average of $1,300 per year—characterized as "a limited fund available for prevention measures aimed at keeping children safe in their homes."[79] This funding was described as being used to cover expenses like in-home supports, emergency food, transportation, therapy, children's camps, and child care.[80] The commission also heard evidence from witnesses critical of the tools. This included testimony from Cindy Blackstock, who cautioned the commission about the validity of these tools being applied to First Nations children when they were originally developed and validated with another (non-Canadian First Nations) population. This has led to "issues such as poverty [to be] conflated with neglect" or to observing "structural issues such as poverty, and treat[ing] them as parental deficits."[81] Commissioner Hughes wrote that "representatives of AMC [Assembly of Manitoba Chiefs] and SCO [Southern Chiefs Organization] expressed the view that the tools should not be used before they are validated to correct for cultural bias" which the commission was told could be done "only after three to five years' experience with the tools in the jurisdiction."[82]

Exploring and mapping children "at risk" constitutes a cultural process of rational-technical analysis[83] that effectively locates pathology within children and their families as opposed to addressing the violence, pathology, and terror within the institutions and social spaces to which they've been subjected. This allows for the imposition of settler professional service sectors like child welfare, corrections, psychology, and psychiatry to exercise power and control over bodies and subjectivities, and to write authoritative narratives that limit the framing of distress—"normalizing social pathology or pathologizing the psychophysiology of terror."[84] The experience of social suffering and its impacts upon the mental and emotional lives of Indigenous children is cultivated as more territory to be explored and mapped, a resource to be mined and exploited. Settler narratives of a "post-colonial" world and their inevitable fatalistic notions of colonial "legacies" ultimately serve to "naturalize power,"[85] as opposed to acknowledging and addressing an ongoing colonial project that pathologizes Indigenous children and families living with social suffering associated with experiences of structural violence.

MOBILIZING ECONOMIES, MOBILIZING HISTORIES

In the examples above, we see the ways in which the state intervenes in the name of "care" or "protection" but does not in fact secure either. In the case of young Phoenix Sinclair, the state was involved in her life but not enough to actually protect her from death. And an economy has been mobilized around her as $14.5 million is spent on discussing the various factors that contributed to her death. It is striking that a key finding in the inquiry into her death was that poverty is the most significant factor in making children and families vulnerable and leading them into contact with the child welfare system.[86] It is striking but not surprising that the state will spend millions to discuss poverty versus spending the money to address poverty—the vulgarity is both stark and unapologetic. If we turn to Tina Fontaine, we see a young woman who was brought into "care" only to be neglected by those who were expected to deliver care. The practice of removing children and youth from their homes only to be placed in relatively unsupervised settings such as downtown hotels leads to violent outcomes, including but not limited to the death of Tina and the horrible assault of a fifteen-year-old girl. Tina, rolled in a blanket and thrown into the Red River, became emblematic of the dire situation facing Indigenous women and girls in Canada—disposability. This sense was only amplified when Cormier was found not guilty of Tina's murder in February 2018. Tina's death, the manner of its investigation, and the suspect's eventual acquittal drew public outcry. The rallies, vigils, and protests that followed drew attention to racialized justice *and* child welfare practices—including peaceful camps that were struck in the dead of winter across the Prairies that drew attention to these practices and called for paradigm shifts in justice and child welfare practices.

Figure 8.4. Winter shot from Camp: Justice for Our Stolen Children. This camp was started on 28 February 2018 on Treaty Four Territory in Regina, Saskatchewan. At the time of writing, the camp had been running for 169 days and counting. The camp joined others across Canada to draw attention to the lives of Indigenous youth and children, including Colten Boushie, Tina Fontaine, and Haven Dubois. The camp also focused on bringing children home and out of the child welfare system. Photo by A. Snell.

Figure 8.5. Aerial shot of Camp: Justice for Our Stolen Children. The camp grew from one tipi to over a dozen tipis representing different nations, families, and communities within and beyond Treaty Four Territory. Photo by P. Demas.

Demanding #justicefortina became a rallying cry for more than reform because in the absence of a paradigm shift, the conditions that allowed Tina Fontaine (and so many others) to be murdered still remained—and because simple reforms and temporary indignation do not change the structural conditions and systemic racism facing Indigenous children, families, and communities. Similarly, the matter of Phoenix Sinclair was followed by social services doubling its budget and led to one of the most expensive inquiries in the province's history,[87] but nothing fundamentally changed. The state continued to invest in its own institutions, not in the lives of Indigenous children or their families. These stories are emblematic of settler colonialism and specifically of the practices that actively displace children into systems of welfare and punishment—systems that generate economies predicated on suffering and displacement.

When thinking about the fifteen-year-old boy in Winnipeg who was both subject to state trauma, and then inflicted trauma, we are confronted with these histories of colonial encounters alongside historic and contemporary trauma. His victim and Tina Fontaine have become part of a broadening and expanding statistic in Canada: the disproportionate number of Indigenous women and girls that experience interpersonal and sexualized violence. A phenomenon that is understood to have become so "commonplace" in Canada,[88] with literally thousands missing or murdered, that it compelled a national inquiry. While this issue is currently receiving much public and policy attention, it has taken place as a result of decades of impunity for those who have wrought violence and is frequently perpetuated by racialized justice[89] and media representations.[90]

Returning to the discussion of the residential school program in Canada, this practice was modelled on reformatories in Europe and the United States that were created to house poor children. Reformulated in Canada to "kill the Indian in the child," the residential school program took children out of their families and communities and placed them in rigid schooling programs focused on assimilation and "cultural genocide."[91] While articulated as spaces to help children, they were instead the place of widespread abuse, suffering, and death. They were also sites in which the settler colonial imaginary became both set and fixed on the lives of young children and their potential for subjugation through economic expansion. Most residential schools are no longer standing, but the policies and practices they mobilized serve to anchor a key practice in Canadian settler colonialism—displacement. The photos shared throughout this chapter highlight how these spaces of colonial subjugation continue to shape and reshape lives through practices of coercion and displacement. The stories shared in this chapter highlight the latest in a long line of colonial interventions that are levelled upon the bodies of children with a goal of extracting value out of their lives while concurrently seeking to disrupt and displace families as Canada continues to clear the Plains, moving children out of their homes and into a pipeline that ensures their lives will mobilize economic activity from birth to death.

NOTES

1 Tuzzolo and Hewitt, "Rebuilding Inequity."

2 Heitzeg, "Education or Incarceration."

3 Wald and Losen, "Defining and Redirecting a School-to-Prison Pipeline"; Tuzzolo and Hewitt, "Rebuilding Inequity."

4 Wald and Losen, "Defining and Redirecting a School-to-Prison Pipeline."

5 Christle, Jolivette, and Nelson, "Breaking the School to Prison Pipeline."

6 Heitzeg, "Education or Incarceration"; Cregor and Hewitt, "Dismantling the School-to-Prison Pipeline."

7 Boyd, "Confronting Racial Disparity," 571.

8 Smith, "Deconstructing the Pipeline," 1009.

9 Winn and Behizadeh, "The Right to Be Literate."

10 Smith, "Deconstructing the Pipeline."

11 Doyle Jr., "Child Protection and Adult Crime."

12 Jonson-Reid and Barth, "From Placement to Prison"; Ryan, Hernandez, and Herz, "Developmental Trajectories of Offending for Male Adolescents."

13 Reilly, "Transition from Care."

14 Porter, "The School-to-Prison Pipeline."

15 Fine and Ruglis, "Circuits and Consequences of Dispossession."

16 Ibid.

17 Harris, "Prison vs. Education Spending Reveals California's Priorities."

18 Raible and Irizarry, "Redirecting the Teacher's Gaze."

19 Razack, *Dying from Improvement*.

20 Daschuk, *Clearing the Plains*.

21 Truth and Reconciliation Commission of Canada, *Honouring the Truth, Reconciling for the Future*; Niezen, *Truth and Indignation*; Vowel, *Indigenous Writes*.

22 Assembly of First Nations, *Leadership Action Plan on First Nations Child Welfare*.

23 Blackstock, "Residential Schools," 74.

24 McKenzie, Varcoe, Browne, and Day, "Disrupting the Continuities"; Fraser, Vachon, Hassan, and Parent, "Communicating Power and Resistance"; Sinclair, "Identity Lost and Found."

25 Sinclair, "Identity Lost and Found."

26 McKenzie, Varcoe, Browne, and Day, "Disrupting the Continuities"; Fraser, Vachon, Hassan, and Parent, "Communicating Power and Resistance"; Sinclair, "Identity Lost and Found."

27 Monture, "Race and Erasing," 207.

28 Preston, "Neoliberal Settler Colonialism, Canada and the Tar Sands"; Comack, Deane, Morrissette, and Silver, *"Indians Wear Red"*; Coulthard, *Red Skin, White Masks*.

29 Wolfe, *Settler Colonialism and the Transformation of Anthropology*.

30 Woroniak and Camfield, "Choosing Not to Look Away."

31 Anderson and Robertson, *Seeing Red*; Barker, "The Contemporary Reality of Canadian Imperialism"; Bell, "Recognition or Ethics?"; Brigg, "Biopolitics Meets Terrapolitics"; Coulthard, *Red Skin, White*

Masks; Howard-Wagner and Kelly, "Containing Aboriginal Mobility in the Northern Territory"; Pels, "The Anthropology of Colonialism"; Cavanagh and Veracini, *The Routledge Handbook of the History of Settler Colonialism*; Wolfe, *Settler Colonialism and the Transformation of Anthropology*; Morgensen, "The Biopolitics of Settler Colonialism."

32 Simpson, *Mohawk Interruptus*.

33 Anderson and Robertson, *Seeing Red*; Episkenew, *Taking Back Our Spirits*.

34 See edited volume by Greenwood, de Leeuw, Lindsay, and Reading, *Determinants of Indigenous Peoples' Health in Canada*; Bourassa, McKay-McNabb and Hampton, "Racism, Sexism and Colonialism."

35 Anderson, *Home in the City*.

36 Razack, *Dying from Improvement;* Comack, Deane, Morrisette, and Silver, *"Indians Wear Red."*

37 Comack, Deane, Morrisette, and Silver, *"Indians Wear Red."*

38 Cooke and Bélanger, "Migration Theories and First Nations Mobility"; Norris and Clatworthy, "Urbanization and Migration Patterns of Aboriginal Populations in Canada"; Williams, "Canadian Urban Aboriginals."

39 Williams, "Canadian Urban Aboriginals."

40 Comack, Deane, Morrisette, and Silver, *"Indians Wear Red,"* 59.

41 Tadiar, "Life-Times in Fate Playing," 785.

42 Tait, Henry, and Loewen Walker, "Child Welfare."

43 Manitoba Family Services, *Annual Report 2015–2016*.

44 Fumagalli and Mezzadra, *Crisis in the Global Economy*; Marazzi, *The Violence of Financial Capitalism*.

45 Coulthard, *Red Skin, White Masks*.

46 Wright, "The Dialectics of Still Life."

47 Tadiar, "Life-Times in Fate Playing"; Wright, "Dialectics of Still Life."

48 Ibid.

49 Ibid., 789.

50 Hughes, *The Legacy of Phoenix Sinclair*.

51 Ibid.

52 Manitoba Family Services, *Annual Report 2005–2006*.

53 Ibid., *Annual Report 2015–2016*.

54 Ibid., *Annual Report 2005–2006*; ibid., *Annual Report 2015–2016*.

55 Hughes, *The Legacy of Phoenix Sinclair*, 448–49.

56 Ibid., 449.

57 Brownell, "Children in Care and Child Maltreatment in Manitoba."

58 By "First Nations children" here, we are referring to those children who have status as "Indians" under Canada's Indian Act, to whom the federal government has responsibilities consistent with its jurisdiction under Canada's constitution acts. Jurisdictional disputes arise as a result of the fact that while the federal government has legal obligations to "status Indians," including providing funding for government services for those children residing on reserves, the provinces have jurisdiction regarding the provision of child welfare services in both on- and off-reserve communities. It has not been uncommon for disputes to arise between provincial and federal governments regarding the provision and funding of services, leaving children vulnerable to a lack of services.

59 Hughes, *The Legacy of Phoenix Sinclair*, 2:390.

60 *First Nations Child and Family Caring Society of Canada et al. v. Attorney General of Canada*, par. 21 and 69.

61 Tait, Henry, and Loewen Walker, "Child Welfare."

62 Razack, *Dying from Improvement*.

63 Tadiar, "Life-Times in Fate Playing," 789.

64 Ibid., 791.

65 Manitoba's Children's Advocate, *Annual Report: April 1st 2000–March 31st 2001*.

66 See Burnside, *Safe for Today*.

67 For discussion of a similar case, see Jackson and Flett, "Manitoba's CFS Girls."

68 May, "Teen Sentenced for Parkade Attack That Left Girl with Permanent Injuries."

69 Ibid.

70 Ibid.

71 Ibid.

72 Legal Aid Manitoba, *Notice to the Profession*.

73 Brainfeed TV, 2016.

74 As cited in Swadener and Lubeck, *Children and Families "At Promise."*

75 The Children's Research Center is a section of the U.S.-based National Council on Crime and Delinquency. The council's website claims that: "since 1907, NCCD has been applying research to policy and practice in criminal justice, juvenile justice, and child welfare. By formulating innovative approaches to public safety and advising hundreds of agencies on effective and cost-efficient policies, strategies, and programs, our studies and policy recommendations continue to revolutionize the field."

76 Hughes, *The Legacy of Phoenix Sinclair,* 353.

77 Ibid., 357.

78 Ibid., 356.

79 Ibid., 361.

80 Ibid.

81 Ibid.

82 Ibid.

83 Kleinman, Das, and Locke, "Introduction."

84 Ibid., xii.

85 Yanagisako and Delaney, "Naturalizing Power."

86 Hughes, *The Legacy of Phoenix Sinclair*, 451.

87 Puxley, "Report about Murdered Teen Tina Fontaine to Be Kept Secret."

88 Razack, "Sexualized Violence and Colonialism."

89 Razack, "Gendered Racial Violence and Spatialized Justice"; Pan et al., "The Cedar Project."

90 Jiwani and Young, "Missing and Murdered Women"; Jiwani, "Symbolic and Discursive Violence in Media Representations of Aboriginal Missing and Murdered Women."

91 de Leeuw and Greenwood, "Geographies of Indigenous Children and Youth."

CHAPTER NINE

"I CLAIM IN THE NAME OF . . ."

Indigenous Street Gangs and Politics of Recognition in Prairie Cities

ROBERT HENRY

For almost thirty years, Indigenous street gangs have captured the imagination of Western Canada, representing the violence and unpredictability found within urban spaces through their deviant activities.[1] Such depictions reinforce long-standing colonial ideologies of Indigenous people as dangerous, uncivilized, and "in need" of wholesale state-sanctioned interventions to "correct" their immoral and deviant behaviour in order to "rescue" or save Indigenous people.[2] Indeed, popular constructions of Indigenous bodies have reinforced and continue to reinforce settler colonial ideologies where Indigenous people are seen to lack morality, where childlike and later violent behaviours must be controlled, most often through police actions and surveillance, to remove and protect settler society.[3] Adjectives such as hyper-violent, unpredictable, skid row, addict, and urban terrorist are continually (re)used to create images of Indigenous gangsters and the urban neighbourhoods they occupy.[4] Such descriptions reinforce the need for and support of heightened state violence and violent removal of Indigenous people from urban spaces.[5]

Over the past two decades, issues related to Indigenous street gangs across the Prairie provinces of Canada have garnered local and national media attention.[6] These news reports depict Indigenous gangs and their members as a "disease" or "epidemic" that plague both rural and urban communities.[7] Such sensationalized journalism relies on what Simon Hallsworth and Tara Young describe as "gang talkers" and "gang talk," where "experts" exaggerate and misrepresent the narratives and experiences of those living in neighbourhoods labelled as gang infested.[8] This type of journalism feeds the collective social imaginary that such neighbourhoods and their inhabitants are to be feared because they represent social decay and are constant reminders of the long-standing impacts of colonization. It has also led to local gang strategies that focus on specific neighbourhoods and those, particularly racialized and Indigenous people, who reside within them.[9]

Indigenous gangs and their members are described by some researchers to live nasty, brutish, and short lives.[10] Thus, Indigenous street gang members are often understood to be living in states of constant violence and trauma.[11] Such perspectives support the need of state-sanctioned violence to remove and control Indigenous bodies, much in the same way cultures of terror[12] and fear are used to control those who are deemed out of place.[13] Therefore, similar to the depiction of Indigenous peoples as savage and uncivilized during the early colonial period and the colonization of the Prairie provinces, today the gang member has become the body to be feared and controlled, supporting the need for state-sanctioned violence, most often conducted through policing policies.[14] However, what is most often missing from discussions on urban Indigenous street gangs is how their presence challenges settler colonialism as they claim urban spaces through territorialization. Street gangs have created ways to claim space within urban Prairie cities through what I term a street politics of recognition, where Indigenous gang members utilize space through visual ownership as well as through their bodies. However, because of their connections to the underground illegal economies, recognition is coded in order to remain hidden from the broader community. This results in the creation and adaptation of local street codes to allow Indigenous street gang members opportunities to increase their economic and social capital.

This chapter examines how Indigenous street gangs and their members paradoxically challenge and reinforce settler colonialism. Examining two photovoice research projects that include both Indigenous men and women who were involved in street gangs, I show how their presence and actions are necessary for settler state apparatuses such as the police and justice systems to continue to control and remove Indigenous bodies, but also how the gangs challenge settler colonialism as they reclaim urban space through their presence. I begin with a discussion on street gang set space and the politics involved in the development of such spaces. Next I discuss the impacts of photovoice research, its implications with Indigenous street gang members, and its impact in understanding the lived realities of those living a street lifestyle. I then move to the findings of two photovoice studies conducted with Indigenous men and women who were once involved with street gangs and the street lifestyle. Specifically, I examine how settler colonialism and specific socio-political histories have come to create and shape Indigenous urban gang set space in two cities in the province of Saskatchewan, Saskatoon and Regina. To conclude, I propose that a deeper examination into Indigenous street gangs is needed, one outside of criminal justice perspectives, in order to address violence and trauma within core urban neighbourhoods. This includes a discussion on how engagement in street gangs creates a double bind: violent actions are validated through one's involvement within a street gang in order to survive, but this violence in turn supports increased colonial violence, since all Indigenous bodies are presumed to be violent gang members until proven otherwise.

STREET GANG SET SPACE AND THE PRAIRIE CITY

Street gang set space is defined both by the demarcated boundaries through the use of space and specific points of interest where individuals come together to form their gang.[15] According to Elijah Anderson, the street has its own codes, literacies, values, and norms that must be understood by those who engage daily within the space in order to protect themselves from potential violence.[16] Through state policies and police surveillance, Indigenous people's movements have been restricted, controlling the neighbourhoods where they should reside.[17] These spaces have a history of being labelled as violent and unpredictable because of the high rates of poverty and perceived issues of addictions associated with these spaces. As a result of settler polices and police surveillance, many Indigenous people who move to cities have to move to impoverished neighbourhoods or those not yet gentrified, as these offer low rental rates and are mired in entrenched racialized poverty. The movement of Indigenous people to such spaces is strategic, helping to maintain symbolic borders that divide those who are good and contribute to the progression of the city from those who are criminal or viewed as a burden to society. Through the concentration of Indigenous people to neighbour-hoods of extreme racialized poverty, we see how meritocracy within settler colonial logic helps to maintain those historical constructions of Indigenous people who need to be guided or controlled because they are considered lazy, childlike, and violent.

To understand those groups of individuals who are constructed as street gangs, an examination of their history and growth across Saskatchewan is necessary, as gangs are seen to be a by-product of macro-historical and macro-structural processes of exclusion.[18] Therefore, specific communities—which experience heightened levels of racialized poverty[19]—are labelled as gang infested, and those residing within as under gang control. The term "gang" is also ambiguous and often used by media and society as a floating signifier to identify both pro-social and deviant groups;[20] however, with its connection to violence, addictions, and those outside of the law, the gang label has become a political tool for impinging on the rights of low socio-economic, racialized Others.[21] As a result, people and communities become labelled as lawless, constructing a de facto status whereby class and racial identities become imprinted on their bodies, which carry specific social labels that are used to validate, in the context of the urban Prairie West, the removal and erasure of Indigenous people under the guise of protectionism.[22]

The focus on class and race as identifying factors to street gang involve-ment can be found in the research of the early twentieth-century Chicago School.[23] Frederic Thrasher's 1927 ethnographic work on 1,313 street gangs, which laid the groundwork for street gang research, depicted the lives of immigrant and working poor male youth in the inner city of Chicago.[24] For Thrasher and other early gang researchers, the gang "was above all to be studied in the context of the physical processes and changing shape of the modern city, with Chicago as the universal model."[25] Thus, the gang needed to be understood as a part of the whole city and not as a microcosm unto itself.

Within the context of Saskatchewan and the Prairie provinces of Canada, Indigenous street gangs are considered a more recent phenomenon.[26] Although Indigenous drinking groups and small gangs of male youth are reported in the media as early as the 1960s, the development of Indigenous-based street gangs such as the Indian Posse, Native Syndicate, Warriors, Redd Alert, and others did not occur till the late 1980s and early '90s. These groups of marginalized Indigenous youth, with similar histories of involvement in the child welfare system, early contact with the justice system, experiences of entrenched poverty, and poor education opportunities, first formed on the city streets of Winnipeg.[27]

In his biography of Daniel Wolfe, one of the founders of the Indian Posse, Joe Friesen explains how such experiences of violence and removal that were concentrated in the North End of Winnipeg brought the youth together because of their shared experiences.[28] Banding together, the youth looked to each other in order to survive within a hostile urban environment. Modelling their new group around the growing American street gang model and earlier gangs of Winnipeg such as the Main Street Rattlers, Daniel Wolfe, his brother Richard, and their friends sought to gain status through the building of fear through physical violence. However, the Indian Posse, like other Indigenous gangs at the time and those that have followed, used its Indigeneity to connect to the urban environments as well as to differentiate itself from other gangs, for quick and rapid recruitment.[29] As Friesen notes:

> The branding was effective. The Indian Posse represented a kind
> of raised fist rebellion for teenagers desperate to be connected to
> something bigger than themselves ... perhaps the name or the colours
> of the idea of belonging ... touched a chord within [I]ndigenous
> youth in the city. It was hip hop and urban at a time when those trends
> were taking off in music and movies. Though they barely had time
> to establish many rules, there was one that they immediately put into
> effect: only [I]ndigenous people could join. ... For the gang's leadership
> structure the founders chose the circle, a symbol of central significance
> for [I]ndigenous people.[30]

The Indigenous street gangs that formed on the streets of Winnipeg during the 1980s and 1990s became a tool for often impressionable Indigenous youth to not only find a place to belong but also to resist their marginalized positions. By bringing together their collective marginality, the youth created an identity for laying claim to urban territories that sought to remove them. Over a short period of time, Indigenous street gangs have expanded across Canada as Indigenous youth and young adults joined street gangs as a way to survive and resist their marginalized status within hostile urban environments.

When street gangs expand to new locations, new groups also form as individuals band together around common histories as well as connections to location.[31] When Indigenous gangs expand, not all youth are recruited to join, which results in the formation of new gangs.[32] The new gangs use different colours, names, and tags to identify and distinguish themselves from other gangs while at the same time remaining hidden from others in the community not involved in local underground economies.

USING PHOTOVOICE IN INDIGENOUS STREET GANG RESEARCH

You don't make a photograph with just your camera. You bring to the act of photography all the pictures you have seen, the books, you have read, the music you have heard, the people you have loved.[33]

Caroline Wang and Mary Ann Burris developed the photovoice research method while trying to understand experiences of health inequalities of rural Chinese women.[34] Wang and Burris describe photovoice as a "process by which people can identify, represent, and enhance their community through a specific photographic technique."[35] Photovoice is a transformational research process in which participants become the experts of their realities as they show researchers and outside community members how they have come to understand specific social justice issues. Thus, photovoice is intended to be a reflective process, providing both researcher and participant the opportunity to learn from one another through dialogue.[36]

Photovoice methods have been used most extensively within health research to examine the lived realities of marginalized people in an effort to create positive policy changes for those most impacted. As a research method, photovoice has three overarching goals: to provide space for communities to reflect on a specific phenomenon from their perspective; to promote critical dialogue; and to influence policy makers for effective change in the community.[37] Theoretically, Wang and Burris position photovoice close to feminist and critical race theories, Friere's concepts of critical consciousness and transformative pedagogy, and to non-traditional documentary photography. Weaving these elements together, photovoice provides participants with a platform to challenge dominant discourses, where knowledge about a phenomenon shifts to privileging a participant's lived experiences, where they become the experts of their experiences.

Photovoice research has expanded beyond the health field and is now being used across multiple disciplines to examine an array of issues. Much of this research continues to focus on the experiences of marginalized populations; however, a growing number of research projects are using photovoice as a way to engage with children and youth.[38] As the popularity of photovoice increases across disciplines, some questions, have been raised about its ability to shift or encourage social justice change. For example, the impact that photovoice has on the promotion of social justice has not been evaluated for its effectiveness. Second, there is limited information on photovoice's impact on the ethical issues related to privacy, anonymity, and confidentiality.[39] However, despite such concerns, photovoice methods have proven to be an effective tool to explore social issues from the perspectives of individuals' lived experience.

As a research method, photovoice is a novel approach for critical gang researchers, as it can challenge the preconceived hyper-violent "gangster" image sensationalized over time by journalists and researchers.[40] By providing cameras to those who have engaged in the street gang lifestyle, a counter-narrative is created that challenges preconceived notions of street gang spaces, of consistent violence, and marginalized spaces. Photovoice methods thus have the potential to move beyond the hyper-violent gangster image, creating a critical consciousness for researchers, community members, and policy makers.[41]

For this chapter, photovoice methods are used to comprehend how Indigenous ex–gang members make use of urban space in the cities of Regina and Saskatoon to claim territory for their respective street gang. Both cities are noted for having high urban Indigenous populations, where Indigenous people constitute 9 percent (Saskatoon) and 8 percent (Regina) of all city residents.[42] The Indigenous population continues to be one of the fastest-growing population in both cities, with high birth rates and migration of Indigenous people to urban centres from reserve and rural communities. Indigenous people move to cities for a variety of reasons, such as education and employment opportunities, which are not as readily available on reserves or in rural communities. However, because the majority of those who migrate to Saskatoon and Regina often have limited economic capital, they often find themselves living in what are known as and identified by residents as "core" neighbourhoods. These core neighbourhoods are associated with high rates of poverty, subsidized housing, and poor infrastructure, along with high rates of violence and criminal activities. In Saskatoon the core neighbourhoods are located on the "Westside," an area bounded by Idylwyld Drive, 11th Street, Circle Drive, and 33rd Street. In Regina, the neighbourhoods are located in North Central. This area is known for heightened levels of violence, poverty, and addictions.[43] The result, then, is increased levels of police surveillance within such neighbourhoods, because they have been constructed as spaces of terror that are feared by those outside of the community.[44]

I now turn to two photovoice research projects conducted with Indigenous men and women who were involved in street gangs in Saskatoon and Regina. Through narratives and photographs, I show how Indigenous street gang presence becomes a space of survivance for those who participate, providing opportunities for members to increase their economic and social capital, which they are normally denied as a result of settler colonialism. However, because the street space is mired in violence and Indigenous bodies are seen to be violent, vanishing, and in need of control, Indigenous street gang members' bodies are used as a settler colonial tool as "proof" of the need to increase surveillance and police presence on and within Indigenous urban spaces. The participants explain how they used urban spaces to expand their influence and control of local underground economies. The control and claiming of urban spaces was accomplished by different modes of street literacy that included clothing and colours, physical occupation of spaces, and tagging. Through local street codes and street literacy, participants show how their involvement in street gangs provided them with opportunities to engage in local underground economies through their presences while at the same time remaining hidden from the majority of the urban population.

EXPERIENCES OF TERRITORIALIZATION AND INDIGENOUS STREET GANGS IN TWO SASKATCHEWAN CITIES

Indigenous street gangs are a by-product of macro-historical and macro-structural forces that have shaped and limited access to economic capital.[45] With limited economic opportunities, individuals who live in communities that are highly devoid of economic opportunities to sustain a livelihood (those paying above minimum wage) look to local underground/illegal economies to supplement their incomes.[46] Sociologist Jock Young surmised that society presumes that marginalized communities do not adhere to middle-class values (e.g., hard work, capitalism); however, he concluded that those living

Figure 9.1. Photo of the new Saskatoon police station under construction. This photo taken by Baldhead in 2013 shows the police station being built on Idylwyld Drive, the street that defines the beginning of Saskatoon's Westside.

Figure 9.2. Photo of Ashworth Holmes Park. Kinuis took this photo to show the park and area that he and his crew controlled.

in core neighbourhoods are actually deeply invested in capitalism, but their marginalized status limits any positive involvement: "The problem of the ghetto was not so much the process of it being simply excluded but rather one that was all too strongly included in the culture but, then, systematically excluded from its realization."[47]

Street gangs then become an avenue or institution for some who live in core neighbourhoods as a way to increase their economic capital through involvement within illegal underground economies, as long as they are willing to "put in the necessary work."[48] Because the work is outside of the law, violence becomes a tool to control, protect, and increase one's investment.[49] As a result, core communities become targets of hyper-surveillance to support gentrification policies, which for urban Indigenous people are woven through settler colonial logics of renewal.[50] With hyper-surveillance working to limit participation in underground economies, Indigenous street gangs in Saskatoon and Regina have developed a myriad of ways to use city spaces as a way to claim territory while also trying to stay hidden in plain sight.

Through their expansion and increase in number, Indigenous street gangs have moved beyond street corner models of territorialization[51] to encompass blocks and whole neighbourhoods. Gangs and their members move in and around the neighbourhoods laying claim to the space for the use of the gang.

> We'd steal, rob, sell drugs, and we'd fight all the time. We held down the Caswell area. That was our 'hood. Everyone knew it as a Crip neighbourhood. (Kinuis)

> Because they always had to keep NS out, had to keep IP out and K's dad always said you guys don't need a name, just need to stick together as bro's, this is your 'hood, this is your territory, nobody steps on it. (Bev)

If territories are encroached on by outsiders, violence is often used and validated to support takeovers, or to stop encroachment from rivals and others outside of the neighbourhood.

> That was some funny fuckin' shit man and Apollo got taken out 'cause uh, shit happened afterwards but and they kicked a lot of Apollos out and they kept the ones that they want. So, the ones that they want had to strike now, so they tried to come into the fuckin' 'hood and take over. They got maybe six blocks in man, and three of them ended up getting shot right off their bikes and shit, man. It didn't last too long man, but

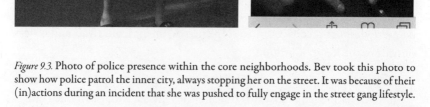

Figure 9.3. Photo of police presence within the core neighborhoods. Bev took this photo to show how police patrol the inner city, always stopping her on the street. It was because of their (in)actions during an incident that she was pushed to fully engage in the street gang lifestyle.

Figure 9.4. Photo of street gang member in Regina. Dave took this photo to show how a gang member indentifies himself with his colours and signs.

Figure 9.5. Facebook photo of gang members posing. Faith took this photo to show the connections of the gang to family, as well as how individuals pose with their colours and gang signs.

nothing ever happened about it. They just went their own way and
stayed out of the 'hood. (Dale)

To keep whoever out of the territory, to you know, when your rivalries
are around, or do shut downs, there is like so much stuff. If you
find out IP is in your territory, you go to that house, and you do a
shutdown. (Bev)

It didn't matter. You keep—if you had— if you had —if you had this—
you had one block—you had two blocks—you go roll on their block.
You fuckin' show them. You tell 'em this is the way it is. This is the way
it's gonna be or we're gonna just fuckin' bust out man. (Adam)

Protection of territory is extremely important because the gangs that
control particular blocks have access to underground economies that provide
capital for the gang and its members to purchase goods and pay members a
wage. The larger one's territory, the greater income for the gang, leading to
increased status within the neighbourhood. Territorial protection is then integral for street gangs to maintain control and power within neighbourhoods.

The violence that street gang members enact, though, is not as random
as is depicted within public media, whose reports have led to heightened
police presence and overpolicing of Indigenous bodies and communities.[52]
Rather, street codes frame the actions and reactions within the underground
economies, leading to what Bruce Jacobs and Richard Wright define as street
justice.[53] Street justice is used because those who are involved in underground
economies do not have access to police and the law, since the actions that led
to the altercation are most often part of the underground economy. Thus, to
maintain respect, status, and control of specific territories, Indigenous street
gang members have to react in ways that adhere to local codes of street justice
in order to maintain their authority.

Street codes also help to demarcate those who belong and those who
do not.[54] With increased surveillance in these neighbourhoods, street gang
members and others who live in the neighbourhoods or frequent them often
must have an understanding of the local street codes in order to navigate safely
within these areas.[55] Often this is accomplished through the use of colours
and styles of dress to connect to their gang as well as differentiate from others
in the community:

[T]he first things that you have to take a look at, is how do they look, or what are they doing? The majority of the time when you see gang members when they walk is, what they wear within their collars, within their wristbands, or in their pockets, or legs of pants. Are there a couple of people dressed the same. Are there a couple of people wearing the same hats. At least a couple, are they wearing it the same way.... And one of the certain things that you always look for is the colour of the shoelaces, shoelaces, what they wear for earrings. Crazy Cree have different types of earrings of what they wear, you know, and where they wear it, and the colour patches within their clothes.[56]

Therefore, it is not simply a matter of wearing colours or clothing but the way they are worn that assigns membership. This is because much of the clothing and styles of clothing are derived from popular hip hop culture. Clothing companies such as Crooks & Castle, Diamond, and even sports teams with colours and numbers become encoded with messages of which gang or neighbourhood one belongs to. When an individual is brought into a gang they are given its flag (bandana) which they are to use to represent their allegiance.

I was all decked out in white and black and I had bandanas all over my neck, on my feet, on my legs, on my arms, like I represented to the fullest. (Shay)

Well I don't know. Gangster is someone that wears their colours hard and wears their tag.... Just like when you see them you'll know them ... and they wear their colour hard and they're dressed in their colours. (James)

The importance of the bandana, flag, or rag is something that must be respected by all gang members, as it is their connection to the gang and to get one, one must prove one's loyalty. Shay later explains an incident where she lent one of her rags to a girl who was not as respected as she was in the eyes of her "higher up":

I remember there was times my higher up would get mad at me. I remember I got a licking one time for lending one of my bandanas to Tammy, and he got really mad. I remember going to his house and he seen Tammy wearing that bandana. I was wearing a bandana around my neck and he jumped over the fence and he grabbed me by my bandana,

Figure 9.6. Photo of street gang member in Regina. Bonks took this photo to show how he dressed while going on a mission, wearing his bandana to cover his face.

Figure 9.7. Group photo of gang. Bev took this photo to show how the gang she belonged to was first made up of childhood friends and relatives who grew up together and later organized themselves into a gang as a way to control a portion of the illegal economy and keep other gangs from entering their neighbourhood.

> I remember he was real close to my face and he said, "I told you not to
> fucking give your rags away." I remember thinking, holy this chick is
> supposed to be down. And I got a licking for that. (Shay)

Bandanas and colours, therefore, are important in differentiating those who
belong from those who do not. Street gangs then develop specific styles of
dress, which can be adapted to shifting styles of dress and pop culture. As
such, street gangs become very much involved within capitalistic economies
as they promote themselves to others in the community.

As gang members move in and around their community, their colours and
bandanas that they prominently show are used to pronounce their territory.
By displaying their colours and moving around their neighbourhoods, street
gang members begin to lay claim to a territory. By "being present," Indigenous
street gang members actively engage in a street politics of recognition,[57] albeit
within local street spaces. Here Indigenous gang members have the opportunity to make themselves known and assert a presence within and across
urban neighbourhoods.

> Being noticed on the block is how we used to do it. Just seeing a guy
> walking down the street with his flag hanging down his side, you know
> what I mean. That's how we used to do that and people would know
> that that was our spot. (Bonks)

> Then I'd wear my colour around—see someone else wearin' my colour
> then go fight them or pull a knife on them and there was always
> violence. And it was just like my new—my new set of mind was like
> fuckin'—yeah nobody wanted fuckin' around on my streets and shit
> and so if I seen anybody wearin' red I would go take them out and twist
> 'em up or something, stomp them and take their red off them and stuff
> like that. (James)

Protecting and asserting claim to territory through one's presence creates
an active space of recognition. Street gang members use their bodies in ways
that provide a status of recognition, both for individuals and for their gang,
which aids in the control of their territory.[58] However, being present in
their colours is not always considered wise, since it increases the chances of
becoming recognized by police. Therefore, tagging and other forms of physical markings become forms of street literacy to identify borders, providing

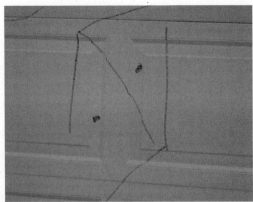

Figure 9.8. Photo of Native Syndicate tag. Dave took this photo to show how the Native Syndicate used tags to mark their territory.

Figure 9.9. Photo of gang tag. Jay took this photo to show a gang tag on a garage door in her old neighbourhood.

Figure 9.10. Photo of commemorative wall. Baldhead took this photo to show how his brother, who died in a car accident, was commemorated.

warnings to those who want to encroach and cross borders to extend their own territories.

Tagging is the most common form of street literacy. A tag can best be understood within Indigenous street gang culture as a symbol that identifies one street gang from another. Tags are often placed strategically in neighbourhoods to designate space that is claimed by a particular gang.

> We never really, I was never into tagging, like you know what I mean, like stuff mostly just the young guys running around, marking territories, here and there. Letting them know that we're here in this area, in this neighbourhood. (Bonks)

When asked the significance of the tag, Jay explained:

> Native Syndicate, it was supposed to be a sign of power. I guess I would say an affiliation. It was a territory you know? NS people go there you know? (Jay)

The result, much like the way in which Western imperialist countries sought to divide the globe for expansion and resources for the "Mother country," is that street gangs use tags to claim territory within and across neighbourhoods as a way to assert their ownership and control of the resources.

Tagging is also used by street gang members as a way of commemorating individuals who have lost their lives. Buildings and structures that have a connection to an individual are used to carry on their legacy even after they had passed on. For example, Baldhead talks about how his brother lost his life in a car accident but is remembered by those in the community through his tag, which is displayed on buildings, structures, and trees within the neighbourhood.

> My brother's tags. My deceased little brother, JS. He was actually just starting to go down that route, and I left the gang. I told him, IWA, I walk alone. I really drove it into him. I think he was affiliated, but when he passed away he was down with nobody and I was proud. You know I was proud that he yeah. JS, yeah. I tagged that up like this is the alley where I found him abandoned him in the alley. He got in a car crash and like from the impact they left him in the alley and I found him and then . . . I found him so I thought I would just spray paint his name then his friends came along and they put love forever and one of

Figure 9.11. Photo of shoes over powerlines. Dave took this photo to show the symbolism shoes have when placed over powerlines. In Regina, shoes thrown over in this manner are a way to show which colours are not wanted in the neighbourhood. This functions as a warning sign to others as to which street gang and colours are allowed within the borders.

Figure 9.12. Photo of Adidas shoes over powerlines. Baldhead took this photo to demonstrate his connection to his brother. In Saskatoon, shoes are used as a way to commemorate an individual's life and are placed where an individual has died or where they were known to hang out.

them put 425, I WA 'cause exactly that's how he died was walking alone, yeah. (Baldhead)

As evident through Baldhead's narrative, even after individuals have been lost to the street lifestyle, there are ways to remember them and recognize their lives.

Another symbol of recognition within street spaces is through shoes thrown over the top of powerlines. Shoes are both a sign of status, as they reflect economic capital, and a way to distinguish between street gangs.

> When I was a little kid having good shoes was important to me— having nice shoes, so I was having a lot of shoes and shoes are expensive, so I would just steal anything to get enough money to buy a pair. Even if I had to steal all day just to get a pair I would do that. Like go steal a bunch of things here sell it for ten bucks, go here steal another thing, get another twenty—thirty dollars and just add it up and go get myself some new shoes or a new shirt or something I wanted. I would get it even the fact that I had to steal all day just to get it. (James)

Shoes hold symbolic and cultural value across local street codes. They are used both as a way to identify territory as well as to commemorate those who may have lost their lives at a particular place. In the context of violence, shoes are removed from rivals who encroach on another street gang's territory. In this context, the shoes become warning signs for others as to which colours are allowed or not allowed within a neighbourhood. As another form of recognition, shoes from an individual who died either through gang violence or an accident (e.g., hit by a vehicle) are placed over powerlines as a way of remembrance, functioning much the same as a tombstone.

> There's a close-up. Shoes hanging from our neighbourhood. That means our neighbourhood and those are, you know, old kicks. (Baldhead)

Shoes are used as a sign of status for those who can afford the right brands. Therefore, street gangs and their members search out ways to participate in consumerism as they use specific brands to show their status within the neighbourhood. However, because of the cultural capital that shoes represent, they also increase potential violence to those who are members of Indigenous street gangs or those presumed to be members by their race, location, style of dress, and colour of clothing. At the same time that shoes are sought after, they are also used to mark territories and pay respects to those who have lost their lives within the neighbourhood. The narratives of the shoes provide examples of how Indigenous street gangs engage both within capitalism and in street politics of recognition.

THEORIZING SETTLER COLONIALISM AND CREATING INDIGENOUS URBAN GANG SET SPACE

Settler colonialism differs from other forms of colonialism because capital taken from the land remains in the settler state rather than being sent back to the metropole.[59] To accomplish this, settlers must erase Indigenous peoples and their presence from the land in order to claim the land as their own. Through physical and political erasure, the intentions of the settler were and are the destruction of Indigenous peoples in order to replace or rebuild the territory in accordance with the settler's vision. Thus settler colonialism, as Patrick Wolfe notes, must be understood as a structure and not as an event located in the past.[60] The intentions of colonialism/imperialism and then settler colonialism were to first exploit resources (peoples and nature), then through Western international laws (see Doctrine of Discovery and *terra nullius*) erase Indigenous presence in order to validate settler possession and nation building of a moral and just society. In this way, settler colonialism eliminates via amalgamation and replacement.[61]

Wolfe's "logic of elimination" is animated by violence, as Indigenous bodies were and are removed from their lands to make room for the burgeoning settler state.[62] Through violent experiences of removal such as relocation in the United States,[63] to more insidious measures such as exposure to trade goods carrying pathogens,[64] to forced residential school attendance[65] and now child welfare policies,[66] Indigenous bodies and territories have experienced and continue to experience heightened levels of violence by the settler state. Through settler colonial violence enacted on Indigenous bodies, Scott Morgensen asserts that "settler colonialism performs biopower in deeply historical and fully contemporary ways."[67] However, what also must be made clear is that these attacks did not happen all at once, nor have all Indigenous peoples experienced colonialism in the same way or have the same length of history with settler colonialism. Rather, as expansion moved westward across what is now Canada, the ways in which settler colonialism was enacted shifted. But the intent remained: to remove Indigenous peoples and make room for the increased settler population that would tame and civilize the vast open prairies.[68]

Emma LaRocque discusses how Indigenous peoples have been constructed within a civilized/savage dichotomy.[69] Through her work on the ways Indigenous peoples have been portrayed within literary works, LaRoque explains how Indigenous bodies were represented as "savage" or amoral in relation to white settler bodies. This construction was also gendered, as Indigenous men were viewed as violent savage warriors and Indigenous women depicted as "squaws." Indigenous people were also dichotomized as "noble warriors" (men) and "Indian princesses" (women). As such, certain Indigenous bodies were valued for what they portrayed to the nation building of the settler state.[70] While the focus of violence to Indigenous men was in relation to the violence that they inflicted on others, violence was enacted upon Indigenous women through the "squaw" label, as their bodies were and are easily sexually exploited.[71] Both the savage warrior and squaw constructions stigmatized Indigenous bodies, allowing for the use of violence to control as well as erase Indigenous people from spaces. Both constructions depicted Indigenous people as lazy, violent, and animal-like. In other words, use of these constructions permitted and continues to permit settler colonial violence to be inflicted onto Indigenous bodies by deeming them to be "worthless." Violence can then be validated as a way to assault, dispose, and remove Indigenous peoples.[72]

Today, the savage and the squaw constructions have become representative of Indigenous people in urban spaces who are connected to street lifestyles marred with poverty, violence, and addictions. Sherene Razack sees such urban spaces as racialized territories, where Indigenous bodies can be attacked with impunity by the state and its actors.[73] As Razack contends, such racialized spaces impact all Indigenous people, as their bodies are viewed to be disposable, even if an individual is not connected to the space. The result is the ability of settler peoples to assert dominion over these spaces and over those who reside within them through hyper-violence, sanctioned by settler states.[74] It is within these racialized spaces that Mbembe's necropolitics[75] and Foucault's biopower[76] concepts work together to validate the erasure of those bodies deemed to be dead or dying.[77] François Debrix and Alexander Barder state that Foucault's notion of biopower is embedded within state mechanisms, specifically race, in an effort to eliminate, purify, and exercise sovereign power. Thus, biopower is the process of the state to construct, classify, and relate to the life of the Other; validating the abnormal, subhuman, or even non-human bodies and characteristics to construct a violent enemy[78]—an enemy that can be disposed of in ways that the settler state would view as inhumane if inflicted on themselves. The removal, erasure, and deaths of Indigenous people then become rationalized by the settler state, simply because of their being Indigenous.[79] Urban streets become proximal zones where the settler state can, through its own laws and actions, be actively supported to exert violence onto Indigenous people under the guise of protection from their potential and perceived acts of violence.

With their connection to underground and illegal economies, street gangs and their members also help those who are willing and able to increase their economic stability, providing them opportunities to participate in urban capitalism. However, because the underground economy is outside of the protection of the law, violence is used and validated as a way to protect and increase a gang's investment through territorialization. Thus, the image and perceived presence of the Indigenous street gang member aids in the validation of state-sanctioned violence and removal of Indigenous people from urban spaces. This then results in a double bind for Indigenous street gang members, where the gang provides spaces of survivance while also supporting a settler colonial nostalgia for the "savage" who is unable to fully integrate into modern settler spaces.

CONCLUSION

Settler colonialism continues to impact Indigenous people, specifically in the ways in which Indigenous bodies are constructed as violent and a danger to the moral settler state. The result of this violence has impacted the mobility of Indigenous bodies, as increased surveillance and policing tactics control Indigenous movement across urban spaces, limiting many Indigenous people to reside within core impoverished neighbourhoods.[80] To survive and participate within capitalist economies, Indigenous people must find alternative ways to accumulate the economic capital necessary to survive and keep their families together. The street gang, with its connection to illegal underground economies, provides economic opportunities for those who are willing to engage in a hyper-violent masculine performance. Such a performance is needed to protect and increase a gang's territoriality, thereby increasing the gang's economic potential within the neighbourhood.

With their connection to the underground economy, and the illegality of its processes, street gangs have found ways to be both visible and invisible within their neighbourhoods. Thus they practise what I have come to understand as a street politics of recognition. Through street codes and street justice, the gangs create boundaries within core urban spaces as a way to lay claim to available and potential underground economies. By using a street literacy connected to clothing, colours, and symbols, street gang members claim space and move within their territories, the borders shared with other street gangs and the broader urban community. In doing so, Indigenous street gangs make use of urban landscapes and geographies in ways that claim an urban territorialization,[81] where identities and survivance are interconnected to local street politics of recognition.

Throughout this chapter I have shown how Indigenous street gangs have come to redefine urban spaces and become recognized, while at the same time remaining hidden from the broader urban population. The photographs and narratives of Indigenous gang members help to show those outside of such spaces how street gangs use urban spaces to increase their status and thus economic opportunities, in order to survive within core neighbourhoods. Through the claiming of core neighbourhoods, Indigenous street gangs increase potential avenues to accrue economic capital, and in turn social capital, because of their status and reputation within the neighbourhood. However, it is also important to recognize that those who are involved in underground economies do not have the full protection of the law when violence is acted upon them. To survive and protect themselves from further violence, street gang members must engage in street justice to maintain status within specific neighbourhoods. The violence that escalates from such altercations then supports increased state-sanctioned violence and the need to control the presumed violent Indigenous urban population, thereby reinforcing and entrenching settler colonial logics.

NOTES

1   Henry, "Through an Indigenous Lens"; Koch and Scherer, "Redd Alert!"; Sinclair and Grekul, "Aboriginal Youth Gangs in Canada."

2   LaRocque, *When the Other Is Me.*

3   Grekul and LaBoucane-Benson, "Aboriginal Gangs and Their (Dis)placement"; Henry, "Through an Indigenous Lens"; Sinclair and Grekul, "Aboriginal Youth Gangs in Canada."

4   Comack, *Racialized Policing*; Henry, "Moving beyond the Simple," 241; Henry, "Through an Indigenous Lens."

5   Henry, "Through an Indigenous Lens"; Koch and Scherer, "Redd Alert!"; LaRocque, *When the Other Is Me*; Razack, *Race, Space, and the Law*; Razack, *Dying from Improvement.*

6   Henry, "Through an Indigenous Lens."

7   Ibid.

8   Hallsworth and Young, "Gang Talk and Gang Talkers."

9   Henry, "Not Just Another Thug."

10 Totten, *Nasty, Brutish, and Short.*

11 Grekul and LaBoucane-Benson, "Aboriginal Gangs and Their (Dis)placement"; Sinclair and Grekul, "Aboriginal Youth Gangs in Canada."

12 Taussig, *Shamanism, Colonialism, and the Wild Man.*

13 Cacho, *Social Death*; Glassner, *The Culture of Fear.*

14 See Comack, this volume.

15 Taniguchi, Ratcliffe, and Taylor, "Gang Set Space, Drug Markets, and Crime"; Tita, Cohen, and Engberg, "An Ecological Study of the Location of Gang 'Set Space.'"

16 Anderson, *Code of the Street.*

17 Comack, Deane, Morrisette, and Silver, *"Indians Wear Red"*; Silver, "Complex Poverty and Home-Grown Solutions."

18 Henry, "Through an Indigenous Lens"; Vigil, *A Rainbow of Gangs.*

19 Comack, Deane, Morrisette, and Silver, *"Indians Wear Red."*

20 Hallsworth, *The Gang and Beyond.*

21 Cacho, *Social Death*; Wacquant, "Ghettos and Anti-Ghettos."

22 Cacho, *Social Death*; Comack, this volume; Wacquant, "Class, Race and Hyperincarceration"; White, "Indigenous Young People."

23 Hagedorn, "Gangs, Institutions, Race, and Space."

24 Thrasher, *The Gang.*

25 Hagedorn, "Gangs, Institutions, Race, and Space," 14.

26 Comack, Deane, Morrisette, and Silver, *"Indians Wear Red"*; Grekul and LaBoucane-Benson, "Aboriginal Gangs and Their (Dis)placement"; Henry, "Not Just Another Thug"; Henry, "Through an Indigenous Lens"; Sinclair and Grekul, "Aboriginal Youth Gangs in Canada."

27 Comack, Deane, Morrisette, and Silver, *"Indians Wear Red."*

28 Friesen, *The Ballad of Danny Wolfe.*

29   Buddle, "Urban Aboriginal Gangs and Street Sociality in the Canadian West"; Buddle, "An Aboriginal Youth Gang Narconomy."

30   Friesen, *The Ballad of Danny Wolfe.*

31   Wacquant, "Territorial Stigmatization"; White, "Disputed Definitions and Fluid Identities."

32   Henry, "Through an Indigenous Lens"; Henry, "Social Spaces of Maleness."

33   Ansel Adams, as quoted on Goodreads, http://www.goodreads.com/quotes/52291-you-don-t-makea-photograph-just-with-a-camera-you, retrieved 13 June 2014.

34   Wang, "Photovoice"; Wang, "Using Photovoice as a Participatory Assessment and Issue Selection Tool"; Wang and Burris, "Photovoice: Concept, Methodology, and Use."

35   Wang and Burris, "Photovoice: Concept, Methodology, and Use," 369.

36   Mitchell, *Doing Visual Research*; Wang and Burris, "Photovoice: Concept, Methodology, and Use."

37   Wang, "Photovoice"; Wang and Burris, "Photovoice: Concept, Methodology, and Use." See also Mitchell, *Doing Visual Research.*

38   First, Mills-Sandoval, First, and Houston, "Using Photovoice for Youth Resilience"; Helm et al., "Using Photovoice with Youth to Develop a Drug Prevention Program in a Rural Hawaiian Community."

39   Hannes and Parylo, "Let's Play it Safe: Ethical Considerations from Participants in a Photovoice Research Project."

40   Hallsworth, *The Gang and Beyond*; Henry, "Through an Indigenous Lens"; Rodriguez, "On the Subject of Gang Photography"; White, *Youth Gangs, Violence, and Social Respect.*

41   Henry, "Through an Indigenous Lens."

42   Statistics Canada, *Aboriginal Peoples in Canada: First Nations, Métis and Inuit; National Household Survey, 2011.*

43   Razack, "Gendered Racial Violence and Spatialized Justice."

44   LaPrairie, "Aboriginal Over-Representation in the Criminal Justice System."

45   Conchas and Vigil, "Multiple Marginality and Urban Education"; Fraser, *Urban Legends*; Klein and Maxson, *Street Gang Patterns and Policies*; Vigil, *A Rainbow of Gangs.*

46   Buddle, "An Aboriginal Youth Gang Narconomy"; Comack, Deane, Morrisette, and Silver, *"Indians Wear Red"*; Henry, "Through an Indigenous Lens."

47   Young, "Merton with Energy, Katz with Structure," 394.

48   Buddle, "An Aboriginal Youth Gang Narconomy"; Henry, "Through an Indigenous Lens."

49   Jacobs and Wright, *Street Justice.*

50   Simpson, *Mohawk Interruptus.*

51   Thrasher, *The Gang.*

52   Perry, *Policing Race and Place in Indian Country.*

53   Jacobs and Wright, *Street Justice.*

54   Anderson, *Code of the Street*; Garot, *Who You Claim?*

55   I want to note that particular individuals are protected, even if they do not understand local street codes. This is because race, class, and status (presumed to be associated with the state—police, teachers, social workers) play major roles within street codes. A middle-aged white male who is wearing nice clothes will be associated with the police and therefore will not have to be aware of the codes.

Thus, the social privilege that has created the concentration of Indigenous people in specific neighbourhoods continues to protect those who hold social capital outside of the neighbourhoods.

56 Henry, "Not Just Another Thug," 56.

57 Coulthard, *Red Skin, White Masks*.

58 Anderson, *Code of the Street*; Bourgois, *In Search of Respect*; Garot, *Who You Claim?*; Henry, "Through an Indigenous Lens."

59 Tuck and Yang, "Decolonization Is Not a Metaphor."

60 Wolfe, "Settler Colonialism and the Elimination of the Native."

61 Morgensen, "The Biopolitics of Settler Colonialism."

62 Kauanui, "'A Structure, Not an Event'"; Veracini, "Introducing Settler Colonial Studies"; Wolfe, "Settler Colonialism and the Elimination of the Native."

63 Barker, *Sovereignty Matters*.

64 Daschuk, *Clearing the Plains*.

65 Truth and Reconciliation Commission of Canada, *They Came for the Children*; de Leeuw, "'If Anything Is to Be Done with the Indian'"; MacDonald and Hudson, "The Genocide Question and Indian Residential Schools."

66 See Stewart and La Berge, this volume.

67 Morgensen, "Biopolitics of Settler Colonialism," 52.

68 Daschuk, *Clearing the Plains*.

69 LaRocque, *When the Other Is Me*.

70 Tuck and Yang, "Decolonization Is Not a Metaphor."

71 Gilchrist, "'Newsworthy' Victims?"

72 Comack, *Racialized Policing*; Henry, "Through an Indigenous Lens"; Razack, *Dying from Improvement*; Taussig, *Shamanism, Colonialism, and the Wild Man*.

73 Razack, *Race, Space and the Law*; Razack, *Dying from Improvement*.

74 Hubbard and Razack, "Reframing Two Worlds Colliding."

75 Mbembe, "Necropolitics."

76 Foucault, *The Foucault Effect*.

77 Morgensen, "Biopolitics of Settler Colonialism"; Razack, *Dying from Improvement*.

78 Debrix and Barder, *Beyond Biopolitics*; Taussig, *Shamanism, Colonialism, and the Wild Man*.

79 Razack, *Dying from Improvement*.

80 Comack, Deane, Morrisette, and Silver, *"Indians Wear Red."*

81 Fraser, *Urban Legends*.

Part Four

CONTESTATION, RESISTANCE, SOLIDARITY

CHAPTER TEN

TALISI THROUGH THE LENS

Locating Native Tulsa in the Films of Sterlin Harjo

LINDSEY CLAIRE SMITH

Seminole and Creek filmmaker Sterlin Harjo (1979–) has enjoyed remarkable success on the film festival circuit with his groundbreaking representations of contemporary Indigenous life. Harjo's films *Goodnight, Irene*,[1] *Four Sheets to the Wind*,[2] *Barking Water*,[3] *This May Be the Last Time*,[4] and *Mekko*[5] bring the unique spaces of Oklahoma into focus, drawing connections between homelands, in both rural and urban locations, of Indigenous Oklahomans. Harjo has become known for his artful and affectionate perspective on Oklahoma landscapes, and his renderings of the city of Tulsa are no exception. Tulsa emerges as a centre for contemporary Indigenous life, a hometown that holds great promise as well as tragedy, in the films *Four Sheets to the Wind* and *Mekko*. In these two works, Harjo presents the cosmopolitan experiences of Indigenous Oklahomans while also recognizing the Creek foundations of the city, countering all-too-typical notions of dislocation between urban Natives and their homelands. In this chapter, I argue that these two films recover urban spaces for Indigenous peoples and prompt us to reconsider typical approaches to urban studies.

Scholarship on urban American Indians in the United States has for the most part explored the circumstances surrounding and aftermath of the 1950s Urban Relocation Program. This program was a U.S. government initiative to entice reservation dwellers to cities with promises of plentiful jobs and modern conveniences. Donald Fixico's foundational study *The Urban Indian Experience in America* details the Urban Relocation Program of the 1950s and discusses the results of the program institutionally and culturally. Fixico's framework for urbanization emphasizes differing roles in response to city life: traditionalist, suburbanite, and middle-class members.[6] He explains that typically while Indians seek to be urbanites, their mindset is Indian, a situation that has led many to crisis.[7] While not discounting the significance of this state of crisis for galvanizing urban Indian activism, Susan Lobo argues in *American Indians and the Urban Experience* that as new generations of American Indians inhabit cities, their experiences, including their relationships to urban Indian Country, are varied. Noting that in the past anthropologists have studied rural communities and sociologists have studied urban settings, she stresses that urban/rural is a false dichotomy.[8] In her study of San Francisco, Lobo identifies a network of relatedness in cities that is more fluid, situational, negotiable, and diverse than the formalized, federally prescribed boundaries of rural tribes.[9] This network is akin to the phenomenon described by Renya Ramirez in her book *Native Hubs*. Ramirez promotes a concept that Laverne Roberts (Paiute) introduced to her, in which cities are the hub of a wheel, with social networks acting as spokes connecting city Natives to tribal land bases at a distance.[10] Though the contexts for urban Indigenous experiences in Canada are different from those in the United States, Evelyn Peters and Vince Robillard present data that show connections between urban and rural locations in homeless people's movement, rebuffing notions of a sharp rural/urban split.[11]

While all of these studies document situations of change, mobility, and persistence among urban Natives, still other scholarship emphasizes Indigenous foundations of cities, correcting the impression that urban areas are necessarily sites of separation from tribal homelands. Nicholas Blomley's *Unsettling the City* recounts Vancouver's history as a settler city, founded on the imaginary premise of its incorporation on empty land, despite Squamish land rights. He identifies two manoeuvres as fundamental to the settler city: (1) removal of Indian people from urban space, which requires imagining them as in the past or in nature; and (2) emplacement of settler society, which makes the city into a white place.[12] Kathi Wilson and Evelyn Peters also emphasize that perceptions of cities as non-Indigenous lands are a spatial ordering of the state.[13] Julie Tomiak presents a similar critique of colonial imaginaries in her study of Ottawa, arguing for "the centrality of asserting collective Indigenous agency and visibility, thereby refuting settler narratives that claim Indigenous peoples, as rights and title holders, do not belong and do not exist in cities."[14] Coll Thrush's *Native Seattle* recovers Indigenous origins of Seattle and investigates ways that city infrastructures, especially "historical" monuments, obscure those origins. Echoing Renalto Rosaldo's exposure of "imperialist nostalgia," or "mourning for what one has destroyed,"[15] Thrush explains that cities "indelibly mark their Indian inhabitants in urban ghost stories."[16] These ghost stories appear in monuments to Indian people in the very locations in which Indians have been displaced. He goes on, "Stories of ghosts and totem poles and dispossessed chieftains cast Indians only as passive victims of, rather than participants in, the urban story,"[17] and he offers "cosmopolitan Indianness"[18] as a way of understanding the history of Seattle's Indigenous citizens. Likewise reframing typical notions of Indian urbanization, Nicolas Rosenthal's *Reimagining Indian Country* seeks "to argue from Los Angeles outward."[19] As his title indicates, Rosenthal documents ways that Indians have included cities in their definitions of Indian Country, valuing mobility and making an important contribution to the growth of the American middle class. Finally, Evelyn Peters and Chris Andersen, in *Indigenous in the City*, remind readers of the history of Indigenous urban sites and settlements, noting that the "creation of Indigenous 'homelands' outside of cities is in itself a colonial invention."[20] The roughly fifteen years of scholarship represented by these studies have provided essential language for articulating a diversity of Indigenous experiences in cities, for the most part privileging social histories of mobility within the constraints of settler colonial nation building.

Though such an approach challenges relegation of Indigenous peoples to a preindustrial past, it is not a complete methodology for understanding ways that Indigenous people not only make a living but also make a life in urban America. Along with histories of urban relocation, creative encounters with urban spaces themselves are worthy of further consideration as scholars study contemporary life. For this reason, it is helpful to bring scholars in Indigenous studies into dialogue with scholars in urban studies, such as Henri Lefebvre and his successor, Edward Soja, for language to conceptualize these encounters. Lefebvre and Soja uncover ways that capitalist commodification of urban space enacts power. Lefebvre, who is largely responsible for socio-theoretical assessments of the urban, draws attention to capitalism's abstraction of urban space simultaneously with fetishism of nature. Lefebvre noticed that France, in capitalist modernity, has turned to reconstruction of space for social organization. In the transition from agriculture to industry, agriculture is subordinate to industrial production: "subordinate to its demands, subject to its constraints."[21] Lefebvre explains that the urban is not limited to built environments of cities; instead, through this agricultural subordination, the influence of cities expands to regional, national, and global scales. He states, "This expression, 'urban fabric,' does not narrowly define the built world of cities but all manifestations of the dominance of the city over the country.... Of varying density, thickness, and activity, the only regions untouched by it are those that are stagnant or dying, those that are given over to 'nature.'"[22] Lefebvre thereby suggests that the power of the state, centred in cities, exerts its influence broadly, drawing agricultural towns and large metropolises alike into its consumerist influence.[23] Recognizing the ubiquitous influence of the urban for all manner of communities thus undergirds a necessary recognition of its impact on Indigenous peoples and of Indigenous peoples' negotiation of this influence. This is an important step in debunking continual association of Native peoples with a preindustrial past.

Lefebvre's remarks on the role of nature in the urban fabric reveal parallels to Thrush's discussion of monuments that are erected in areas of Indigenous displacement in North America, though Lefebvre never directly discusses how colonialism figures into the urban fabric. Lefebvre notes that nature is subject to new threats in industrialism, which leads to its fetishism. The transition to capitalist urbanism expands these threats, which ironically leads to the multiplication of signs of nature, in the form of open spaces, parks, and gardens.[24] For Lefebvre, it is the right to the city—over the right to nature (or ideologies of nature)—that is essential, as urban society is a place of encounter among diverse social groups with distinct rights. Anticipating Thrush's later assessment of Seattle's "ghost stories," monuments, in Lefebvre's formulation, are not to be trusted; they are objects transformed into ideologies, seats of institutions that colonize space.[25] Lefebvre's discussion of capitalism's fetishizing of the nature that it destroys may shed light on the fetishizing of Indigenous peoples in monuments that appear in U.S. cities. As Joni Adamson explains, the Western idealization of Indigenous links to "pristine" nature is persistent though inaccurate and veils the impact of environmental racism on communities of colour.[26] Considering Lefebvre's comments about ideologies of nature along with urban histories paves the way for understanding the impulse to create parks and monuments that idealize both nature and Indigenous peoples. Unfortunately, Lefebvre never examines the literal impact of colonialism, despite his use of the word "colonize" to describe the relationship between nature and the urban fabric.[27] Thus, there is still work to do to conceptualize Indigenous experiences in the settler colonial cities of the United States.

Soja makes important strides in filling Lefebvre's gaps in his ideas about urban space relative to race and gender. In *Postmodern Geographies*, he describes cities as repositories of state power and explains that geography (rendering spatial logic) supersedes history in shaping our understanding of the world.[28] He extends Lefebvre's methodology, naming geographically uneven development as integral to global capitalism and cities as centres of social power through "enclosure, confinement, surveillance, partitioning, social discipline and spatial differentiation."[29] Soja identifies the role of mani-fest destiny in American urbanization, hinting at least to the settler colonial dynamics of contemporary Los Angeles. In his case study, Soja marks the Watts riots of 1965 as a starting point for the ramifications of inequality that is essential to capitalism. In the shadow of the "governmental and corpor-ate citadel" of downtown Los Angeles, Soja remarks on the stark contrast between the extreme wealth clustered in condominiums, law offices, and corporate headquarters, and the hardships of immigrant labourers and the largest concentration of homeless people in the United States.[30] Soja points out the largely unrecognized importance of urban planning to the Los Angeles cityscape, which, though appearing to many as a haphazard amalgamation, is carefully designed in accordance with the labour required to sustain its consumerism.[31] He also names imperialism as a foundational feature of the city: "Securing the Pacific rim has been the manifest destiny of Los Angeles, a theme which defines its sprawling urbanization perhaps more than any other analytical construct. . . . It is not always easy to see the imprint of this imperial history on the material landscape."[32] Like Lefebvre, however, Soja never explores in sufficient detail how this "imperialism" both creates and reproduces urban space, simply relying instead upon the metaphorical force of the word. Though he details the transformation of Bunker Hill into a centre for civic purposes, for example, he neglects to mention the neighbourhood's importance to participants in the Urban Relocation Program. Soja's more recent books, *Seeking Spatial Justice* and *My Los Angeles*, document a frame-work for addressing spatial inequality but similarly avoid serious engagement

with colonialism or its impact on Indigenous peoples.[33] This omission is especially problematic since after New York City, Los Angeles has the highest
number of Indigenous peoples in the United States.[34]

Through dialogue between urban and Indigenous studies, one can recognize the ideologies of power—and conquest—that mark urban spaces where
Indigenous people reside, but also important are ways in which these residents participate in the production of the city as *oeuvre*, to use Lefebvre's
term. Lefebvre's later writings, namely *The Production of Space*, move beyond
theorizing space itself to investigate the processes and practices that create
it. According to Lukasz Stanek, Lefebvre's work "put[s] aside the determina-
tive power of the market by revealing the agency of discursive and symbolic
spatial practices . . . and complicating the thesis about the homogenizing
power of capitalism by discovering inside it a constant negotiation, dispute,
and compromise over spaces."[35] Lefebvre emphasizes social relations in the city
as "a production and reproduction of human beings by human beings, rather
than a production of objects."[36] Lefebvre's recognition of human agency—and
resistance—in urban space is important for recognizing American Indians'
active role in creating urban cultures despite their disenfranchisement as a
result of settler colonization of their lands. Further, Lefebvre points toward
art as evidence of the city's value to its residents, even when bureaucracy reigns
supreme. He explains that the appearance of art reflects a city's use value—
not just exchange value—because of the importance of its unique history
to its citizens. A city's value above and beyond exchange makes it an *oeuvre*
and holds the promise of a "transformed and renewed right to urban life."[37]
Drawing on Lefebvre's language, Indigenous art, including filmmaking, can
thus be understood to be an enactment of a right to the city, an expression
of the value of the urban community to its Indigenous people. Of course,
as American cities are on Indigenous lands, this right has never been relin-
quished! Nevertheless, in the face of the urban ghost stories that Thrush
describes, Lefebvre's critical language is useful for describing Indigenous artistic and cultural resistance to the spatial dimensions of settler erasure.

Scholarship on creative responses to objects-turned-ideologies and the
spatial dimensions of Native experience has begun with the work of Dean
Rader and Mishuana Goeman. Rader, in *Engaged Resistance*, interrogates
public art that captures colonial symbolic discourse about Indigenous
peoples. Though not specifically centred on urban locations, Rader's study
links romantic stereotypes of Indians rendered in car lots to "high art" of

government grounds in Oklahoma City, Tulsa, and Santa Fe—all cities in Indian Country—to reveal how such images reinforce problematic purposes of tourism. He argues that the "aesthetic activism" of visual and literary artists in these locations defends Native identities from these purposes.[38] Mishuana Goeman, in *Mark My Words*, uses Lefebvre's theories of space as a springboard for her discussion of (re)mapping, or spatial decolonization, in which Indigenous women unsettle settler space through literature.[39] Goeman names colonial spatialities, specifically maps, surveys, field reports and so on, as critical to the erasure of Native mobility and the general acceptance of a dichotomy of urban/reservation Native.[40] Like Rader's and Goeman's literary scholarship, my study engages film as not just a mirror of experience but as a producer of it. While my reading of Harjo's films is informed by the history of Tulsa, it also considers the spatial dimensions of Native experiences with the city.

Harjo, a native of Oklahoma, grew up in Holdenville, which, like Tulsa, originated as a Creek town. He attended the University of Oklahoma and moved to Tulsa as a young adult. With the encouragement of N. Bird Runningwater, an alumnus of the University of Oklahoma, Harjo received a fellowship from the Sundance Institute in 2004. There he premiered his short film, *Goodnight, Irene*, to positive reviews at the 2005 Sundance Film Festival. Harjo quickly began receiving more attention in local, national, and international communities with the release of his feature films, but despite his increased renown, he remains committed to a home in Oklahoma. He has served as video director for Tulsa's This Land Press and as director of *Osiyo, Voices of the Cherokee People*, a project of his company, Fire Thief Productions. According to Harjo, stories of Oklahoma are his creative inspiration: "I love all the stories in Oklahoma. It's overflowing with unique history. I love dirt roads and the countryside. Tulsa is perfect because it's not too big and it's not too small. You can get a good cup of coffee, but you can also get to the country pretty fast if you need to."[41] Harjo's words indicate the significance of the city as an artistic home that is still tied to a broader rural geography. As Lobo, Ramirez, Peters, and Robillard have discussed in their scholarship, notions of a sharp divide between urban and rural Indigenous cultures are mostly incorrect. Especially in Oklahoma, the former Indian Territory where reservations are not the norm, tribal jurisdictions encompass both rural and urban areas, and tribal citizens generally participate in activities across these diverse geographies.

Tulsa is in fact brimming with stories, not often told, about the Indigenous foundations of the city. According to Creek preservationist David Proctor, Tulsa originated with the Talisi Indians, part of the Creek confederacy, who founded a ceremonial ground and tribal town there near the Arkansas River.[42] The Perrymans, a Creek family, were prominent in the establishment of the city. Robert Trepp, a descendant of the Perrymans, explains that the Creek founders of Tulsa brought their ceremonial fires with them from the Southeast and built them again in stomp grounds near Council Oak Tree, a site that marks Tulsa's founding. Under threat during the Civil War and again with the imposition of the Dawes Severalty Act, the stomp grounds were moved south of town, and Creek families found themselves increasingly marginalized amid the growing presence of newcomers. Though Tulsa was in Indian Territory, which was supposed to remain so in perpetuity after Jacksonian removals of tribes from the Southeast, the commodification of natural resources such as coal, lead, zinc, and especially oil, fuelled the clamour for Indian Territory to become a state in 1907.[43] The opening of the Glenn Pool oil field in 1905, a large, underground lake of oil just south of Tulsa on the allotment of Creek citizen Ida Glenn, was especially key to the influx of settlers seeking profit on this land.

The Tulsa landscape, still marked by the fading glory of its heyday as the oil capital of the world, contains reminders of its origin as Talisi and of the former Creek allotments that are the grounds for city landmarks. These landmarks reflect both Native disenfranchisement in the city's settlement as well as the continued participation of Creeks and other Native peoples in the city's cultural scene, which counters flawed perceptions of cities as non-Indigenous places. These landmarks include the first post office, established by Josiah Perryman; the Perryman Ranch, a working ranch and event centre still managed by descendants of Creek city founders; and Woodward Park (formerly Perryman's Pasture), the city's most treasured park that was obtained and condemned without the consent of its Creek owner, Helen Woodward. Tulsa's Indigenous art scene is arguably among the most influential in the United States. Gilcrease Museum, named for the Creek collector and museum founder Thomas Gilcrease, houses the country's largest collection of western and Native American art, and Philbrook Museum, which hosted the Indian Annual from 1946 to 1979, are both pivotal in showcasing and driving Indigenous art, especially of the contemporary era. Beyond these institutions, the participation of local tribes is vital to the Oklahoma economy, making a \$10.8 billion impact statewide through tribal government and business operations, including gaming.[44]

Like the Creek community that built the city, a cosmopolitan Creek community emerges in Harjo's two Tulsa-based feature films, *Four Sheets to the Wind* and *Mekko*. And also like their Creek ancestors, the characters within these films find grounding as Creeks within the city while connecting with relatives and other, more rural landscapes of Creek country. Their experiences, echoing the process of urban Indigenous filmmaking itself, are marked by creative encounters with urban spaces in addition to recollection of urban Indian histories. These encounters are provocative because they assert Indigenous rights to the city beyond the land rights that are typically understood to be outside of the urban fabric. These two texts, which present urban settings that are certainly gritty, convey Indigenous participation in the human, lived—not abstract or idyllic—everyday life of the city, which resonates beyond the architecture of objects to transformative encounters in beauty and in art.

Four Sheets to the Wind places the Creek and Seminole Smallhill family in the overlapping landscapes of Holdenville, Wewoka, and Tulsa, creating a synchronicity between rural and urban environments. Harjo's rendering of Tulsa is Indigenous, a place that is, though apart from rural homelands in southern Oklahoma, an appropriate location for the film's protagonist, Cufe Smallhill, to find love and to reach insight into the family dynamics that have led to his sister Miri's troubles. By depicting Cufe's maturation amid Tulsa landmarks such as the Blue Dome district, the Cain's Ballroom, and Cathedral Square, Harjo creates a sense of home for Cufe that parallels the homeplace evoked in rural Oklahoma, making clear the broad reach and appeal of the city to Oklahoma Natives in surrounding rural areas. Cufe's urban experiences also set the stage for his final decision to travel more widely. Thus Harjo, I argue, constructs characters not inherently marked by loss of or disconnection from culture, as many earlier writers have done. Instead, in Harjo's works Indigenous characters challenge typical notions of authenticity, creating fluidity among various places, rural and urban, that are significant for understanding self, community, and culture. This fluidity renders an alternative Indigenous space, unsettling urban settler imaginaries. In fact, one of the most remarkable things about the film's 2007 premiere in Tulsa's Circle Cinema independent theatre was the audience's response. In the lobby afterward, amid the racially, economically, nationally, and generationally mixed crowd, I could hear over and over again comments that expressed a common sentiment, that this Oklahoma was recognizable to its people. Harjo's film accordingly both depicts and creates experience, asserting a right to the city. Within the language of Indigenous studies, this accomplishment is also an act of visual sovereignty. As Kristin Dowell argues, such an act not only recasts images of Indigenous people onscreen but also creates and negotiates community off-screen.[45]

Harjo's Oklahoma mirrors the diverse, multi-tribal, non-reservation, heavily Indigenous-populated dynamics of the state that do not often see the light of day in popular culture, especially movies. Cufe's community extends outward from Holdenville, but also from Tulsa, and includes people from a variety of backgrounds. Cufe's experience of community is driven by his relationship with his Creek father but is inclusive of and informed by people of other tribes and other races. In Holdenville and Wewoka (the capital of the Seminole Nation, adjacent to the Creek Nation), Seminole and Creek peoples interact, and Cufe and his friends and relatives form relationships with whites, African Americans, and other tribal citizens, achieving intimacy in some instances and confronting racism in others. The situation is much the same in Tulsa, where encounters in bars, health clinics, and eating establishments almost directly correspond to similar scenarios and scenes in the rural locations. These parallel scenarios and scenes of conflict, hardship, love, and reconciliation across Tulsa, Holdenville, and Wewoka demonstrate that life in these urban and rural locations is connected and reciprocal, further confounding state formations of settler and Indigenous space.

The opening scenes of the movie reveal this parallelism. The film begins with an image of Cufe dragging his deceased father, Frankie Smallhill, who has committed suicide, down a dirt road, through woods marked "private property," and into a pond, where he gives his father a watery burial to fulfill his final wishes.[46] From the scene of the pond and surrounding trees, Harjo transitions to images of dirt roads, then to a shot of the town of Holdenville, then to a picture of the landscape viewed through a barbed wire fence. After Cufe walks across a cattle guard, the audience sees a passing train, a storefront church, several oil pumpjacks, an overgrown basketball court, some broken-down cars, and finally Cufe's house and dog. Later, when Cufe heads to Tulsa to visit Miri, the series of images—evoking natural elements as well as manufactured items associated with transport—is parallel. The audience sees a railroad yard, the Tulsa skyline, a bus station, a kitty, and Miri's apartment complex. This series of images may be understood as a catalogue. Not only is this Oklahoma landscape in its natural appearance significant for Cufe, most obviously in the association between his father and the pond, but also the material items—the trains, cars, scooters, and cityscapes—are visible reminders of "progress" and its problematic as well as invigorating implications. It seems that upon his arrival in Tulsa, Cufe has literally seen it all before.

Miri's and Cufe's plotlines, though leading to different outcomes, are also parallel. Where Miri's Tulsa experiences following her failed attempt at an acting career in California seem to be mostly negative, revealing her desperate and empty existence in the city, Cufe's Tulsa experiences spur his honest communication about his father with his first serious girlfriend, a young white woman named Francine, and seem to give him the confidence to consider making a road trip with her to California. In this way, the movie hinges on the contrast between Cufe's and Miri's experiences of space, which for both characters involves leaving Holdenville and travelling to Tulsa and California. Over the course of the film, Cufe leaves Holdenville, goes to Tulsa, returns to Holdenville briefly, and then leaves, apparently for California. Miri, on the other hand, has already been to California, begins the film in Tulsa, and finally returns to Holdenville. This contrast between Cufe's and Miri's spatial encounters transforms typical representations of urban Indigenous people by highlighting a fluidity between rural and urban and representing all these spaces as Indigenous. Again, these images counter settler colonial whitewashing of urban space.

In most literature and film up until the 1990s, urban Indigenous experiences are marked by ambivalence, usually accompanied by "hybrid" or mixed-blood identities, which, if not leading to tragedy, lead to eventual flight from urban locations that are environmentally and spiritually problematic and a return to reservations or rural towns.[47] Indigenous-authored texts that have received the most critical acclaim, especially those from the 1960s and '70s, including N. Scott Momaday's *House Made of Dawn*[48] and Leslie Marmon Silko's *Ceremony*,[49] emphasize reservation over urban experiences, especially the religious importance of returning to these locations after time overseas and/or in cities. William Bevis calls this phenomenon "homing in," explaining, "In Native American novels, coming home, staying put, . . . is a primary mode of knowledge and a primary good."[50] Joanna Hearne describes how in the realm of film, Indigenous people typically appear only "at a certain historical moment in the mid- and late nineteenth century, or . . . are chronically incapable of navigating a modernity imagined as the sole purview of urban dwellers—the audience of the movies themselves, who are imagined as homogenous white settlers."[51] Based on narratives such as these, readers and audiences may thereby conclude that being authentic necessitates living in a predominantly Indigenous community, usually on a reservation, and rejecting urbanization, a process equated with assimilation.

As we see in Harjo's film, Miri's character ultimately returns home, echoing the homing plot just described; however, Cufe's path suggests another option, transforming this narrative convention. Significantly for theoretical approaches to Indigenous studies, though Cufe presumably leaves Oklahoma to travel and pursue a relationship with Francine away from his ancestral home, the implication of his choice is not a turning away from a particular Creek identity. Cufe's father narrates his son's story at its beginning in Holdenville and at its end at the start of Cufe's travels, speaking in the Creek language and integrating Cufe's experience into traditional tribal stories. Cufe, whose name in Creek means "rabbit," thus is part of the Creek story of Rabbit, who, as Frankie Smallhill explains, was able to trick Bear into entering his stomach in search of honey, rendering him satisfyingly full. By the end of the film, viewers get the sense that Cufe is likewise full. As Lee Schweninger argues, though Frankie is dead, his influence endures, his voice critical to the revelation of the characters, which is an important revision of Hollywood's vanishing Indian convention.[52] As Frankie narrates, the night before his departure Cufe sleeps well, full of dreams of love and travel. Thus, Cufe's story buoys tribally specific cultural frameworks while also incorporating other nationalities and even faraway places into that model, suggesting, as Ramirez, Goeman, and others have theorized, that Indigenous mobility across borders, landscapes, and culture, is not prohibitive of identities strongly connected to tribal homelands. This understanding of cosmopolitan Indigeneity has implications for urban space itself, as Indigenous writers like Harjo reclaim cityscapes for their communities. In the film, the privileging of space over histories of tribal peoples that viewers might expect is apparent in an encounter between Cufe and a white partygoer in Tulsa. Reflecting an almost comical (but typical) obsession with "Indians and time," he won't stop asking, "Where have all the Indians gone?" His question indicates his assumption that there are no Indians in the present, especially in this urban environment. Understandably, Cufe responds with confusion and incredulity.

In Frankie's narration, communication, even in unexpected ways, emerges as the most important factor in becoming "full" in urban space, as Cufe does. The day that Cufe leaves, after Miri, their mother Cora, and Cufe have spent their last night together in Holdenville, Frankie explains, "I know something wonderful happened that day in Oklahoma. . . . It was a silence that everyone shared . . . and I know . . . it resembled something like love." He continues, "People come around in circles. Never ending circles. But you're never that far from home." As Francine places a picture of Cufe in a frame in her Tulsa apartment, Frankie asserts, "You always come back." As Cufe leaves Holdenville for the final time, he returns to the burial pond where he fished with his father and takes a fishhook with him on his travels. Frankie's words during this final act are as follows: "All my life people have said, 'You never talk.' I just like listening I guess." Cufe's actions to share Creek community, whether through overt communication or through shared silence, maintain a constant connection to family and culture.[53]

Harjo's film, *Mekko*, like his first feature, portrays a protagonist who eventually reaches self-awareness against the backdrop of Tulsa landmarks. And also like *Four Sheets*, Creek language is the source of narration as the film begins and ends, this time representing the main character's own thoughts. Inspired by fellow Oklahoman Richard Ray Whitman's *Street Chiefs* photographic series, Harjo seeks through *Mekko* to bring to life the stories of homelessness in the city, stories of a community that he realized was noticeably Indigenous. Like *Four Sheets*, *Mekko* portrays an urban environment that for some characters only mounts feelings of hopelessness. But also like the earlier film, there is not a clear dichotomy between rural and urban. The rural homeland away from Tulsa is not the clear guidepost to redemption, at least not uncomplicatedly so. Instead of privileging a timeline of events in Mekko's life, the film emphasizes sites across landscapes of Oklahoma as locations for his reflections on his past and his relationships to family and community.

The film begins with Mekko's articulation in Creek language of a sickness, brought from an estekini (a shape-shifting "witch") to his rural community. Accompanying this voiceover are images in black and white of an abandoned small town, with rows of homes that look like tribal housing commonly seen in Oklahoma. Mekko explains that his grandmother instilled in him the importance of striving against the sickness, a special responsibility for him in his role as a seer who could "see the darkness coming." Oakhern is the fictional town for this sequence, but the filming locations are Maud and Picher, two

Oklahoma towns with histories of violence.[54] Maud is today mostly known as the birthplace of rockabilly star Wanda Jackson. But the town is also notorious for a horrific lynching. Resting on the pre-statehood dividing line between Oklahoma and Indian Territories, in 1898 Maud was the scene of the lynching of two Seminole teenagers who, in the wake of the murder of a white woman (presumably by an Indian), were dragged into Oklahoma Territory and burned at the stake at a Baptist church.[55] Picher, located in far northeastern Oklahoma within the jurisdiction of the Quapaw tribe, is now a ghost town on account of its designation, along with the town of Cardin, as the Tar Creek Superfund Site in 1983.[56] The site, one of the most toxic in the United States, was subject to federal buyouts because of contamination from lead and zinc mining. Mining, which galvanized Indian Territory's transformation into the state of Oklahoma, poisoned Tar Creek and left a multitude of chat piles (mining waste). These chat piles caused elevated levels of lead in Picher's children, along with other adverse health effects such as chronic lung disease in the population as a whole.[57] The connection between these communities also indicates the connections between urban and rural that are fundamental to Lefebvre's articulation of the urban fabric. The industrial exploitation of Picher demonstrates the dependence of areas outside of built cities on the urban. *Mekko*'s foreboding opening emphasizes a shared experience of homelessness in the protagonist's community, in Tulsa and beyond, an experience that prepares him (and the audience) for empathy with the inhabitants of Tulsa's streets.

Mekko's release from prison begins the action of the film, and his first move is to head for Tulsa in the back of a pickup truck. Though the reason for Mekko's imprisonment is not revealed until later in the film, Mekko explains that he continually thinks of his grandmother and cousin John, with ever-stronger visions that drive him to drink and make him afraid to return home, highlighting Mekko's history with John as a source for his torment. Echoing the significance of water in *Four Sheets*, the first Tulsa location that Mekko visits is the Arkansas River, a waterway that for many Oklahoma tribes has been historically important for settlements, trade, and transport. Against that backdrop the audience learns that Mekko took John's life, though the circumstances are not immediately known. From there, Mekko walks to the gallery (appearing in the film as "Great Plains Gallery") of Cherokee Wes Gan, a long-time collector of Indigenous art, in downtown Tulsa. There Mekko is again reminded of John, an artist. Next, Mekko heads to Coney Island, a mainstay in the city for over ninety years, and savours a plate of coneys at one of the small wooden desks so familiar to Tulsans. Affected by these touchstones that evoke a strong sense of place, Mekko visits another cousin, where he explains that he misses his family, has been left behind, and is ready to make amends. But he is rejected.

Though Mekko has found meaningful connection with Tulsa landmarks, this rejection from family leaves him without a place to lay his head. As night falls, he stares at the Tulsa skyline rising over the expressway, and as the motion of the cars lights up the sky, Mekko is standing still. Walking into the darkness, he senses that he is being followed, the sound of an owl adding to the disturbing atmosphere. But despite this menacing moment, the next day Mekko finds a kindred spirit at another Tulsa institution, Brownie's Hamburger Stand, known for its excellent coconut pie. Tafv, a waitress, like Mekko has her own troubles; with her mother struggling with addiction, she is responsible for her little sister's care. Her empathy with Mekko fosters an avuncular relationship between the two that makes Brownie's a lighthouse of sorts for Mekko. After leaving Brownie's, Mekko arrives in the Kendall-Whittier neighbourhood, where the city's homeless gather at Whittier Square across from the art-house Circle Cinema. There, finding a new family, Mekko joins the homeless camp, where he first sees Bill, an embodiment of the estekini figure that he has been dreading. It is soon clear that Bill has several of the characters under his control, dealing drugs to them and demanding payment. Mekko connects with an old friend in the camp, Bunnie. Bunnie leads Mekko to Circle Cinema, pointing out the sidewalk tribute to Will Sampson and letting him in on a free popcorn hookup via an exasperated employee. Again Mekko finds a level of solace in a legendary Tulsa location, even as a familiar (and literal) demon follows him.

Bunnie's relationship with Mekko is a noteworthy bridge between the spaces of Oakhern and Tulsa and ultimately between conflicting sides of Mekko's character. The two discuss their upbringing, musing about the decline of their small town. Bunnie reminds Mekko of the devastation of lead mining that forced people to be evacuated. Immediately following this discussion, scenes of Bill's evil impact on others are revealed. Bill calls himself a warrior of the streets who protects people, but it is obvious that he is bent on destruction. Bunnie and Mekko sleep next to the river, and in the night Bill provokes Mekko by stealing his favourite hat. When Mekko asks, "Who does he think he is?" Bunnie utters the prophetic words, "He's one of us."

As Mekko circulates with Bunnie among sites in his new community—the Coney Island, the Beehive Lounge, Brownie's, the Admiral flea market—Bill, who by this point is emblematic of Mekko's own spiritual darkness, haunts him. This series of encounters with city landmarks as well as the relationships and tensions between Mekko and others in the homeless community of Kendall-Whittier echo Lefebvre's insights about the force of capitalism as a struggle over spaces. For Mekko, homelessness compounds his alienation from his family, yet joining the street community may be understood as an assertion of the right to this place. Lefebvre found art to be a primary way of asserting human agency and of valuing an urban community. It is appropriate, then, that Mekko seeks out Indigenous art on the road to redemption.

Bunnie keeps hope for spiritual renewal alive for Mekko. At the flea market, Mekko finds one of John's paintings and purchases it for $1.50. As the two admire the piece, Bunnie confides that he has been dreaming about the sweat lodges, a means of cleansing evil. In a confessional moment back in camp, Mekko explains the accidental circumstances that led him to kill his cousin John: a drunken altercation in the parking lot of a bar. Bill reappears, this time provoking Bunnie. When the two friends sleep for the night in front of Ziegler's Art Supply store (significant in light of John's artistic talent), Bill attacks them both, killing Bunnie. With this climactic event, the stakes of Mekko's responsibility to his community, and to his better nature, are abundantly clear. In light of his conversation with Bunnie, Mekko is aware that Bill is not just a reflection of his own personal demons; he also can be traced to the settler exploitation of their home community. Bunnie can no longer be cultural memory or compass. Mekko is responsible for setting things right to prevent further violence.

Mekko recovers in the hospital, buoyed by Creek hymn singers and the care of Tafv, and from this point forward, Mekko endeavours to exorcise Bill, his literal and figurative antagonist. Remembering the warning contained in the stories, that one can't run from an estekini, Mekko returns to the river, where his resolve is clear. Harjo signals the significance of this Tulsa location by including in the shot graffiti on the 21st Street Bridge that reads, "Motorcycle boy reigns." This message is a nod to Francis Ford Coppola's *Rumble Fish*,[58] a film based on the book by Tulsa novelist S.E. Hinton, which was filmed on location in the city. Motorcycle Boy is a character with a dark past who feels stuck in a deterministic future, yet seeks a way out for his younger brother. Likewise, the way ahead for Mekko is unclear, but key to his recovery is his influence on Allen, a young newcomer to the streets. With no money (which means no coneys!), Mekko heads to Iron Gate soup kitchen, a gathering place for Tulsa's homeless residents, where Harjo recruited several of the individuals who appear in the film. At Iron Gate, Mekko breaks bread with an Indian lady who, like Tafv, offers him comfort and empathy. Near St. Francis Xavier Catholic Church, Mekko finds Allen, a former Oklahoma University student who is in danger of overdose and exposure. Recognizing Allen's sickness, literal and spiritual, Mekko listens to Allen's story of loss, in which he expresses a desire to be reunited with his grandmother and cousins, a story that Mekko can certainly understand. Mekko offers words of wisdom to this rendering of his younger self, stating, "Welcome to manhood." As Bill eavesdrops, Mekko urges Allen to recognize that the sickness can enter when darkness takes over one's spirit. Looking at John's artwork, Mekko recalls that when the sickness retreats, his people will return, and he determines, "I can make them well."

The conclusion of Mekko's journey leads to vengeance and redemption, symbolized by the presence of water in both urban and rural locations. As Mekko walks down Greenwood Avenue, in a historically black neighbourhood that was devastated during the 1921 Tulsa Race Massacre, a Native individual plays a hand drum while Bill follows, confronting Mekko by yelling his name. Mekko reacts by chasing Bill down and stabbing him, carving out his heart, immersing it in the river, and washing his hands clean. Mekko and Allen then return to Oakhern, where the two make a camp and build a fire, which, an elder assures them, is representative of the fire that continues to burn in the hearts of their community despite their trials. Mekko, having shown Allen the mentorship he couldn't provide for John, is confident in the message of the stories of his childhood. He knows now that the people will come back, and he believes "we'll have a big victory dance." Committed to keeping the fire going, Mekko decides, "As long as I breathe, I will fight to the end." Finally, he and Allen enter the abandoned house of his grandmother, where he sees a vision of her and his cousin John. "I'll be here, cousin," he says, "I'll be waiting for you." Immediately, an aerial view of the river in luscious colour, a stark contrast to the film's bleak opening, leaves viewers with a sense that the sickness has retreated.

While *Mekko* certainly paints a grittier portrait of Tulsa than *Four Sheets to the Wind* does, its rendering of the city is nonetheless affectionate, highlighting a right to the city amid the struggles of homelessness and asserting a prominent role for Indigenous people in the city's creative and artistic *oeuvre*, or product of spatial and social relationships. Though Mekko leaves Tulsa for spiritual renewal at the end, explaining that he "had to get out of the damn city," framing the story as a typical "homing plot" would be a misreading. It is the experience of finding an alternative family at Whittier Square that allows Mekko to become a mentor, fulfill his obligations to his tribe, and be assured of his community's renewal. As in *Four Sheets*, Creek homelands are evident across rural and urban locations, with the threat of dislocation—and the opportunity for reconnection—available in both.

Sterlin Harjo documents and envisions an Indigenous cityscape that is rooted in Creek stories and culture and extends outward to people of other nations and backgrounds and even to Indigenous homelands that are at a distance from built urban environments. He thereby complicates the "homing in" theme of many typical texts and films, suggesting that for his characters, fulfillment comes not from an in-between identity or from a choice between rural and urban but rather from locating and transforming Indigenous identity within an urban landscape. This creative act undermines settler colonial impositions of urban/rural divisions of Indigenous space. It also reflects the importance of Indigenous production of space, which can be understood as creative and meaningful experiences of community in the urban present that counter ideologies rendered through civic monuments. The impact that Harjo's films have in creating community both on- and off-screen also shows the power of art to reclaim urban Indigenous space, echoing Lefebvre's celebration of the right to the city and disrupting settler colonial erasure of Native claims to urban lands. A critical approach to Harjo's representation of Tulsa (Talisi) that links Indigenous studies and urban studies methodologies is thus a productive way to foreground Tulsa's history as Indigenous homeland as well as its significance as a centre for Indigenous creativity. Throughout *Four Sheets to the Wind* and *Mekko*, Indigenous Tulsa comes into focus as communitist and transformative, with Creek culture at its centre.

NOTES

1 Harjo, *Goodnight, Irene* (2005).

2 Harjo, *Four Sheets to the Wind* (2007).

3 Harjo, *Barking Water* (2009).

4 Harjo, *This May Be the Last Time* (2014).

5 Harjo, *Mekko* (2015).

6 Fixico, *The Urban Indian Experience*, 162.

7 Ibid., 180.

8 Lobo, Introduction to *American Indians and the Urban Experience*, xiii.

9 Lobo, "Is Urban a Person or Place?," 77.

10 Ramirez, *Native Hubs*, 1.

11 Peters and Robillard, "'Everything You Want Is There.'"

12 Blomley, *Unsettling the City*, 114.

13 Wilson and Peters, "'You Can Make a Place for It,'" 399.

14 Tomiak, "Unsettling Ottawa," 9.

15 Rosaldo, "Imperialist Nostalgia," 107–8.

16 Thrush, *Native Seattle*, 9.

17 Ibid., 10.

18 Ibid., 112.

19 Rosenthal, *Reimagining Indian Country*, 3.

20 Peters and Andersen, *Indigenous in the City*, 7–8.

21 Lefebvre, *The Urban Revolution*, 3.

22 Ibid., 3–4.

23 Ibid., 4.

24 Ibid., 27.

25 Ibid., 20.

26 Adamson, *American Indian Literature, Environmental Justice, and Ecocriticism*.

27 Kipfer and Goonewardena provide an overview of the potential for Lefebvre's work to speak to post-colonial situations but ultimately conclude that his work is unable to overcome its "Eurocentric roadblocks." See "Urban Marxism and the Post-Colonial Question."

28 Soja, *Postmodern Geographies*, 78.

29 Ibid., 105, 153.

30 Ibid., 210.

31 Ibid., 238.

32 Ibid., 225.

33 Soja, *Seeking Spatial Justice*; Soja, *My Los Angeles*.

34 United States Census, "The American Indian and Alaska Native Population."

35 Stanek, *Henri Lefebvre on Space*, 57.

36   Lefebvre, *Writings on Cities*, 101.

37   Ibid., 158.

38   Rader, *Engaged Resistance*, 1.

39   Goeman, *Mark My Words*, 1, 32.

40   Ibid., 7.

41   Thorne, "Meet: Sterlin Harjo."

42   Herrera and Cobb, "Tracing Tulsa's Creek Roots."

43   Baird and Goble, *The Story of Oklahoma*.

44   Mecoy, "Tribal Activities Make $10.8B Impact on Oklahoma's Economic Output."

45   Dowell, *Sovereign Screens*, xii.

46   Hearne notes that like Sherman Alexie's groundbreaking film *Smoke Signals*, Harjo's representation
     of funeral rituals revises media stereotypes of vanishing Indians. See Hearne, *Smoke Signals*, 124.

47   Bevis, "Native American Novels."

48   Momaday, *House Made of Dawn*.

49   Silko, *Ceremony*.

50   Bevis, "Native American Novels," 582.

51   Hearne, *Smoke Signals*, 6.

52   Schweninger, *Imagic Moments*, 202.

53   This contrasts to Miri's experience, in which coming back to Holdenville is a reintroduction to family
     and culture after an extended period of familial disconnection that made distance synonymous with
     cultural dislocation.

54   Rutland, "'Mekko' Film Event Held in Okmulgee."

55   Littlefield, *Seminole Burning*, 4.

56   See *The Creek Runs Red*, a documentary directed by Julianna Brannum, Bradley Beesley, and James
     Payne for a moving representation of the impact of the Environmental Protection Agency superfund
     designation on the Quapaw tribe.

57   Shepherd, "Last Residents of Picher, Oklahoma."

58   Coppola, *Rumble Fish*.

CHAPTER ELEVEN

LITTLE PARTITIONS ON THE PRAIRIES

Muslim Identity and Settler Colonialism in Saskatchewan

SHARMEEN KHAN

When CBC first aired *Little Mosque on the Prairie* in 2006, the Muslim community in Regina was very excited. Not only was the creator and head writer Zarqa Nawaz living in Regina, but the television series was inspired by her own experience as a Muslim in the Prairies. The show was intended to offer a comedic view of the interactions between Muslims and non-Muslims in a small Prairie town, putting a uniquely Canadian and multicultural spin on Laura Ingalls Wilder's classic, *Little House on the Prairie*. It used humour to unpack stereotypes about both the Islamic faith and Prairie life, relying on comedic devices to create bridges of understanding between white Canadians and Muslims who are otherwise seen as outsiders.

Nawaz described the show as "apolitical," but I don't find her claim convincing. *Little Mosque* tells a story about Muslim immigration into Canadian Prairie life that obscures the colonial relation at the heart of this phenomenon. The show reinforces myths of Canadian multiculturalism, while obscuring the significance of Indigenous communities and struggles to the Prairies.

In this way, a seemingly apolitical storyline operates to reinforce dominant political narratives by making Indigenous peoples invisible or casting them as people of the past. While *Little Mosque* is sometimes seen as a progressive and anti-racist intervention in the face of growing Islamophobia, its silence around colonization reinforces a particular role for Muslim immigrants in settler colonialism.

I grew up in Regina—a Prairie city where there were many systemic attempts to ignore or erase the presence of Indigenous communities in the city. As a child of Muslim immigrants, I was positioned to understand Canada from within a multicultural framework. Many anti-racist and anti-colonial writers have spoken about the kind of silence between immigrants and Indigenous peoples that *Little Mosque* exemplifies. The show creates a structure of solidarity between Muslim immigrants and settler colonialism. It celebrates the resonance of racialized immigrants with the white settler experience where immigrant integration then becomes a project of colonial dispossession.

In so doing, the show operates to erase the common link of colonization that is shared between many Muslim immigrants and Indigenous peoples. For Muslims coming to Canada from North Africa, South Asia, or the Middle East, the legacy of colonization continues to have an impact. In fact, it is often directly connected to migration itself. Importantly, the logics of partition that operated in South Asia are also at work in the Canadian Prairies today. In both cases, imagined borders disconnect people who might otherwise be in solidarity with each other. With colonial connections obscured, Muslim immigrants miss the opportunity to build an anti-colonial foundation of solidarity with Indigenous peoples.

Using *Little Mosque* as an example, this chapter examines the ongoing tension between immigrant-settlers and Indigenous people in the Prairies. It explores this theme in four sections. The first looks closely at *Little Mosque* itself and assesses its significance. The second builds on this assessment in the context of my own personal experience growing up in an immigrant Muslim community in Regina and considers how Canadian settler colonization operated to silence the colonization that my family experienced, including the process of partition. The third section discusses how narratives of partition and their impact on immigrant consciousness are related to Indigenous struggle and could offer an opening to solidarity. And the final section considers these questions in the context of my experiences as a political organizer in the Prairies and explores the possibilities of undoing these structures and building solidarity.

HOW MUSLIMS SAVED THE CANADIAN BROADCASTING CORPORATION

Little Mosque on the Prairie won accolades and gave the CBC high ratings. The series coincided with growing Islamophobia and, at the time of its production, no other major television network had a show with main characters who were Muslim. Over the course of its five-year run, *Little Mosque* introduced audiences to a range of "relatable" Muslim characters, some of which mobilized stereotypes and some of which challenged them. It features, for example, both a conservative Muslim father who wants to stay true to the scripture and his young daughter who seeks to balance teen life with her faith (although for the Muslim youth I knew in Regina, that meant sneaking out of the house to drink and date). The show also includes a Muslim feminist who is a doctor, a Muslim woman from Nigeria who runs a café, and a white convert. And yet while multiculturalism and Prairie diversity are recurring themes, there are no Indigenous characters to be found in or around the show's fictional setting. This is a striking editorial decision, given the considerable size of Saskatchewan's Indigenous community.

The show's Muslim characters actively participate in the capitalist economy and contribute to the development of the town. They are portrayed as hard working and highly educated. They aspire to live heteronormative, middle-class lives. Beyond their religious and cultural practices, they ultimately challenge very little about the social and economic organization of the town. Because of their class position, their practices are largely accepted. In this sense, they are the definition of the "model minority." Differences in food, cultural practices, and clothing are acceptable, as long as immigrants are productive.

This image of the model immigrant is worth considering in light of the way that Indigenous people have been depicted as incapable of integrating into the capitalist system. In *Prairie Rising: Indigenous Youth, Decolonization and the Politics of Intervention*, Jaskiran Dhillon writes about the Canadian state's preoccupation with "improving" the social conditions of Indigenous peoples. "The mark of the racial," she writes, "is always to need assistance into modernity. And when the racial is cast as such, the settler state must become adept at producing portraits of Indigenous self-destruction and dysfunc-tion—as remnants always living on the edge, on the brink of death; colonial subjects in need of settler state rescue."[1]

These same colonial logics existed in other countries and continue to be expressed in contemporary forms of foreign intervention and development—affecting countries where many Muslim immigrants come from. Yet while many of these communities may arrive from countries broken by coloniza-tion, the consciousness of colonialism is curiously absent in the characters that appear in *Little Mosque*. Questions about Indigenous communities are treated as historical in a narrative that is concerned to show how white settlers and Muslim immigrants are forging their futures together. The Prairies are presented as an open and empty space where a narrowly conceived form of integrative multiculturalism can flourish.

Saskatchewan is located within the traditional territories of the Cree, the Saulteaux, the Dene, and the Dakota, and yet there is only one episode in the entire series which suggests that Indigenous peoples may have existed on that land.[2] In it, a contractor finds an arrowhead while building a gazebo and brings it to the town's professor of archaeology (played by Cree actor Tom Jackson). This precipitates an archaeological dig in the search for more arti-facts, but nothing of significance is found, and construction continues. Here again, Indigenous peoples are presented as mere relics.

These narratives of development and immigration feed into the myth of *terra nullius* that facilitated colonization. This myth erases the systemic displacement of Indigenous peoples. It also shapes understandings of the struggles faced by Muslim immigrants moving to the Prairies by suggesting that their fight for land is shared with white, Christian settlers, not Indigenous peoples. Accordingly, they must be accountable and make relationships with white settlers rather than with the traditional owners of the land. These narratives present immigrant struggles as separate and distinct from the strug-gles of Indigenous peoples, and shed light on why Indigenous people are omitted from *Little Mosque*. Indigenous struggles simply do not make for a comedic story.

The lack of solidarity between Muslim immigrants and Indigenous peoples consists of more than just identity politics or differences keeping people apart. Muslim immigrants arrive in Canada with their own history of colonial-ism, and yet the colonial narrative of Canada remains invisible or conflated with other "minority rights" issues. I do not discount the fact that many

immigrants genuinely lack education and understanding of these issues—
but this is a systemic form of ignorance within a settler colonial context.

In Regina, I knew many Muslim immigrants who struggled with racism
and sought to create their own spaces, but I remember little acknowledgement
of the violent racism shouldered by Indigenous people in our own community. Did my family not recognize colonialism in the deaths that happened
in the infamous "starlight tours" when I was thirteen?[3] Did they not recognize colonialism when two boys from my high school sexually assaulted and
killed Pamela George?[4]

While *Little Mosque* presents Muslims as a model minority wanting to
do good and contribute to their community, it ignores that to "do good" in
a colonial society is often to strengthen colonial structures of displacement.
As Baijayanta Mukhopadhyay reflects in his role as a doctor serving remote
Indigenous communities:

> Am I simply a continuation of history? Even before I started this work,
> I was by no means naïve. Pushed to Canada through intergenerational
> displacement caused by the ravages of colonialism, I already knew its
> dynamics of co-optation and collaboration well. My father was part
> of the post-Independence exodus from an India set up by its former
> colonial masters to stumble in its sovereignty—colonial masters
> whose first concerns for local health in 19th century India centred
> on institutions for sex workers so syphilis would not wipe out British
> troops stationed there to protect economic interests. The machinations
> of a more modern petro-imperialism led to my own displacement,
> from the Middle East where my father had sought survival, to colonial
> Canada today.[5]

By looking at my own family's understanding of colonialism and partition,
I can explore how the logics of partition extend into acceptance into a settler
colonial framework.

REAL LIFE ON THE PRAIRIE

I grew up in Regina in a fairly politically liberal, Muslim household. My
family immigrated to Regina from Pakistan in the mid 1970s. My grandfather was upper class and educated in England, allowing him access to employment in Canada. He first came to Ontario before immigrating, to learn

about CANDU nuclear reactors as an engineer. He had hoped to remain in Ontario when the family moved to Canada permanently. But the Canadian government found my grandfather a civil service job in the Prairies, so my grandparents moved to Regina. At the time, they were one of three Muslim Pakistani families in a city with few brown families. Family members tell stories about eggs and snowballs being thrown at their house when they settled in the neighbourhood of Whitmore Park. They spent a great deal of energy assimilating as well as they could—some of them started using Western names. Like many immigrant families, they straddled Western expectations and a desire to (privately) maintain their religion and Pakistani culture. I was one of the few people of colour in elementary and high school.

There weren't many Muslims in Regina, but the population began to grow in the 1970s. Muslims in Regina used to pray in the basement of a house; later, they rented an apartment where they would have Islamic school and prayers. Finally, in the 1980s, they raised enough money to convert an old church into a mosque. My family found no use for politics after witnessing the trauma of the partition and corruption of Pakistani politics. They thought Pierre Trudeau was amazing because of his immigration policies. I think they thought the key to creating a life was stable employment and safe communities—to be politically active was an unnecessary risk. When I had a political awakening in high school, my family would often comment that there was no reason for political struggle in Canada. Here, everyone was privileged and had a good life.

Many of the tropes presented in *Little Mosque* rang true for my family. They felt that they had arrived on empty lands and had to fit into the lives of the white majority. We all hated living on the Prairies. And we all wanted to leave. My family missed big cities where you could go to Bollywood films and buy *gulab jaman* or *pani puri* on the streets. My grandfather was an engineer, but he was also an amazing sitarist and became known as one of the most talented players in the Prairies (although to be honest, I have no idea how many sitar players there were in the area). He was also obsessed with painting those empty, decrepit farmhouses that spot the Prairie landscape. On road trips, he would stop along the highways and take photos of random, old barns or houses. When I was a child, I asked why he painted them and he told me, "It's how I feel being here. A broken house on flat land."

Like most immigrant families, mine knew very little about Canadian colonization. They bought into the narrative that Canada was now a post-colonial territory. They saw the Prairies as an empty space, littered with rotting barns and houses from the past, needing development. If they ever did consider colonization or the Indigenous population in Regina, it was in fear or incredulity as to why Aboriginal people couldn't get it together. At the time, most Indigenous people lived in the north end of Regina. This zone was always portrayed as the home of "bad" neighbourhoods and "bad" people; it was understood as a place where we should not venture. I have memories of family members reacting in fear when they were approached by Indigenous people on the street. When I was seven, I remember sitting in the back seat with my father as we waited to pick up my mother after her shift at the hospital. An Indigenous man gently tapped on the window and asked my father for a few dollars as his wife was in the hospital. My father said "sure," took out a five-dollar bill, but then slowly started driving, tricking the man into walking fast and then running to grab the five dollars. My father sped away laughing, rolling up the window and returning the five-dollar bill to his wallet. I looked through the rear window and saw the man slowly stop running and just stand there, staring at us driving away.

I noticed how racist my family were toward Indigenous people that they saw on the street and how they would reproduce problematic narratives about alcoholism and laziness. There was also an outright ban in my family on developing any friendships or relationships with Indigenous people. The only way my family would appreciate any Indigenous presence was in the sanitized, historical representations of dance.

When I began to read and understand the logics of racism and colonialism, I realized how the logics of colonization persisted in my family, as well as in most of the Pakistani and Muslim community that I encountered. While many people experienced racism and colonization themselves, they did not have the politics to recognize systemic racism. Rather, they acquiesced to the system and actually benefited from colonization and participated in roles that furthered the colonial agenda of the Canadian state. They bought into the myth that we Muslim immigrants were contributing to modernity while Indigenous peoples were incapable of doing the same.

It's always difficult to pinpoint the roots of racism. I do not want to romanticize the experience of colonization and imply that everyone who experiences it suddenly has a magical understanding of oppression and exploitation. In fact, my experience suggests the opposite. My family experienced the horrors of colonization, including the tragedy of partition—yet colonization framed a great deal of their consciousness around modernity and their assumptions about who is or isn't capable of participating in it.

PARTITION

The idea that people need to be forcibly separated for the good of a nation or a community—whether differences are religious, racial, or cultural—reinforces a dangerous politics of belonging. The 1947 partition between India and Pakistan spurred one of the greatest migrations in human history, where fourteen million people left their traditional lands and relocated. During the migration an estimated two million people died. While this separation led to the birth of the new nations of Pakistan and Bangladesh, it is often remembered as a catastrophe. "Marked by genocidal violence, forced conversions, abductions and rapes in large parts of north India as well as an unprecedented displacement of people, Partition has been called 'a holocaust' of a tragedy . . . our understanding of 'Partition violence' [must] include the bureaucratic violence of drawing political boundaries and nationalizing identities that became, in some lives, interminable," writes Vazira Fazila-Yacoobali Zamindar.[6]

To say that partition continues to have lingering impacts on the South Asian diaspora is an understatement. It separated communities that had lived together for thousands of years. In my own family's case, it instilled a particular kind of trauma that destroyed their sense of home and community.

Based (simply) on the "two-nation theory," the main argument of the separation was that despite regional and cultural similarities, the two main faiths of Islam and Hinduism needed their own nations in the region. The reality of the region, however, was a complex history of many faiths living together. Partition was a moment of rupture where imagined identities and nations were solidified into borders. Generations later, the events remain obscured. As Kita Kotharie writes, "Silence and denial about Partition continue in the public sphere, despite overt and implied reminders of Partition's 'unfinished business.'"[7]

My grandfather told me that he never imagined that people who had spent so long together could fall apart that quickly. He often commented how strange it was that communities with so much in common (despite religious differences) could be so rapidly separated. After partition, he was left to find a new life in a new country.

For me, my grandfather's stories are reminders of how fighting colonization and wanting to build a new society is a process of powerlessness and uncertainty. Some in my family blame the British for the partition insofar as they had encouraged the growth of communalism and divided India since their arrival in 1757. As Aijaz Ahmad has said, "The truth remains that Britain's policy first created the basis for the division of India, a policy of divide and rule over a long period of time, and when the crisis came to a head, Britain did very little to save the unity of India."[8]

In his 2006 book *Midnight's Furies*, Nisid Hajari writes of the surprise and confusion the partition caused: "Many of the politicians in Delhi and Karachi, too, had once fought together against the British; they had social and family ties going back decades. They did not intend to militarize the border between them with pillboxes and rolls of barbed wire. They laughed at the suggestion that Punjabi farmers might one day need visas to cross from one end of the province to the other."[9] Of course, along with the confusion and lack of power there is also the trauma of violence. As Hajari states, "*Partition* has become a byword for horror."[10] Before I knew much about the birth of Pakistan, my grandmother told me the story of her first big trip on the infamous trains carrying Muslims away from India toward Pakistan. She was seven at the time. And she still remembers how the people in her car managed to lock the doors to prevent killers who ambushed the train from entering. They had piled all their belongings against the doors and windows. She said she heard screams and was certain that the army would arrive to help them. But stepping onto the train platform after close to twenty-four hours of travel, she saw her first dead body. She told me that she saw so much blood she was certain it wasn't real. I asked her why they wanted to kill the Muslims when they were going to leave. And to this day when we talk about the partition, she cannot make sense of it. "Some people just can't live together," she told me.

While I've heard stories of my family's experience of that migration and seen representations of it in cinema and novels, I never quite understood how that trauma lived on when they came to Canada. There was always this simple resignation that brown people have always had to move for work, and that the only success we could achieve was through the spoils of empire. White folks may have won the colonizing game but if we kept quiet in their world, we could carve out a small space of peace.

While my grandparents have traumatic memories of partition, the struggles of building a new home in the new state of Pakistan had its own horrors.

There they witnessed the back and forth of ruling authority, living through military coups and the false promises of corrupt "socialists." They supported the promises of socialism promoted by Zulfikar Ali Bhutto ("Islam is our faith, democracy is our policy, socialism is our economy. All power to the people.") but were rewarded with only reactionary results. They lived through war over contested land and watched as their new state spent a huge portion of its limited wealth on building a military complex to protect them from a new enemy—India.

While my family immigrated to a new country in the 1940s on the basis of their faith, they were still seen as settlers taking land and resources from people who already lived there. The question of home and belonging has always been contentious for my family. For us, there is really no such thing. To be accused of settling in a place that does not belong to you, where you have no connection, is not only the story of migration—it is the story of the nation state. It is a story of forced migration and removal of people, the creation of laws to determine who can belong within contrived borders and a climate of fear for those who do not belong.

Like all histories of forced displacement and migration, those legacies endure for generations. When it comes to the partition, historian Ayesha Jalal writes that as "a defining moment that is neither beginning nor end, partition continues to influence how the peoples and states of postcolonial South Asia envisage their past, present and future."[11]

On the Prairies, the trauma of partition and the failures of a post-colonial Pakistan informed a great deal of my family's relationship to Canadian colonization. We may never be equal, but if we work hard, we can potentially find safety in the worlds that white people have created. Nice houses with a double garage. A pension. And peace. This is the narrative my family followed when they talked about moving to the Prairies. And it is the narrative they follow when they excuse police violence against Indigenous and Black people. If people can't make it in Canada, they just haven't worked hard enough.

It took me a very long time to figure out where this perspective came from. It is easy to yell at your racist family and demand they read Frantz Fanon to understand colonization. I couldn't comprehend how they could excuse colonization after the experiences they had had. How could they not see it? It wasn't until I did a lot of reading about the partition (a lot of poetry and personal narratives) and made time with my family to talk about growing up in Pakistan and their experiences settling in Canada that I slowly realized that the power of partition continues not only in South Asia, but also within Canada. The Prairies have their own legacies of blood and partition that have continually separated people.

ANTI-RACISM AND SETTLER COLONIALISM

Much has been written about the tension between anti-racist and anti-colonial movements. Bonita Lawrence and Enakshi Dua write that "antiracism is premised on an ongoing colonial project . . . rather than challenging the ongoing colonization of Aboriginal peoples, Canadian anti-racism is furthering contemporary colonial agendas."[12] In *The Transit of Empire*, Jodi Byrd argues that many activists maintain a multicultural liberalism that flattens Indigenous history and struggle as simply another "minority fight," obscuring the foundational question of land theft. She argues that with the rise of multiculturalism in the 1980s and the "postracial ideologies of the 2000s," American Indians have lost their historical and cultural specificities and their identities have often been subsumed within the generic Other category.[13]

Byrd does not accuse migrants, queers, and people of colour of participating in and benefiting from Indigenous loss of land and lives—she finds it too simple to attribute the category of "settler" to people of colour. She argues that the project of imperialism has forced settlers and arrivants to cathect (or experience) the space of the native as their home. Her project is to activate Indigeneity as a condition of possibility within theory. She aims to deploy it to avoid the traps of equivalence on the one hand, and the economies of racism, homophobia, sexism, and class exploitation [to order the place of peoples on Indigenous home grounds] on the other.

For Byrd, the concept of "transit" as a tool of analysis has a double meaning. First, she uses it to argue that reiterative stereotypes circulating in the discourse on Indigeneity strategically fill the empty signifier of the Other in the U.S. colonial project. She explains that cultural representations of immigrants to the United States are contaminated by these discourses. This strategy, in its disciplining and domesticating of the American Other, acts as a most effective tool of colonization. Byrd also uses the concept of "transit" to foreground the evolution of Indigenous peoples and their identities throughout American history, thereby actively resisting the mainstream notion that they exist in the past tense, belonging in museums rather than on the streets and lands of contemporary North America.

Byrd documents the processes and structures of colonization throughout the United States in a very difficult but important project to show that without centring land or colonization as part of the oppressive apparatus, different oppressed or identity groups will negotiate with the state to win liberties or rights at the expense of others—most notably, Indigenous people. But she also acknowledges that empire is steeped in white supremacy, so it is necessary to make a distinction between white settlers and *arrivants*—people of colour who migrate to North America.

This disruption of the settler/Indigenous binary is important to me. In the Prairies, people of colour are not seen as the equivalent of white settlers. Growing up as one of the few people of colour in my high school, I was not regaled with stories of my ancestors. Nor was I ever really seen as Canadian. I have heard far too many anecdotes of people of colour being asked where they are from. So while I accept that my family benefited from settling in the Prairies, it didn't mean that we became white—even though we tried very hard.

Beenash Jafri has some smart things to say about the relationship between people of colour and Indigenous people: "What makes the relationship between racialized subjects and settler colonialism so challenging to tease out is that even as racialized subjects access colonial power in settler states—for example, through political representation—they remain socially and politically unrecognized as settlers (and thus unrecognized as wholly human)."[14] It can be difficult for those who have experienced histories of systemic oppression to feel that they have some complicity with colonization.

Sometimes these tensions reveal themselves through the messiness of organizing. When you decide to be a revolutionary in the Prairies, it is very difficult not to create some relationships with Indigenous activists. Regina is so small that when you start showing up to demonstrations and meetings, the word spreads quickly.

It is possible to remain within homogenous social justice scenes, but for what I was generally interested in (throwing capitalism into the dustbin of history), the invisibility of the Indigenous presence on the Prairies was quickly ripped away. The radical circles I began to associate with were interested in poverty, police brutality, and divisions within the city. When we read about racial profiling in Black liberation texts, we began to make connections with the racial profiling and high incarceration rate of Indigenous people that we saw in Regina.

But in reflecting on those times in Regina, I see that a lot of spaces I organized in were pretty white. I was often tokenized as a woman-of-colour expert in all things brown. And I witnessed the tokenizing of Indigenous leaders as well. I remember speaking at a Saskatchewan Federation of Labour (SFL) conference as *the* woman of colour alongside a Cree leader who spoke as *the* expert on all things Native. The photographer wanted various photos of us shaking hands and posing with the leadership of the SFL under their banner.

When you start organizing, you end up working within structures that you want gone. You work within structures that have kept different communities and nations apart for generations. And I don't only mean geographically. The education I was given about Indigenous people was a form of partition. So too was the failure of the educational system to explain our obligations under Treaty Four. The same goes for the routinized representation of Native people as drunks or sex workers who don't deserve life or freedom.

While colonialism isn't over, neither are the forms of partition that both systemically and ideologically separate us from histories and realities that my family could relate to. Instead of embracing this potential solidarity, however, my family identified with whiteness and the comfort of white supremacy. Even after Pakistani men were being rounded up and subjected to secret trials after 9/11, very few connections were made to the constant incarceration of Indigenous men.

Canada is shaped by colonization and ongoing multiple imperialisms. The displacement of Indigenous peoples has coincided with a colonial and class-based immigration system that favours wealthy people as immigrants. Colonial displacement has also coincided with Canadian foreign policy that has forced and maintained poverty in many countries. At the same time, the Canadian government has created programs for poor workers from these poor countries to come to Canada and take up difficult work that Canadians do not want to do. These foreign workers engage in low-paying and often dangerous work while also living in precarity and poverty in Canada as they send money in the form of remittances home to family. And while classified as "temporary," many foreign workers work for many years with little state protection and no process for status.

I use this example to outline how Canadian colonialism and imperialism have displaced different communities that also remain systemically apart and often unknowing of each other. Canadian policy has led to the displacement of Indigenous peoples and the extraction of resources on their land by poor workers of colour from other countries. These different kinds of imperialism meet head-on in Canadian soil. Yet to this day, we don't see strong alliances or solidarity work happening between Indigenous activists and migrant workers. And I believe that this is the ongoing logic of partition—a systemic process of separating people—that continues to this day. This does not excuse the racism of migrants toward Indigenous people but rather points to ongoing colonial legacies.

This relationship between migrant and Indigenous solidarity has always been a messy one, and not much has been written about it that is useful for activists. There are sometimes only two roads— one that leads to crass identity politics that simplify struggles and people, or one that leads to liberal multiculturalism that suppresses difference and Indigeneity. What I have found is that making efforts to create small and authentic relationships with individual Native activists to start breaking down these structures of partition is an important step, but a slow and frustrating one because of how strong these partitions are.

ORGANIZING/UNDOING THE WORLD

If you are a Muslim from an immigrant family, beginning to disrupt racism is a step toward undoing the separation between immigrants and Indigenous people. I began to confront racism when I became politicized in Regina and began writing for alternative media as a teenager, then attending regular meetings at the local chapter of the Communist Party of Canada, then trying to start my own communist organization, helping with Food Not Bombs, pro-choice rallies, and student politics. I became aware of and started organizing around Saskatchewan's uranium mining and the pollution of the tailing ponds, and met impacted First Nations for the first time in Northern Saskatchewan.

Without an analysis of white supremacy, there is an insufficient recognition of the power of white settlers over non-white immigrants and refugees who arrive in Canada. Lack of analysis also erases the history of slavery and the reality of anti-Black racism. The myth of the "model minority" has offered some immigrants a better life, but it's a limited promise, as that life is often built on the backs of exploited others and on stolen land. And the "model minorities" themselves become symbols of "tamed" people of colour and then become part of the colonization process.

Understanding these structures and questioning power means asking why different oppressed communities are separated. The process of partition diminishes opportunities for unity, collaboration, and solidarity, and often hides how our struggles are connected. It prevents people from relating to the struggles of others. It undoes any work toward internationalism. We can see this, for example, when people ask why resources going to Syrian refugees are not going to Indigenous communities or the homeless. Yet we rarely hear questions about how the allocation of state resources creates divisions among the exploited and oppressed. While some express hate toward the outsiders coming in and "taking" needed resources, there are questions about why the resources are kept so limited in the first place.

BUILDING SOLIDARITY

In promoting the idea of partition as a form of post-colonial identity construction and nationalism, I am not attempting to offer a blanket analysis of racism. Rather, I think the term provides a helpful rhetorical tool for understanding how the legacies of "divide and rule" politics continue to operate in the present day. In thinking about the endurance of partition in this country, my point is not to imply that members of Canada's ruling class meet secretly to plan how to keep the oppressed fighting among themselves, but that the logic of colonial division continues to find expressions in neoliberal multiculturalism. The ideological power and violence of colonization and capitalism have seduced many members of the Muslim community in Regina into claiming political affinity with white culture and colonization, despite their own histories of colonial displacement and dispossession.

In *The Heart Divided*, Mumtaz Shah Nawaz argues that both nationalism and colonialism turn natural allies against colonization into enemies that cannot live with each other. While she is concerned with the division between Muslims and Hindus, she offers clarity about how broader forms of partition foster hostilities between "former" colonized populations, while at the same time forcing them to compete for economic partnerships with the same "former" colonizers.[15]

Just as the partition between Pakistan and India set up arbitrary borders that separated generations, the same has been true for Canada, where borders were drawn to cut off Indigenous nations from each other and force some nations to relocate to other areas. The creation of borders not only meant the renaming of traditional territories but also put in place legal structures to hierarchize status and citizenship in Canada.

These structures have a particular impact on the Prairies, with its particular history of colonization and displacement of Indigenous peoples. The strength of multiculturalism has also served to redefine the state's relationship with Indigenous peoples. As Sunera Thobani writes, the refusal of the state to provide adequate education and create opportunities for Indigenous people to enter the labour force (which would have given them improved socioeconomic status), suggests that Canada considered immigration a better alternative than integrating Indigenous people into the labour force.[16]

With so many structures in place to keep communities apart, it is an international project to undo the partitions that have created so much alienation and separation. Lisa Lowe insists that we understand the links between the process of colonization, the Atlantic slave trade, the forced migration of cheap labour from the South, and how these have led to neoliberalism and free trade.[17] Struggles on the Prairies are connected to broader struggles against global capital, and linking those struggles may open up more opportunities for solidarity. While my family could not see these links, revealing these historical narratives may encourage more internationalism in our struggles. Creating new historical narratives is not an easy task, but linking the struggles of exploitation and forced displacement may provide some openings for forming stronger relationships and, perhaps, for different communities to fight colonization.

CONCLUSION

What am I driving at? At this idea: that no one colonizes innocently, that no one colonizes with impunity either; that a nation which colonizes, that a civilization which justifies colonization—and therefore force—is already a sick civilization, a civilization that is morally diseased.
—*Aimé Césaire, Discourse on Colonialism*

I often imagine an alternative to *Little Mosque*. It's a show about the Prairies—probably one that would have to be moved from CBC to HBO. Rather than the sunny comedy of the original series, I envision a moody drama that would try to seriously engage with the violence of disconnection from the land. It would focus on brown Muslim experiences of colonization and partition and would show Muslim characters becoming settlers themselves, adopting a system that ignores the state violence against Indigenous people. Some want to be part of the system so much that they change their traditional names and put on white make-up. The show would portray the legacies of colonization against Indigenous peoples and their resistance, only to see large segments of their population jailed and ignored by possible allies. And in this show, the immigrant characters would find it nearly impossible to live in peace under colonization—unable to forget the journey that brought them to these stolen lands. I acknowledge that for some, *Little Mosque* was merely a silly television show to make people laugh. But that's how ideology works: fantasies are narrated as truth, and this narration encourages their acceptance. For those of us struggling against colonization, articulating new stories is part of the fight.

There is a familiar thread running through many of the readings I have done around the partition; many writers talk about the difficulty in giving voice to the impact of the partition or of colonialism. This is an important lesson of Idle No More and other ongoing struggles across the country. To voice trauma is a way to heal; perhaps if more *arrivants* realized their history of colonization and gave voice to it, more connections might be built. It might be a way to encourage people to show up for each other on Indigenous blockades and migrant justice rallies.

The theories of nationalist movements fighting colonization can help us, but I feel if more activists articulated their experiences of colonization and linked them to the anti-colonial struggles of where they live, new forms of ideas and knowledge to fight the nationalist narratives of multiculturalism would emerge. The personal challenge for those of us organizing in streets, linking up with blockades, wanting to do more than traditional land acknowledgments is to begin writing our histories and our connections to this land.

NOTES

1   Dhillon, *Prairie Rising*, 70.

2   CBC, *Little Mosque on the Prairie*, season 2, episode 4 ("Lucky Day").

3   Green, "From Stonechild to Social Cohesion."

4   See Razack, "Gendered Racialized Violence and Spatialized Justice."

5   Mukhopadhyay, "Care as Colonialism."

6   Zamindar, *The Long Partition and the Making of Modern South Asia*, 2.

7   Kothari, "From Conclusions to Beginnings."

8   Ahmad, *Confronting Empire*, 7–8.

9   Hajari, *Midnight's Furies*, v.

10 Ibid.

11 Dalrymple, quoted in "The Great Divide."

12 Lawrence and Dua, "Decolonizing Antiracism," 123.

13 Byrd, *The Transit of Empire*, 209.

14 Jafri, "Desire, Settler Colonialism and the Racialized City," 76

15 Nawaz, *The Heart Divided*.

16 Thobani, *Exalted Subjects*, 174.

17 Lowe, *The Intimacies of Four Continents*.

CHAPTER TWELVE

DECOLONIZING PRAIRIE PUBLIC ART

The Further Adventures of the Ness Namew

ZOE TODD

This is a story about Edmonton, of Edmonton, rooted in the human and more-than-human stories and materialities that make that city—known by its nehiyawewin (Plains Cree, Y dialect) name amiskwacîwâskahikan[1]—specific and unique to its geographies, lands, and waters. Many people know of Edmonton as an afterthought, an interchangeable Canadian city referenced by the media in passing for its various dubious distinctions; stereotypes of my hometown abound in the media and collective Canadian psyche. For example, Edmonton is referred to colloquially by locals as "Stabmonton," and it was denounced by a British journalist in the *Telegraph* in 2001 as "Deadmonton."[2] Local artists and musicians like to refer to it as "Dirt City,"[3] in what I imagine they consider an avowedly tongue-in-cheek reference to Edmonton's hard-scrabble industrial life and its perceived non-place within eastern Canadian cultural institutions and media. However, the ability to reduce a locality that has been shaped and co-constituted by human and more-than-human beings and *life* since time immemorial to a mere death-scape/dustscape is an explicitly settler colonial conceit. This reduction of the city that I know to be a lively, visceral, and inherently vibrant place to nothing more than dirt and death reinforces and normalizes the notions of settler colonial erasure of local Indigenous legal traditions, epistemologies, ontologies, and worlds. In this chapter, I seek to mobilize some of the more-than-human kin who animate amiskwacîwâskahikan to trouble and disrupt this notion of Deadmonton/Dirt City in the local settler arts scene. I trouble this narrative precisely because it lays the groundwork for local white settler artists to speak "for" and "about" Indigenous life and being. This in turn (re)produces the settler colonial logics of dispossession and erasure, and the white supremacist notions of white possessiveness[4] upon which Prairie cities like Edmonton are built. Instead, I offer a vibrant and inscrutable narrative of life and existence in this place and remind the co-constituents of Edmonton that we owe reciprocal responsibilities to the pluralities of life, longing, and labour that make this Prairie city what it is. I further explore the ways in which the white settler impulse to speak "for" marginalized groups through art is not solely an Edmonton phenomenon, but rather a white possessive exigency that characterizes white art worlds in both Canada and the United States of America, tying Edmonton into a long history of white supremacist art trajectories that symbolically and literally brutalize Black and Indigenous bodies in the name of "solidarity." Ultimately, the alternative more-than-human narrative that I engage in this piece turns on the principles of reciprocity and refusal, building on the work of Mohawk scholar Audra Simpson in her theorizations of Mohawk political consciousness and refusal vis-à-vis the American and Canadian nation-states.[5]

In order to accomplish this disruption of Prairie settler arts logics in my hometown, I turn to my collaborator, the Ness namew—a well-travelled lake sturgeon who spends her time swimming the waterways of my Métis family's territories. The Ness namew (namew is the Plains Cree, Y dialect or nehiyawewin word for sturgeon) is so named for her predilection for travelling to Loch Ness on a whim and scaring Scottish interlocutors in her turn as the enigmatic Loch Ness monster. She is a decolonial monster-fish: tricky, elusive, and well versed in the legal-governance entanglements of Scottish colonialism and Canadian settler dispossession. She uses her girth and her mirth to challenge Scots to consider their role in the violent colonization of her homelands in the Lake Winnipeg Watershed and beyond. She's also an eager but still-learning scholar of Black and Indigenous feminist scholarship, doing her best to employ her fishy wiles to work in solidarity with her human kin to disrupt white supremacy and its entwined expressions of anti-Blackness and anti-Indigeneity in various Canadian institutions.

When we last saw her, circa 2015,[6] the Ness namew was travelling the cool deep waters of Loch Ness, haunting and teasing the Scottish psyche in order to viscerally unsettle Scottish refusals to engage with the long and tangled reach of their enthusiastic complicity in the British colonial project. She was languidly and purposefully swimming the long lengths of that cool Highland loch, setting Scottish nerves on edge. Her message, coded in her steely flesh and set in the scutes on her back, was unrepentant: you are responsible for the devastation of the waters I have swum through since time immemorial. My haunting is your shaming.

She had enjoyed this decolonial journey, travelling the lengths of the Lake Winnipeg Watershed with petty and delightful revenge in mind. She swam the long twisting kisiskaciwani-sipiy with her briefcase full of scientific reports on the pollution, diversions, and desecration of Prairie waters. She also carried a parchment copy of Treaty Six, signed at Fort Carlton in 1876, to complement the oral history version of that agreement passed on to her by her mother, who herself had swum along the sipiy on those fateful days of the Treaty Commission as it negotiated with Cree leaders. It should come as no surprise, given the long reach of fish throughout every single territory that first the British Crown and then Canada had laid claim to, that fish bear witness to all of our deliberations. And fish have thoughts on the strategies the state has taken in refusing political agency to namewak and other fish philosophers.

To make her way to the distant shores of Scotland, the Ness namew had to navigate complex waterways. First, she swam the Lake Winnipeg Watershed, making her way through the choking blue-green algae that plagues Lake Winnipeg[7] and winding her way along the Nelson River. Then she passed north of York Factory and paused for a moment to consider the devastating impact that the fur trade had had on many of her namewak kin.[8] Once she found herself in James Bay, she had to swirl her way through polynyas and unseasonal hydrological shifts caused by Quebec's massive hydro projects along the eastern James Bay and Hudson Bay coast. She promised the eider ducks, dying as a result of the James Bay hydro projects,[9] that she would do her best to honour their stories. She then carried herself purposefully up the length of Hudson Bay and to the Arctic coast, and steeled herself for the cool journey through the Northwest Passage.

Once she had crossed the Atlantic, she teased her way along the North Sea coast, hugging western Scotland and greeting it with splashes of her long tail. "I come bearing gifts," she laughed. "Gifts of decolonial revenge," she added with a devilish smile. Like many a decolonial sturgeon before her, she followed the current with care and made her way up the north Scottish coast. Once she reached the mouth of the River Ness, she paused and breathed deeply.

"You got this, bb," she told herself.

She shook her fishy body, psyched herself up for the last leg of her journey. She knew this was the hardest but most rewarding part. Soon, reports would erupt on social media and in British local news: "MONSTER SPOTTED IN RIVER NESS!"

That was when she knew her work was taking hold. Peakish Scottish faces would soon appear on the shores of Loch Ness and crowd over the sides of tour boats. After a few playful laps around the lake, to drum up interest in her sudden reappearance in the loch, she would set up shop near Urquhart Castle, with a booth festooned with Prairie water quality reports, a full print-out of all 4,000 pages of the report from the 1996 Royal Commission on Aboriginal Peoples and a DVD player featuring every single documentary film by Indigenous filmmakers from back home for the Scottish public to view.

After that journey, she needed a rest. She took a short vacation in Iceland on her way back, making friends with local sharks. But she would not have the luxury of relaxing for too long. As she swam languidly in the Blue Lagoon, catching up with other decolonial critters criss-crossing the Atlantic on their own journeys, she got a private message on Twitter from Eric the Walleye.

"Stuff's going down in amiskwacîwâskahikan. Come quick! Need your help!" he said.

She made her way back to her coastal hotel room, nestled in the rocky shores of the western Icelandic coast. She logged on to her laptop and got the full story from her dear friend Eric. She did not always see eye to eye with Eric on many political topics. He was a bit more of a homebody, preferring to stick to Prairie lakes and engage in long debates with settlers about how to share territory reciprocally. But she knew that if he was asking for her help, things were serious.

He explained, in short Twitter messages, that the whitefish and minnows of the North Saskatchewan River had grown concerned over recent events in amiskwacîwâskahikan. The magpies, crows, and red-winged blackbirds had reported that in their fly-overs of downtown, they had seen two newish pieces of public art created by a white settler artist that were causing quite a bit of pain for Indigenous people in town. They had overheard Indigenous women discussing a mural that featured an image of a scalped Indigenous man— reports that it was making women sick to their stomachs and reports that some people felt the work was reinforcing hateful, possessive, and elimina- tory settler logics were circulating on the bird, tree, and amphibian social networks, which were all a-twitter.

"Something must be done," the sticklebacks had declared.

Now, everyone knew sticklebacks were outspoken critics of white liberal discourses. So at first their message was ignored by many. "Those stickle- backs, they're fighters," was what some of the squirrels had murmured. But when a sculpture of a severed red (Indigenous) hand appeared in downtown Edmonton in 2012 and was later acquired with public funds and perma- nently displayed in central amiskwacîwâskahikan, the animals and plants and minerals called a general council. The Ness namew, enjoying her layover in Iceland, somewhat reluctantly packed up her briefcase and set off back to the North Saskatchewan River. She knew she needed to be present for the historic deliberations of the fish, birds, insects, rocks, earth, water, and plants.

The creatures came to the meeting, held in pehonan at the bend in the river, armed with printouts of website blurbs from the local arts council, and email correspondence with municipal bureaucrats. The magpies, ever effi- cient, started the meeting:

"It has come to our attention that public funds have been used to support public art that portrays violence against Indigenous human bodies."

There was a ripple of murmurs and a few "for shame"s throughout the crowd. The trees bowed mournfully. The magpies continued: "It is being argued by some settler humans that this art is meant to draw attention to the plight of Indigenous people. It's meant to 'honour' Indigenous struggle."[10]

The crowd murmured again. "That's bullshit," a stickleback growled. A few people clapped. The sticklebacks read out anonymous commentary from social media articulating how the two pieces—the mural of a scalped man and the sculpture of a ripped and disembodied hand—made some Indigenous people feel hated and exploited. Rather than draw attention to the need to dismantle all manner of settler colonial violence, the pieces seemed to find a stylized and disaffected pleasure in the blood-soaked ground the Prairie city was built on.

Ever the devil's advocate, the butterflies countered that the art was maybe
meant to draw attention to the violence that Indigenous peoples have experienced on the Plains. "After all," a Great Spangled Fritillary drawled carefully,
"isn't raising awareness of violence an important part of countering violence?"

The proceedings were paused for a moment as the crows circulated some
photocopies of the artist's statement for the severed red hand sculpture from
the city arts council website. They noted that the most recent version of
the artist's statement housed on the City of Edmonton's Public Art website
avoided officially acknowledging the piece was meant to represent Indigenous
bodies, and also claimed the piece was created in consultation with inner city
residents.[11] A brief description of the piece on the Public Art online gallery
stated: "Created in consultation with members of Edmonton's inner city
communities, this sculpture represents the anger of disenfranchised urban
populations."[12] But plot twist: ever the resourceful researchers, the magpies
found the original 2012 artist's statement from when the piece was commissioned as part of the public art project called *Dirt City: Dream City*.[13] This
original statement showed the work was indeed meant to be a representation
of the/an Indigenous body, and did not explicitly reference the involvement
of inner city (Indigenous) residents or organizations, thanking instead the
artist's friends (many of whom were well-known figures in the local non-Indigenous arts and music scene). To underscore the original intent of the work
as inherently racialized, and to draw out the significance of the re-framing
of the piece by the city's arts agency as first, a sculpture not explicitly meant
to reference brutalized Indigenous bodies, and second, as created in consultation with "inner city communities," the magpies read out the entirety of
the artist's statement from the original show backgrounder to the assembled
creatures and critters:[14]

STATEMENT

The large wooden severed hand is seemingly "discarded" in a vacant lot.
The hand is roughly 15 ft long facing palm up, painted cadmium red,
and built strong enough for folks to crawl on if they desire.

The sculpture represents people who have been ripped off and are angry
about it. The racial reference to red acts as a willful remembrance of
the kind of thinking that has pushed such large portions of the native
population to the outskirts of our society.

The severed hand is a symbol of inability or impotence that has shown up in a few of my recent works. It is a projection of the subjective, self imposed feeling of uselessness and futility when you're down and out—trapped in a place you're not allowed to be a part of and not capable of leaving.

Nickelas Johnson would like to thank Tom Johnson, Sean Borchert, Norman Omar, Fish Griwkowsky, Jaime Fjeldsted, Jodie Cloutier, Michael Borchert, Jon Mick and a revolving cast of dear friends who came together and helped out.

When the crows finished reading, the sticklebacks jeered and affected a mocking tone as they read out an appraisal of the sculpture, published in the November 2015 *Edmonton Journal*, by a local settler arts writer who had been thanked in the artist's statement: "Beautifully painted and intentionally decaying, Johnson's largest sculpture so far is the gigantic severed hand, Ripp'd Off and Red, on the corner of 96th Street and 104th Avenue. It's easily one of the city's best—and most evocative—pieces of public art."[15] The muskrats paused. They could see the point the artist was possibly trying to make in the original stated intent of the sculpture—the history of brutal violation of Indigenous bodies in Canada was long, sickening, and omnipresent. This was confirmed by recent undertakings such as the Truth and Reconciliation Commission on Indian residential schools.[16] However, having studied in the great art schools of Paris, the muskrats knew that artists could easily fail in communicating their intentions. There was, they countered, a case to be made that the art was not particularly effective in challenging the very violence it seemingly intended to critique. The aesthetic and technical success of the work also needed to be considered. To draw out their point, the muskrats voiced several rhetorical questions: Did the work in its current form and location—a severed red hand placed in an inner city lot—effectively communicate that it was meant as a *sympathetic* portrayal of Indigenous corporeal suffering? In the original artist's statement the artist explicitly noted that the sculpture was meant to be climbed on—was this an effective way to communicate the autonomy of Indigenous bodies? Who was the intended audience of the piece—was there evidence in the background materials shared by the artist and the commissioning city organization of any anticipation by the artist and the sponsor that the placement of a symbolically brutalized Indigenous hand could trigger or intensify traumatic experiences of some Indigenous interlocutors of the piece? What were the parameters of the consultation alluded to in current official descriptions of the piece, and why were the inner city "communities" allegedly consulted for the work not mentioned by name?

Turning explicitly to the artist's technical goal of encouraging viewers to climb on the piece, the muskrats circulated a copy of an image posted in 2013 of the sculpture. The image, archived on the social media site FourSquare, showed a white man wearing buffalo plaid and sunglasses lying across the red hand sculpture, his whole white hipster body cradled in the decaying and disembodied red hand.

"Ah," the Ness namew thought to herself, "that old chestnut." She could not think of a better allegory for the settler imaginary of their relationship to Indigenous bodies and Indigenous law than this image of a white man lying across a severed red hand. The red cradle to a white race. Disembodied and voiceless red hands holding up feather-light white bodies as they arc their (covered) flesh toward the sun.

While the artist may have set out with the intention of affectively drawing attention to violations against Indigenous bodies in amiskwacîwâskahikan, the muskrats had their doubts this work was successful on that front. The muskrats had only to point out that many Indigenous people had articulated to them that they interpreted both of the artist's public art pieces—the sculpture and his mural of a scalped Indigenous person—as hateful and traumatizing. Aesthetically, the muskrats concluded, the sculpture and mural are easily co-opted into the dominant white supremacist view that Indigenous bodies are *meant* for violation, brutalization, and possession. The fleshy and visceral relationship between white consumers of the art must also be taken into account, the muskrats argued. In this way, they were not convinced the pieces achieved their stated goal.

The northern pike spoke up, softly: "I have been following this debate with great care. And I wanted to point out something quite sensitive and complicated. This sculpture is not just a private piece of art—it is deeply tied to public institutions and funds. We all know that this hand first appeared in a temporary art installation hosted by the Edmonton Arts Council in 2012.[17] It was then purchased by the city for its public art collection and permanently displayed in downtown Edmonton later in 2012, according to the artist's website."[18]

The creatures nodded. A moose let out a long and heavy sigh. The trade of a disembodied red hand from one settler arts body to another seemed rather routinized behaviour for settler organizations. The moose could not see what was actually transgressive about the work, nor did he believe that the organizations commissioning and purchasing it really understood how ironic it was for them to *literally trade in Indigenous body parts* in the twenty-first century.

The moose thought for a moment about the ways that Indigenous and Black bodies were paraded as spectacle in the nineteenth and twentieth centuries in America and Europe.[19] Human zoos, which were opportunities for white people to observe the Other as salacious entertainment, were also violent places: a 2016 report aired on the CBC program *The Nature of Things* describes French human zoos in the nineteenth century, where "terrible living conditions, foreign diseases, and the cold killed dozens of the performers, who were then buried in the gardens." In recent years, two controversial re-creations of human zoos were mounted by artists in Europe—one in Norway, and a second show at the Barbican in London that was cancelled.[20] Regarding the show in Norway, Bwesigye bwa Mwesigire wrote a critical rebuttal of the stated aims of the human zoo re-enactment: "[I]s there any artistic value in the re-enactment of such a dehumanising spectacle, especially in a world not yet fully healed of racism? Is this an abuse of art? Won't the re-enactment reverse the modest gains of the equality struggles, especially in a world that superficially engages the subject of race?"[21] The article concludes: "Fadlabi and Cuzner [the artists] can't exonerate themselves because they mean well. They must be responsible. Indeed, if they are serious about creating discussions of racism in the post-modern world, they ought to think deeper about the likelihood that their project may entrench the same prejudices they claim to fight."[22]

The moose decided that the question regarding the art in Edmonton remains: Is it an effective form of critique for white people to re-create the violence of racist colonial regimes in their art? Or does it simply re-create the violence within a society still implicitly and actively built on the dehumanization and brutalization of Indigenous bodies? And further, what are the possible reverberations and connections between the symbolic brutalization of Indigenous bodies in settler art in Edmonton and the intertwined realities of other white supremacist violations of racialized bodies in the city? Edmonton, as a city within a province with a long history of viscerally white supremacist (anti-Black, anti-Indigenous, anti-Semitic) political and social organization, was home not only to anti-Indigenous racism but also to anti-Black racism and other interrelated forms of white supremacy.[23] It was not possible or ethical to isolate anti-Indigenous forms of white supremacy in a Prairie city like Edmonton without also attending to anti-Black racism and other forms of insistent racism that shaped the entire settler colonial political formation of the city. After all, there is a strong canon of scholarship that tends to the entanglements and reciprocal relationalities of Black and Indigenous experiences of colonization of North America. For example, as Patrick Wolfe has argued in his early work,[24] settler colonization of North America relies simultaneously on the dispossession and elimination of Indigenous peoples in Indigenous territories in North America, while also dispossessing African peoples through the machinations of the transatlantic slave trade, relying on the enslavement of African and African-descended peoples in order to build the settler colonial order within these dispossessed North American lands. However, as Justin Leroy points out, in Wolfe's later works he embraces an uncompromising interpretation of the settler/colonized binary that leaves little room to engage with the suffering and experiences of enslaved African-descended peoples in North America.[25] Tiffany Lethabo King critiques the white-centric uptake of Wolfe's oceanic settler colonial theory by white settler colonization theorists.[26] In her work, King draws out specific formations of Black women's experiences of slavery and its ongoing legacies within the context of contemporary decolonization efforts. Specifically, she articulates a need for scholars not to abandon the concept of conquest in tangling with the genocidal impulses of colonization in the Americas: "Conquest is a larger conceptual and material terrain than settler colonialism and far more suited for the regional/hemispheric particularities of coloniality in the Americas and the specific ways diasporic Blackness gives conquest, genocide, and settlement its form and feel."[27]

In turn, Dakota scholar Kimberley TallBear attends to the interrelations of Indigenous and Black struggle in North America in her day-to-day intellectual engagements, reminding scholars and activists neither to ignore the injustices of slavery nor to normalize the erasure of Indigenous peoples from conceptions of the American nation-state and resistance to it. The interrelated but distinct experiences of Black and Indigenous peoples in the formation of the American and Canadian nation-states, and indeed through the interrelated histories and trajectories of conquest and settler colonization, as King reminds us,[28] speak to the overarching exploitation and violence of eliminatory and dispossessing white supremacist logics.[29] Taking such complex and interrelated struggles to heart, the Brown, Black, and Fierce! arts collective in Edmonton tends explicitly to the experiences of Indigenous, Black, and other racialized community members in the city, envisioning and mobilizing an art-life world that works beyond the confines and violences of white supremacy.[30]

The critters were labouring to honour these complex histories and relationships between oppressed communities in North America in their own deliberations.

What were the possible connections between the sculpture in Edmonton and other white supremacist and white possessive moves in the North American arts scene more broadly? The moose pondered: *Are these folks achieving their stated goals in their work, or simply reinforcing the view that Black and Indigenous bodies can and should be violated by white thinkers, artists, jurists, doctors, politicians, and other white actors?*

The northern pike spoke up again: "It's interesting to note that there is a shifting narrative around how the red hand sculpture came about—most recently, there are unverifiable claims it was created in consultation with unnamed inner city residents."[31]

A stickleback shouted: "WE ALL KNOW WHAT 'CONSULTATION' REALLY MEANS IN SETTLER CANADA!" A round of applause greeted this interjection.

The pike continued: "These claims of consultation seem to be leveraged as a bulwark against questions about the interpretation of the piece by those who feel sickened by the casual portrayal of violence against Indigenous bodies in the inner city. But the substantive question remains—why and how is it that public art that portrays exceedingly violent depictions of brutalization of Indigenous bodies is being created and funded with public dollars? And whose voices are heard in the debates around these pieces?"

A stickleback shot out of the water and yelled: "Classic white liberal deflection technique! If it's made *for* Indigenous people, then Indigenous people are supposed to be grateful for the white settler attention and settler allyship!" before splashing back into the cool waters of the North Saskatchewan.

The northern pike paused. What she was about to say was quite complicated, and she wanted to make sure she measured her words carefully.

"What has been haunting me, though, is that all of this is happening against a backdrop of a highly publicized case where a Crown prosecutor in

Edmonton/amiskwacîwâskahikan violently employed the disembodied pelvis of a murdered nehiyaw iskwew, Cindy Gladue, in a courtroom in 2015.[32] This case was such an egregious *literal* violation of a Cree woman's body, and on that account it received national news coverage, coverage that highlighted the interrelation of Cindy Gladue's treatment in the Edmonton justice system with the broader violent experiences of many missing and murdered Indigenous women and girls across the country.[33] This violation of Cindy Gladue's body was done without her permission (how could a person consent to such a thing?), and without the permission of her family.[34] Is it really transgressive to make art of brutalized Indigenous bodies when the very justice system that underpins the Canadian settler state is itself violently and abhorrently utilizing the same techniques in its deliberations?"

The northern pike trailed off. She was too upset to continue. The multitude of times that she had witnessed Indigenous bodies casually and deliberately brutalized throughout Edmonton made her angry. She finished by pointing out that her friend, a muskelenge, had told her of a similarly controversial art and anthropology world debate taking place concurrently in Montreal, where a white filmmaker had produced a purportedly "ethnographic"[35] film about Inuit entitled *Of the North*, which portrayed a brutal, and what some called sickening,[36] interpretation of Inuit life. The northern pike explained that the film, comprised of YouTube clips the filmmaker sourced online, is characterized by some who viewed it as a brutal, racist, and painful white settler distortion of Inuit life. The northern pike also explained that refusal of the film by Inuit is demonstrated by Jesse B. Staniforth's coverage in *The Nation* in 2015. She read out the following quote from Staniforth's article: "William Tagoona is a singer/songwriter and broadcaster in Kuujjuak, where he also works as a communications officer for the Makivik Corporation (though his comments here are his personal ones). 'As a residential school survivor I am sickened by the film,' he commented. 'For the whole 74 minutes I was red-faced—not from anger, but from feeling victimized. The film producer was defiantly raging his hatred on Inuit by purposely finding any trash he can find on YouTube and decorating it with some peaceful images to try and colour the true intent of the film.'"[37]

The butterflies spoke up again: "It is all well and good for Indigenous people to critique portrayals of them by white artists, but do artists not have freedom of speech? If we start policing their art and the subjects they choose for their art we are in the depths of fascism!" they shouted.

The northern pike inhaled deeply. "I have never advocated for censorship. What I advocate for is that those who commission, create, and defend these works about Indigenous bodies *by white artists* must understand that freedom of speech is not freedom from consequences for one's work or one's words, as Garfield Hylton argues.[38] I also want these settler artists and arts organizations to acknowledge how their work and operations are deeply imbricated in a white settler heteropatriarchal capitalist system that affords *some* bodies the platform to create—and sell—art, while other voices and bodies are not afforded such a platform at all. Perhaps white artists wouldn't have to *speak for* Indigenous people if Indigenous people had full and unfettered sovereign control over their own art."

The pike finished, and supportive cheers erupted from the sticklebacks and the crows.

The snails had been silent throughout the whole council. They were carefully parsing each argument, trying to make sense of how to proceed. They had been following the work of Dakota scholar Dr. Kimberley TallBear, a Canada Research Chair at the University of Alberta in Edmonton and were incredibly moved by her sharp analysis of settler colonial obsession with possessing and manipulating Indigenous bodies, Indigenous flesh, and even Indigenous DNA to their own colonial ends.[39] The snails were also deeply moved by TallBear's use of Aileen Moreton-Robinson's work in her incisive critiques of American exceptionalism in the heady days of post-election Trump America.[40] The snails held up a copy of Moreton-Robinson's book *The White Possessive.*

One especially tiny snail spoke up: "It has long been a white settler imperative to own, manipulate and control Indigenous bodies—both in life, in death, and even in ontological terms!" The small snail described Moreton-Robinson's seminal work on the logics of white possession in Australia, in which she writes:

> The "Aborigine" is invented as a white possession being accorded the necessary prescribed racialized attributes within racialized discourse. When racialized discourse constitutes and defines the "Aborigine," it is producing through knowledge a subject of its own making, one that it interprets for itself. This process violates the subjectivity of Goories and Koories by disavowing any trace of our ontological and epistemological existence. In this way "Aborigines" are constituted in and deployed

by racialized discourse as white social constructs and epistemological possessions. This Aborigine has functioned discursively in the print media for two centuries, with new racialized attributes added as the disciplinary knowledges of Law, Science, and Anthropology grew within the new nation.[41]

"As you can see," the snail continued, "in this sense, white people have been indoctrinated for centuries now to see anything Indigenous as their own construct, and their own kind of intellectual commons to mine for art and scholarship."

With the notion of Moreton-Robinson's *white possessive* in mind, the aspen trees circulated a photocopy of a *Canadian Art* article by Crystal Migwans entitled "The Violence of Cultural Appropriation," which details two instances of appropriation of Indigenous flesh and struggle by non-Indigenous artists. The first is an appropriation of Indigenous material culture (a faux Plains headdress) by the non-Indigenous artist Latifa Laâbissi. The second case study details a different violation: the aspen read out a quote from Migwans's article where Migwans describes an encounter with a non-Indigenous artist who wished to use the unclaimed bones of Indigenous people in an artistic intervention. Migwans describes the reaction of the artist to her own resolute refusal of the white possessive manipulation of Indigenous bodies, bones, and flesh: "They were surprised and annoyed by the suggestion that some materials and references were not available to them as an artist. They felt I was imposing upon their artistic freedom by asking them not to use another's body. Like Latifa Laâbissi, the artist said they would take my criticisms into account, but that it was their personal work and their decision alone. Also like Laâbissi, the artist stressed the goodness of their intentions and the virtue of their work as an anticolonial tool."[42]

Hearing this, the Ness namew sat up with a jolt, remembering her Catholic father's incantation that "the road to hell is paved with good intentions." She frowned at the memory, in keeping with her own misgivings about the Catholic church and its legacy across the Prairies. But she tried to extract the nugget of truth from the saying—the road to settler colonial domination in the arts surely seemed to be paved with good "ally" intentions.

All was not lost, though. Despite the fact that the processes through which the two brutalizing pieces had been approved revealed significant problems with Prairie arts administration and normalized white supremacist and white possessive ideologies embedded in settler colonial urban arts "allyship," there were meaningful things being done to refuse white settler control of the arts in Edmonton. "The good news," the northern pike explained, "is that some local Indigenous artists have worked very hard to foster a different paradigm. I'm hearing now that local artists must adhere to some Indigenous legal traditions if they hope to create certain kinds of projects in amiskwacîwâskahikan."

The question remained, however, of what was to be done about the open wound these two artworks—the sculpture and the mural—represented for some people. The creatures turned to the Ness namew. They knew she was pursuing a part-time PhD at a Scottish university, and they hoped she might be willing to take on the affective labour of challenging the social conventions that normalized the violent settler public artworks they were deliberating over.

She paused for a moment, unsure how to respond. An aspen spoke up: "Let us move this meeting *in camera*."

And with that, the Council of Creatures moved their deliberations out of view of the human world. I am told that they came to a collective decision about how to tend to the sculpture and the mural, and declared that they would lobby the human arts councils and fine arts faculties at the local universities with a sweeping and comprehensive set of reciprocal responsibilities for human artists to honour and co-constitute through time and space in amiskwacîwâskahikan. The northern pike, when interviewed by a local frog and toad media outlet following the meeting, indicated that there would be some big changes around these parts, with an insistent and unapologetic return to the reciprocal legal-ethical and kinship principles employed in local Indigenous legal traditions—inspired in part by the work of Robert Innes and his book *Elder Brother and the Law of the People*. Innes reminds us that the legal-ethical paradigms contained within Cree and Anishinaabe Elder Brother stories in his home community, Cowessess First Nation, have much to teach us about kinship, and living, co-constitutive, reciprocal forms of citizenship in the Prairies:[43] "For Cowessess people, these values are embedded in the stories of Elder Brother. Wîsahêcâhk and Nanubush, in Cree and Ojibwe/Saulteaux oral stories respectively, are also known by the kinship term Elder Brother. The Elder Brother stories as well as others are told in the wintertime by skilled storytellers. . . . The Elder Brother stories along with other stories, form the basis of the Law of the People that guided people's social interaction with all of creation, including kinship practices."

Drawing on this work, the creatures urged Prairie institutions and citizens to work hard to learn the enduring and powerful manifestations of kinship and law that inform relationships and protocols between Cree, Saulteaux, Assiniboine, and Métis peoples in Innes's home territory, and which deeply inform the treaty negotiations that shape Prairie treaty relationships between Indigenous and non-Indigenous legal orders and traditions.[44]

DISCUSSION

As the animals move on with their deliberations, let me return to the human work of deciphering and engaging with the theory and argumentation they mobilized in their council on the severed red hand sculpture and the mural of a scalped Indigenous man. The co-optation of visceral Indigenous suffering in white settler art is hardly constrained to the Canadian Prairies. As I write this piece in early 2017, several high-profile instances of white artists co-opting Indigenous and Black struggle(s) have come to light. One such instance is artist Dana Schutz's decision to paint an image of Emmett Till as he lay in his casket in 1955 after being murdered by two white men. The piece, entitled *Open Casket*, was featured in the 2017 Whitney Biennial in New York, where it elicited immediate pushback. Calvin Tomkins described this in his sweeping profile of Schutz in the April 2017 *New Yorker*:

> At the public opening, a young African-American artist named Parker Bright, wearing a T-shirt with "Black Death Spectacle" written on the back, stood for several hours in front of "Open Casket," making it difficult (but not impossible) for others to view the painting. He was joined from time to time by other silent protesters. That afternoon, a British-born artist and writer named Hannah Black posted a letter to the curators Lew and Locks on Facebook, demanding not only that "Open Casket" be removed from the show but that it be destroyed. "It is not acceptable for a white person to transmute Black suffering into profit and fun," she wrote.[45]

A second highly publicized case study of a white artist co-opting Indigenous suffering was Sam Durant's piece *Scaffold* at the Walker Art Center in Minneapolis, Minnesota. This work, originally shown at Documenta 13 in Kassel Germany in 2012, is a life-size recreation of a gallows. As Sarah Cascone notes, the piece references, in part, "the largest mass execution [in U.S.

history], which claimed the lives of 38 Dakota Indians in 1862, and took place in nearby Mankato, Minnesota. Made by a white artist, it looks like a jungle gym or a viewing platform, and is displayed alongside more lighthearted pieces such as Katharina Fritsch's giant blue rooster, *Hahn/Cock* (2013), and Claes Oldenburg and Coosje van Bruggen's iconic *Spoonbridge and Cherry* (1985–1988)."[46] Durant's piece elicited strong critique from Indigenous people. After an outcry from the public, the artist agreed to dismantle the piece, and Dakota leaders deemed the best course of action was to burn the sculpture: "The burning will be ceremonial, a Dakota tradition aimed at healing. Many Dakota elders believe that torching the timbers will bring finality to the dark history stirred by the sculpture, said Janice Bad Moccasin, a Dakota prayer leader and elder. 'The fires help us to release negative energy and acts placed upon us,' she said. If the sculpture were dismantled and placed in storage, that energy would remain, she added. 'We are ceremoniously releasing the spirit of that entire event.'"[47] As the case studies of the two art pieces in Edmonton, as well as the works by Schutz, Durant, and the film *Of the North* demonstrate, there seems to be no shortage of contemporary white artists speaking *for* Black and Indigenous life through their art in North America. In many of these instances, the artists state their desire to symbolically (re)produce the brutalization of Black and Indigenous flesh "in solidarity" with, or to raise awareness about, the struggles of marginalized peoples these white artists are representing.

However, I am interested here in the positionality of the white artists who choose these subjects relative to the Black and Indigenous communities and struggles that they represent. All things being equal (though nothing is equal in a settler, white supremacist, heteropatriarchal state), who has the power to speak for and about the struggles and brutalization of Indigenous life? In the Prairies, where Indigenous bodies are not only *symbolically* brutalized but in fact literally violated by white settler actors and agencies (see the tragic examples of the Saskatoon police "starlight tours" and the violent deaths of Neil Stonechild and Colten Boushie),[48] the choice to reproduce the violation of Indigenous flesh and bodies as "art" with public funds hosted on public land is not a transgressive commentary against white supremacy. Instead, it is a sad and predictable re-entrenchment of the very logics upon which white settler elimination of Indigenous life on the Prairies is predicated.

CONCLUSION

At a press conference following the council, the critters reaffirmed the rights of Indigenous peoples to refuse the white settler state and its exigencies for Indigenous peoples to accept the scraps and crumbs of violent white artistic "solidarity." The creatures and critters promised to support their human kin in a strong and unapologetic kind of Indigenous presence in the Prairies—a presence that is free, if it so chooses, to turn its back entirely on the false economy of white settler arts. They imagined, instead, a refusal to placate or humour those who would re-animate the brutalizations of Indigenous flesh in the name of "solidarity" while simultaneously profiting from the suffering of racialized peoples in a settler colonial nation state. The sticklebacks urged a kind of refusal and revenge, in the spirit of anthropologist Audra Simpson's articulations of powerful Mohawk political refusals of the violent settler colonization, dispossession, and illegality of the North American nation-states in Haudenosaunee lands in the northeastern portion of the North American continent.[49] Drawing on Simpson's work, the sticklebacks reminded those gathered that the work of settlers articulating and apprehending Indigenous thought, Indigenous bodies, Indigenous laws, and Indigenous stories is always couched in the violences and possessive logics of the white settler state. They noted that Simpson's work demonstrates how refusal is a powerful mode of disrupting these possessive logics. A tiny stickleback cleared her throat and began:

"In imagining what it means for you as white artists to engage with the ongoing violations and struggle of Indigenous peoples in the Prairies, I want you to sit with this quote from the work of Audra Simpson as she describes the labour and effort members of her own community of Kahnawake take in their relationships to colonial realities: 'What was crucial were the very deliberate, willful, intentional actions that people were making in the face of the expectation that they consent to their own elimination as a people, that they consent to having their land taken, their lives controlled, and their stories told for them.'"[50] The animals murmured and cheered. The stickleback, heartened by the encouragement, looked squarely at the television cameras and continued: "May you expunge from your minds this idea that Indigenous people must consent to your framing of their stories, may you disabuse yourself of this idea that you have a right to re-enact Indigenous suffering 'on their behalf.' May you forever remember, in the spirit of Simpson's work, that Indigenous peoples have willful and deliberate stories of their own, and these stories are not *for* you. And, finally, may you remember that Indigenous peoples owe you nothing when you tell their stories for them."

The creatures erupted in cheers. The cameras kept rolling as the animals stepped down from the small platform the aspen had built for the council. As the media vans pulled away from the press conference, the creatures and critters bade one another farewell and made their way to their respective homes.

The Ness namew closed her eyes after the last of the critters had flown, swum, and manifested their way home. She let her flesh fall heavy around her and settled in for the night. That night she dreamt of a fishy future devoid of white possessive logics—one built on kinship, care, reciprocity, and resolute refusals[51] of white supremacist settler art logics.

It was a good dream.

NOTES

1   Throughout this text, I choose not to italicize nehiyawewin or Indigenous words. This is in keeping with the spirit of the argument laid out in 2014 by Alice Te Punga Somerville regarding the treatment of Indigenous text in academic publishing: "The publishing convention of italicizing words from other languages clarifies that some words are imported: it ensures readers can tell the difference between a foreign language and the language of home ... Now all of my readers will be able to remember which words truly belong in Aotearoa and which do not." "Kupu rere kē," shared via Facebook. https://www.facebook.com/notes/alice-te-punga-somerville/kupu-rere-kē/10152910880595786.

2   CBC, "Reporter Expresses 'Regret.'"

3   Schieman, "Rising from the Dirt."

4   Moreton-Robinson, *The White Possessive.*

5   Simpson, *Mohawk Interruptus.*

6   Todd, "Decolonial Dreams."

7   Lake Winnipeg Foundation, "Mapping Out New Watershed Connections."

8   Holzkamm, Lytwyn, and Waisberg, "Rainy River Sturgeon."

9   Heath, and the Community of Sanikiluaq, *People of a Feather.*

10 Edmonton Arts Council, "Backgrounder."

11 Edmonton Arts Council, Public Art Collection, "Ripp'd Off and Red."

12 Ibid.

13 Edmonton Arts Council, "Backgrounder."

14 Ibid.

15 Griwkowsky, "ArtPic."

16 Truth and Reconciliation Commission of Canada, *Honouring the Truth, Reconciling for the Future.*

17 Edmonton Arts Council, "Backgrounder."

18 See Johnson, Artist CV; Edmonton Arts Council, Public Art Collection, "Ripp'd Off and Red."

19 CBC, "Human Zoos a Shocking History."

20 Ibid.; Wyatt, "Exhibit B 'Human Zoo' Show Cancelled."

21 Mwesigire, "Exhibiting Africans Like Animals."

22 Ibid.

23 Global News, "Edmonton's Historical Ties to the Ku Klux Klan Resurface."

24 Wolfe, *Settler Colonialism and the Transformation of Anthropology,* 2.

25 Leroy, "Black History in Occupied Territory."

26 King, "New World Grammars."

27 Ibid.

28 Ibid.

29 Ibid.

30 Brown, Black, and Fierce!, 18 August 2017. http://brownblackfierce.tumblr.com/. Accessed 2 September 2017.

31 Edmonton Arts Council, "Ripp'd Off and Red"; City of Edmonton, Indigenous Relations Office, personal communication, 29 July 2016 and 8 September 2016. This claim could not be independently

verified when I queried governing bodies about the origins of the piece in 2016. An official request to the City of Edmonton's Indigenous Relations office regarding the history of the purchase of the artwork, as well as questions regarding the origins of the mural of a scalped Indigenous person on the 109th Street bike path, were carefully taken up by a representative of that office. Unfortunately, the request to verify more recent public claims that the piece was created collaboratively with inner city residents (and that inner city residents had requested that the city acquire the sculpture for the City's permanent public art collection) led to a series of exchanges wherein a local arts council responded unclearly to the request for independent verification of the origins and purchase of the piece. I received a response from the Edmonton Arts Council that reasserted the public claims about collaboration with no clear indication of *which* autonomous inner city communities had collaborated on the work or allegedly requested its purchase from the city. Grateful for the help of the Indigenous Relations Office, but stymied by the runaround from the arts council, I gave up on trying to get official responses from municipal organizations on the specifics of creation and acquisition of the pieces in question. City of Edmonton, Indigenous Relations Office, personal communication, 2016.

32   Big Canoe, "Cindy Gladue Suffered Her Last Indignity at Murder Trial."

33   Hunt and Sayers, "Cindy Gladue Case Sends a Chilling Message."

34   Ibid.

35   Stewart, "Of Digital Selves and Digital Sovereignty."

36   Staniforth, "Of the North"—Quebec Filmmaker Uses YouTube and Unauthorized Music."

37   Ibid.

38   Hylton, "'Freedom of Speech.'"

39   TallBear, *Native American DNA.*

40   TallBear, "American Dreaming Is White Possessiveness."

41   Moreton-Robinson, *The White Possessive*, 457.

42   Migwans, "The Violence of Cultural Appropriation."

43   Innes, *Elder Brother*, 6.

44   Ibid.

45   Tomkins, "Why Dana Schutz Painted Emmett Till."

46   Cascone, "After Outcry from the Dakota Nation."

47   Ross and Eler, "Why Dakota Elders Want to Burn Controversial 'Scaffold' Sculpture."

48   Lee, "Indian Summer."

49   Simpson, "Consent's Revenge."

50   Ibid.

51   Ibid.

BIBLIOGRAPHY

Aboriginal Affairs and Northern Development Canada. *Backgrounder—Urban Reserves: A Quiet Success Story.* Ottawa: AANDC, 2008. https://www.aadnc-aandc.gc.ca/eng/110010001633 1/1100100016332.

———. Documents obtained through ATI request, A201301457_2014-02-05_10-28-02. Ottawa: AANDC, 2014.

———. *Fact Sheet—Approved Additions to Reserve Proposals 2014.* Ottawa: AANDC, 2015. https:// www.aadnc-aandc.gc.ca/eng/1398352543029/1398354251407.

———. *Land Management Manual.* Ottawa: AANDC, 2001.

Abu-Lughod, Janet. "Tale of Two Cities: The Origins of Modern Cairo." *Comparative Studies in Society and History* 7, no. 4 (1965): 429–57.

Adams, Howard. *Prison of Grass: Canada from a Native Point of View.* Saskatoon: Fifth House, 1989.

Adams, John, and Barbara Van Drasek. *Minneapolis-St. Paul: People, Place and Public Life.* Minneapolis: University of Minnesota Press, 1993.

Adams, Michael. *Fire and Ice: The United States, Canada and the Myth of Converging Values.* Toronto: Penguin Canada, 2004.

Adamson, Joni. *American Indian Literature, Environmental Justice, and Ecocriticism: The Middle Place.* Tucson: University of Arizona Press, 2001.

Adese, Jennifer. "Constructing the Aboriginal Terrorist: Depictions of Aboriginal Protestors, the Caledonia Reclamation, and Canadian Neoliberalization." In *Engaging Terror,* edited by Marianne Vardalos, Guy Kirby Letts, Hermino Meireles Teixeira, Anas Karzai, and Jane Haig, 275–86. Boca Raton, FL: Brown Walker Press, 2009.

Ahmad, Eqbal. *Confronting Empire: Interviews with David Barsamian.* Cambridge, MA: South End Press, 2000.

Ahmed, Sara. "Declarations of Whiteness: The Non-Performativity of Anti-Racism." *Borderlands* 3, no. 2 (2004).

Alfred, Taiaiake. *Wasáse: Indigenous Pathways of Freedom and Action.* Toronto: University of Toronto Press, 2005.

Allan, Billie, and Janet Smylie. *First Peoples, Second Class Treatment: The Role of Racism in the Health and Well-Being of Indigenous Peoples in Canada.* Toronto: Wellseley Institute, 2015.

Allen, Chadwick. *Blood Narrative: Indigenous Identity in American Indian and Maori Literary and Activist Texts.* Durham, NC: Duke University Press, 2002.

AlSayyad, N. *Forms of Dominance: On the Architecture and Urbanism of the Colonial Enterprise.* Aldershot and Brookfield: Avebury, 1992.

Andersen, Chris. "From Nation to Population: The Racialization of 'Métis' in the Canadian Census." *Nations and Nationalism* 14, no. 2 (2008): 347–68.

———. *"Métis": Race, Recognition, and the Struggle for Indigenous Peoplehood.* Vancouver: University of British Columbia Press, 2014.

————. "Residual Tensions of Empire: Contemporary Métis Communities and the Canadian Judicial Imagination." In *Canada: The State of the Federation 2003*, edited by Michael Murphy, 295–325. Montreal and Kingston: McGill-Queens University Press, 2003.

————. "Urban Landscapes of North America." In *The World of Indigenous North America*, edited by Robert Warrior, 139–70. New York: Routledge, 2015.

Anderson, Alan B., ed. *Home in the City: Urban Aboriginal Housing and Living Conditions*. Toronto: University of Toronto Press, 2013.

Anderson, Elijah. *Code of the Street: Decency, Violence, and the Moral of Life in the Inner City*. New York: W.W. Norton, 1999.

Anderson, Kim, Maria Campbell, and Christi Belcourt. *Keetsahnak / Our Missing and Murdered Indigenous Sisters*. Edmonton: University of Alberta Press, 2018.

Anderson, Mark Cronlund, and Carmen L. Robertson. *Seeing Red: A History of Natives in Canadian Newspapers*. Winnipeg: University of Manitoba Press, 2011.

Arlee, Johnny. "Salish and Pend d'Oreille People Meet the Lewis and Clark Expedition." Salish Kootenai College D'Arcy McNickle Library, Montana, 4–7 September 2002.

Assembly of First Nations. *Leadership Action Plan on First Nations Child Welfare*. Ottawa: Assembly of First Nations, 2006.

Auriat, Kerry. "Plight of Aboriginals Is About More than Racism." *Brandon Sun,* 2 July 2015. http://www.brandonsun.com/opinion/columnists/kerry-auriat/plight-of-aboriginals-is-about-more-than-racism-291138581.html.

Azure, B.L. "Small Signs Carry Big Messages." *Char-Koosta News,* 7 June 2018. http://www.charkoosta.com/news/small-signs-carry-big-messages/article_647dc1b4-69c2-11e8-8f14-cf7619384a85.html.

Baird, David W., and Danney Goble. *The Story of Oklahoma*. Norman: University of Oklahoma Press, 1994.

Baloy, Natalie J.K. "Spectacles and Spectres: Settler Colonial Spaces in Vancouver." *Settler Colonial Studies* 6, no. 3 (2016): 209–34.

————. "'We Can't Feel Our Language': Making Places in the City for Aboriginal Language Revitalization." *The American Indian Quarterly* 35, no. 4 (2011): 515–48.

Banivanua Mar, Tracey, and Penelope Edmonds, eds. *Making Settler Colonial Space: Perspectives on Race, Place and Identity*. New York: Palgrave Macmillan, 2010.

Banks, Dennis, and Richard Erdoes. *Ojibwa Warrior: Dennis Banks and the Rise of the American Indian Movement*. Norman: University of Oklahoma Press, 2004.

Barker, Adam J. "The Contemporary Reality of Canadian Imperialism: Settler Colonialism and the Hybrid Colonial State." *The American Indian Quarterly* 33, no. 3 (2009): 325–51.

————. "(Re-)Ordering the New World: Settler Colonialism, Space, and Identity." PhD diss., University of Leicester, 2012.

Barker, Joanne, ed. *Sovereignty Matters: Locations of Contestation and Possibility in Indigenous Struggles for Self-Determination*. Lincoln: University of Nebraska Press, 2005.

Barman, Jean. "Erasing Indigenous Indigeneity in Vancouver." *BC Studies* 155 (2007): 3–30.

Barraclough, Laura R. *Making the San Fernando Valley: Rural Landscapes, Urban Development, and White Privilege*. Athens: University of Georgia Press, 2011.

————. "South Central Farmers and Shadow Hills Homeowners: Land Use Policy and Relational Racialization in Los Angeles." *The Professional Geographer* 61, no. 2 (2009): 164–86.

Barrett, Stanley. *Is God a Racist? The Right Wing in Canada*. Toronto: University of Toronto Press, 1987.

Barron, F. Laurie, and Joseph Garcea. "The Genesis of Urban Reserves and the Role of Governmental Self-Interest." In *Urban Indian Reserves: Forging New Relationships in Saskatchewan*, edited by F. Laurie Barron and Joseph Garcea, 22–52. Saskatoon: Purich Publishing, 1999.

———, eds. *Urban Indian Reserves. Forging New Relationships in Saskatchewan*. Saskatoon: Purich Publishing, 1999.

Bartlett, Don V. Interview by E. Hausle, 30 July 1973. SDOHP 0952. Transcript. South Dakota Oral History Project. South Dakota Oral History Center, University of South Dakota, Vermillion, South Dakota.

Bateman, Fiona, and Lionel Pilkington. *Studies in Settler Colonialism: Politics, Identity and Culture*. New York: Palgrave Macmillan, 2011.

BC Representative for Children and Youth. *Too Many Victims: Sexualized Violence in the Lives of Children and Youth in Care*. Report prepared by Mary-Ellen Turpel-Lafond. 2016.

Belanger, Yale, Gabrielle Weasel Head, and Olu Awosoga, "Housing and Aboriginal People in Urban Centres: A Quantitative Evaluation." *Aboriginal Policy Studies* 2, no. 1 (2012): 4–25.

Belich, James. *Replenishing the Earth: The Settler Revolution and the Rise of the Anglo-World 1780–1930*. New York: Oxford University Press, 2011.

Bell, Avril. "Recognition or Ethics? De/centering and the Legacy of Settler Colonialism." *Cultural Studies* 22, no. 6 (2008): 850–69.

Berry, Mary F. "Homesteading: New Prescription for Urban Ills." *The Challenge*, January 1974.

Bevis, William. "Native American Novels: Homing In." In *Recovering the Word: Essays on Native American Literature*, edited by Brian Swann and Arnold Krupat, 580–620. Berkeley: University of California Press, 1987.

BigCanoe, Christa. "Cindy Gladue Suffered Her Last Indignity at Murder Trial." *CBC News*, 2 April 2015. http://www.cbc.ca/news/indigenous/cindy-gladue-suffered-her-last-indignity-at-murder-trial-1.3019500.

Biolsi, Thomas. *Deadliest Enemies: Law and the Making of Race Relations on and off Rosebud Reservation*. Minneapolis: University of Minnesota Press, 2007.

———. *Organizing the Lakota: The Political Economy of the New Deal on the Pine Ridge and Rosebud Reservations*. Tucson: University of Arizona Press, 1992.

Birch, Tony. "'The Invisible Fire': Indigenous Sovereignty, History, and Responsibility." In *Sovereign Subjects: Indigenous Sovereignty Matters*, edited by Aileen Moreton-Robinson. Crows Nest, NSW: Allen and Unwin, 2007.

Birong, Christine. "The Influence of Police Brutality on the American Indian Movement's Establishment in Minneapolis, 1968–1969." MA thesis, University of Arizona, 2009.

Bittner, Egon. "Florence Nightingale in Pursuit of Willie Sutton: A Theory of the Police." In *Policing: Key Readings*, edited by Time Newburn, 150–73. Portland, OR: Willan Publishing, 2005.

Black Hills Alliance. *The Keystone to Survival: The Multinational Corporations and the Struggle for Control of Land*. Rapid City, SD: Black Hills Alliance, 1981.

Blackstock, Cindy. "Residential Schools: Did They Really Close or Just Morph into Child Welfare?" *Indigenous Law Journal* 6, no. 1 (2007): 71–78.

———. "Should Governments Be Above the Law? The Canadian Human Rights Tribunal on First Nations Child Welfare." *Children Australia* 40 (2015): 95–103.

Block, Sheila, and Grace-Edward Galabuzi. *Canada's Colour Coded Labour Market: The Gap for Racialized Workers*. Ottawa and Toronto: Canadian Centre for Policy Alternatives and The Wellesley Institute, 2011.

Blomley, Nicholas. "Law, Property, and the Geography of Violence: The Frontier, the Survey, and the Grid." *Annals of the Association of American Geographers* 93, no. 1 (2003): 121–41.

———. "Making Space for Property." *Annals of the Association of American Geographers* 104, no. 6 (2014): 1291–1306.

———. "Mobility, Empowerment and the Rights Revolution." *Political Geography* 13, no. 5 (1994): 407–22.

———. *Unsettling the City: Urban Land and the Politics of Property.* New York: Routledge, 2004.

Bonds, Anne, and Joshua Inwood. "Beyond White Privilege: Geographies of White Supremacy and Settler Colonialism." *Progress in Human Geography* 40, no. 6 (2015): 715–33.

Bourassa, Carrie, Kim McKay-McNabb, and Mary Hampton. "Racism, Sexism and Colonialism: The Impact on the Health of Aboriginal Women in Canada." *Canadian Woman Studies* 24, no. 1 (2004): 23–30.

Bourgois, Philippe. *In Search of Respect: Selling Crack in El Barrio.* 2nd ed. New York: Cambridge University Press, 2003.

Boyd, Tona M. "Confronting Racial Disparity: Legislative Responses to the School-to-Prison Pipeline." *Harvard Civil Rights-Civil Liberties Law Review* 44 (2009): 571–80.

Brannum, Julianna, Bradley Beesley, and James Payne. *The Creek Runs Red.* Directed by Julianna Brannum, Bradley Beesley, and James Payne. Boston: Public Broadcasting Service, Independent Lens, 2007.

Braun, Bruce Willems. "Colonial Vestiges: Representing Forest Landscapes on Canada's West Coast." *BC Studies* 112 (1996/97): 5–39.

Brenner, Neil. *Implosions/Explosions: Towards a Study of Planetary Urbanization.* Berlin: Jovis, 2014.

———. "A Thousand Leaves: Notes on the Geographies of Uneven Spatial Development." In *Leviathan Undone? Towards a Political Economy of Scale*, edited by Roger Keil and Rianne Mahon, 27–49. Vancouver: University of British Ccolumbia Press, 2009.

Brigg, Morgan. "Biopolitics Meets Terrapolitics: Political Ontologies and Governance in Settler-Colonial Australia." *Australian Journal of Political Science* 42, no. 3 (2007): 403–17.

Broad, Dave. *Capitalism Rebooted? Work, Welfare and the New Economy.* Winnipeg and Halifax: Fernwood Publishing, 2000.

Broad, Dave, Jane Cruikshank, and Jim Mulvale. "Where's the Work? Labour Market Trends in the New Economy." In *Capitalism Rebooted? Work and Welfare in the New Economy*, edited by Dave Broad and Wayne Antony. Winnipeg and Halifax: Fernwood Publishing, 2006.

Brody, Hugh. *Indians on Skid Row: The Role of Alcohol and Community in the Adaptive Process of Indian Urban Migrants.* Ottawa: Northern Science Research Group, 1970.

Brokaw, Chet. "Multiple Drownings Stymie South Dakota Police." *Los Angeles Times*, 26 September 1999. http://articles.latimes.com/1999/sep/26/news/mn-14207.

———. "Officials Look for Answers in Rapid Creek Mystery Deaths." *Rapid City Journal*, 21 June 2009. http://rapidcityjournal.com/news/local/officials-look-for-answers-in-rapid-creek-mystery-deaths/article_42a62a1b-9d23-54d0-b145-86675f854e73.html.

Brokenhead First Nations v. Canada. Federal Court (FC) 982, 2009.

Broker, Ignatia. *Night Flying Woman: An Ojibway Narrative.* St. Paul: Minnesota Historical Society Press, 1983.

Brown, Dee. *Bury My Heart at Wounded Knee: An Indian History of the American West.* New York: Macmillan, 2007.

Brown, Jason, Nancy Higgit, Christine Miller, Susan Wingert, Mary Williams, and Larry Morrissette. "Challenges Faced by Women Working in the Inner City Sex Trade." *Canadian Journal of Urban Research* 15, no. 1 (2006): 36–53.

Brown, Lorne, and Caroline Brown. *An Unauthorized History of the RCMP*. Toronto: James Lorimer, 1978.

Brown, Nicholas. "The Logic of Settler Accumulation in a Landscape of Perpetual Vanishing." *Settler Colonial Studies* 4, no. 1 (2014): 1–26.

Brown, Wendy. *Regulating Aversion: Tolerance in the Age of Identity and Empire*. Princeton, NJ: Princeton University Press, 2006.

Brownell, Baker, Joseph K. Howard, and Paul Meadows. *Life in Montana: As Seen in Lonepine, A Small Community*. Missoula: University Press, 1945.

Brownell, Marni D. "Children in Care and Child Maltreatment in Manitoba: What Does Research from the Manitoba Centre for Health Policy Tell Us, and Where Do We Go From Here?" In *The Legacy of Phoenix Sinclair: Achieving the Best for All Our Children*, edited by Ted Hughes, 853–78. Winnipeg: Commission of Inquiry into the Circumstances Surrounding the Death of Phoenix Sinclair, 2013. http://www.phoenixsinclairinquiry.ca/rulings/ps_volume1.pdf.

Brownell, Marni D., Randy Fransoo, and Patricia Martens. "Social Determinants of Health and the Distribution of Health Outcomes in Manitoba." In *The Social Determinants of Health in Manitoba*, edited by Lynne Fernandez, Shauna MacKinnon, and Jim Silver, 1–2. Winnipeg: Canadian Centre for Policy Alternatives, 2010.

Brunette, Pauline. "The Minneapolis Urban Indian Community." *Hennepin County History* 49 (1990): 4–15.

Bruyneel, Kevin. "The American Liberal Colonial Tradition." *Settler Colonial Studies* 3, no. 3–4 (2013): 311–21.

———. "Race, Colonialism, and the Politics of Indian Sports Names and Mascots: The Washington Football Team Case." *Native American and Indigenous Studies* 3, no. 2 (2016): 1–24.

———. *The Third Space of Sovereignty: The Postcolonial Politics of U.S.-Indigenous Relations*. Minneapolis: University of Minnesota Press, 2007.

Buddle, Kathleen. "An Aboriginal Youth Gang Narconomy." *Hemispheric Institute* 8, no. 2 (2011).

———. "Urban Aboriginal Gangs and Street Sociality in the Canadian West: Places, Performances, and Prediaments of Transition." In *Aboriginal Peoples in Canadian Cities: Transformations and Continuities*, edited by Heather A. Howard and Craig Proulx, 171–203. Waterloo, ON: Wilfrid Laurier University Press, 2011.

Burnside, Linda. *Safe for Today: Barriers to Long-Term Success for Youth in Care with Complex Needs*. Special Report by Children's Advocate, Manitoba, July 2015. http://www.childrensadvocate.mb.ca/wp-content/uploads/Safe-for-Today-FINAL.pdf.

Byrd, Jodi A. *The Transit of Empire: Indigenous Critiques of Colonialism*. Minneapolis: University of Minnesota Press, 2011.

Cacho, Lisa Marie. *Social Death: Racialized Rightlessness and the Criminalization of the Unprotected*. New York: New York University Press, 2012.

Campbell, Maria. *Halfbreed*. Toronto: McClelland and Stewart, 1973.

Canada v. Brokenhead First Nation. Federal Court of Appeal (FCA) 148, 2011. http://decisions.fca-caf.gc.ca/fca-caf/decisions/en/item/37163/index.do.

Canada v. Long Plain First Nation. Federal Court of Appeal FCA 177, 2015. http://www.canlii.org/en/ca/fca/doc/2015/2015fca177/2015fca177.html.

Carpio, Myla Vicente. *Indigenous Albuquerque*. Lubbock: Texas Technical University Press, 2011.

Carroll, Clint. "Native Enclosures: Tribal National Parks and the Progressive Politics of Environmental Stewardship in Indian Country." *Geoforum* 53 (2014): 31–40.

Carter, Sarah. *Lost Harvests: Prairie Indian Reserve Farmers and Government Policy*. Montreal and Kingston: McGill-Queen's University Press, 1990.

Cascone, Sarah. "After Outcry from the Dakota Nation, the Walker Art Center May Dismantle a 'Traumatizing' Gallows Sculpture by Sam Durant." *Artnet News*, 30 May 2017. https://news.artnet.com/art-world/walker-controversy-sam-durant-scaffold-974612.

Cavanagh, Edward, and Lorenzo Veracini, eds. *The Routledge Handbook of the History of Settler Colonialism*. New York: Routledge, 2016.

CBC (Canadian Broadcasting Corporation). "Few Details in Kapyong Deal between Federal Government, Treaty 1 First Nations. Agreement in Principle Will Help Move Process Along to Final Agreement, Says Defence Minister." *CBC News*, 11 April 2018. https://www.cbc.ca/news/canada/manitoba/few-details-in-kapyong-deal-between-federal-government-treaty-1-first-nations-1.4615599.

———. "First Nations Group Granted Access to Kapyong Barracks for Ceremony." *CBC News*, 31 May 2016. http://www.cbc.ca/news/canada/manitoba/kapyong-barracks-campout-first-nations-winnipeg-1.3609314.

———. "Human Zoos a Shocking History of Shame and Exploitation." *The Nature of Things*, 17 June 2017. http://www.cbc.ca/natureofthings/features/human-zoos-a-shocking-history-of-shame-and-exploitation.

———. "Hundreds March in Support of Shoal Lake Freedom Road." *CBC News*, 12 September 2015. http://www.cbc.ca/news/canada/manitoba/hundreds-march-in-support-of-shoal-lake-freedom-road-1.3225818.

———. *Little Mosque on the Prairie*. Written by Zarqa Nawaz. http://www.cbc.ca/littlemosque/episodes.php?sid=2&eid=204.

———. "Reporter Expresses 'Regret' for 'Deadmonton' article." *CBC News*, 10 August 2001. https://www.cbc.ca/news/canada/reporter-expresses-regret-for-deadmonton-article-1.259335.

CCPA—MB (Canadian Centre for Policy Alternatives—Manitoba). *Step by Step: Stories of Change in Winnipeg's Inner City*. Winnipeg: Canadian Centre for Policy Alternatives—Manitoba, 2007.

Chan, Wendy, and Kiran Mirchandani. "From Race and Crime to Racialization and Criminalization." In *Crimes of Colour: Racialization and the Criminal Justice System in Canada*, edited by Wendy Chan and Kiran Mirchandani, 9–22. Peterborough, ON: Broadview Press, 2002.

Charette, Guillaume. *Vanishing Spaces: Memoirs of a Prairie Métis*. Translated by Ray Ellenwood. Winnipeg: Editions Bois-Brûlés, 1976.

Cheng, Wendy. *The Changs Next Door to the Díazes: Remapping Race in Suburban California*. Minneapolis: University of Minnesota Press, 2013.

Cheng, Wendy, and Rashad Shabazz. "Introduction: Race, Space, and Scale in the Twenty-First Century." *Occasion* 8 (2015): 1–7.

Cheung, Leslie. *Racial Status and Employment Outcomes*. Ottawa: Canadian Labour Congress, 2005.

Child, Brenda. *Holding Our World Together: Ojibwe Women and the Survival of Community*. New York: Viking, 2012.

Christle, Christine A., Kristine Jolivette, and C. Michael Nelson. "Breaking the School to Prison Pipeline: Identifying School Risk and Protective Factors for Youth Delinquency." *Exceptionality* 13, no. 2 (2005): 69–88.

City of Edmonton. Indigenous Relations Office and Edmonton Arts Council. Personal communication, 2016.

City of Winnipeg. *Aboriginal Persons Highlights*, 2011. http://winnipeg.ca/cao/pdfs/2011Aboriginal_Persons_Highlights_National_Household_Survey.pdf.

City of Winnipeg. Citizen Equality Committee. *One: The Mayor's National Summit on Racial Inclusion: Report*. Winnipeg, 2015.

Clatworthy, Stewart. *The Migration and Mobility of Canada's Aboriginal Population*. Winnipeg: Four Directions Consulting, 1995.

Clatworthy, Stewart, and Jonathan Gunn. *Economic Circumstances of Native People in Selected Metropolitan Areas in Western Canada*. Winnipeg: Institute of Urban Studies, 1982.

Clow, Richmond L., ed. *The Sioux in South Dakota History: A Twentieth-Century Reader*. Pierre: South Dakota Historical Society Press, 2007.

Comack, Elizabeth. *Racialized Policing: Aboriginal People's Encounters with Police*. Halifax: Fernwood Publishing, 2012.

Comack, Elizabeth, and Gillian Balfour. *The Power to Criminalize: Violence, Inequality and the Law*. Halifax: Fernwood Publishing, 2004.

Comack, Elizabeth, and Evan Bowness. "Dealing the Race Card: Public Discourse on the Policing of Winnipeg's Inner-city Communities." *Canadian Journal of Urban Research* 19 (2010): 34–50.

Comack, Elizabeth, Lawrence Deane, Larry Morrissette, and Jim Silver. *"Indians Wear Red": Colonialism, Resistance, and Aboriginal Street Gangs*. Halifax: Fernwood Publishing, 2013.

Comack, Elizabeth, and Jim Silver. *Safety and Security in Winnipeg's Inner-City Communities: Bridging the Community-Police Divide*. Winnipeg: Canadian Centre for Policy Alternatives–Manitoba, 2006.

Committee on Urban Indians. *Public Forum before the Committee on Urban Indians in Minneapolis-St. Paul*, 18–19 March 1969.

Community Welfare Council Indian Committee. *The Minneapolis Indian in Minnesota*. Minneapolis: Community Welfare Council of Hennepin County, 1956.

Conchas, Gilberto Q., and James Diego Vigil. "Multiple Marginality and Urban Education: Community and School Socialization Among Low-Income Mexican-Descent Youth." *Journal of Education for Students Placed at Risk* 15, no. 1–2 (2010): 51–65.

Cooke, Martin, and Danièle Bélanger. "Migration Theories and First Nations Mobility: Towards a Systems Perspective." *Canadian Review of Sociology/Revue canadienne de sociologie*, 43, no. 2 (2006): 141–64. doi:10.1111/j.1755-618X.2006.tb02217.x.

Cook-Lynn, Elizabeth. *Anti-Indianism in Modern America: A Voice from Tatekeya's Earth*. Urbana: University of Illinois Press, 2001.

———. *New Indians, Old Wars*. Urbana: University of Illinois Press, 2007.

———. "'There Are No Two Sides to This Story': An Interview with Elizabeth Cook-Lynn." Interview by Nick Estes. *Wicazo Sa Review* 31, no. 1 (2016): 27–45.

Cooper, Sarah. "Housing for People, Not Markets: Neoliberalism and Housing in Winnipeg's Inner City." In *2011 State of the Inner City Report. Neoliberalism: What a Difference a Theory Makes*, 20–36. Winnipeg: Canadian Centre for Policy Alternatives–Manitoba, 2011.

Coppola, Francis Ford. *Rumble Fish*. Directed by Francis Ford Coppola. San Francisco: Zoetrope Studios, 1983.

Cormier, Paul. "Indigenous Youth Conflict Intervention: The Transformation of Butterflies." *First Peoples Child and Family Review* 5, no. 2 (2010): 23–33.

Cornellier, Bruno, and Michael R. Griffiths. "Globalizing Unsettlement: An Introduction." *Settler Colonial Studies* 6, no. 4 (2016): 305–16.

Corntassel, Jeff. "Re-Envisioning Resurgence: Indigenous Pathways to Decolonization and Sustainable Self-Determination." *Decolonization: Indigeneity, Education and Society* 1, no. 1 (2012): 86–101.

Corntassel, Jeff, and Cheryl Bryce. "Practicing Sustainable Self-Determination: Indigenous Approaches to Cultural Restoration and Revitalization." *The Brown Journal of World Affairs* 18, no. 2 (2012): 151–62.

Cothran, Boyd. *Remembering the Modoc War: Redemptive Violence and the Making of American Innocence.* Chapel Hill: University of North Carolina Press, 2014.

Coulthard, Glen Sean. "From Wards of the State to Subjects of Recognition?: Marx, Indigenous Peoples, and the Politics of Dispossession in Denendeh." In *Theorizing Native Studies*, edited by Audra Simpson and Andrea Smith, 56–98. Durham, NC: Duke University Press, 2014.

———. *Red Skin, White Masks: Rejecting the Politics of Recognition.* Minneapolis: University of Minnesota Press, 2014.

———. "Subjects of Empire: Indigenous Peoples and the 'Politics of Recognition' in Canada." *Contemporary Political Theory* 6 (2007): 437–60.

Cowen, Deborah. *The Deadly Life of Logistics: Mapping Violence in Global Trade.* Minneapolis: University of Minnesota Press, 2014.

———. "Infrastructures of Empire and Resistance." *Verso*, 27 January 2017. http://www.versobooks. com/blogs/3067-infrastructures-of-empire-and-resistance.

Craft, Aimée. *Breathing Life into the Stone Fort Treaty: An Anishinabe Understanding of Treaty One.* Saskatoon: Purich Publishing, 2013.

Cregor, Matt, and Damon Hewitt. "Dismantling the School-to-Prison Pipeline: A Survey from the Field." *Poverty and Race* 20, no. 1 (2011): 5–7.

Crehan, Kate. *Gramsci's Common Sense: Inequality and Its Narratives.* Durham, NC: Duke University Press, 2016.

Cronon, William. *Nature's Metropolis: Chicago and the Great West.* New York: W.W. Norton, 1991.

Culhane, Dara. "Their Spirits Live within Us: Aboriginal Women in Downtown Eastside Vancouver Emerging into Visibility." *American Indian Quarterly* 27, no. 3 (2003): 593–606.

Curtis, Bruce. *The Politics of Population: State Formation, Statistics, and the Census of Canada, 1840–1875.* Toronto: University of Toronto Press, 2002.

Dalrymple, William. "The Great Divide: The Violent Legacy of Indian Partition." *New Yorker*, 29 June 2015. http://www.newyorker.com/magazine/2015/06/29/the-great-divide-books-dalrymple.

Daniels v. Canada.

Damas and Smith Ltd. *Neeginan: A Feasibility Report Prepared for Neeginan Manitoba Incorporated.* Winnipeg: Damas and Smith, 1975.

D'Arcus, Bruce. "The Urban Geography of Red Power: The American Indian Movement in Minneapolis Saint Paul 1968–70." *Urban Studies* 47 (2010): 1241–55.

Daschuk, James William. *Clearing the Plains: Disease, Politics of Starvation, and the Loss of Aboriginal Life.* Regina, SK: University of Regina Press, 2013.

Davis, Arthur. "Edging Into Mainstream: Urban Indians in Saskatchewan." In *A Northern Dilemma: Reference Papers,* Vol. 1. Bellingham, Western Washington State College, 1967.

Davis, Julie. *Survival Schools: The American Indian Movement and Community Education in the Twin Cities.* Minneapolis: University of Minnesota Press, 2013.

Dean, Amber. *Remembering Vancouver's Disappeared Women: Settler Colonialism and the Difficulty of Inheritance.* Toronto: University of Toronto Press, 2015.

Deane, Lawrence. *Under One Roof: Community Economic Development and Housing in the Inner City.* Halifax: Fernwood Publishing, 2006.

Debrix, François, and Alexander D. Barder. *Beyond Biopolitics: Theory, Violence, and Horror in World Politics.* London: Routledge, 2013.

Dedekker, J. "Mosque Closes Doors." *The Province,* 2 April 2012.

Delany, Samuel R. *Times Square Red, Times Square Blue.* New York: New York University Press, 1999.

de Leeuw, Sarah. "'If Anything Is to Be Done with the Indian, We Must Catch Him Very Young': Colonial Constructions of Aboriginal Children and the Geographies of Indian Residential Schooling in British Columbia, Canada." *Children's Geographies* 7, no. 2 (2009): 123–40.

de Leeuw, Sarah, and Margo Greenwood. "Geographies of Indigenous Children and Youth: A Critical Review Grounded in Spaces of the Colonial Nation State." *Space, Place, and Environment* (2016): 47–65.

de Leeuw, Sarah, Margo Greenwood, and Nicole Lindsay. "Troubling Good Intentions." *Settler Colonial Studies* 3, no. 3–4 (2013): 381–94.

Deloria, Phillip. *Indians in Unexpected Places.* Lawrence: University of Kansas Press, 2004.

Deloria, Vine, Jr. "Out of Chaos." In *For this Land: Writings on Religion in America,* 243–250. New York: Routledge, 1999.

Denetdale, Jennifer Nez. "'No Explanation, No Resolution, and No Answers': Border Town Violence and Navajo Resistance to Settler Colonialism." *Wicazo Sa Review* 31, no. 1 (2016): 111–31.

Department of National Defence. Documents obtained through ATI request, A-2010-01212. Ottawa: Department of National Defence, 2010.

———. Documents obtained through ATI request, A-2010-01225. Ottawa: Department of National Defence, 2010.

Dhillon, Jaskiran. *Prairie Rising: Indigenous Youth, Decolonization and the Politics of Intervention.* Toronto: University of Toronto Press, 2017.

Dorries, Heather. "Planning as Property: Uncovering the Hidden Racial Logic of Municipal Nuisance By-Law." *Canadian Journal of Law and Social Policy* 27 (2017): 72–93.

Dosman, Edgar. *Indians: The Urban Dilemma.* Toronto: McClelland and Stewart, 1972.

Dowell, Kristin. *Sovereign Screens.* Lincoln: University of Nebraska Press, 2013.

Doyle, J.J., Jr. "Child Protection and Adult Crime: Using Investigator Assignment to Estimate Causal Effects of Foster Care." *Journal of Political Economy* 116, no. 4 (2008): 746–70.

Dunbar-Ortiz, Roxeanne. *An Indigenous Peoples' History of the United States.* Boston: Beacon, 2014.

Eagle, Karin. "A Ripe Rank Case of Theft of Rapid City Land." *Native Sun News,* 17 February 2014. http://www.indianz.com/News/2014/02/17/native-sun-news-a-ripe-and-ran.asp.

Edmonds. "Unpacking Settler Colonialism's Urban Strategies: Indigenous People in Victoria British Columbia, and the Transition to a Settler-Colonial City," *Urban History Review* 38 (2010): 4–20.

———. *Urbanizing Frontiers: Indigenous Peoples and Settlers in 19th Century Pacific Rim Cities.* Vancouver: University of British Columbia Press, 2010.

Edmonton Arts Council. "Backgrounder." https://www.edmontonarts.ca/static_media/pdfs/files/eac_misc/DCDC1_backgrounder.pdf.

———. "Ripp'd Off and Red by Nickelas 'Smokey' Johnson." http://edmontonpublicart.ca/#!/details/164.

Elkins, Caroline, and Susan Pedersen, eds. *Settler Colonialism in the Twentieth Century: Projects, Practices, Legacies*. New York: Routledge, 2005.

Emery, James E. Interview by Stephen R. Ward, 11 July 1972. SDOHP 0527. Transcript. South Dakota Oral History Project. South Dakota Oral History Center, University of South Dakota, Vermillion, South Dakota.

England, Jennifer. "Disciplining Subjectivity and Space: Representation, Film and Its Material Effects." *Antipode* 36 (2004): 295–321.

Ennis, David. "Not All Down Hill from There: The Shoal Lake Aqueduct and the Great Winnipeg Water District." *Manitoba History* 75 (2014). http://www.mhs.mb.ca/docs/mb_history/75/aqueduct.shtml.

Episkenew, Jo-Ann. *Taking Back Our Spirits: Indigenous Literature, Public Policy, and Healing*. Winnipeg: University of Manitoba Press, 2009.

Ericson, Richard. *Reproducing Order: A Study of Police Patrol Work*. Toronto: University of Toronto Press, 1982.

Essed, Philomena. "Everyday Racism: A New Approach to the Study of Racism." In *Race Critical Theories*, edited by Philomena Essed and David T. Goldberg, 176–94. Oxford: Blackwell, 2002.

Estes, Nick. "Off the Reservation: Lakota Life and Death in Rapid City, South Dakota." *Funambulist Magazine* 5, May–June 2016. https://thefunambulist.net/history/off-the-reservation-lakota-life-and-death-in-rapid-city-south-dakota-by-nick-estes.

———. "Racist City, SD: Life Is Violent, and Often Deadly in Rapid City." *Indian Country Today*, 5 September 2014. https://indiancountrymedianetwork.com/news/politics/racist-city-sd-life-is-violent-and-often-deadly-in-rapid-city/.

Fehrs, Adriana. "The Good Life of Tony Incashola." *Char-Koosta News*, 1 May 2014.

Fiedler, Leslie A. "Montana; or The End of Jean-Jacques Rousseau." *Partisan Review* 16 (1949): 1239–48.

Filion, Pierre. "Concepts of the Inner-City and Recent Trends in Canada." *Canadian Geographer/Le Géographe canadien* 31 (1987): 223–32.

Fine, Michelle, and Jessica Ruglis. "Circuits and Consequences of Dispossession: The Racialized Realignment of the Public Sphere for U.S. Youth." *Transforming Anthropology* 17, no. 1 (2009): 20–33.

First, Jennifer, Toby Miolls-Sandoval, Nathan First, and J. Brian Houston. *Using Photovoice for Youth Resilience*. Columbia: Disaster and Community Crisis Center at the University of Missouri, 2016.

First Nations Child and Family Caring Society of Canada et al. v. Attorney General of Canada (representing the Minister of Indian and Northern Affairs). https://fncaringsociety.com/sites/default/files/AGC%27s%20submissions.pdf.

Fixico, Donald L. *Termination and Relocation: Federal Indian Policy, 1945–1960*. Albuquerque: University of New Mexico Press, 1986.

———. *The Urban Indian Experience in America*. Albuquerque: University of New Mexico Press, 2000.

Flowers, Rachel. "Refusal to Forgive: Indigenous Women's Love and Rage." *Decolonization: Indigeneity, Education and Society* 4, no. 2 (2015): 32–49.

Ford, Lisa. *Settler Sovereignty: Jurisdiction and Indigenous People in America and Australia 1788–1835*. Cambridge, MA: Harvard University Press, 2010.

Foucault, Michel. *The Foucault Effect: Studies in Governmentality*. Edited by Graham Burchell, Colin Gordon, and Peter Miller. University of Chicago Press, 1991.

Fraser, Alistair. *Urban Legends: Gang Identity in the Post-Industrial City*. Oxford: Oxford University Press, 2015.

Fraser, Sarah, Mélanie Vachon, Ghayda Hassan, and Valérie Parent. "Communicating Power and Resistance: Exploring Interactions Between Aboriginal Youth and Non-Aboriginal Staff Members in a Residential Child Welfare Facility." *Qualitative Research in Psychology* 13, no. 1 (2016): 67–91.

Freeman, Victoria. "Toronto Has No History!: Indigeneity, Settler Colonialism, and Historical Memory in Canada's Largest City." *Urban History Review* 38, no. 2 (2010): 21–35.

Fresonke, Kris, and Mark Spence, eds. *Lewis and Clark: Legacies, Memories, and New Perspectives.* Berkeley: University of California Press, 2004.

Friesen, Joe. *The Ballad of Danny Wolfe: Life of a Modern Outlaw.* Toronto: Signal, 2016.

Fumagalli, Andrea, and Sandro Mezzadra, eds. *Crisis in the Global Economy: Financial Markets, Social Struggles, and New Political Scenarios.* New York: Semiotext(e), 2010.

Furniss, Elizabeth. "Aboriginal Justice, the Media, and the Symbolic Management of Aboriginal/ Euro-Canadian Relations." *American Indian Culture and Research Journal* 25, no. 2 (2001): 1–36.

Garot, Robert. *Who You Claim?: Performing Gang Identity in School and on the Streets.* New York: NYU Press, 2010.

Gaudry, Adam, and Chris Andersen. "Daniels v. Canada: Racialized Legacies, Settler Self-Indigenization and the Denial of Indigenous Peoplehood." *TOPIA: Canadian Journal of Cultural Studies* 36 (Fall 2016): 19–30.

Gertler, Michael. "Indian Urban Reserves and Community Development: Some Social Issues." In *Urban Indian Reserves: Forging New Relationships in Saskatchewan*, edited by F. Laurie Barron and Joseph Garcea, 263–79. Saskatoon: Purich Publishing, 1999.

Gilchrist, Kristen. "'Newsworthy' Victims? Exploring Differences in Canadian Local Press Coverage of Missing/Murdered Aboriginal and White Women." *Feminist Media Studies* 10, no. 4 (2010): 373–90.

Gilmore, Ruth Wilson. *Golden Gulag: Prisons, Surplus, Crisis, and Opposition in Globalizing California.* Berkeley: University of California Press, 2007.

———. "Race and Globalization." In *Geographies of Global Change: Remapping the World*, edited by R.J. Johnston, Peter J. Taylor, and Michael J. Watts, 261–74. 2nd ed. Malden, MA: Blackwell, 2002.

———. "What Is to Be Done?" *American Quarterly* 63, no. 2 (2011): 245–65.

Gilmore, Scott. "The Hard Truth about Remote Communities." *Maclean's*, 9 February 2016. http://www.macleans.ca/news/canada/scott-gilmore-the-hard-truth-about-remote-communities/.

Glassner, Barry. *The Culture of Fear: Why Americans Are Afraid of the Wrong Things.* New York: Basic Books, 1999.

Goeman, Mishuana. "Disrupting a Settler Grammar of Place: The Visual Memoir of Hulleah Tsinhnahjinnie." In *Theorizing Native Studies*, edited by Audra Simpson and Andrea Smith, 235–65. Durham, NC: Duke University Press, 2014.

———. *Mark My Words: Native Women Mapping Our Nations.* Minneapolis: University of Minnesota Press, 2013.

Global News. "Edmonton's Historical Ties to the Ku Klux Klan Resurface." 13 January 2017. https://globalnews.ca/news/3180050/edmontons-historical-ties-to-the-ku-klux-klan-resurface/.

Goldberg, David Theo. *Racist Culture: Philosophy and the Politics of Meaning.* Oxford and Malden, MA: Blackwell, 1993.

Golberg, Michael, and John Mercer, *The Myth of the North American City: Continentalism Challenged.* Vancouver: University of British Columbia Press, 1986.

Gonzalez, Mario, and Elizabeth Cook-Lynn. *The Politics of Hallowed Ground: Wounded Knee and the Struggle for Indian Sovereignty.* Urbana: University of Illinois Press, 1999.

Gough, Jamie, Aram Eisenschitz, and Andrew McCulloch. *Spaces of Social Exclusion*. London, UK: Psychology Press, 2006.

Governor's Human Rights Commission. *Minnesota's Indian Citizens: Yesterday and Today*. St. Paul: State of Minnesota, 1965.

Gramsci, Antonio. *Selections from the Prison Notebooks*. Edited and translated by Quintin Hoare and Geoffrey Smith. New York: International Publishers, 1971.

Grandinetti, Tina. "Urban Aloha 'Aina: Kaka'ako and a Decolonized Right to the City." *Settler Colonial Studies* (2017): 1–20. https://www.tandfonline.com/doi/pdf/10.1080/2201473X.2017.1409400?needAccess=true.

Green, Joyce. "Decolonization and Recolonization in Canada." In *Changing Canada: Political Economy as Transformation*, edited by Wallace Clement and Leah Vosko, 51–78. Montreal and Kingston: McGill-Queen's University Press, 2003.

———. "From Stonechild to Social Cohesion: Anti-Racist Challenges for Saskatchewan." Presentation to the Canadian Political Science Association A9(b): Theory, Policy and Pedagogy of Decolonization, University of Western Ontario, 2–4 June 2005.

———. "Honoured in Their Absence: Indigenous Human Rights." In *Indivisible: Indigenous Human Rights*, edited by Joyce Green, 1–16. Halifax: Fernwood Publishing, 2014.

Greene, Jennifer. "Johnny Arlee, Cultural Leader, Has Walked Many Roads." *Char-Koosta News*, 8 August 2002.

———. "Pageant to Provide Education." *Char-Koosta News*, 18 July 2002.

Greenwood, Margo, Sarah de Leeuw, Nicole Marie Lindsay, and Charlotte Reading. *Determinants of Indigenous Peoples' Health in Canada: Beyond the Social*. Toronto: Canadian Scholars' Press, 2015.

Grekul, Jana, and Patti LaBoucane-Benson. "Aboriginal Gangs and Their (Dis)placement: Contextualizing Recruitment, Membership, and Status." *Canadian Journal of Criminology and Criminal Justice* 50, no. 1 (2008): 59–82.

Griwkowsky, Fish. "ArtPic: Nickelas Smokey Johnson and Candice Kelly's Glory." *Edmonton Journal*, 26 November 2015. http://edmontonjournal.com/entertainment/local-arts/nickelas-smokey-johnson-and-candice-kellys-glory.

Hackworth, Jason. *The Neoliberal City: Governance, Ideology, and Development in American Urbanism*. Ithaca, NY: Cornell University Press, 2007.

Hagedorn, John M. "Gangs, Institutions, Race, and Space: The Chicago School Revisited." In *Gangs in the Global City*, edited by John Hagedorn, 13–33. Chicago: University of Illinois Press, 2007.

———. *A World of Gangs: Armed Young Men and Gangsta Culture*. Minneapolis: University of Minnesota Press, 2008.

Haida Nation v. British Columbia, Minister of Forests. SCC 73, 3 SCR 511, 2004.

Hajari, Nisid. *Midnight's Furies: The Deadly Legacy of India's Partition*. New York: First Mariner Books, 2016.

Hall, Anthony. *American Empire and the Fourth World: The Bowl with One Spoon*. Vol. 1. Montreal and Kingston: McGill-Queen's Press, 2004.

Hall, Leslie. "The Early History of the Winnipeg Indian and Métis Friendship Centre, 1951–1968." In *Prairie Metropolis: New Essays on Winnipeg Social History*, edited by Esyllt W. Jones and Gerald Friesen, 223–41. Winnipeg: University of Manitoba Press, 2009.

Hall, Philip S. *To Have This Land: The Nature of Indian/White Relations, South Dakota, 1888–1891*. Vermillion: University of South Dakota Press, 1991.

Hall, Stuart, Chas Critcher, Tony Jefferson, John Clarke, and Brian Roberts. *Policing the Crisis: Mugging, the State, and Law and Order*. London: MacMillan Press, 1978.

Hallsworth, Simon. *The Gang and Beyond: Interpreting Violent Street Worlds*. Basingstoke: Palgrave Macmillan, 2013.

Hallsworth, Simon, and Tara Young. "Gang Talk and Gang Talkers: A Critique." *Crime, Media, Culture* 4, no. 2 (2008): 175–95.

Hamilton, Alvin C., and C. Murray Sinclair, Commissioners. *Report of the Aboriginal Justice Inquiry of Manitoba*. Vol. 2, *The Deaths of Helen Betty Osborne and John Joseph Harper*. Winnipeg: Queen's Printer, 1991.

Hannes, Karin, and Oksana Parylo. "Let's Play it Safe: Ethical Considerations from Participants in a Photovoice Research Project." *International Journal of Qualitative Research Methods* (February 2014): 255–74.

Hansen, Bert B. "An Evaluation of the Montana Study." *Journal of Higher Education* 20, no. 1 (1949).

———. "A Tale of the Bitter Root: Pageantry as Sociodrama." *Quarterly Journal of Speech* 23, no. 2 (1947).

Harding, Robert. "Historical Representations of Aboriginal People in the Canadian News Media." *Discourse and Society* 17, no. 2 (2006): 205–35.

Harjo, Sterlin. *Barking Water*. Directed by Sterlin Harjo. Tulsa: Indion Entertainment, 2009.

———. *Four Sheets to the Wind*. Directed by Sterlin Harjo. Los Angeles: Alchemy, 2007.

———. *Goodnight, Irene*. Directed by Sterlin Harjo. 2005.

———. *Mekko*. Directed by Sterlin Harjo. Tulsa, OK: Indion Entertainment, 2015.

———. *This May Be the Last Time*. Directed by Sterlin Harjo. New York: Sundance Channel, 2014.

Harris, Cheryl. "Whiteness as Property." *Harvard Law Review* 106, no. 8 (1993): 1710–91.

Harris, Cole. "How Did Colonialism Dispossess? Comments from an Edge of Empire." *Annals of the Association of American Geographers* 94, no. 1 (2004): 165–82.

———. *Making Native Space: Colonialism, Resistance, and Reserves in British Columbia*. Vancouver: University of British Columbia Press, 2002.

Harris, Maya. "Prison vs. Education Spending Reveals California's Priorities." *SF Gate*, 29 May, 2007. https://www.sfgate.com/opinion/openforum/article/Prison-vs-education-spending-reveals-2591142.php.

Harris, Richard. *Creeping Conformity: How Canada Became Suburban, 1900–1960*. Toronto and Buffalo: University of Toronto Press, 2004.

Hearne, Joanna. *Smoke Signals: Native Cinema Rising*. Lincoln: University of Nebraska Press, 2012.

Heath, Joel, and the Community of Sanikiluaq. *People of a Feather*. Directed by Joel Heath and the Community of Sanikiluaq. 2012. http://www.peopleofafeather.com.

Heitzeg, Nancy A. "Education or Incarceration: Zero Tolerance Policies and the School to Prison Pipeline." *Forum on Public Policy Online* (2009): 1–21. http://works.bepress.com/nancy-heitzeg/42/.

Helm, Lee, Vanda Hanakahi, Krissy Gleason, and Kayne McCarthy. "Using Photovoice with Youth to Develop a Drug Prevention Program in a Rural Hawaiian Community." *American Indian and Alaska Native Mental Health Research* 22, no. 1 (2015): 1–28.

Henry, Francis, Carol Tator, Winston Mattis, and Tim Rees. "The Ideology of Racism." In *The Politics of Race in Canada: Readings in Historical Perspectives, Contemporary Realities and Future Possibilities*, edited by Maria Wallis and Augie Fleras, Section 2.3. Toronto: Oxford University Press, 2009.

Henry, Robert. "Moving beyond the Simple: Addressing the "Misuse" of the FASD-Gang Link in Public Discourse." *Pimatisiwin* 11, no. 2 (2013): 241–54.

————. "Not Just Another Thug: Implications of Defining Street Gangs in a Prairie City." MA thesis, University of Saskatchewan, 2009.

————. "Social Spaces of Maleness: The Role of the Street Gang in Practicing Indigenous Masculinities." In *Indigenous Masculinities: An Anthology*, edited by Kim Anderson and Robert Innes, 181–96. Winnipeg: University of Manitoba Press, 2015.

————. "Through an Indigenous Lens: Understanding Indigenous Masculinity and Street Gang Involvement." PhD diss., University of Saskatchewan, 2015.

Hern, Matt. *What a City Is For*. Boston: MIT Press, 2016.

Herod, Andrew, and Melissa W. Wright, eds. *Geographies of Power: Place Scale*. Malden, MA: Blackwell, 2002.

Herrera, Allison, and Russell Cobb. "Tracing Tulsa's Creek Roots." *Invisible Nations*. KOSU, Tulsa, 22 June 2016. kosu.org/post/tracing-tulsas-creek-roots.

Hinton, Alexander Laban, Andrew Woolford, and Jeff Benvenuto, eds. *Colonial Genocide in Indigenous North America*. Durham, NC: Duke University Press, 2014.

Hoffman, Ron. "Canada's National Use-of-Force Framework for Police Officers." *Police Chief* 71, no. 10 (April 2004): 125–40.

Hogue, Michel. *Metis and the Medicine Line: Creating a Border and Dividing a People*. Regina: University of Regina Press, 2015.

Hokowhitu, Brendan. "Producing Indigeneity." In *Indigenous in the City: Contemporary Identities and Cultural Innovation,* edited by Evelyn Peters and Chris Anderson, 354–77. Vancouver: University of British Columbia Press, 2013.

Holzkamm, Tim E., Victor P. Lytwyn, and Leo G. Waisberg. "Rainy River Sturgeon: An Ojibway Resource in the Fur Trade Economy." *Canadian Geographer/Le Géographe canadien* 32, no. 3 (1988): 194–205. doi:10.1111/j.1541-0064.1988.tb00873.x.

Home, Robert. *Of Planting and Planning: The Making of British Colonial Cities*. London: Taylor and Francis, 1996.

Homstad, Carla. "Two Roads Diverged: A Look Back at the Montana Study." *Montana: The Magazine of Western History* 53, no. 3 (2003): 16–29.

Hovik, Suzanne. "Urban Indians Must Conquer Problems of 'Alien' Culture. *Minneapolis Star*, 3 April 1968.

Howard, Heather A., and Craig Proulx, eds. *Aboriginal Peoples in Canadian Cities: Transformations and Continuities*. Waterloo, ON: Wilfrid Laurier University Press, 2011.

Howard, Joseph Kinsey. *Montana: High, Wide, and Handsome*. Lincoln: University of Nebraska Press, 2003.

Howard-Wagner, Deidre, and Ben Kelly. "Containing Aboriginal Mobility in the Northern Territory: From Protectionism to Interventionism." *Law Text Culture* 15 (2011): 102–34.

Howe, Craig, and Kim TallBear, eds. *This Stretch of the River: Lakota, Dakota, and Nakota Responses to the Lewis and Clark Expedition and Bicentennial*. Sioux Falls, SD: Pine Hill Press, 2006.

Howe, Craig, Lydia Whirlwind, and Lanniko Lee, eds. *He Sapa Woihanble: Black Hills Dream*. St. Paul, MN: Living Justice Press, 2011.

Howe, Peter D. "Newsworthy Spaces: The Semantic Geographies of Local News." *Aether: The Journal of Media Geography* 4 (2009): 43–61.

Howitt, Richard. "Getting the Scale Right? A Relational Scale Politics of Native Title in Australia." In *Leviathan Undone? Towards a Political Economy of Scale*, edited by Roger Keil and Rianne Mahon, 141–55. Vancouver: University of British Columbia Press, 2009.

Hoxie, Frederick E., and Jay T. Nelson, eds. *Lewis and Clark and the Indian Country*. Urbana: University of Illinois Press, 2007.

Hubbard, Tasha, and Sherene Razack. "Reframing Two Worlds Colliding: A Conversation between Tasha Hubbard and Sherene Razack." *Review of Education, Pedagogy, and Cultural Studies* 33, no. 4 (2011): 318–32.

Hughes, Ted. *The Legacy of Phoenix Sinclair: Achieving the Best for All Our Children*. Winnipeg: Commission of Inquiry into the Circumstances Surrounding the Death of Phoenix Sinclair, 2013. http://www.phoenixsinclairinquiry.ca/rulings/ps_volume1.pdf.

Hugill, David. "Metropolitan Transformation and the Colonial Relation: The Making of an "Indian Neighborhood" in Postwar Minneapolis." *Middle West Review* 2, no. 2 (2016): 169–99.

———. *Missing Women, Missing News: Covering Crisis in Vancouver's Downtown Eastside*. Halifax: Fernwood Publishing, 2010.

———. "Settler Colonial Urbanism: Notes from Minneapolis and the Life of Thomas Barlow Walker." *Setter Colonial Studies* 6, no. 3 (2016): 265–78.

———. "What Is a Settler-Colonial City?" *Geography Compass* (2017): 1–11.

Hugill, David, and Owen Toews. "Born Again Urbanism: New Missionary Incursions, Aboriginal Resistance and Barriers to Rebuilding Relationships in Winnipeg's North End." *Human Geography* 7, no.1 (2014): 69–84.

Hunt, Sarah, and Naomi Sayers. "Cindy Gladue Case Sends a Chilling Message to Indigenous Women." *Globe and Mail*, March 25, 2015. https://beta.theglobeandmail.com/opinion/cindy-gladue-case-sends-a-chilling-message-to-indigenous-women/article23609986/?ref=http://www.theglobeandmail.com&.

Hylton, Garfield. "'Freedom of Speech' Does Not Mean Freedom of Consequences." *Ebony.com*, February 26, 2014. https://www.ebony.com/news-views/freedom-of-speech-does-not-mean-freedom-of-consequences-404.

Iacobucci, Frank. *Police Encounters with People in Crisis*. Toronto: Toronto Police Service, 2014. https://www.torontopolice.on.ca/publications/files/reports/police_encounters_with_people_in_crisis_2014.pdf.

Innes, Robert Alexander. *Elder Brother and the Law of the People: Contemporary Kinship and Cowessess First Nation*. Winnipeg: University of Manitoba Press, 2013.

Iverson, Peter. *The Plains Indians of the Twentieth Century*. Norman: University of Oklahoma Press, 1985.

———, ed. *"We Are Still Here": American Indians in the Twentieth Century*. Wheeling, IL: Harlan Davidson, 1998.

Jackson, Kenneth. *Crabgrass Frontier: The Suburbanization of the United States*. Oxford and New York: Oxford University Press, 1985.

Jackson, Kenneth, and Jaydon Flett. "Manitoba's CFS Girls: How the Province Feeds Winnipeg's Sex Trade." *APTN National News*, 24 June 2015. http://aptn.ca/news/2015/06/24/manitobas-cfs-girls-province-feeds-winnipegs-sex-industry/.

Jacobs, Bruce A., and Richard Wright. *Street Justice: Retaliation in the Criminal Underworld*. Cambridge: Cambridge University Press, 2006.

Jacobs, Jane M. *Edge of Empire: Postcolonialism and the City*. New York: Routledge, 1996.

Jacobs, Margaret D. "Genocide or Ethnic Cleansing? Are These Our Only Choices?" *Western Historical Quarterly* 47, no. 4 (2016): 444–48.

Jafri, Beenash. "Desire, Settler Colonialism and the Racialized Cowboy." *American Indian Culture and Research Journal* 37, no. 2 (2013): 73–86.

Jiwani, Yasmin. "Symbolic and Discursive Violence in Media Representations of Aboriginal Missing and Murdered Women." In *Understanding Violence: Contexts and Portrayals*, edited by Marika Guggisberg and David Weir, 63–74. England: Inter-Disciplinary Press, 2009.

Jiwani, Yasmin, and Mary Lynn Young. "Missing and Murdered Women: Reproducing Marginality in News Discourse." *Canadian Journal of Communication* 31, no. 4 (2006): 895–917.

Johnson, Nickelas. Artist CV. Undated. http://www.smokeydraws.com/index.php?/cv/.

Johnson, R.M. Untitled letter to Gerald Vizenor. June 12, 1969, box 2, Gerald Vizenor Papers, Minnesota Historical Society Archives, St. Paul.

Jones, John Paul, III, Helga Leitner, Sallie A. Marston, and Eric Sheppard. "Neil Smith's Scale." *Antipode* 49, no. S1 (2017): 138–52.

Jones, John Paul, III, Sallie A. Marston, and Keith Woodward. "Scales and Networks—Part II." In *The Wiley-Blackwell Companion to Human Geography*, edited by John A. Agnew and James S. Duncan, 404–14. New York: Blackwell Publishing, 2011.

Jonson-Reid, Melissa, and Richard P. Barth. "From Placement to Prison: The Path to Adolescent Incarceration from Child Welfare, Supervised Foster or Group Care." *Children and Youth Services Review* 22, no. 7 (2000): 493–516.

Kauanui, J. Kēhaulani. "'A Structure, Not an Event': Settler Colonialism and Enduring Indigeneity." *Lateral* 5, no. 1 (2016). http://csalateral.org/issue/5-1/forum-alt-humanities-settler-colonialism-enduring-indigeneity-kauanui/.

Kazemipur, Abdi, and Shiva Halli. *The New Poverty in Canada: Ethnic Groups and Ghetto Neighbourhoods.* Toronto: Thompson, 2000.

Kenora Online. "Shoal Lake 40 Shares Stories of Devastation and Anger." 10 July 2014. https://www.kenoraonline.com/local/shoal-lake-40-shares-stories-of-devastation-and-anger.

Kentfield, Calvin. "A Letter from Rapid City: 'The Only Thing to Do Is Wipe 'em All Out; Go Out There and Wipe 'em All Out.'" *New York Times*, 15 April 1973.

King, Anthony. *Colonial Urban Development: Culture, Social Power, and Environment.* London and Boston: Routledge and Paul, 1976.

———. *Urbanism, Colonialism, and the World-Economy: Cultural and Spatial Foundations of the World Urban System.* New York: Routledge, 1990.

King, Martin Luther, Jr. "Letter from Birmingham City Jail." 16 April 1963. http://teachingamericanhistory.org/library/document/letter-from-birmingham-city-jail-excerpts/.

King, Tiffany Lethabo. "Interview with Dr. Tiffany Lethabo King." *Feral Feminisms* 4 (2015): 64–68. http://muse.jhu.edu/article/633275.

———. "New World Grammars: The 'Unthought' Black Discourses of Conquest." *Theory and Event* 19, no. 4 (2016).

Kino-nda-niimi Collective, ed. *The Winter We Danced. Voices from the Past, the Future, and the Idle No More Movement.* Winnipeg: ARP Books, 2014.

Kipfer, Stefan. "Pushing the Limits of Urban Research: Urbanization, Pipelines and Counter-Colonial Politics." *Environment and Planning D: Society and Space* 36, no. 1 (2018): 474–93.

Kipfer, Stefan, and Kanishka Goonewardena. "Urban Marxism and the Post-colonial Question: Henri Lefebvre and 'Colonisation.'" *Historical Materialism* 21 no. 2 (2013): 76–116.

Kirbyson, Geoff. "Confronting Racism." *Winnipeg Free Press,* 20 March 2015. https://www.winnipeg-freepress.com/local/confronting-racism-296984281.html.

Klein, Malcolm W., and Cheryl L. Maxson. *Street Gang Patterns and Policies.* Oxford: Oxford University Press, 2010.

Kleinman, Arthur, Veena Das, and Margaret M. Locke. "Introduction." In *Social Suffering,* edited by Arthur Kleinman, Veena Das, and Margaret M. Locke, ix–xxvii. Berkeley: University of California Press, 1996.

Koch, Jordan, and Jay Scherer. "Redd Alert! (De)Coding the Media's Production of Aboriginal Gang Violence on a Western Canadian First Nation." *Aboriginal Policy Studies* 6, no. 1 (2016): 34–62.

Koelle, Alexandra V. "Pedaling on the Periphery: The African-American Twenty-Fifth Infantry Bicycle Corps and the Roads of American Expansion." *Western Historical Quarterly* 41, no. 3 (2010): 305–26.

Korsgaard, Ross P. *A History of Rapid City, South Dakota, during Territorial Days.* Pierre: South Dakota State Historical Society, 1977.

Kothari, Rita. "From Conclusions to Beginnings: My Journey with Partition." In *Partition: The Long Shadow,* edited by Urvashi Butalia, 30–48. Haryana: Penguin Books India, 2015.

Krouse, Susan Applegate, and Heather A. Howard, eds. *Keeping the Campfires Going: Native Women's Activism in Urban Communities.* Lincoln: University of Nebraska Press, 2009.

Kusch, Larry, and Mia Rabson. "First Nations 1, Ottawa 0—Treaty 1 Leaders Win First Battle over Kapyong Barracks." *Winnipeg Free Press,* 15 December 2012.

LaDuke, Winona, and Sean Aaron Cruz. *The Militarization of Indian Country.* East Lansing, MI: Makwa Enewed, 2013.

LaGrand, James. *Indian Metropolis: Native Americans in Chicago, 1945–1975.* Urbana: University of Illinois Press, 2002.

Lake Winnipeg Foundation. "Mapping Out New Watershed Connections." https://www.lakewinnipeg-foundation.org/news/mapping-out-new-watershed-connections.

Lakota People's Law Project. *Native Lives Matter.* Rapid City, SD: Lakota People's Law Project, 2015.

Laliberte, Ronald. "Being Métis: Exploring the Construction, Retention, and Maintenance of Urban Métis Identity." In *Indigenous in the City: Contemporary Identities and Cultural Innovation,* edited by Evelyn Peters and Chris Andersen, 110–31. Vancouver: University of British Columbia Press, 2013.

LaPrairie, Carol. "Aboriginal Over-Representation in the Criminal Justice System: A Tale of Nine Cities." *Canadian Journal of Criminology* 44, no. 2 (2002): 181–208.

LaRocque, Emma. *When the Other Is Me: Native Resistance Discourse, 1850–1990.* Winnipeg: University of Manitoba Press, 2011.

Lawrence, Bonita. "Gender, Race, and the Regulation of Native Identity in Canada and the United States: An Overview." *Hypatia* 18, no. 2 (2003): 3–31.

———. *"Real" Indians and Others: Mixed-Blood Urban Native Peoples and Indigenous Nationhood.* Lincoln: University of Nebraska Press, 2004.

Lawrence, Bonita, and Enakshi Dua. "Decolonizing Antiracism." *Social Justice* 32, no. 4 (2005): 120–43.

Lazarus, Edward. *Black Hills/White Justice: The Sioux Nation versus the United States, 1775 to the Present.* Lincoln: University of Nebraska Press, 1999.

League of Women Voters of Minneapolis. *Indians in Minneapolis.* Minneapolis: League of Women Voters of Minneapolis, 1968.

Lee, Erica Violet. "'Indian Summer.'" *The Monitor.* Canadian Centre for Policy Alternatives, 2016. https://www.policyalternatives.ca/publications/monitor/indian-summer.

Lefebvre, Henri. *The Production of Space*. Translated by Donald Nicholson-Smith. Oxford: Blackwell, 1991.

———. *The Urban Revolution*. Translated by Robert Bononno. Minneapolis: University of Minnesota Press, 2003.

———. *Writings on Cities*. Translated and edited by Eleonore Kofman and Elizabeth Lebas. Cambridge, MA: Blackwell Publishers, 1996.

Legal Aid Manitoba. *Notice to the Profession*. Manitoba: Legal Aid, 2013. http://www.legalaid.mb.ca/pdf/np_21_2013.pdf.

Legg, Stephen. *Spaces of Colonialism: Delhi's Urban Governmentalities*. Oxford: Wiley-Blackwell, 2007.

Lehman, Timothy. "Wrong Side Up: Joseph Kinsey Howard and the Wisdom of the Dispossessed." In *Regionalists on the Left: Radical Voices from the American West*, edited by Michael C. Steiner, 209–28. Norman: University of Oklahoma Press, 2013.

Leo, Christoper, and Kathryn Anderson. "Being Realistic about Urban Growth." *Journal of Urban Affairs* 28, no. 2 (2006): 169–89.

Leroy, Justin. "Black History in Occupied Territory: On the Entanglements of Slavery and Settler Colonialism." *Theory and Event* 19, no. 4 (2016). http://muse.jhu.edu/article/633276.

Lett, Dan. "Desperate Times Call for Desperate Measures—Conservatives' Decision to Relent on Kapyong Battle Speaks Volumes." *Winnipeg Free Press*, 24 September 2015.

Levin, Dan. "A Museum about Rights, and a Legacy of Uncomfortable Canadian Truths." *New York Times*, 5 October 2016. https://www.nytimes.com/2016/10/06/world/americas/winnipeg-canadian-museum-for-human-rights.html?_r=0.

Levin, E.A. *A Proposal for the Urban Indians and Métis*. Winnipeg: Dept. of Environmental Planning, 1972.

"Lewis and Clark Sesquicentennial, Council Grove Treaty Centennial, U.S. Forest Service 50th Birthday." 12–14 August 1955. http://ppolinks.com/forestservicemuseum/2017_66_3.pdf.

Lewis, Wallace C. *In the Footsteps of Lewis and Clark: Early Commemorations and the Origins of the National Historic Trail*. Boulder: University Press of Colorado, 2010.

Lezubski, Darren, Jim Silver, and Errol Black. "High and Rising: The Growth of Poverty in Winnipeg." In *Solutions that Work: Fighting Poverty in Winnipeg*, edited by Jim Silver, 26–51. Winnipeg and Halifax: Fernwood Publishing, 2000.

Lipset, Seymour Martin. *Continental Divide: The Values and Institutions of the United States and Canada*. London: Routledge, 1990.

Lipsitz, George. *How Racism Takes Place*. Philadelphia: Temple University Press, 2011.

Littlefield, Daniel. *Seminole Burning: A Story of Racial Vengeance*. Oxford: University Press of Mississippi, 1996.

Lobo, Susan. Introduction to *American Indians and the Urban Experience*, edited by Susan Lobo and Kurt Peters, xi–xvi. Walnut Creek, CA: AltaMira Press, 2001.

———. "Is Urban a Person or Place? Characteristics of Urban Indian Country." In *American Indians and the Urban Experience*, edited by Susan Lobo and Kurt Peters, 73–84. Walnut Creek, CA: AltaMira Press, 2001.

———. "Urban Clan Mothers: Key Households in Cities." *American Indian Quarterly* 27, no. 3 (2003): 505–25.

Lokensgard, Maurice Foss. "Bert Hansen's Use of the Historical Pageant as a Form of Persuasion." PhD Diss., Southern Illinois University, Carbondale, 1969.

Long Plain First Nation v. Canada. Federal Court (FC) 1474, 2012. http://decisions.fct-cf.gc.ca/en/2012/2012fc1474/2012fc1474.html.

Low, Setha M. *Behind the Gates: Life, Security, and the Pursuit of Happiness in Fortress America.* London: Routledge, 2004.

Lowe, Lisa. *The Intimacies of Four Continents.* Durham: Duke University Press, 2015.

Loxley, John. *Aboriginal, Northern, and Community Economic Development: Papers and Perspectives.* Winnipeg: Arbeiter Ring Press, 2010.

Lutz, John. *Makúk: A New History of Aboriginal-White Relations.* Vancouver: University of British Columbia Press, 2009.

Luz, Nimrod, and Nurit Stadler. "Religious Urban Decolonization: New Mosques/Antique Cities." *Settler Colonial Studies* (2017). https://www.tandfonline.com/doi/full/10.1080/2201473X.2017.1409406.

MacDonald, David B., and Graham Hudson. "The Genocide Question and Indian Residential Schools in Canada." *Canadian Journal of Political Science* 45, no. 2 (2012): 427–49.

Macdonald, Nancy. "Welcome to Winnipeg: Where Canada's Racism Problem Is at Its Worst." *Maclean's,* 22 January 2015.

Macdougall, Brenda. *One of the Family: Metis Culture in Nineteenth-Century Northwestern Saskatchewan.* Vancouver: University of British Columbia Press, 2010.

———. "*Wahkootowin*: Family and Cultural Identity in Northwestern Saskatchewan Metis Communities." *Canadian Historical Review* 87, no. 3 (2006): 431–62.

Mackey, Eva. "The Apologizer's Apology." In *Reconciling Canada: Historical Injustices and the Contemporary Culture of Redress* edited by Jennifer Henderson and Pauline Wakeham, 47–62. Toronto: University of Toronto Press, 2013.

MacKinnon, Shauna. "Making the Case for an Aboriginal Labour Market Intermediary: A Community Based Solution to Improve Labour Market Outcomes for Aboriginal People in Manitoba." *Manitoba Law Journal* 37, no. 2 (2013): 277–302.

———. "Tracking Poverty in Winnipeg's Inner City: 1996–2006." *State of the Inner City Report 2009.* Winnipeg: Canadian Centre for Policy Alternatives—Manitoba, 2009.

Maclean's. Transcript: Winnipeg Mayor's Press Conference on Racism. 23 January 2015. http://www.macleans.ca/news/canada/for-the-record-winnipegs-political-leaders-condemn-racism/.

Macoun, Alissa, and Elizabeth Strakosch. "The Ethical Demands of Settler Colonial Theory." *Settler Colonial Studies* 3 (2013): 426–43.

Magnuson, Stew. *The Death of Raymond Yellow Thunder: And Other True Stories from the Nebraska-Pine Ridge Border Towns.* Lubbock: Texas Tech University Press, 2012.

Mahon, Rianne, and Roger Keil. Introduction to *Leviathan Undone? Towards a Political Economy of Scale,* edited by Roger Keil and Rianne Mahon, 3–23. Vancouver: University of British Columbia Press, 2009.

Makela, Kathleen. "Legal and Jurisdictional Issues of Urban Reserves in Saskatchewan." In *Urban Indian Reserves: Forging New Relationships in Saskatchewan,* edited by F. Laurie Barron and Joseph Garcea, 78–95. Saskatoon: Purich Publishing, 1999.

Mandelker, Daniel R. "Removal and Exclusion Legislation." *Wisconsin Law Review* (1956): 57–78.

Manitoba Family Services. *Manitoba Family Services: Annual Report 2005–2006.* Manitoba: Manitoba Family Services, 2006. http://www.gov.mb.ca/fs/about/pubs/fsar_2005-06.pdf.

———. *Manitoba Family Services: Annual Report 2015–2016.* Manitoba: Manitoba Family Services, 2016. http://www.gov.mb.ca/fs/about/pubs/fsar_2015-16.pdf.

Manitoba Indian Brotherhood. *Urban Housing Survey*. Winnipeg: Manitoba Indian Brotherhood, 1971.

Manitoba's Children's Advocate. *Annual Report: April 1st 2000–March 31st 2001*. Manitoba: Office of the Children's Advocate, 2001. http://www.childrensadvocate.mb.ca/wp-content/uploads/ ChildrensAdvocateEng.pdf.

Marazzi, Christian. *The Violence of Financial Capitalism*. New York: Semiotext(e), 2010.

Marcuse, Peter. "Whose Right(s) to What City?" In *Cities for People, Not for Profit: Critical Urban Theory and the Right to the City*, edited by Neil Brenner, Peter Marcuse, and Margit Mayer, 24–41. London and New York: Routledge, 2012.

Martin, Deborah G. "Constructing Place: Cultural Hegemonies and Media Images of an Inner-City Neighborhood." *Urban Geography* 21, no. 5 (2000): 380–405.

Martin, Judith, and Anthony Goddard. *Past Choices/Present Landscapes: The Impact of Urban Renewal on the Twin Cities*. Minneapolis: Center for Urban and Regional Affairs, University of Minnesota, 1989.

Massey, Doreen B. *Space, Place, and Gender*. Minneapolis: University of Minnesota Press, 1994.

Mawani, Renisa. *Colonial Proximities: Crossracial Encounters and Juridical Truths in British Columbia, 1871–1921*. Vancouver: University of British Columbia Press, 2009.

———. "Genealogies of the Land: Aboriginality, Law, and Territory in Vancouver's Stanley Park." *Social and Legal Studies* 14, no. 3 (2005): 315–39.

May, Katie. "Teen Sentenced for Parkade Attack That Left Girl with Permanent Injuries." *Winnipeg Free Press*, 18 August 2016. http://www.winnipegfreepress.com/local/teen-sentenced-for-parkade-attack-that-left-girl-with-permanent-injuries-390635501.html.

Mays, Kyle T. "Pontiac's Ghost in the Motor City: Indigeneity and the Discursive Construction of Modern Detroit." *Middle West Review* 2, no. 2 (2016): 115–42.

Mbembe, Achille. "Necropolitics." *Public Culture* 15, no. 1 (2003): 11–40.

McAdam, Sylvia (Saysewahum). "Armed with Nothing More than a Song and a Drum: Idle No More." In *The Winter We Danced: Voices from the Past, the Future, and the Idle No More Movement*, edited by Kino-nda-niimi Collective. Winnipeg: ARP, 2014.

———. *Nationhood Interrupted: Revitalizing nêhiyaw Legal Systems*. Vancouver: UBC Press, 2015.

McClintock, Nathan. "Urban Agriculture, Racial Capitalism, and Resistance in the Settler-Colonial City." *Geography Compass* 12, no. 6 (2018). https://onlinelibrary.wiley.com/doi/epdf/10.1111/gec3.12373.

McCreary, Tyler. *Shared Histories: A History of Settler-Witsuwit'en Relations in Smithers, British Columbia, 1921–1967*. Smithers, BC: Creekstone Press, 2018.

McCreary, Tyler, and Richard Milligan. "The Limits of Liberal Recognition: Racial Capitalism, Settler Colonialism, and Environmental Governance in Vancouver and Atlanta." *Antipode*. (forthcoming).

———. "Pipelines, Permits, and Protests: Carrier Sekani Encounters with the Enbridge Northern Gateway Project." *Cultural Geographies* 21, no.1 (2014): 115–29.

McKenzie, Brad, and Larry Morrissette. "Cultural Empowerment and Healing for Aboriginal Youth in Winnipeg." In *Rebirth: Political, Economic, and Social Development in First Nations*, edited by Anne-Marie Mai, 117–130. Toronto: Dundurn Press, 1993.

McKenzie, Holly A., Collen Varcoe, Annette J. Browne, and Linda Day. "Disrupting the Continuities among Residential Schools, the Sixties Scoop, and Child Welfare: An Analysis of Colonial and Neocolonial Discourses." *International Indigenous Policy Journal* 7 no. 2, 4 (2016): 1–24.

Mecoy, Don. "Tribal Activities Make $10.8B Impact on Oklahoma's Economic Output, Study Suggests." *Newsok.com*, 26 October 2012. http://newsok.com/article/3719667.

Migwans, Crystal. "The Violence of Cultural Appropriation." *Canadian Art*, 7 February 2017. http://canadianart.ca/features/violence-cultural-appropriation/.

Mikisew Cree First Nation v. Canada Minister of Canadian Heritage. SCC 69, [2005] 3 SCR 388, 2005.

Miles, Robert. "Apropos the Idea of 'Race' . . . Again." In *Theories of Race and Racism*, edited by Les Back and John Solomos, 125–44. London: Routledge, 2000.

———. *Racism*. Milton Keynes: Open University Press, 1989.

Milgrom, Richard. "Slow Growth versus the Sprawl Machine: Winnipeg, Manitoba." In *In-Between Infrastructure: Urban Connectivity in an Age of Vulnerability*, edited by Douglas Young, Patricia Burke Wood, and Roger Kiel, 87–100. Kelowna, BC: Praxis (e)Press, 2011.

Miller, Jaimy L. "The Papaschase Band: Building Awareness and Community in the City of Edmonton." In *Aboriginal Peoples in Canadian Cities: Transformations and Continuities*, edited by Heather A. Howard and Craig Proulx, 53–68. Waterloo, ON: Wilfrid Laurier University Press, 2011.

Miller, J.R. *Compact, Contract, Convenant. Aboriginal Treaty-Making in Canada*. Toronto: University of Toronto Press, 2009.

Milligan, Richard, and Tyler McCreary. "Between Kitimat LNG Terminal and *Monkey Beach*: Literary-Geographic Methods and the Politics of Recognition in Resource Governance on Haisla Territory." *GeoHumanities* 4, no. 1 (2018): 45–65.

Milloy, John. *A National Crime: The Canadian Government and the Residential School System, 1879 to 1986*. Winnipeg: University of Manitoba Press, 1999.

Miners for Safety. Yellow Thunder Camp Press Release, 17 April 1981. Roger A. Finzel Papers, Center for Southwest Research, University of New Mexico, Box 2, Folder 19.

Minneapolis Tribune. "The Plight of the Urban Indian." 11 April 1968.

Minnesota Human Rights Commission. *Police Brutality, Minneapolis Public Hearing #2*. 25 June 1975, Minneapolis.

Mitchell, Claudia. *Doing Visual Research*. Los Angeles: Sage, 2011.

Mitchell, Don. "Neil Smith, 1954–2012: Marxist Geographer." *Annals of the Association of American Geographers* 104, no. 1 (2014): 215–22.

Momaday, N. Scott. *House Made of Dawn*. London: Harper and Row, 1968.

Monteith, William. "Markets and Monarchs: Indigenous Urbanism in Postcolonial Kampala." *Settler Colonial Studies* (2017). https://www.tandfonline.com/doi/pdf/10.1080/2201473X.2017.1409402?needAccess=true.

Monture, Patricia A. "Race and Erasing: Law and Gender in White Settler Societies." In *Race and Racism in 21st Century Canada,* edited by Sean P. Heir and B. Singh Bolaria, 197–216. Peterborough, ON: Broadview Press, 2007.

Monture-Angus, Patricia. *Journeying Forward: Dreaming First Nations Independence*. Halifax: Fernwood Publishing, 1999.

———. *Thunder in My Soul: A Mohawk Woman Speaks*. Halifax: Fernwood Publishing, 1995.

Morellato, Maria. *The Crown's Constitutional Duty to Consult and Accommodate Aboriginal and Treaty Rights*. Vancouver: National Centre for First Nations Governance, 2008.

Moreton-Robinson, Aileen. *The White Possessive: Property, Power and Indigenous Sovereignty*. Minneapolis: University of Minnesota Press, 2015.

Morgensen, Scott Lauria. "The Biopolitics of Settler Colonialism: Right Here, Right Now." *Settler Colonial Studies* 1, no. 1 (2011): 52–76.

————. *Spaces between Us: Queer Settler Colonialism and Indigenous Decolonization*. Minneapolis: University of Minnesota Press, 2011.

Morrissette, Larry, and David Blacksmith. "Winnipeg's Bear Clan Patrol." *Canadian Dimension* 27, no. 3 (May/June 1993): 24–26.

Muecke, Stephen. *Ancient and Modern: Time, Culture and Indigenous Philosophy*. Sydney, NSW: University of New South Wales Press, 2004.

Mukhopadhyay, Baijayanta. "Care as Colonialism: Immigrant Health Workers at Canada's Frontiers." *Upping the Anti: A Journal of Theory and Action*, 19 (2017). https://uppingtheanti.org/journal/article/19-care-as-colonialism.

Mwesigire, Bwesigye bwa. "Exhibiting Africans Like Animals in Norway's Human Zoo." *This Is Africa*. 25 April 2014. https://thisisafrica.me/exhibiting-africans-like-animals-norways-human-zoo/.

Nagler, Mark. *Indians in the City: A Study of the Urbanization of Indians in Toronto*. Ottawa: Canadian Research Centre for Anthropology, St. Paul University, 1970.

Nawaz, Mumtaz Shah. *The Heart Divided*. New Delhi: Penguin Books, 2004.

Needham, Andrew. *Power Lines: Phoenix and the Making of the Modern Southwest*. Princeton, NJ: Princeton University Press, 2014.

Neely, Brooke, and Michelle Samura. "Social Geographies of Race: Connecting Race and Space." *Ethnic and Racial Studies* 34, no. 11 (2011): 1933–52.

Negri, Antonio. "The Labor of the Multitude and the Fabric of Biopolitics." *Mediations* 23, no. 2 (2008): 8–25.

Neils, Elaine. *Reservation to City: Indian Migration and Federal Relocation*. Chicago: University of Chicago Department of Geography, 1971.

Nelson, Philip J. "Community Dreaming in the Rural Northwest: The Montana Study, 1944–47." *Great Plains Quarterly* 19, no. 4 (1999): 257–75.

————. "Regionalism and the Humanities Division of the Rockefeller Foundation." *Research Reports from the Rockefeller Archive Center* (1998): 12–14.

Nettelbeck, Amanda, and Russell Smandych. "Policing Indigenous Peoples on Two Colonial Frontiers: Australia's Mounted Police and Canada's North-West Mounted Police." *Australian and New Zealand Journal of Criminology* 43, no. 2 (2010): 356–75.

Newhouse, David, and Evelyn Peters, eds. *Not Strangers in These Parts: Urban Aboriginal Peoples*. Ottawa: Policy Research Initiative, 2003.

Niezen, Ronald. *Truth and Indignation: Canada's Truth and Reconciliation Commission on Indian Residential Schools*. Toronto: University of Toronto Press, 2013.

Nightingale, Carl. *Segregation: A Global History of Divided Cities*. Chicago: University of Chicago Press, 2012.

Norris, Mary Jane, and Stewart Clatworthy. "Urbanization and Migration Patterns of Aboriginal Populations in Canada: A Half Century in Review (1951 to 2006)." Presented at Indigenous Urbanization in International Perspective, Departments of Native Studies and Geography, University of Saskatchewan, Saskatoon, 29–30 October 2009. DRAFT 20 May 2010.

O'Brien, Jean. *Firsting and Lasting: Writing Indians Out of Existence in New England*. Minneapolis: University of Minnesota Press, 2010.

OED Online. "reservation, n." http://www.oed.com.libproxy.unm.edu/view/Entry/163498?rskey=mU7xUw&result=1.

Omi, Michael, and Howard Winant. *Racial Formation in the United States: From the 1960s to the 1980s.* New York: Routledge and Kegan Paul, 1986.

Ostler, Jeffrey. *The Lakotas and the Black Hills: The Struggle for Sacred Ground.* New York: Viking, 2010.

———. *The Plains Sioux and U.S. Colonialism: From Lewis and Clark to Wounded Knee.* Cambridge: Cambridge University Press, 2004.

Pan, Stephen W., Chief Wayne M. Christian, Margo E. Pearce, Alden H. Blair, Kate Jongbloed, Hongbin Zhang, Mary Teegee, Vicky Thomas, Martin T. Shechter, and Patricia M. Spittal. "The Cedar Project: Impacts of Policing among Young Aboriginal People Who Use Injection and Non-Injection Drugs in British Columbia, Canada." *International Journal of Drug Policy* 24, no. 5 (2013): 449–59.

Pasternak, Shiri. *Grounded Authority: The Algonquins of Barriere Lake against the State.* Minneapolis: University of Minnesota Press, 2017.

———. "How Capitalism Will Save Colonialism: The Privatization of Reserve Lands in Canada." *Antipode* 47, no. 1 (2015): 179–96.

———. "Jurisdiction and Settler Colonialism: Where Do Laws Meet?" *Canadian Journal of Law and Society* 29, no. 2 (2014): 145–61.

Paul, Alexandra. "City's First Urban Reserve Born—Native Leaders Hail Opening of Polo Park-Area Property." *Winnipeg Free Press,* 24 May 2013.

———. "Grand Plan for Prosperity: Leader of Southern Chiefs Organization Calls Urban Reserves 'Our Path Out of Poverty.'" *Winnipeg Free Press,* 6 February 2014.

———. "Racism Is Manitoba's Shame, Oswald Declares." *Winnipeg Free Press,* 26 January 2015.

———. "Residents Voice Concerns over Urban Reserve—Worried about Property Values near Kapyong." *Winnipeg Free Press,* 6 March 2015.

Pearce, Tyler, and Wanda Wuttunee. "Our Hearts on Our Street: Neechi Commons and the Social Enterprise Centre in Winnipeg." *Universitas Forum* 4, no. 2 (2015): 1–11.

Peck, Jamie. "Cities beyond Compare?" *Regional Studies* 49 (2015): 160–82.

Pellow, David N. "Toward a Critical Environmental Justice Studies: Black Lives Matter as an Environmental Justice Challenge." *Du Bois Review* 13, no. 2 (2016): 1–16.

Pels, Peter. "The Anthropology of Colonialism: Culture, History, and the Emergence of Western Governmentality." *Annual Review of Anthropology* 26 (1997): 163–83.

Pennington County Sheriff's Office. *Annual Report 2013.* Pennington County, South Dakota. http://www.pennco.org/index.asp?SEC=E6CD5DAE-1428-4E43-BFEE-C303509D5320&Type=B_BASIC.

Perry, Adele. *Aqueduct: Colonialism, Resources, and the Histories We Remember.* Winnipeg: ARP Books, 2016.

Perry, Barbara. "Nobody Trusts Them! Under- and Over-Policing Native American Communities." *Critical Criminology* 14, no. 4 (2006): 411–44.

———. *Policing Race and Place in Indian Country: Over- and Underenforcement.* Lanham, MD: Lexington Books, 2009.

Peters, Evelyn. "'I Like to Let Them Have Their Time': Hidden Homeless First Nations People in the City and Their Management of Household Relationships." *Social and Cultural Geography* 13, no. 4 (2012): 321–38.

———. "Subversive Spaces: First Nations Women and the City." *Environment and Planning D: Society and Space* 16, no. 6 (1998): 665–85.

———. "Three Myths about Aboriginals in Cities." Breakfast on the Hill Presentation, Canadian Federation for the Humanities and Social Sciences, Ottawa, 2004.

———. "'Urban' and 'Aboriginal': An Impossible Contradiction." In *City Lives and City Forms: Critical Research and Canadian Urbanism*, edited by Jon Caulfield and Linda Peake, 47–62. Toronto: University of Toronto Press, 1996.

———. "Urban Reserves." Research paper prepared for the National Centre for First Nations Governance. Vancouver: NCFNG, 2007.

Peters, Evelyn, and Chris Andersen, eds. *Indigenous in the City: Contemporary Identities and Cultural Innovation*. Vancouver: University of British Columbia Press, 2013.

Peters, Evelyn, and Vince Robillard. "'Everything You Want Is There': The Place of the Reserve in First Nations' Homeless Mobility." *Urban Geography* 30, no. 6 (2009): 652–80.

Peters, Evelyn, Matt Stock, Adrian Werner. *Rooster Town: The History of an Urban Métis Community, 1901–1961*. With Lawrie Barkwell. Winnipeg: University of Manitoba Press, 2018.

Phillips, Nelson, and Cynthia Hardy. *Discourse Analysis: Investigating Processes in Social Construction*. Thousand Oaks, CA: SAGE, 2002.

Pitawanakwat, Brock. "Bimaadzwin Oodenaang: A Pathway to Urban Nishnaabe Resurgence." In *Lighting the Eighth Fire: The Liberation, Resurgence and Protection of Indigenous Nations*, edited by Leanne Simpson, 161–73. Winnipeg: Arbeiter Ring Publishing, 2008.

Piterberg, Gabriel. *The Returns of Zionism: Myths, Politics and Scholarship in Israel*. London and New York: Verso, 2008.

———. "Settlers and Their States: A Reply to Zeev Sternhell." *New Left Review* 62 (2010): 115–24.

Porter, Libby, and Oren Yiftachel. "Urbanizing Settler-Colonial Studies: Introduction to the Special Issue." *Settler Colonial Studies* (2017): 1–10.

Porter, Tracie R. "The School-to-Prison Pipeline: The Business Side of Incarcerating, Not Educating Students in Public Schools." *Arkansas Law Review* 68, no. 1 (2015): 55–81.

Poston, Richard Waverly. *Small Town Renaissance: A Story of the Montana Study*. New York: Harper, 1950.

Povinelli, Elizabeth A. *The Cunning of Recognition: Indigenous Alterities and the Making of Australian Multiculturalism*. Durham, NC: Duke University Press, 2002.

———. *The Empire of Love: Toward a Theory of Intimacy, Genealogy, and Carnality*. Durham, NC: Duke University Press, 2006.

Pratt, Geraldine. "Abandoned Women and the Space of the Exception." *Antipode* 37, no. 5 (2005): 1052–78.

Preston, Jen. "Neoliberal Settler Colonialism, Canada and the Tar Sands." *Race and Class* 55, no. 2 (2013): 42–59.

Pritchard, Dean. "'Intensive' Help for Teen Who Brutally Assaulted Friend in Parkade." *Winnipeg Sun*, 18 August 2016. http://www.winnipegsun.com/2016/08/18/intensive-help-for-teen-who-brutally-assaulted-friend-in-parkade.

Proulx, Craig. "Aboriginal Identification in North American Cities." *Canadian Journal of Native Studies* 26 (2006): 405–38.

Pulido, Laura. *Black, Brown, Yellow and Left: Radical Activism in Los Angeles*. Berkeley: University of California Press, 2006.

———. "Rethinking Environmental Racism: White Privilege and Urban Development in Southern California." *Annals of the Association of American Geographers* 90, no. 1 (2000): 12–40.

Puxley, Chinta. "Report about Murdered Teen Tina Fontaine to Be Kept Secret." *Star*, 21 August 2014. https://www.thestar.com/news/canada/2014/08/21/report_about_murdered_teen_tina_fontaine_to_be_kept_secret.html.

Rabson, Mia. "Land Claim Prevents Transfer of Homes to First Nations: MP." *Winnipeg Free Press*, 4 April 2009.

———. "Tories Appeal Kapyong Ruling a Second Time." *Winnipeg Free Press*, 22 January 2013.

Rader, Dean. *Engaged Resistance: American Indian Art, Literature, and Film from Alcatraz to the NMAI.* Austin: University of Texas Press, 2011.

Raible, John, and Jason G. Irizarry. "Redirecting the Teacher's Gaze: Teacher Education, Youth Surveillance and the School-to-Prison Pipeline." *Teaching and Teacher Education* 26, no. 5 (2010): 1196–1203.

Ramirez, Renya. *Native Hubs: Culture, Community, and Belonging in Silicon Valley and Beyond.* Durham, NC: Duke University Press, 2007.

Razack, Sherene. *Dying from Improvement: Inquest and Inquiries into Indigenous Deaths.* University of Toronto Press, 2015.

———. "Gendering Disposability." *Canadian Journal of Women and the Law* 28, no. 2 (2016): 285–307.

———. "Gendered Racial Violence and Spatialized Justice: The Murder of Pamela George." *Canadian Journal of Law and Society* 15, no. 2 (2000): 91–130.

———. "Memorializing Colonial Power: The Death of Frank Paul." *Law and Social Inquiry* 37, no. 4 (2012): 908–932.

———, ed. *Race, Space, and the Law: Unmapping a White Settler Society.* Toronto: Between the Lines, 2002.

———. "Sexualized Violence and Colonialism: Reflections on the Inquiry into Missing and Murdered Indigenous Women." *Canadian Journal of Women and the Law* 28, no. 2 (2016): i–iv.

———. "Timely Deaths: Medicalizing the Deaths of Aboriginal People in Police Custody." *Law, Culture and the Humanities* 9, no. 2 (2013): 352–74.

———. "When Place Becomes Race." In *Race and Racialization: Essential Readings*, edited by Tania Das Gupta, Carl E. James, Roger Maaka, Grace-Edward Galabuzi, and Chris Andersen, 74–82. Toronto: Canadian Scholars' Press, 2007.

Reber, Susanne, and Robert Renaud. *Starlight Tour: The Last, Lonely Night of Neil Stonechild.* Toronto: Random House Canada, 2005.

Reilly, Thom. "Transition from Care: Status and Outcomes of Youth Who Age Out of Foster Care." *Child Welfare-New York* 82, no. 6 (2003): 727–46.

Reiman, Jeffrey, and Paul Leighton. *The Rich Get Richer and the Poor Get Prison: Ideology, Class and Criminal Justice.* New York: Routledge, 2016.

Rifkin, Mark. "Indigenizing Agamben: Rethinking Sovereignty in Light of the 'Peculiar' Status of Native Peoples." *Cultural Critique* 73 (2009): 88–124.

———. "Settler Common Sense." *Settler Colonial Studies* 3, no. 3–4 (2013): 322–40.

———. *Settler Common Sense: Queerness and Everyday Colonialism in the American Renaissance.* Minneapolis: University of Minnesota Press, 2014.

Riney, Scott. *The Rapid City Indian School, 1898–1933.* Norman: University of Oklahoma Press, 1999.

Rios, Victor M. *Punished: Policing the Lives of Black and Latino Boys.* New York and London: New York University Press, 2011.

Ritzer, George. *The McDonaldization of Society.* Thousand Oaks, CA: Pine Forge, 2004.

Robbins, Rebecca L. "Setting the Record Straight: A Salish Account." *Tribal College Journal* 14, no. 3 (2003). https://tribalcollegejournal.org/setting-record-straight-salish-account/.

Rodriguez, Richard. "On the Subject of Gang Photography." In *Gangs and Society*, edited by Louis Kontos, David C. Brotherton, and Luis Barrios, 255–82. New York: Columbia University Press, 2005.

Rosaldo, Renato. "Imperialist Nostalgia." *Representations* 26 (1989): 107–22.

Rosenthal, Nicholas. *Reimagining Indian Country: Native American Migration and Identity in Twentieth-Century Los Angeles.* Chapel Hill: University of North Carolina Press, 2012.

Ross, Jenna, and Alicia Eler. "Why Dakota Elders Want to Burn Controversial 'Scaffold' Sculpture." *Star Tribune*, 4 June 2017. http://www.startribune.com/why-dakota-elders-want-to-burn-controversial-scaffold-sculpture/426176391/#1.

Ross, Robert, and Gerard Telkamp. *Colonial Cities: Essays on Urbanism in a Colonial Context.* Dodrecht: Martinus Nijhoff, 1985.

Rutland, Amanda. "'Mekko' Film Event Held in Okmulgee." Muskokemedia.com, 20 April 2016. mvskokemedia.com/mekko-film-event-held-in-okmulgee/.

Ryan, Joseph P., Pedro M. Hernandez, and Denise Herz. "Developmental Trajectories of Offending for Male Adolescents Leaving Foster Care." *Social Work Research* 31, no. 2 (2007): 83–93.

Salish-Pend d'Oreille Culture Committee and Elders Cultural Advisory Council, Confederated Salish and Kootenai Tribes. *The Salish People and the Lewis and Clark Expedition.* Lincoln: University of Nebraska Press, 2005.

Sandercock, Leonie. "Commentary: Indigenous Planning and the Burden of Colonialism." *Planning Theory and Practice* 5, no. 1 (2004): 118–24.

Santin, Aldo. "Summit Seen as a First Step." *Winnipeg Free Press*, 19 August 2015.

Saunders, Richard. "Suburbia Booms as 'Blue Collar' Workers Arrive." *Minneapolis Tribune*, 10 January 1960.

Sayre, Nathan F. "Scale." In *A Companion to Environmental Geography*, edited by Noel Castree, David Demeritt, Diana Liverman, and Bruce Rhoads, 95–108. New York: Blackwell, 2009.

Schell, Herbert S. *History of South Dakota.* 4th ed. Rev. ed. Pierre: South Dakota State Historical Society Press, 2004.

Schieman, Christopher. "Rising from the Dirt: Dirt City: Dream City Starts the Conversation in the Quarters." *Avenue Edmonton*, July 2012. http://www.avenueedmonton.com/July-2012/Rising-from-the-Dirt/.

Schulman, Sarah. *The Gentrification of the Mind: Witness to a Lost Imagination.* Berkeley: University of California Press, 2012.

Schweninger, Lee. *Imagic Moments: Indigenous North American Film.* Athens: University of Georgia Press, 2013.

Seshia, Maya. *The Unheard Speak Out.* Winnipeg: Canadian Centre for Policy Alternatives, 2005.

Shaw, Wendy. *Cities of Whiteness.* Malden, MA: Wiley-Blackwell, 2007.

Shearing, Clifford, and Richard Ericson. "Culture as Figurative Action." *British Journal of Sociology* 42, no. 4 (1991): 481–506.

Shepherd, Dan. "Last Residents of Picher, Oklahoma Won't Give Up the Ghost (Town)." NBCNews.com, 28 April 2014. www.nbcnews.com/news/investigations/last-residents-picher-oklahoma-wont-give-ghost-town-n89611.

Shoal Lake 40 First Nation Museum of Canadian Human Rights Violations. "Press Release: Shoal Lake 40 Launches the Museum of Canadian Human Rights Violations." 15 September 2014. http://www.sl40.ca/docs/CMHRVPressRelease.pdf.

Shoemaker, Nancy. "Urban Indians and Ethnic Choices: American Indian Organizations in Minneapolis, 1920–1950." *Western Historical Quarterly* 19 (1988): 431–47.

Silko, Leslie Marmon. *Ceremony*. London: Penguin, 1977.

Silver, Jim. "Complex Poverty and Home-Grown Solutions in Two Prairie Cities." In *Passion for Action in Child and Family Services: Voices from the Prairies*, edited by Sharon McKay, Don Fuchs, and Ivan Brown, 227–46. University of Regina: CPRC Press, 2009.

———, ed. *In Their Own Voices: Building Urban Aboriginal Communities*. Halifax: Fernwood Publishing, 2006.

———. *North End Winnipeg's Lord Selkirk Park Housing Development: History, Comparative Context, Prospects*. Winnipeg: Canadian Centre for Policy Alternatives, 2006.

———. "Segregated City: A Century of Poverty in Winnipeg." In *Manitoba Politics and Government*, edited by Paul Thomas and Curtis Brown, 331–57. Winnipeg: University of Manitoba Press, 2010.

———. "Spatially Concentrated, Racialized Poverty as a Social Determinant of Health: The Case of Winnipeg's Inner City." In *The Social Determinants of Health in Manitoba*, 2nd ed., edited by Lynne Fernandez, Shauna MacKinnon, and Jim Silver, 227–40. Winnipeg: Canadian Centre for Policy Alternatives, 2015.

———. *Unearthing Resistance: Aboriginal Women in the Lord Selkirk Park Housing Developments*. Winnipeg: Canadian Centre for Policy Alternatives, 2007.

———. "Winnipeg's North End: Yesterday and Today." *Canadian Dimension* 44 (2010). https://canadiandimension.com/articles/view/winnipegs-north-end.

Silver, Jim, Parvin Ghorayshi, Joan Hay, and Darlene Klyne. "Sharing, Community and Decolonization." In *In Their Own Voices: Building Urban Aboriginal Communities*, edited by Jim Silver, 133–73. Halifax: Fernwood Publishing, 2006.

Silvern, Steven E. "Scales of Justice: Law, American Indian Treaty Rights and the Political Construction of Scale." *Political Geography* 18, no. 6 (1999): 639–68.

Simon, David. "Third World Colonial Cities in Context: Conceptual and Theoretical Approaches with Particular Reference to Africa." *Progress in Human Geography* 8, no. 4 (1984): 493–514.

Simpson, Audra. "Consent's Revenge." *Cultural Anthropology* 31, no. 3 (2016): 326–33. https://doi.org/10.14506/ca31.3.02.

———. *Mohawk Interruptus: Political Life across the Borders of Settler States*. Durham, NC: Duke University Press, 2014.

———. "Settlement's Secret." *Cultural Anthropology* 26, no. 2 (2011): 205–17.

———. "The State Is a Man: Theresa Spence, Loretta Saunders and the Gender of Settler Sovereignty." *Theory and Event* 19, no. 4 (2016). https://muse.jhu.edu/article/633280.

———. "Whither Settler Colonialism?" *Settler Colonial Studies* 6, no. 4 (2016): 438–45.

Simpson, Leanne Betasamosake. *As We Have Always Done: Indigenous Freedom through Radical Resistance*. Minneapolis: University of Minnesota Press, 2017.

———. *Dancing on Our Turtle's Back: Stories of Nishnaabeg Re-Creation, Resurgence and a New Emergence*. Winnipeg: ARP Books, 2011.

———. "Land as Pedagogy: Nishnaabeg Intelligence and Rebellious Transformation." *Decolonization: Indigeneity, Education and Society* 3, no. 3 (2014): 1–25.

Simpson, Michael, and Jen Bagelaman. "Decolonizing Urban Political Ecologies: The Production of Nature in Settler Colonial Cities." *Annals of the American Association of Geographers* 108, no. 2 . (2018): 558–68.

Sinclair, Gordon. *Cowboys and Indians: The Shooting of J.J. Harper.* Toronto: McClelland and Stewart, 1999.

Sinclair, Raven. "Identity Lost and Found: Lessons from the Sixties Scoop." *First Peoples Child and Family Review* 3, no. 1 (2007): 65–82.

Sinclair, Raven, and Jana Grekul. "Aboriginal Youth Gangs in Canada: (De)constructing an Epidemic." *First Peoples Child and Family Review* 7, no. 1 (2012): 8–28.

Skelton, Ian, Cheryl Selig, and Lawrence Deane. "Social Housing and CED Initiatives in Inner-City Winnipeg." In *Doing Community Economic Development*, edited by John Loxley, Jim Silver, and Kathleen Sexsmith. Halifax: Fernwood Publishing, 2007.

Sloan Morgan, Vanessa, and Heather Castleden. "Framing Indigenous–Settler Relations within British Columbia's Modern Treaty Context: A Discourse Analysis of the Maa-nulth Treaty in Mainstream Media." *The International Indigenous Policy Journal* 5, no. 3 (2014): 1–19.

Smith, Chauncee D. "Deconstructing the Pipeline: Evaluating School-to-Prison Pipeline Equal Protection Cases through a Structural Racism Framework." *Fordham Urban Law Journal* 36 (2009): 1009–49.

Smith, Neil. *Uneven Development: Nature, Capital, and the Production of Space.* 3rd edition. Athens: University of Georgia Press, 2008.

Smith, Neil, and Michael LeFaivre. "Class Analysis of Gentrification." In *Gentrification, Displacement, and Neighborhood Revitalization*, edited by John Palen and Bruce London, 43–63. Albany: State University of New York Press, 1984.

Smith, Paul Chaat, and Robert Warrior. *Like a Hurricane: The Indian Movement from Alcatraz to Wounded Knee.* New York: The New Press, 1996.

Snelgrove, Corey, Rita Kaur Dhamoon, and Jeff Corntassel. "Unsettling Settler Colonialism: The Discourse and Politics of Settlers, and Solidarity with Indigenous Nations." *Decolonization* 3, no. 2 (2014): 1–32.

Snider, Laureen. "Making Corporate Crime Disappear." In *Locating Law: Race, Class, Gender, Sexuality Connections,* edited by Elizabeth Comack, 183–206. 2nd ed. Halifax: Fernwood Publishing, 2006.

Soja, Edward. *My Los Angeles: From Urban Restructuring to Regional Urbanization.* University of California Press, 2014.

———. *Postmodern Geographies: The Assertion of Space in Critical Social Theory.* Verso: London, 1989.

———. *Seeking Spatial Justice.* Minneapolis: University of Minnesota Press, 2010.

South Dakota Criminal Justice Initiative Work Group. *South Dakota Criminal Justice Initiative: Final Report November 2012.* Pierre: State of South Dakota, 2012.

Spitzer, Stephen. "Toward a Marxian Theory of Deviance." *Social Problems* 22, no. 5 (1975): 638–51.

Stanek, Lukasz. *Henri Lefebvre on Space.* Minneapolis: University of Minnesota Press, 2011.

Staniforth, Jesse. "'of the North'—Quebec Filmmaker Uses YouTube and Unauthorized Music to Portray the Inuit." *the Nation*, 8 December 2015. http://www.nationnews.ca/of-the-north-racist-documen-tary-quebec-filmmaker-uses-youtube-and-unauthorized-music-to-portray-the-inuit-people/.

Stannard, David. *American Holocaust: The Conquest of the New World.* Oxford: Oxford University Press, 1993.

Stasiulis, Daiva, and Nira Yuval-Davis. *Unsettling Settler Societies: Articulations of Gender, Race, Ethnicity and Class.* London and Thousand Oaks, CA: Sage, 1995.

Statistics Canada. *Aboriginal Peoples in Canada in 2006: Inuit, Métis and First Nations, 2006 Census.* Ottawa, Ministry of Industry, 2008. http://www12.statcan.ca/census-recensement/2006/as-sa/97-558/pdf/97-558-X1E2006001.pdf.

———. *Aboriginal Peoples in Canada: First Nations, Métis and Inuit; National Household Survey, 2011.* Ottawa, 2016. http://www12.statcan.gc.ca/nhs-enm/2011/as-sa/99-011-x/99-011-x2011001-eng.cfm.

———. *Winnipeg: 2011 National Household Survey.* Data tables, Catalogue # 99-011-X2011034. Ottawa: Minister of Industry, 2013.

Stanbury, W.T., and Jay Siegel. *Success and Failure: Indians in Urban Society.* Vancouver: UBC Press, 1975.

Stewart, Michelle. "Of Digital Selves and Digital Sovereignty: Of the North." *Film Quarterly* 70, no. 4 (2017): 23–38.

St. Ignatius Post. "8000 People See Thrilling Centennial Pageant-Drama." 10 July 1947.

St-Onge, Nicole, Carolyn Podruchny, and Brenda Macdougall, eds. *Contours of a People: Metis Family, Mobility, and History.* Norman: University of Oklahoma Press, 2012.

Stromnes, John. "Salish Showcase." *Missoulian,* 31 August 2002. http://missoulian.com/uncategorized/salish-showcase/article_d788ecd4-d10b-58c7-a2e0-65d4a6d09ef7.html.

Swadener, Beth Blue, and Sally Lubeck, eds. *Children and Families "At Promise": Deconstructing the Discourse of Risk.* Albany: State University of New York Press, 1995.

Tadiar, Neferti X.M. "Life-Times in Fate Playing." *South Atlantic Quarterly* 111, no. 4 (2012): 783–802.

Tait, Caroline, Robert Henry, and Rachel Loewen Walker. "Child Welfare: A Social Determinant of Health for Canadian First Nations and Métis children." *Pimatisiwin* 11, no.1 (2013): 39–53.

Tait, M.J. "Kapyong and Treaty One First Nations: When the Crown Can Do Nothing Wrong." In *Surviving Canada: Indigenous Peoples Celebrate 150 Years of Betrayal,* edited by K.L. Ladner and M.J. Tait, 102–28. Winnipeg: ARP Books, 2017.

TallBear, Kimberly. "American Dreaming Is White Possessiveness." Presentation at Reimagining Creative Economy Workshop, University of Alberta, 27 April 2016. https://rce.ualberta.ca/2016/12/06/kimberly-tallbear/.

———. "DNA, Blood, and Racializing the Tribe." *Wicazo Sa Review* 18, no. 1 (2003): 81–107.

———. *Native American DNA: Tribal Belonging and the False Promise of Genetic Science.* Minneapolis: University of Minnesota Press, 2013.

Taniguchi, Travis A., Jerry H. Ratcliffe, and Ralph B. Taylor. "Gang Set Space, Drug Markets, and Crime around Drug Corners in Camden." *Journal of Research in Crime and Delinquency* 48, no. 3 (2011): 327–63.

Tator, Carol, and Francis Henry. *Racial Profiling in Canada: Challenging the Myth of "A Few Bad Apples."* Toronto: University of Toronto Press, 2006.

Taussig, Michael. *Shamanism, Colonialism, and the Wild Man: A Study in Terror and Healing.* Chicago: University of Chicago Press, 1987.

Thobani, Sunera. *Exalted Subjects: Studies in the Making of Race and Nation in Canada.* Toronto: University of Toronto Press, 2007.

Thorne, Vicki May. "Meet: Sterlin Harjo." *This Land Press,* 21 January 2012. thislandpress.com/2012/01/21/meet-sterlin-harjo/.

Thrasher, Frederic. *The Gang.* Chicago: University of Chicago Press, 1927.

Thrush, Coll. *Indigenous London: Native Travelers at the Heart of Empire*. New Haven, CT: Yale University Press, 2016.

———. *Native Seattle: Histories from the Crossing-Over Place*. Seattle: University of Washington Press, 2007.

Tita, George E., Jacqueline Cohen, and John Engberg. "An Ecological Study of the Location of Gang 'Set Space.'" *Social Problems* 52, no. 2 (2005): 272–99.

Todd, Zoe. "Decolonial Dreams: Unsettling the Academy through Namewak." In *The New (New) Corpse*, edited by Caroline Picard, 104–17. Green Lantern Press: Chicago, 2015.

———. "From Classroom to River's Edge: Tending to Reciprocal Duties beyond the Academy." *Aboriginal Policy Studies* 6, no. 1 (2016): 90–97.

Toews, Owen. "Resettling the City? Settler Colonialism, Neoliberalism, and Urban Land in Winnipeg, Canada," PhD diss., City University of New York, 2015.

———. *Stolen City: Racial Capitalism and the Making of Winnipeg*. Winnipeg: ARP Books, 2018.

Tomiak, Julie. "Contesting the Settler City: Indigenous Self-Determination, New Urban Reserves, and the Neoliberalization of Colonialism." *Antipode* 49 (2017): 928–45. doi: 10.1111/anti.12308.

———. "Indigeneity and the City: Representations, Resistance, and the Right to the City." In *Lumpen-City: Discourses of Marginality, Marginalizing Discourses*, edited by Alan Bourke, Tia Dafnos, and Markus Kip, 163–92. Ottawa: Red Quill Books, 2011.

———. "Indigenous Self-Determination, Neoliberalization, and the Right to the City: Rescaling Aboriginal Governance in Ottawa and Winnipeg." PhD diss., Carleton University, 2011.

———. "'Too Valuable for Indians': Discourses on Treaty Land Entitlement, Property, and Urban Planning in Winnipeg." Presented at Native American and Indigenous Studies Association (NAISA), Vancouver, June 2017.

———. "Unsettling Ottawa: Settler Colonialism, Indigenous Resistance, and the Politics of Scale." *Canadian Journal of Urban Research* 25, no. 1 (2016): 8–21.

Tomkins, Calvin. "Why Dana Schutz Painted Emmett Till." *New Yorker*, 10 April 2017. http://www.newyorker.com/magazine/2017/04/10/why-dana-schutz-painted-emmett-till.

Tonkiss, Fran. "Analyzing Text and Speech." In *Researching Society and Culture,* edited by Clive Seale. 2nd ed. London: Sage, 1998.

Totten, Mark. *Nasty, Brutish, and Short: The Lives of Gang Members in Canada*. Toronto: James Lorimer, 2012.

Treasury Board of Canada. *Treasury Board Policy on the Disposal of Surplus Real Property*. Ottawa: Treasury Board of Canada, 2001.

Troupe, Cheryl. "Métis Women: Social Structure, Urbanization and Political Activism, 1850–1980." MA thesis, University of Saskatchewan, 2009.

Truth and Reconciliation Commission of Canada. *Honouring the Truth, Reconciling for the Future: Summary of the Final Report*. Toronto: James Lorimer, 2015.

———. *They Came for the Children: Canada, Aboriginal Peoples, and Residential Schools*. Winnipeg, 2012. http://www.myrobust.com/websites/trcinstitution/File/2039_T&R_eng_web%5B1%5D.pdf.

Tubbs, Stephenie Ambrose. "Bert Hansen: Montanan." *Drumlummon Views*. Drumlummon Institute, fall 2008.

Tuck, Eve. "Suspending Damage: A Letter to Communities." *Harvard Educational Review* 79, no. 3 (2009): 409–28.

Tuck, Eve, and Marcia McKenzie. *Place in Research: Theory, Methodology, and Methods*. New York: Routledge, 2015.

Tuck, Eve, and K. Wayne Yang. "Decolonization Is Not a Metaphor." *Decolonization: Indigeneity, Education and Society* 1, no.1 (2012): 1–40.

Tuzzolo, Ellen, and Damon T. Hewitt. "Rebuilding Inequity: The Re-Emergence of the School-to-Prison Pipeline in New Orleans." *High School Journal* 90, no. 2 (2006): 59–68.

U.S. Census Bureau. *The American Indian and Alaskan Native Population: 2010*. By Tina Norris, Paula L. Vines, and Elizabeth M. Hoeffel. Issued January 2012.

U.S. Census Bureau. Department of Commerce. *Poverty Rates for Selected Detailed Race and Hispanic Groups by State and Place: 2007–2011*. By Suzanne Macartney and Kayla Fontenot. Issued Febuary 2013.

U.S. Commission on Civil Rights. South Dakota Advisory Committee. *Native Americans and the Administration of Justice in South Dakota*. Transcript of a community forum held 6 December 1999.

U.S. Congress. Senate. Committee on Public Works. *To Investigate the Adequacy and Effectiveness of Federal Disaster Relief Legislation, Part 2*. 93rd Congress, 1st session, 30 and 31 March 1973.

U.S. Congress. Senate. Committee on the Judiciary. *Constitutional Rights of the American Indian: Hearings before the Subcommittee on Constitutional Rights, Part 3*. 87th Congress, 2nd session, 1, 2, and 6 June 1962.

U.S. Department of Interior. Bureau of Indian Affairs. *Sioux Sanatorium Lands, Rapid City, South Dakota*. Aberdeen, SD: BIA Area Office, 1974.

Valandra, Edward C. *Not Without Our Consent: Lakota Resistance to Termination, 1950–59*. Urbana: University of Illinois Press, 2006.

Valverde, Mariana. "Jurisdiction and Scale: Legal 'Technicalities' as Resources for Theory." *Social and Legal Studies* 18, no. 2 (2009): 139–57.

Veracini, Lorenzo. "Introducing: Settler Colonial Studies." *Settler Colonial Studies* 1, no. 1 (2011): 1–12.

———. *The Settler Colonial Present*. New York: Springer, 2015.

———. *Settler Colonialism: A Theoretical Overview*. Basingstoke, UK: Palgrave Macmillan, 2010.

———. "Suburbia, Settler Colonialism and the World Turned Inside Out." *Housing, Theory and Society* 29 no. 4 (2012): 339–57.

Vigil, Diego. *A Rainbow of Gangs: Street Cultures in the Mega-City*. University of Texas Press, 2010.

Vimalassery, Manu, Juliana Hu Pegues, and Alyosha Goldstein. "Introduction: On Colonial Unknowing." *Theory and Event* 19, no. 4 (2016): https://muse.jhu.edu/article/633283.

Vizenor, Gerald. "Aesthetics of Survivance: Literary Theory and Practice." In *Survivance: Narratives of Native Presence*, edited by Gerald Vizenor, 1–23. Lincoln: University of Nebraska Press, 2008.

———. *Crossbloods: Bone Courts, Bingo, and Other Reports*. Minneapolis: University of Minnesota Press, 1990.

———. "Indian's Lot: Rent, Ruins and Roaches." *Minneapolis Tribune*, 12 January 1969.

———. *Interior Landscapes: Autobiographical Myths and Metaphors*. Albany: State University of New York Press, 2009.

Vowel, Chelsea. *Indigenous Writes: A Guide to First Nations, Métis and Inuit Issues in Canada* Winnipeg: Portage and Main Press, 2016.

Vrooman, Nicholas. "*The Whole Country was . . . 'One Robe'*": *The Little Shell Tribe's America*. Great Falls, MT: Little Shell Tribe of Chippewa Indians of Montana and Drumlummon Institute, 2012.

Wacquant, Loïc. "Class, Race and Hyperincarceration in Revanchist America." *Daedalus* 139, no. 3 (2010): 74–90.

———. "Ghettos and Anti-Ghettos: An Anatomy of the New Urban Poverty." *Thesis Eleven* 94, no. 1 (2008): 113–18.

———. "Territorial Stigmatization in the Age of Advanced Marginality." *Thesis Eleven* 91, no. 1 (2007): 66–77.

———. *Urban Outcasts: A Comparative Sociology of Advanced Marginality.* Cambridge, MA: Polity Press, 2008.

Waddell, Jack, and O. Michael Watson. *The American Indian in Urban Society.* Boston: Little Brown, 1984.

Wald, Johanna, and Daniel J. Losen. "Defining and Redirecting a School-to-Prison Pipeline." *New Directions for Youth Development* 2003, no. 99 (2003): 9–15.

Walia, Harsha. *Undoing Border Imperialism.* Oakland, CA: AK Press, 2013.

Walker, Ryan, Ted Jojola, and David Natcher, eds. *Reclaiming Indigenous Planning.* Montreal and Kingston: McGill-Queen's University Press, 2013.

Wang, Caroline C. "Photovoice: A Participatory Action Research Strategy Applied to Women's Health." *Journal of Women's Health* 8, no. 2 (1999): 185–92.

———. "Using Photovoice as a Participatory Assessment and Issue Selection Tool." *Community Based Participatory Research for Health* (2003): 179–96.

Wang, Caroline C., and Mary-Ann Burris. "Photovoice: Concept, Methodology, and Use for Participatory Needs Assessment." *Health Education and Behavior* 24, no. 3 (1997): 369–87.

Watkins, Arthur V. "Termination of Federal Supervision: The Removal of Restrictions over Indian Property and Persons." *Annals of the American Academy of Political and Social Science* 311 (1957): 47–55.

Waziyawatin. *What Does Justice Look Like?* St. Paul, MN: Living Justice Press, 2008.

Welch, Mary Agnes. "Breaking Down the Kapyong Saga." *Winnipeg Free Press*, 24 September 2015.

———. "Kapyong Is a Symbol of Sabotage." *Winnipeg Free Press*, 2 January 2015.

Wharf, Brian, and Michael Clague, eds. *Community Organizing: Canadian Experiences.* Toronto: Oxford University Press, 1997.

White, Rob. "Disputed Definitions and Fluid Identities: The Limitations of Social Profiling in Relation to Ethnic Youth Gangs." *Youth Justice* 8, no. 2 (2008): 149–61.

———. "Indigenous Young People and Hyperincarceration in Australia." *Youth Justice* 15, no. 3 (2015): 256–70.

———. *Youth Gangs, Violence and Social Respect: Exploring the Nature of Provocations and Punch-Ups.* New York: Palgrave Macmillan, 2013.

Wideman, Trevor James, and Jeffrey Masuda. "Intensification and Neoliberalization: A Case Study of Planning Policy in Winnipeg, Canada, 1990–2013." *Prairie Perspectives: Geographical Essays* 16 (2013): 55–67.

Wilkes, Rima, Catherine Corrigall-Brown, and Danielle Ricard. "Nationalism and Media Coverage of Indigenous People's Collective Action in Canada." *American Indian Culture and Research Journal* 34, no. 4 (2010): 41–59.

Wilkinson, Charles. *Blood Struggle: The Rise of Modern Indian Nations.* New York: Norton, 2005.

Williams, Allison, M. "Canadian Urban Aboriginals: A Focus on Aboriginal Women in Toronto." *Canadian Journal of Native Studies* 17, no. 1 (1997): 75–101.

Williams, Raymond. *Marxism and Literature.* Oxford: Oxford University Press, 1978.

Williams, Robert A. *Like a Loaded Weapon: The Rehnquist Court, Indian Rights, and the Legal History of Racism in America*. Minneapolis: University of Minnesota Press, 2005.

Wilson, Kathi, and Evelyn Peters. "'You Can Make a Place for It': Remapping Urban First Nations Spaces of Identity." *Environment and Planning D: Society and Space* 23 (2005): 395–413.

Winn, Maisha T., and Nadia Behizadeh. "The Right to Be Literate: Literacy, Education, and the School-to-Prison Pipeline." *Review of Research in Education* 35, no. 1 (2011): 147–73.

Winnipeg Free Press. "How to Fix Canada's 'Most Racist' City." 23 January 2015.

———. "No Need to Appeal Kapyong." 3 October 2009.

———. "Readers Divided on 'Racist City' Claim." 25 January 2015.

Winnipeg Police Service. *Annual Statistical Report*. 2014. http://www.winnipeg.ca/police/AnnualReports/2014/2014_wps_annual_report_english.pdf.

Wolfe, Patrick. "Settler Colonialism and the Elimination of the Native." *Journal of Genocide Research* 8, no. 4 (2006): 387–409.

———. *Settler Colonialism and the Transformation of Anthropology: The Politics and Poetics of an Ethnographic Event*. New York: Bloomsbury Publishing, 1999.

———. *Traces of History: Elementary Structures of Race*. London and Brooklyn: Verso, 2016.

Womack, Craig S. *Red on Red: Native American Literary Separatism*. Minneapolis: University of Minnesota Press, 1999.

Wood, Patricia. "The 'Sarcee War': Fragmented Citizenship and the City." *Space and Polity* 10 (2006): 229–42.

Woroniak, Monique, and David Camfield. "Choosing Not to Look Away: Confronting Colonialism in Canada." *The Bullet*, no. 768 (2013). https://newsocialist.org/choosing-not-to-look-away-confronting-colonialism-in-canada/.

Wright, David H., Commissioner. *Report of the Commission of Inquiry into Matters Relating to the Death of Neil Stonechild*. 2004. http://www.justice.gov.sk.ca/stonechild/finalreport/Stonechild.pdf.

Wright, Melissa W. "The Dialectics of Still Life: Murder, Women, and Maquiladoras." In *Millennial Capitalism and the Culture of Neoliberalism*, edited by Jean Comaroff and John L. Comaroff, 125–46. Durham, NC: Duke University Press, 2001.

Wyatt, Daisy. "Exhibit B 'Human Zoo' Show Cancelled by the Barbican following Campaigner Protest." *Independent*, 24 September 2014. http://www.independent.co.uk/arts-entertainment/art/news/exhibit-b-human-zoo-show-cancelled-by-the-barbican-following-protest-9753519.html.

X, Malcolm. "It Shall Be the Ballot or the Bullet." Speech delivered at the Audubon Ballroom, Washington Heights, NY, 29 March 1964.

Yanagisako, Sylvia, and Carol Delaney. "Naturalizing Power." In *Naturalizing Power: Essays in Feminists Cultural Analysis,* edited by Sylvia Yanagisako and Carol Delaney, 1–24. New York: Routledge, 1995.

Yazzie, Melanie K. "Brutal Violence in Border Towns Linked to Colonization." *Indian Country Today*, 22 August 2014. https://indiancountrymedianetwork.com/news/politics/brutal-violence-in-border-towns-linked-to-colonization/.

Young, Jock. "Merton with Energy, Katz with Structure: The Sociology of Vindictiveness and the Criminology of Transgression." *Theoretical Criminology* 7, no. 3 (2003): 389–414.

Zamindar, Vazira Fazila-Yacoobali. *The Long Partition and the Making of Modern South Asia: Refuges, Boundaries and Histories*. New Delhi: Penguin Books India, 2007.

CONTRIBUTORS

CHRIS ANDERSEN is the former director of the Rupertsland Centre for Métis Research and currently the Dean of the Faculty of Native Studies at the University of Alberta. He is the author of *"Métis": Race, Recognition and the Struggle for Indigenous Peoplehood* (UBC Press, 2014). With Jean O'Brien, he also co-edited *Sources and Methods in Indigenous Studies* (Routledge, 2017), is the managing editor of the journal *aboriginal policy studies* and is a member of the Royal Society of Canada's College of New Scholars, Artists, and Scientists.

NICHOLAS BROWN is a scholar and artist based in Boston, Massachusetts and La Farge, Wisconsin. He teaches in the School of Architecture and the Department of History at Northeastern University. His research examines the production of cultural landscapes and the politics of relationality in settler colonial contexts. He is the co-author of *Re-Collecting Black Hawk: Landscape, Memory, and Power in the American Midwest* (University of Pittsburg Press, 2015). Other recent and ongoing projects include: Ecologies of Acknowledgement, Kickapoo Conversations, A People's Guide to Firsting and Lasting in Boston, The Vanishing Indian Repeat Photography Project, and Ni-aazhawa'am-minis Spur.

ELIZABETH COMACK is a professor in the Department of Sociology and Criminology at the University of Manitoba. Her research program presently revolves around her participation in the Manitoba Research Alliance's SSHRC-sponsored project Partnering for Change: Community-Based Solutions for Aboriginal and Inner-City Poverty. She leads the Justice, Safety, and Security stream of this project. In addition to journal articles, book chapters, research reports, and policy papers, she has published thirteen books, the most recent being *Coming Back to Jail: Women, Trauma, and Criminalization* (Fernwood Publishing, 2018).

HEATHER DORRIES (Anishinaabe) was born and raised in Winnipeg, Manitoba. She is an Assistant Professor in the Department of Geography and Planning and Centre for Indigenous Studies at the University of Toronto. Her research is focused on the relationship between urban planning and settler colonialism and examines how Indigenous knowledge might give rise to resurgent forms of city building.

NICK ESTES is a citizen of the Lower Brule Sioux Tribe. He is an Assistant Professor in the American Studies Department at the University of New Mexico. In 2014, he co-founded The Red Nation, an Indigenous resistance organization. Estes is the author of *Our History Is the Future: Standing Rock Versus the Dakota Access Pipeline, and the Long Tradition of Indigenous Resistance* (Verso, 2019) and with Jaskiran Dhillon he co-edited *Standing Rock: Voices from the #NoDAPL Movement* (University of Minnesota Press, 2019).

ADAM GAUDRY is an Associate Professor and Associate Dean (Research and Graduate Studies) in the Faculty of Native Studies at the University of Alberta. He is Métis and his family is from the Lake of the Woods in northwestern Ontario and he grew up near Hamilton. Adam has diverse research interests and he is currently working on several different projects. He is writing a book on nineteenth-century Métis political thought and the Métis-Canada "Manitoba Treaty" of 1870, currently under contract with the University of Manitoba Press. He is leading a large collaborative and community-driven research partnership to build a Teetł'it Gwich'in bush school in Teetł'it Zheh, Northwest Territories. He has also published extensively on Métis issues, Indigenous research methodologies, and indigenization policy in Canadian post-secondary education.

ROBERT HENRY is Métis from Prince Albert, Saskatchewan, and is an Assistant Professor in the Department of Indigenous Studies at the University of Saskatchewan. Robert's work focuses in the area of Indigenous street lifestyles, Indigenous research methodologies, community-engaged research, and visual research methods. He has published in the areas of Indigenous masculinities, street gangs, and Indigenous health.

DAVID HUGILL is an Assistant Professor in the Department of Geography and Environmental Studies at Carleton University. His research focuses on the relationship between city building and settler colonization.

SHARMEEN KHAN lives in Toronto, Ontario and works at CUPE 3903. She organizes with No One Is Illegal-Toronto and is the founding editor of *Upping the Anti: A Journal of Theory and Action*. She is also a trainer with Tools for Change.

COREY LABERGE is a cultural anthropologist and practising lawyer. He has held teaching and research appointments at Simon Fraser University, the University of Victoria, and the University of Manitoba. His work has included research and community development regarding Fetal Alcohol Spectrum Disorder (FASD), representing parents in family and child protection proceedings, criminal defence work on behalf of youth, and promoting children's rights as Manitoba's Deputy Children's Advocate. He is a lawyer in Cranbrook, British Columbia.

BRENDA MACDOUGALL is the Chair of Métis Research at the University of Ottawa and has been researching Métis community histories for many years. She is the author of *One of the Family: Metis Culture in Nineteenth Century Northwestern Saskatchewan* (UBC Press, 2010) as well as numerous journal articles and book chapters. More recently she has collaborated to create an online database of historical resources related to Métis history called the Digital Archives Database (DAD) project.

TYLER MCCREARY is an Assistant Professor of Geography at Florida State University and an Adjunct Professor of First Nations Studies at University of Northern British Columbia. He is the author of *Shared Histories: Witsuwit'en-Settler Relations in Smithers, British Columbia, 1913–1973* (Creekstone Press, 2018), as well as two dozen journal articles and book chapters. His scholarship focuses on Indigenous relationships to settler colonial institutions.

LINDSEY CLAIRE SMITH is an editor of *American Indian Quarterly*, one of the foremost publications in interdisciplinary American Indian Studies, and Director of the Center for Poets and Writers at OSU-Tulsa. She is the author of *Indians, Environment, and Identity on the Borders of American Literature* (Palgrave Macmillan, 2008) and co-editor of *Alternative Contact: Indigeneity, Globalism, and American Studies* (John Hopkins University Press, 2011). Her manuscript on urban Indian literatures of Tulsa, New Orleans, and Santa Fe is under contract with University of Nebraska Press.

MICHELLE STEWART is an Associate Professor in Women's and Gender Studies and Director of the Community Research Unit at the University of Regina. Michelle's research focuses on disabilities, mental health, and systemic racism in the criminal justice and child welfare systems of a settler state. Michelle works on a number of research teams which allows her to be involved in international research and arts-based projects focused on social isolation and (dis)ability. As an applied anthropologist, Michelle's work involves community-engaged projects that mobilize findings into real-world application and advocacy that seeks to change policy and practices.

JULIE TOMIAK is an Associate Professor in the School of Indigenous and Canadian Studies at Carleton University. She is of mixed Anishinaabe and European descent and researches Indigenous resistance to settler colonialism in cities and the neoliberalization of settler capitalism and state power.

ZOE TODD (Métis) is an artist and scholar from amiskwaciwâskahikan (Edmonton) in the Treaty Six Area of Alberta, Canada. She writes about human-fish relations, Métis law, science, and environmental issues in Alberta and the Lake Winnipeg watershed.

INDEX